郑作时 ◎ 著

第二版中英文精装版

追梦人

陈爱莲与万丰控股集团

中信出版集团 · 北京

图书在版编目（CIP）数据

追梦人 / 郑作时著. -- 2 版. -- 北京：中信出版
社，2017.1
　　ISBN 978-7-5086-5981-7

　　I.①追… 　II.①郑… 　III.①汽车－车轮－铝合金－
制造厂－民营企业－工业企业管理－经验－中国　IV.
①F426.471

　　中国版本图书馆CIP数据核字（2016）第 047109 号

追梦人

著　　者：郑作时
译　　者：陈爱民　曹亚昌
出版发行：中信出版集团股份有限公司
　　　　　（北京市朝阳区惠新东街甲 4 号富盛大厦 2 座　邮编　100029）
承　印　者：北京楠萍印刷有限公司

开　　本：787mm×1092mm　1/16　　印　　张：38.75　　字　　数：530 千字
版　　次：2017 年 1 月第 2 版　　　　印　　次：2017 年 1 月第 1 次印刷
广告经营许可证：京朝工商广字第 8087 号
书　　号：ISBN 978-7-5086-5981-7
定　　价：85.00 元

封面人物
陈爱莲

　　万丰控股集团董事局主席，出生于浙江新昌。中共十七大代表、全国第十二届人大代表、全国党建研究会非公专委会委员，中共浙江省委第十一、十二、十三次党代表，中共绍兴市委第五、六、七次党代表，绍兴市第四、五、七届人大代表（人大常委会委员），中共新昌县委三届委员；担任中国企业联合会副会长、浙江省工商联副主席、上海市浙江商会执行会长等。

　　曾获全国优秀中国特色社会主义建设者、中国经营大师、全国优秀创业企业家、全国三八红旗手、中国十大杰出女性、首届风云浙商、全国光彩事业特殊贡献奖等荣誉。

万丰控股集团

　　万丰控股集团创立于 1994 年，是以先进制造业为核心的国际化企业集团，遵循"永恒提升价值，不断奉献社会"的经营理念，涉足汽车部件、航空工业、智能装备、金融投资等领域。致力于"营造国际品牌，构筑百年企业"，名列中国民营企业综合实力 500 强前列、中国近 3000 家上市公司综合实力第 39 位，是名副其实的"隐形冠军"企业。

　　本书记录了万丰及其创始人 20 余年的发展历程。作者实地深入访谈，获得了众多鲜为人知的故事，并试图分析其高速发展并保持行业领先地位的秘密。"万丰人"发扬实事求是、艰苦奋斗、雷厉风行、一抓到底的作风，为中国民营制造业的发展壮大树立了典范。

郑作时

财经作家，曾任《南风窗》高级记者，中国本土最佳商业作者之一。著有《阿里巴巴：让天下没有难做的生意》、中国首富刘永行自述《希望永行——成为首富的短路径》、《汽车"疯子"李书福》、《阳光基业：一家金融保险新锐企业的崛起路径》、《领先的背后：一家港资企业的百年成长经验》、《商学有道：徐万茂与华茂的教育之路》等。

目　录

CONTENTS

追梦人

掌舵梦想①

复旦大学管理学院院长　陆雄文

　　爱莲是复旦大学 2003 年春高级管理人员工商管理硕士（EMBA）班的优秀学员，她不仅是万丰奥特的创始人，也是中共十七大代表，是浙江唯一的民营女企业家代表，她还是第十二届全国人大代表。我认识她近 12 年，自以为对她和万丰奥特很了解，然而当她让我为《追梦人》这本记述万丰奥特创业 20 年的纪实作品写序的时候，我仍然禁不住好奇，想了解更多万丰奥特成功背后的故事和秘密。

　　我用了一个晚上加一个早晨读完了全书。我看到了爱莲在她积极向上、乐观自信之下的那份百折不挠、坚持不懈的成长基因，以及成就她事业的内在逻辑。我也明白了为何在过去十年，宏观经济多次经历起伏，她一直保有着

---

　　①　本文写于 2014 年，本书初次出版时。——编者注

那份淡定和自信。当经济下行时，每当我关心地问她万丰奥特的状况，她总是告诉我："是有些困难，但我们有我们的对策"，"我们企业仍然在稳定地扩张发展中"。她永远充满活力，充满激情，脸上永远挂着灿烂的笑容。

万丰奥特 20 年的奋斗史是中国经济奇迹般增长的真实写照；是一代民族企业家创业创新、奋力拼搏、勇于竞争、善于竞争的真实写照；是一家企业由小变大、由弱变强，由单一产品走向多元产业，由国内市场走向全球市场的真实写照；是中国一代企业家从早期凭直觉、凭悟性、凭刻苦、凭冒险的"野蛮"生长，向凭学习、凭借鉴、凭创新、凭视野的有机发展而蜕变，并赢得国际同行尊重的真实写照。

20 年持续成长的万丰奥特，同中国过去 20 年来许多发展壮大的民营企业一样，它们的领导者基因有着以下五个方面的共性：

一、有敏锐的、独到的市场先见，善于捕捉市场机会，发现并拓展市场空间；

二、有很强的领导力，身先士卒，带领团队勇于拼搏；

三、重视创新，尤其是技术研发，不断积累技术基础，发展核心竞争力；

四、重视人才，引进与培养人才，以事业、报酬和情感凝聚人心，并愿意为人才发展提供培训和专业学习机会，形成人才梯队；

五、在战略上也知道如何顺应经济发展周期，有进有退，从而避过险滩，实现在低谷时期积蓄能量、继而乘势而起，跨越发展。

然而，爱莲还有两点特别的地方，可能是很多其他企业家所不具备的：

一、非常注重管理制度的建设，善于亲自设计管理架构和规章制度，奖罚分明、集思广益、理性决策。

二、她自己非常勤奋好学、求知若渴。她参加过许多总裁研修班、MBA 课程班的学习，除了在复旦大学获得 EMBA 学位外，她几乎每年都要到高校进修，求学足迹遍布大江南北。她不仅善于向同行学习、向国际先进学习，而且更强调要形成系统化的知识体系，并且与时俱进，不断更新和升级自己的知识储备。

当然，如果还要加一点，那就是作为女性企业家，她也善于用自己的情商来拓展新兴市场、发展合作伙伴、凝聚团队士气。

《追梦人》非常真实而贴切地反映了爱莲的成长轨迹，以及背后的动力和成功的原因，她也一直把自己今天的成就归为她过去几十年的好学，尤其是在复旦大学管理学院EMBA班的学习。

我也经常审视，作为一所大学的管理学院，一个以致力于培养既具有国际视野又深谙本土情势的领袖人才为使命的管理学院，应该如何来评价自己。尽管我们已经有4个EMBA项目，一个MBA项目被英国《金融时报》列入全球百强，但我仍然觉得，这不足以更本质地反映我们的教育使命是否已经达成。我和我的同事们说，我可能并不在乎我们现在的毕业生工资可以拿多少，或者毕业几年内工资的增长幅度有多高，我也可能并不在乎我们的国际排名在前多少位，我更在乎的是，在我离开院长岗位的二三十年之后，再来看看我们曾经的学生，他们的事业成就、他们为国家和世界的贡献有多大。我真切地希望10年以后，爱莲的事业有更高的高度，在全球范围内成为更强大的行业领导者。

这本《追梦人》以其非常坦诚、真实、开放的风格还原了万丰奥特20年创业奋斗发展史，还原了一个丰富丰满、性格爽朗、心地坦荡的爱莲的形象。她也想以这本书作为自己的一个总结。同时，这本书也是商学院的一个很好的案例，也能为更多的企业家、职业经理和商学院学生所借鉴。

我一直认为，一个处于行业领导地位的企业的掌舵人是不能在商言商的，他们一定要承担起归属于他们的社会责任。这种责任不仅仅只是行善捐款、关注环保、体恤顾客，它必然也是企业家以其思想和行为溢出企业的边界从而影响社会文明进程的担当。所以，一个真正的企业家不仅在贡献着社会的物质财富，也在创造着社会的精神财富。《追梦人》这本书的写作和出版也反映了爱莲同我在这一点上的共识。

Dream to steer[1]

by Lu Xiongwen, Dean of Fudan University

Ailian was an outstanding student in 2003 Executive MBA Spring Semester Program at Fudan University. She is not only the founder of Wanfeng Auto but also a member of the 17th Communist Party Congress, the only CPC member representing female entrepreneurs from Zhejiang private enterprises, as well as the member of 12th National People's Congress. I have known her and Wanfeng Auto well enough for nearly 12 years and still when she asked me to write a preface to this book, I could not help my curiosity to know more about Wanfeng Auto's story behind its success.

With a whole night and a morning, I finished reading the

---

[1] This article was written in 2014, when the book was first published.— editor's note

book, in which I saw persistent growth gene and inherent logic of her career achievements behind Ailian's optimism and confidence. I also understand how she maintained her calm and positiveness through those macroeconomic ups and downs in the past decade. Whenever the economy was down and I was concerned about Wanfeng Auto's situation, she would tell me, "there is a bit difficulty, but we have our strategies," "our company is still expanding steadily ." She is such a lady full of energy, passion, always wearing a brilliant smile on her face.

Wanfeng Auto's 20-year venture is a portrait of China's miracle in economic growth; and a portrait of innovation, hard work, as well as the courage and wisdom of a generation of Chinese entrepreneurs to compete. It is about how a business grows from small to large, from weak to strong, from single-product to multi-industry, from domestic market to global market; how this generation of Chinese entrepreneurs transform from "barbaric" growth in their early times with instinctive understanding, hard work, risk-taking to organic growth with learning, reference, innovation and vision, and won respect from their international counterparts.

Wanfeng Auto's 20 years of continuous growth should be attributed to the following five aspects in its leader's gene, which are shared by many developed and expanded private Chinese enterprises in the past 20 years:

First, they have a keen, unique vision to capture opportunities, discover and expand the market;

Second, they have strong leadership to lead their team to compete;

Third, they place emphasis on innovation, research and development of technology in particular, continue to accumulate technical basis, core competencies;

Fourth, they value talents and attract talents with career opportunities, incentives and emotion,and are willing to provide those talented with career training and opportunities for growth, which give birth to a benign reserve of human resources;

Fifth, they know how to adapt to economic development cycle , when to advance and retreat, and thus how to avoid traps and wait for the future rising at low tides.

Besides, Ailian possesses two special traits that many other entrepreneurs may not have:

First, she attaches great importance to building up management system and is good at designing management scheme and setting rules and regulations, penalties and rewards with brainstorming and rational decision-making.

Second, she is very studious and eager to learn. She participated in many CEO Seminars, MBA courses, in addition to getting EMBA degree from Fudan University. She goes to universities for further education almost every year and leaves her footprints all over China. She is good at learning not only from her peers, but also from her international counterparts.She puts more emphasis on building a systematic scheme of knowledge, and advancing with the times, constantly upgrading her knowledge reserve.

Moreover, as a woman entrepreneur, she is also good at using her own emotional intelligence to expand, to find business partners, and to cheer up her team's morale.

Dream Chaser is a vivid portrait of Ailian's growth, as well as the driving force of her success. She personally would rather attribute her success today to her studious learning in the past decades, especially her learning in the EMBA program at School of Management, Fudan University.

I often ponder, as a School of Management in a university committed to cultivating leaders with both global perspectives and local awareness, how we should evaluate ourselves. Although we already have four EMBA programs and an MBA program ranking top 100 globally by British "Financial Times" , I still think that is not enough to demonstrate the fulfillment of our mission. Once I said to my colleagues,I may not care about the wage of our graduates, or the rate of their pay-rise within a few years after graduation; I may not even care about the international ranking of my school; instead, I care more about my students'career achievements and their contribution to the country and the world in the following two or three decades, maybe after my retiring from the post of President. I sincerely hope that Ailian's career will mount on a new height and Wanfeng will become a more powerful industry leader globally.

Dream Chaser portraits Wanfeng Auto's 20 years of entrepreneurial struggle in a candid, truthful and open style and Ailian, an open-minded leader with rich fullness. She personally would like to take this book as a summary to her experience. At the same time, Dream Chaser can be a good case of Business Schools, as well a reference for more entrepreneurs, professional managers and business school students.

I always hold that a leading enterprise in the industry is not doing business for business's sake, they must bear more social responsibility than charity,concerns over environmental protection and caring customers. It should also be about entrepreneurs'spilling corporate boundaries and thus affecting the process of social civilization with their thinking and behaviors. Therefore, a true entrepreneur, not only contributes to the material wealth of society, but also creates social wealth. Luckily, the publishing of Dream Chaser shows that Ailian sees eye to eye with me.

不忘初心，二十年后"再创业"
是幸福的 ①

上海复星高科技集团董事长　郭广昌

与爱莲董事长的相识已经有很多年了，因为我们都是上海浙江商会的成员，她还是商会女企业家联谊会的会长，在一起交流得也多，早就与她成了很好的朋友。而且，我还一直觉得爱莲董事长就像位大姐一样，经常给我们些很好的启发，非常受人尊敬。

今年正好是她创办的万丰奥特成立 20 周年，这本《追梦人》就是爱莲董事长过去艰辛创业历程的缩影。作为同时期的创业者，它激起了我心中的万般思考与共鸣。

民营企业是改革开放和中国现代化的产物，复星与万丰奥特一样，刚刚走过了自己的第一个 20 年。在复星集团（以下简称复星）创立 20 年的时候，我们非常明确地提出

---

①　本文写于 2014 年，本书初次出版时。——编者注

要"再创业"。为什么？不是因为我们是苦行僧，要再创业；恰恰相反，我们感觉"再创业"很幸福，因为我们觉得成为一名创造者是最幸福的。所以，在面对未来20年的选择时，我们一定会选择再创业，要重新开始，有能力、有信心、有干劲，把企业的发展带上一个新的高度。

当然，创业不易，再创业更是难上加难。以我和复星为例，经过20年的不断发展，我们终于找到了一个可以为未来复星20年发展提供持续动力的"保险＋投资"双轮驱动的战略。但是，在将战略落地的时候，我们还是一定要十分注重、强调两点内容，它们正如爱莲董事长过去20年经历的一样，一个是关注细节和产品力，另一个是不断地国际化。

马云和马化腾是我们中国成功企业家中的翘楚，虽然表面看起来两个人的行事风格很不一样，但在不一样的背后，我觉得他们都是在不断寻求战略和细节的配合与深化。马云的战略思想一般人很难理解，但是他有一群非常务实的合作伙伴，这些人在执行力和对产品的深化上是非常强的；马化腾不仅是位极其优秀的产品经理，他现在写的一些文章，也很有战略思维，很有高度。我觉得他们最后会是殊途同归，因为都是要抓住客户的需求，要为了客户体验去积极努力，关注细节、提升产品力。所以，未来的再创业，关键问题还是看我们能不能继续深入下去。而不是说已经有了20年积累就可以高高在上，正如书中谈到爱莲董事长对于产品创新、质量细节的孜孜追求，我们要真正能接地气，一点一滴地去推动一个企业的发展。这就是我对未来"再创业"的第一点思考。

第二点，中国的企业想在未来取得更大的发展，我们的国家要成为最强有力的经济体，那么我们就必须要更加主动地融入全球经济，中国的企业也必须要更积极、更主动地开始全球化。在这方面，我们有全球最大的市场，以前，我们的市场是被人家整合，现在我们为什么不能利用自己的市场去整合别人的资源呢？所以我的观点是，我们可以用中国动力嫁接全球资源，去主动整合全球资源，比如整合全球最好的品牌、渠道、技术和资金资源，等等。所以，当下我深刻地感受到中国企业全球化的压力非常大，我们必须要用一个更开放、更淡定的姿态学习和融入。这方面爱莲董事长和万丰奥特也给了我们很好的示范。胸怀全球走向国际化，并购全球行业细分市场的领跑者是我们中国企业做大、做强的有效途径。当然，我还想说的是，在融入当中，我们所有的中国企业还应当更广泛地合作起来，中国也应该站在世界经济的角度来综合地考虑发展经济。

以上，即是我的一些思考。我们浙商团队共同见证了爱莲董事长的创业历程，勇气和决心是她 20 年不断发展的最大支持；与创立之初一样，勇气和决心，仍将是未来 20 年"再创业"最重要的力量。所以，此时此刻，我再次向爱莲董事长道一句祝贺，祝贺她已成为最幸福的创造者；也再表一声共勉，希望爱莲董事长不忘初心，享受，20 年后"再创业"的幸福。

让我们不忘初心，从容向前。

SEQUENCE

Holding to original dreams and "re–start" after two decades[①]

Guo Guangchang, chairman of Shanghai Fosun High-Tech Group

I've been knowing chairwoman Ailian for many years as both members of the Commerce Chamber of Shanghai and Zhejiang. She is also the chair of Female Entrepreneur Association in the chamber. We have much communication and cooperation and have long become good friends. And, I always respect her as an elder sister who often inspires us.

This year happens to be the 20th anniversary of the foundation of Wanfeng Auto. Dream Chaser is a miniature of Ailian and Wanfeng Auto's story of 20 years' arduous pioneering journey. The book also aroused my thought and

---

① This article was written in 2014, when the book was first published.— editor's note

sympathy as an entrepreneur in the same era with her.

Private enterprises are the product of reform and opening-up policy as well as the modernization of China, and Fosun and Wanfeng Auto, have both gone through their first 20 years. In the 20th anniversary of Fosun Group (hereinafter referred to as Fosun), we proposed a " re-start" not because we are ascetic and wanted to be mean to ourselves. On the contrary, we feel happy to be a creator. So, facing the next 20 years, we will choose to start all over again,from the beginning. We have the ability, the confidence and energy to bring our enterprises to a new era.

To start a business is difficult, not to mention restarting. For me and Fosun, for example, after 20 years of continuous development, we finally found a development strategy of "insurance plus investment" which can provide continuous driving force for the next 20 years. However, to employ the strategy, we must still attach great importance to two elements, as were experienced in the past 20 years by Ailian, one being details of products and the other being constant internationalization.

Jack Ma and Ma Huateng are considered as the role models by many Chinese entrepreneurs. Although they two have seemingly very different acting styles, they share in their constant search for a balance between strategies and details. Jack Ma's strategic thinking is astounding and even difficult to understand to general people, but he has a group of very pragmatic partners to execute and deepen the products. Ma Huateng is not only a very good product manager, but also one with strategic thinking. He wrote articles of profound perspectives recently. I think they will eventually become the same people, since they are both committed to seize the customers' needs,to go for positive customer experiences, to think highly of details and product competitiveness.

The future re-starting is about whether we can carry on.It is not about feeling superior with 20 years accumulation. Ailian diligently pursues product innovation, quality details. And that's the way to be, to promote the development of an enterprise with an down-to-earth manner. And that's my opinion of restarting.

Second, Chinese enterprises' greater development in the future depends on the nation's future as a most powerful economy, a more active player in the global economy and Chinese enterprises being more positive in globalization. We have the world's largest market. In the past, our market used to be integrated by the world, now it's time we used our market to integrate the global resources. So my point is that we can graft global resources to Chinese engine and take initiatives to integrate global resources, such as the world's best brands, channels, technology and financial resources,etc. So,at the moment I deeply felt the pressure for globalization of Chinese enterprises.We must adapt with a more open and calm attitude of learning and integration.

On this regard, Ailian also makes a good demonstration that it is effective for Chinese enterprises to go stronger and global by merging the global leader in a particular market segment. Of course, I would like to say that, in the process of globalization, Chinese enterprises should co-operate more extensively and China should consider economic development from a perspective of an integrated world economy.

Zhejiang entrepreneurs witnessed Ailian starting her business. What supported her through the 20 years' entrepreneurial process is her courage and determination, which will surely continue to encourage her to"re-start"for the next 20 years. At this moment, I would like to congratulate Ailian once again on her being the happiest creator of her dream and also encourage her not to forget her original determination and restart with a confident pace. May that also be a spur on me.

序 3

"隐形冠军"的标本意义^①

著名财经作家、"蓝狮子"出版人　吴晓波

　　拿到这份书稿的时候，我正在准备一个关于企业失败案例的课程，相对应的，成功者的经验与失败者的教训构成为商业智慧的两面。万丰奥特的发展历程，引起了我的浓厚兴趣。著名财经作家郑作时通过一年多的时间，潜心研究了这样一家好公司，我对它的直观印象是：行业领军者、国际化、现金流充裕、低调且充满活力。

　　毫无疑问，这是真正的"隐形冠军"——在一份关于"2013 年中国汽车行业 30 强"的榜单中，在包含了上汽、一汽、广汽等整车品牌商的排名中，万丰奥特以"汽配商"的身份新晋榜单即名列 22 位。如今，万丰奥特涉足汽车部件、机械装备、金融投资等领域，其中，集团旗下的实业板块 5 个产业当中，铝轮毂产业和新材料镁合金

---

　　① 本文写于 2014 年，本书初次出版时。——编者注

产业已实现行业细分市场的全球领跑，新工艺涂覆产业、新能源混合动力产业和智能工业机器人产业已实现行业细分市场的国内领跑。

1986年，德国管理大师赫尔曼·西蒙通过对德国400多家卓越中小企业的研究，创造性地提出"隐形冠军"（Hidden Champion）的概念。西蒙把他对这些企业的研究成果著成《隐形冠军：全球最佳500名公司的成功之道》一书。在随后的10多年当中，该书被译成20种语言，包括简体中文和繁体中文版，广为传播，成为继柯林斯的《基业长青》之后的又一部管理学经典著作。

西蒙指出，全球最优秀的企业更多是一些"闷声发大财"的行业冠军企业。他归纳了这些企业的三个特点：一是行业领军者，市场份额占据世界前列；二是专业化程度很高，年销售收入一般都不超过10亿美元；最后，非常专注，以世界级企业为标杆，投入最大的资源，执着地在一个行业细分市场做到最优。通过书中的论述，我们可以发现，这三个特点，万丰奥特都基本契合。

记得2012年的8月份，我曾亲赴位于浙江东部地区的新昌，参观万丰科技园，并与掌舵人陈爱莲交谈，谈起万丰奥特的创业历程，谈未来10年的发展方向。她的大气豪爽、敢想敢干的品格，哪怕在男企业家之中也不多见。

经过30多年的改革开放，企业家阶层中，女企业家作为特殊的一个分支，也逐渐走进了大众的视野。在基本上还是男人主导的商业社会里，那些通过自己努力，白手起家而成就功名的就更值得嘉许，比如董明珠、张兰、杨澜、王利芬等，当然，还有陈爱莲。

陈爱莲的创业故事书中已有详述，我只想说一点，万丰奥特所在的轮毂制造行业，恐怕是最不适合女人的职业选择之一，这个女人不仅乐在其中，甚至于能够掌控全局，的确令人惊叹。作者写道，"在她众多的照片当中，经常可以看得到一大群男人当中，她是唯一的女性。'万绿丛中一点红'，自然格外引人注目"。

当然，万丰奥特"格外引人注目"的远远不止这些，至少还有以下三点：

第一，品质的原则。作为汽车轮毂的配件商，并不与消费者直接打交道，一般都是依附于整车商。这样，万丰奥特在与客户谈判的时候，是很难占据主动地位的，能够拿出来谈判的只有品质和价格。90 年代的大多数企业，喜欢用价格来打动客户，这样销售效果立竿见影。陈爱莲却清楚地意识到"品质才是生命"。

很有意思的是，品质原则的确立，陈爱莲的做法与当年张瑞敏"砸冰箱"的办法如出一辙：1995 年，刚创立不久的万丰，一批赶工生产出来的价值 60 万元的轮毂虽然达到行业的一般标准，但离万丰自己的要求仍有差距，陈爱莲带领创业团队成员，在创业资金非常紧张的情况下，仍然毫不犹豫地全部砸掉了，并重新回炉。

如今，当年与万丰奥特同时创立的 100 多家竞争对手消失了一大半，市场份额逐步集中到了少数关注品质的行业领导者手中。

第二，失败的启示。我在研究企业失败案例的时候总结过，"如果你面对的是一家在几年乃至十几年的经营历程中一帆风顺、从来就没有遭遇过挫折和失败的企业，那么，要么它是一个上帝格外呵护的异类，要么它根本就是一个自欺欺人的泡沫"。万丰奥特决然不是异类，它在创业历程中，也经历过整车策略的失误。

我所知道的浙商企业家中，曾有过"汽车梦"的大致有三位，李书福、鲁冠球和本书的主人公陈爱莲，三人都以不同的方式追求和诠释。李书福创立吉利，通过大胆坚毅且披肝沥胆的折腾，如今把沃尔沃收入囊中，站上了一个新的高度。鲁冠球很早就跟我说过想要造车，如今，万向成为特斯拉的合作伙伴，据说万向钱潮的股票还因此连连涨停，也算修得正果。

相比之下，陈爱莲浓厚的汽车情结，早在年轻时成为全县第一位女拖拉机驾驶员的时候就显露无遗，而领导万丰奥特进军整车制造，是把汽车梦付诸实践的尝试。从 2000 年开始的 7 年中，万丰汽车"性价比高"而受到消费者欢迎，总销量超过十万辆，最后却因为团队的管理问题而不得不暂停，令人扼腕。不过，从万丰奥特妥善处理善后事宜的表现来看，在未来的某个时候，重新启动万丰汽车项目，仍具有很大的想象空间。同时，从另外一个角度来看，任何一家企业，只有懂得进退相间，才有可能迎来"柳暗花明又一村"。

第三，政治经济学。毫无疑问，作为民营企业家，陈爱莲深谙政治经济学的基本原理，在她的集团董事长称谓之外，还有诸如党的十七大代表、全国人大代表、浙江省工商联副主席等一连串社会职务。在政治舞台上，这应是民营企业家所能达到的少有的政治高度了。

几千年下来，中国的经济史说到底是一部政商博弈史。如何处理企业与政府的关系，是每一位企业家都绕不过去的永恒课题。很多企业家不理解这一点，折戟商海甚至身陷囹圄。

陈爱莲对于万丰奥特的企业管理，始终围绕着"社会责任"、"历史使命"、"时代召唤"展开，用高度的政治思想和觉悟来要求中高层管理者，企业内部的党委、组织部、书记并非摆设，对于任人用钱都是有实权的，这在民营企业中恐怕也不多见。

看完全书，我突然意识到，其实，用"隐形冠军"来形容今天的万丰奥特恐怕已经不够了。她两年前谈起的很多发展战略，如今都成了现实，比如以"高、精、尖"为特征的工业城市综合体"万丰高科精品园"已经开始建设，入园项目将涉及新能源汽车及混合动力、飞机及零部件制造、高科技军工等战略新兴产业项目，在鸟瞰图上，国际化的百万平方现代化厂房、万丰研究院、万丰商学院、万丰博物馆、万丰花园别墅等一一展现。

陈爱莲在媒体上最新的两次亮相，一是斥资 15.3 亿元，收购加拿大的镁瑞丁公司（Meridian），一举成为镁合金产业的全球领跑者，具有核心技术和市场话语权，成为与特斯拉、保时捷、路虎等世界最高端品牌的长期战略伙伴，在国际化的道路上迈出了坚实的步伐；二是豪掷千万购买了私人专机，这说明，她像赵本山、成龙、李连杰、马云等人一样，已经意识到时间比金钱更宝贵。无论哪一条，都可以说是她作为企业家，更加成熟、更加成功的表现。也许，再过 10 年，我们将看到一个更加杰出的女企业家和前程远大的万丰奥特控股集团。

"Hidden champion", a role model[①]

Wu Xiaobo, financial writer, publisher of Blue Lion

I was preparing for a course on cases of business failure, which is one side of the coin of business wisdom, the other side being successful cases, when I got the manuscript of Dream Chaser. The development process of Wanfeng Auto immediately grabbed my interest. Thanks goes to Mr. Zheng Zuoshi, financial writer and the creating consultant of Blue Lion for his thorough and painstaking research on such a good company. My impression on Wanfeng is: an industry leader, its international vision, ample cash flow, low-key and vitality.

There is no doubt that it is a real "hidden champion" — in a report on "China's auto industry Top 30 in 2013" Wan Feng

---

① This article was written in 2014, when the book was first published.— editor's note

Auto ranked 22nd as an "auto parts supplier" ,the list covering competitive vehicle brands including SAIC, FAW, Guangzhou Auto, etc. Today, Wanfeng Auto gets involved in fields including automotive parts, machinery equipment and financial investment,among which, in industry such as aluminum wheels and new material industry of magnesium alloy, it has taken a dominant global position in its market segment. While in the coating technology industry, new energy and hybrid vehicle industry as well as intelligent robot industry, it has achieved a leading role domestically.

In 1986, Hermann Simon, a German management master creatively put forward the concept of "hidden champion" through his study of more than 400 outstanding SMEs in Germany. Simon published his research on these companies in his book□ Hidden Champions: Lessons from 500 of the World's Best Unknown Companies, which was translated into 20 languages in the following decade including simplified Chinese and traditional Chinese version, widely read as another classic in management after Built to Last by Jim Collins and Jerry I. Porras.

Simon pointed out that the world's best companies are industry champions with some of the more "muffled fortune" . He summed up the three characteristics of these companies: first, they are industry leaders occupying more market share in the world; second, they have a high degree of specialization, their annual sales volume being generally no more than 1 billion US dollars; and finally, they are very focused, taking world-class enterprise as a benchmark, pouring the largest investment of resources into one particular industry segment and dedicated to be the best. Interestingly, I found Wanfeng Auto's traits basically fit the Simon's finding.

In August 2012, I went to Wanfeng Technology Park in Xinchang, eastern Zhejiang and had a talk with Ailian about Wanfeng Auto's adventure as a new business and her blueprint of Wanfeng's next 10 years. Her forthright and bold character,as well as her vision amazed me as rare even among male entrepreneurs.

After China's 30 years of reform and opening up, female entrepreneurs as a special branch have gradually entered into the public view. In such a substantially male-dominated community as business, female entrepreneurs who earned their achievements and fame from scratch are even more commendable; Dong Mingzhu, Zhang Lan, Yang Lan, Wang Lifen, and of course, Chen Ailian, to name some of them.

Ailian's business story has been described in details in this book. What I want to stress is that, Wanfeng Auto is in the wheel manufacturing industry, which is probably one of the worst career choice for a woman, which this woman not only enjoys, and even manages to steer. It's really amazing! The authors wrote, "She was usually the only girl among a large group of men in numerous photos. Just like 'a single red flower in the midst of thick foliage', she was outstanding and naturally in the spotlight".

Of course, Wanfeng Auto is eye-catching for more reasons,the following three being at least in list:

First, its principle of quality. As an auto parts supplier, it generally depends on auto producers and does not deal directly with consumers. Thus, in negotiation with customers,the only ground Wanfeng Auto could take is quality and price. Most enterprises in the 1990s like to tempt clients with low price which is an instant stimulus to the sales volume. However, Ailian was better aware of "quality as life."

Interestingly, she implemented quality principles in exactly the same way as the famous practice of "smashing refrigerators" by Zhang Ruimin, the founder of

Haier Group. In 1995, the newly founded Wanfeng produced a batch of wheel hubs in a rush,which unfortunately didn't meet Wanfeng's quality standard though good enough according to the general industry standard. Despite the tight budget, Ailian led her entrepreneurial team members to smash and melt all the products worth 600 thousand yuan.

Today, Wanfeng Auto found half of its former competitors disappear from the market, the market share gradually concentrating in the hands of a small number of industry leaders who concerned about the quality.

Second, its lesson of failure. In the cases of business failure I studied, my finding is that "If you are faced with an enterprise that has never been struck with any setbacks in a few years or even ten years, it is either specially blessed by the God or simply a bubble of self-deception." Wanfeng Auto is definitely not specially blessed and it did ever make wrong decision to step into vehicle producing field in its entrepreneurial history.

Among the Zhejiang entrepreneurs I know, there are three who harbor the dream of making automobiles — Li Shufu, Lu Guanqiu and Chen Ailian, the heroine of this book. They have been pursuing their dreams in separate ways. Li Shufu,the founder of Geely merged Volvo with bold determination and thorn-breaking courage and is now standing on a new height. Lu guanqiu talked to me about his dream very early, and now Wanxiang Group has become a universal partner of Tesla and its stock price has reportedly surged to limit-up continually, which can also be considered a successful case.

In contrast, Ailian's chasing of her dream can be traced back to her youth as the county's first female tractor driver. The vehicle manufacturing of Wanfeng Auto is to put her dream into practice. Since 2000, seven years afterwards, Wanfeng's vehicles were welcomed by consumers for their "cost-effectiveness" and achieved a total sales of more than one hundred thousand, but sadly had to be called to a halt because of the management problem. Still the performance of Wanfeng Auto's properly handling the aftermath left us a great room for imagination of restarting Wanfeng car project.Meanwhile, a lesson to learn in the case is that only those who know when to advance and when to retreat will be possible to welcome new opportunities.

Third, the political economy. There is no doubt that as a private entrepreneur, Ailian understands the basic principles of political economy.In addition to her title of chairwoman of Wanfeng Group, she is entitled with the member of 17th CPC, National People's Congress, vice chairwoman of Zhejiang Federation of Industry. Such is a rare reputation that a private entrepreneur can enjoy in the political arena.

For thousands of years, Chinese economic history can be interpreted as a game of business and politics. How to handle the relationship between business and government is an eternal topic for every entrepreneur. Many entrepreneurs did not understand this and ended out of the business or even in prison.

Ailian disciplines her senior management team with political thought and conscientiousness and manages Wanfeng Auto with notions such as "social responsibility" , "historical mission" and "time calls", which are probably also rare in private enterprises.

After reading the book, I suddenly realized that "hidden champion" is not enough to describe today's Wanfeng Auto. Ailian's vision two years ago has all been put into practice. For instance, "Hi-Tech Wanfeng Park" which features "high, fine, sharp" industrial city complex has begun construction. Projects to be conducted in the park will involve new energy and hybrid cars, aircraft and parts manufacturing, high-tech military and other strategic new industrial projects. In the aerial view, million square meters of modern workshops, Wanfeng Research Institute, Wanfeng School of Business, Wanfeng Museum, Wanfeng garden villas have all been planned.

Ailian's latest appearance before the media was about her purchasing Canadian Meridian with 1.53 billion yuan and becoming a global leader in industrial magnesium alloy with the core technology and market control right; and establishing long-term strategic partnership with Tesla , Porsche, Land Rover, the world's most high-end brands, which marked a solid pace on its road to internationalization. The other was to spend dozens of million yuan on a private jet, which shows that she, like Zhao Benshan, Jackie Chan, Jet Li and Jack Ma, has realized that time is more valuable than money. Either appearance can be symbol of her maturity as a successful entrepreneur. In another 10 years, we will be bound to see a more outstanding female entrepreneur and promising future of Wanfeng Auto Holding Group.

自 序

常怀感恩之情，常存敬畏之心 ①

万丰控股集团创始人　陈爱莲

如果历史是一条滚滚向前的长河，那么万丰奥特 20
年便是那潮头激情绽放的一朵美丽浪花。经过将近一年的
辛勤付出，蓝狮子创作团队以非常平实的风格为我们撰写
了《追梦人——陈爱莲与万丰奥特 20 年》一书，我们写
作这本书的目的主要有两个：

一方面，是为了在历史长河中积淀宝贵的精神财富，
为万丰奥特未来发展奠定基础；另一方面，我们也非常
愿意把企业成长过程当中的成功经验和挫折教训毫无保
留地奉献出来，如果能对企业的经营管理者以及正在梦
想路上奋勇前行的创业者们有所启迪，此书也就有了它
存在的价值。

---

① 本文写于 2014 年，本书初次出版时。——编者注

作为改革开放大背景下成长起来的民营企业，万丰奥特生逢其时，碰上了一个好环境，赶上了一个好时代。每年大年三十晚上，当新年钟声敲响的那一刻，我总会赤脚踩在黄土地上，仰望浩瀚宇宙，诉说感恩之情：

一是感恩天时。我们每个人都有自己不同的人生观、事业观、价值观。我的父母都是老党员干部，一生光明磊落、克己奉公、宽厚待人，在乡里有口皆碑。这使我从小在骨子里信任党，发自内心地"听党话、跟党走"。这句话听起来很简单，但内蕴很丰富，不是一句口号，如今更是已经成为全体万丰人的共识，也是万丰奥特20年实现稳健发展的方向标。

创业路上，我最大的切身感受是，中国正处于近代历史以来最好的时期。我们回顾一下历史就知道，没有哪一代人像我们这一代人过得这么和平，从1840年以来的170多年里，国家经历鸦片战争、辛亥革命、抗日战争、解放战争等，民不聊生、颠沛流离，直到1949年新中国成立，中国人民站了起来，1978年改革开放，中国人民富了起来。特别是从党的十四大以来，确立了市场经济体制，民营经济从"有益补充"到"重要组成部分"，再到"两个毫不动摇"，党中央在政治经济体制上的不断创新，激发了民营企业的活力，尤其是十八届三中全会提出"使市场在资源配置中起决定性作用"，民营经济又迎来了新的春天。

所以，我常常感慨这个时代很美好，社会给了每一个有梦想的人一个能够充分体现价值的舞台，我觉得自己实在是太幸运了。当我们感觉自己为社会所需要，个人价值得到体现，那真的是一件很幸福的事情！

二是感恩地利。万丰奥特已经成长为一家国际化企业，从产品国际化走向了资本、人才、品牌的国际化，但我们的"根"仍然在浙江。这缘于中华民族五千年的"寻根"传统文化，我们身在浙江、长在浙江，后来出去闯天下了，但俗话说"树高千丈、叶落归根"，浙江就是我们的根。

浙江作为中国民营经济的发祥地，改革开放30多年来，为什么能够从资源小省一跃成为民营经济大省，除了浙商群体发扬了"历经千辛万苦、说尽千言万语、走遍千山万水、想尽千方百计"的精神，还有浙江省历来务实而开放的行政文化，在市场上采取"无为"的态度，按市场经济规律办事；在行政上采取"有为"的手段，服务意识非常强，使浙江民营企业具备了"一有雨露就发芽、一有阳光就灿烂"的强大活力。

最近，浙江省提出了独特的"店小二"文化，要求各级干部要跑得了断腿，服务要勤快；要受得了委屈，角色要无我；要做得了生意，绩效要考核。企业在前方"冲锋陷阵"，各级政府就要在后方提供强有力的支援保障，非常真诚、非常务实。正是处于这样的良好土壤和环境里，我常常想，作为企业来说，我们做好是应该的，做不好是不应该的！

三是感恩人和。万丰奥特 20 年经历了数轮行业大洗牌，很多企业都在时代滚滚向前的洪流中被淘汰了、销声匿迹了，而我们却每洗一次就壮大一次，平均每年诞生或并购一家企业，达到了"并购一家、盘活一家，整合一家、成功一家"的效果，万丰奥特大旗扛到哪里，哪里就能创造奇迹，哪里就能创造样板，最终成长为行业细分市场的全球领跑者。有不少人这样问我，"万丰奥特现象"到底是怎么产生的？我总是笑着回答说，我没有什么特别高的水平，是我们来自五湖四海、由各种专业人才组合起来的各级团队很优秀，我们正是拥有了一批批能征善战的精兵强将，锻造了"敬业、竞争、实干、学习、团队"五种精神，锤炼了"实事求是、艰苦奋斗、雷厉风行、一抓到底"的工作作风，铸就了"永恒提升价值，不断奉献社会"的理想信念，才成就了万丰奥特，同时，万丰奥特也成就了我们。大家虽然工作很辛苦，但都很快乐，有成就感、有归属感、有幸福感，这说明我们各级团队的价值取向、思维方式、行为准则都达到了高度一体。只有价值取向一体了，我们才能在大浪淘沙的残酷竞争中稳步前进。当然，在我们身后还站立着千千万万的好父亲、好母亲、好妻子、好丈夫、好孩子，他们用无声的大爱，铸就了万丰人坚实温暖的后方家园！

在这里，要感恩尊贵客户的厚爱。市场是企业生存的根基，万丰奥特从创立以来，就以"一览众山小、再览众山无"的战略定位，选择了业界最精英的客户群，从而使万丰形成了较好的市场集中度。更重要的是，万丰跟随着精英客户的壮大而迅速成长，始终引领和创造着高端市场。还要感恩一路上众多良师益友的教诲与启迪，总是让我受益良多。

在这个世上，有两样东西值得敬畏——我们头上的星空，我们心中的道德法则。敬畏"头上的星空"，就是要按自然规律、按市场经济规律做事；敬畏"心中的道德法则"，则是要敬畏国家的法律。我认为，做企业不在于做得有多大，而在于做得有多稳、走得有多远。我常常要求每位万丰人都要有法律意识，做到学法、懂法、知法、守法，国家的法律底线不能碰、公司的规章制度要执行好，从而确保企业依法经营，确保自身能够健康成长。我们每一个人只有真正懂得感恩和敬畏，才能保持积极乐观的精神状态，以美丽的眼睛看世界，以阳光的心态做工作！

万丰人喜欢梦想，并始终以强烈的愿望、必胜的信念、锲而不舍的精神，一次次将美好的梦想转化成灿烂的现实。总结过去20年，万丰奥特形成了以百亿先进制造业为核心的国际化企业。展望未来20年，我们将继续走先进制造业的专业化道路，从汽车零部件、工业机器人、新能源混合动力产业向航天航空、飞机及零部件制造、航空大物流等战略新兴产业转型升级；走国际化道路，利用资本市场平台整合全球优质资源；走法治化道路，做有社会责任的美丽企业，不断地做精做专、做强做久，最终实现"营造国际品牌、构筑百年企业"的战略目标。作为万丰奥特创始人，我对万丰奥特的未来充满了信心！让每一个万丰人"快乐工作、幸福生活"，是伟大"中国梦"的组成部分，是我心中的梦，也是全体万丰人共同的"梦"！

生命不息，奋斗不止。我们，追梦在创业路上！

With grateful affection, always keep the awe[①]

Ailian,founder of Wanfeng Auto Holding Group

If history is a river rolling forward, then the 20 years of Wanfeng Auto's entrepreneurial venture is a beautiful spray at the forefront of its tide. After nearly a year of hard work, Blue Lion completed the writing of Dream Chaser—20 years of Chenailian and Wanfeng Auto, with a plain style. We wrote this book for two main purposes:

on the one hand, we want to treasure the precious spiritual wealth accumulation in the history as lay the foundation for Wanfeng Auto's future development; on the other hand, we are very willing to contribute our successful experiences

---

① This article was written in 2014, when the book was first published.— editor's note

and setbacks as lessons to the enterprise managers and entrepreneurs who are courageously on their way of chasing their dreams. If only it could bring about some inspiration, the book may have its value of existence.

As a private enterprise developing in the context of China's reform and opening up, Wanfeng Auto was born at the right time. On every New Year's Eve, when the bell sounded the coming of the New Year, I would express my gratitude with bare foot on the earth and facing the sky:

First thanks given to the era. Each of us has a different outlook on life, career and values. My parents are both CPC members and cadres, known for their honorable life, austerity and generosity in the village. This makes me grow with a trust to the Party in nature. In my heart, "listen to the Party and follow the Party" is not a slogan, but a motto with rich connotation. And now it has become the consensus of all Wanfeng people and also the light house which has directed us to achieve the 20 years'steady development.

On my way to start the business, my personal feeling is that China is in its golden era of the modern history. No generations had ever enjoyed such a long period of peace like us. In the 170 years after 1840, China had suffered the Opium War, Xinhai Revolution , Anti-Japanese War, the Civil War until the founding of PRC when Chinese people rose to their feet. Since 1978, with the reform and opening-up policy, Chinese people are getting rich. Especially since the 14th Party Congress when market economy was established, the private economy has shifted its role from "useful supplement" to "important part" to China's economy". A series of creative and innovative policy reforms in economic and political system has greatly stimulated the vitality of private enterprises, among which, the principle of"letting markets play a decisive role in resource allocation" proposed on the third session of 18th PC brought about a blossom of the private economy.

So, I often feel grateful for this time which gives each person a platform to realize his dream. I feel lucky and happy to live in this time, when we feel needed by the society and our personal values can be fully expressed!

My second thanks go to the location privilege. Wanfeng Auto has developed into an international enterprise,transforming from product internationalization into that of capital, talent and international brand, but we are still rooted in Zhejiang. This is due to China's 5,000 years of "root-seeking" tradition. We were born in Zhejiang,grow in Zhejiang and step out into the world, but we are always rooted here just as the saying goes "A tree may grow a thousand feet high, but its leaves fall back to the roots."

Thanks to the reform and opening-up policy implemented for 30 years, Zhejiang, as the birthplace of China's private economy, can become the top province of the private economy. Its success should be attributed to Zhejiang entrepreneurs'hardship and perseverance, as well as the practical and open administrative culture of the local authority. Their loose control over markets and supportive attitude towards service brought about a privilege environment to the booming private economy.

Recently, Zhejiang Province even proposed a unique "waiter" culture and asked the government official at all levels to act as "waiters" who serve enterprises without complaining. It is for such strong, sincere and practical support that I hold gratitude, as a business it is our duty not to mess up.

Third, my thanks go to my team.In the past 20 years, Wanfeng Auto has gone through several rounds of major reshuffle in the industry, in which many enterprises could not survive and were washed out by the torrent of time. However, we manage to grow stronger in every shuffle, set up or merge a business every year and all the merging are successful by far. Wanfeng has been creating miracles and models and eventually develops into a global leader in our industry market segment. When asked about the secret, I always smiled and replied: I'm not particularly brilliant. I just have a team of professionals at all levels, with a "dedicated, competitive, hard working, and learning"spirit, their working style being "realistic, vigorous,resolute and down to earth" . Our motto is to "enhance the value and constantly contribute to the society" which fulfills the achievements of Wanfeng Auto and at the same time, fulfills our dream. My team have a strong sense of accomplishment, belonging and happiness, which means we share the values, ways of thinking, acting modes at all levels. Behind us, are our supportive family, who always back up Wanfeng people.

My thanks also go to my distinguished customers. Market is the foundation of business survival. Since its founding, Wanfeng Auto has decided on a strategic positioning as market leader and thus selected the industry's most elite customers. More importantly, with the development of its customer group, Wanfeng grows rapidly, always leading and creating the high-end market. Thanks to the teaching and inspiration of my friends and customers, I always benefit.

In this world, there are two things worthy of awing - the starry sky above our heads, the moral law in our hearts. To awe the sky above is to respect the laws of nature, to follow the rules of market economy; while to awe the morals within is to fear the laws of the country. I hold that to run a business does not necessarily mean to expand, but rather how to walk on stably and far. I often ask each Wanfeng person to be legally aware, to study , understand and abide by the law. Should national laws be followed and the company's rules and regulations be performed well, we can ensure our business grow healthily. Each of us should be grateful and fearful, in order to maintain an optimistic state of mind and work with positive attitude.

Wanfeng people like to chase our dreams, and always hold strong desire and perseverance to win. We have time and time again made beautiful dreams into a brilliant reality.As a conclusion to the past 20 years, Wanfeng Auto has developed into an international enterprise of advanced manufacturing with billions of asset as the core. Looking forward to the next 20 years, we will continue our pursuit for specialized advanced manufacturing industry, transforming from automotive parts, industrial robots, the new hybrid energy to aerospace manufacturing industry, aircraft and parts, aviation logistics and other strategic new industry. We will maintain the road of internationalization, by making use of the capital market platform and integrate global quality resources.

We will stick to the rules of law and be responsible to the society, continue to compete in the fine, and specified industry and pursue a long life and ultimately to create an international brand, and build a century-old enterprise. As the founder of Wanfeng Auto, I hold confidence in Wanfeng's future. To let each Wanfeng person "work happily and live happily" is my dream and a part of the grand Chinese dream, and that is the common dream of all the Wanfeng people!

"Cease to struggle and you cease to live." We are always on the road of chasing our dreams!

第一章

亮相

ISO 8644

1998 年的溪口中信花园酒店，在当时当地算是一家非常好的酒店。这是因为它的位置在宁波溪口风景区中最为著名的景点——蒋介石家族故居的边上。

现在去看，还可以看到它当时时尚的一面：早在 20 世纪 90 年代中期，这家酒店的外立面就已经选用了蓝色的玻璃幕墙，饭店内部有挑高的大堂，院落里有迂回的沿廊，颇具中国江南园林的韵味。加上它处于溪口镇的主街——武岭东路上，按当时的话说，住在这家酒店，就是"住在风景里"。

除了酒店本身，位于浙江奉化的溪口镇也是个好地方。相信大多数人都知道，溪口是蒋介石的老家。但只有去过溪口的人才会知道，它还是一个传统和现代结合得不错的小镇。这当然与蒋氏家族有关系。

溪口地处宁波奉化，大致位于一处江南丘陵和平原的交界处，既有雪窦山的秀美风光，又有剡溪的蜿蜒温顺，是一个非常典型的江南小镇。而它与传统江南市镇的不同之处在于，蒋氏家族在镇上经营多年，这里还一度成为蒋氏在国内的政权中心，所以镇上有修建良好的基础设施和底蕴深厚的中国文化的各种院落，是旅游的好去处。

虽然拥有得天独厚的资源，不过在很长时间内因为历史原因，溪口一直默默无名。但在20世纪90年代中期之后，因为两岸关系趋向缓和，而国内又掀起了旅游热潮，有着秀美风光和深厚历史背景的溪口，迅速成为旅游胜地。

也正因此，1998年9月14日，刚刚筹备成立的万丰奥特控股集团有限公司（以下简称万丰奥特）选择这个地方迎接由ISO 8644国际标准组织召开的修订这一标准的会议，这应该算得上是非常精心的安排。

就当时而言，万丰奥特能在风景秀丽的溪口镇召开ISO 8644标准修订会议，并不寻常。

1998年的中国对外开放程度还并不高，而ISO 8644会议是一次高标准的国际会议，会议的参与者来自于中、德、日、意等多个国家。在会议上，可以听到一连串令人注目的名字，比如本田、丰田、哈雷、宝马、大众等，这些大公司都派出代表来参加这次会议。

这在见到外国人都还觉得很稀奇的90年代的中国来说，确实是很少见的。

要理解为什么欧美这些大牌厂商会出现在这次会议上，我们需要大致了解ISO 8644标准。ISO 8644标准的全称是《摩托车-轻合金轮-试验方法》，在国内，它目前对应的是国标GB/T 22435—2008《摩托车和轻便摩托车的轻合金轮》。而ISO 8644标准修订会议，对于国家标准化组织（简称ISO）来说，其实是一次正常的工作会议，它要修订的是当时摩托车车轮生产当中的检测标准。

不过，ISO 8644标准修订会议到中国来召开，其背景倒不是那么简单。

首先当然是因为摩托车生产的标准组织看好中国的未来。

在奉化溪口召开的这一次国际标准会议，组织人叫王颂秦，是天津大学摩托车技术中心的专家，一位女博导。这个技术中心创建于1958年，创始人是我国著名内燃机专家、中国科学院院士、天津大学原校长史绍熙教授。

由中国作为东道主来发起这次国际标准会议，并由王颂秦教授来组织会议，除了天津大学与王教授对于国内摩托车生产和测试的标准有举足轻重的影响力之外，更为重要的有两大原因。

第一，中国当时正在成长为全球摩托车最大的市场。在会议中，摩托车标准组织的主席援引数据说："当前中国国内的摩托车销售量达到了800万辆，再过两年，这个数字将达到2 000万辆之多，构成了一个足以让所有主机生产商都竞相低头的巨大市场。"

如此巨大的市场，加上国内当时非常有优势的价格要素，使得国内摩托车生产企业极为活跃，形成了一大批强有力的竞争厂商，也形成了一大批强有力的配件生产企业。就全球范围来说，这也是一股相当强大的力量。即便当时中国国内的这些厂商规模并不算大，配件生产企业起步的时间也很晚，但由于市场庞大，而且企业领导者的进取心都不小，所以全球大型厂商也都愿意来合作。

1998年，在全球范围内，无论是企业、非政府组织还是政府，都非常积极，兴起一股"到中国去"的热潮。而经过多年的努力，入世的大门也已经基本向中国敞开。所以能在中国市场施加影响，对于摩托车车轮生产的国际标准化组织来说，也是非常重要的。

第二，中国除了是一个规模巨大的潜在市场，还可能是一个规模庞大的生产基地。在当时摩托车产业正在兴起的全球化浪潮中，中国是个非常重要的国家。

1998年，全球化是当时正在兴起的一股浪潮。所谓的全球化，指的是企业在全球范围内配置资源、制造产品、供应市场。20世纪90年代末期正是西方的传统工业向亚洲转移的时期，相较于欧美地区，亚洲地区一方面是新兴市场的所在国家的集中地，另一方面各类资源都有一定优势，是全球化浪潮的得益一方。

而汽车和摩托车制造企业，可以说是得益于当时方兴未艾的全球化浪潮最多的企业。因为摩托车和汽车生产都是对标准化程度要求很高的产品，其标准几乎是全世界通用的。因此全球化非常有利于大型企业扩展自己的市场，而亚洲，尤其是中国，正是这些企业非常在意的市场。

通常情况下，大型跨国企业会在本国进行整车的设计和研发，在各地发布统一的新车型。而生产的工厂，则分布于各个销售区域内。这显然是企业追求生产成本最低化的结果——只有生产工厂靠近销售区域，才能对市场做出最快的反应。

在业内举足轻重的整车厂（业内俗称主机厂）既然已经有了全球化的布局安排，那么随之而来的当然是配件生产企业的全球化。1998 年这种趋势正在蔓延。以摩托车为例，当时主要生产摩托车的几大企业，如美国的哈雷、德国的宝马、日本的本田、铃木、川崎等，都已经在全球范围内布局生产，而配件商也已形成全球供应和当地供应两种体系。根据配件在采购体系当中的不同重要性，主机厂会选择不同的供货方式。比如车轮对于主机厂来说，是一个重要的安全配件，所以其生产分布既可以分散，也可以集中，为此车轮的生产厂在全球范围内有很多。

主机厂的相对集中，与车轮生产厂的相对分散，造成了一个问题，即各国的厂商都按各自国家的标准生产，而主机厂则要求生产相对统一。因此跨越各个国家标准，寻找行业统一标准的需求很大，也因此，ISO在各国厂商内都很活跃。

而把举办这次国际会议的机会给中国，一方面能让国际上的大型企业都有机会深入了解中国以及它的摩托车产业，另一方面也让中国的摩托车企业有机会接触到这些国际企业。ISO 8644 工作会议组织者的这一行动，可谓是用心良苦。

东道主

接住组织ISO 8644 会议的这个好"球"的，是一家新生的浙江民营企业，这是一家生产车轮毂的企业。它就是本书的主人公——万丰奥特。在当时，万丰奥特的规模其实还很小，举办一次国际会议，对它来说算得上一次挑战。

从严格的工业意义上说，1998 年的时候，万丰奥特其实还是一家刚刚走出规模试验达到量产状态的工业企业。这一年，万丰的第一家摩托车轮毂工厂刚刚有了自己的新厂址，它的第二个项目——汽车轮毂项目也才刚刚进入试验状态。就企业历史而言，它不过才创建了四年而已，此时才刚刚定名。

但以业内的影响力而言，这已经是一家不可小觑的企业了。就在 1997 年，中国汽车工程学会、中国汽车流通协会、中国名牌战略促进会联合举办的市场竞争力调查中，万丰奥特的摩托车轮毂一举夺得"品牌市场占有率、品牌质量满意率、客户购买首选率、品牌综合竞争力"四项行业冠军。只是论销售额和企业规模，由这样一家企业来代表中国承办国际会议，多少令人有点意外。一般而言，在 20 世纪 90 年代中期，代表中国的事，基本都是大型国企操办。就当时而言，万丰奥特既非国企，在摩托车行业里也绝非大型企业，怎么会轮得上它来承办这次会议呢？

机会是万丰奥特争取来的。

听说中国将举办 ISO 8644 会议的，是当时万丰奥特的办公室主任夏越璋。他一直在负责公司的品牌策划工作，核心是使万丰奥特熟悉整个产业内的企业并掌握国际通行的游戏规则。

早在 1997 年，他就从国家机械部汽车司摩托车处了解到，天津大学摩托车研究所收到了 ISO 的意向询问，询问中国有没有可能来承办 ISO 8644 标准修订会议。

主办大型国际会议，对于天津大学摩托车研究所来说当然是一个机会。不过，国内的大学与国外的不同，办学经费都是由政府拨给的。所以摆在摩托车研究所面前的问题是，需要找有合作意向的企业来出资承办这次会议。这其中就存在一定的障碍，国内当时已经有了一些摩托车车轮企业，投资比较大的都是国企下属厂，而民营企业当时对于这种花钱的项目都比较谨慎，再加上天津大学摩托车研究中心的学者们又都是知识分子，自尊心很强，不太肯求人，因此在落实承办单位时，出现了一段时间的空白。

万丰奥特敏锐地抓住了这个机会。

夏越璋一听到这个信息，马上向陈爱莲进行了汇报。陈爱莲非常认同夏越璋的意见，觉得应该把这个机会拿下来。

作为一家建立时间不太长的企业，陈爱莲觉得学习应该是万丰奥特最为重要的事情：让公司技术人员知道全球行业专家们在讨论什么，对万丰奥特是有好处的，而承办 ISO 8644 标准修订会议对于这家新生企业而言，是能迅速接触全球业内专业人脉的好机会。不过，1998 年的万丰奥特虽然规模不大，却是一家有规范治理体系的企业，陈爱莲马上召开董事会进行决策。

在获得董事会批准之后，夏越璋专程去了一趟天津，找到摩托车研究所的王颂秦教授，把承办会议的事情承担了下来。

之后我们将会看到，就万丰奥特 22 年的历史而言，承办这次会议确实有它的关键意义。在承办 ISO 8644 标准修订会议之前，新生的万丰奥特更多是在独自摸索产业门道，而在此之后，万丰奥特开始全方位接触它所涉及的全球产业脉络，更自觉地在全球范围内布局自己的产能。另外，万丰奥特在这次会议上，在全球知名主机厂面前，亮了个相。

至此，由天津大学摩托车研究中心主办，并由万丰奥特承办的 ISO 8644 标准修订会议，成为一个多赢的选择。当然，从当时的历史阶段来说，初入摩托车领域的万丰奥特，获利更多些。

从万丰奥特的公司历史来看，用"初入"这个词来形容 1998 年时的万丰奥特，是恰如其分的。万丰奥特当时只是刚刚投产了几条摩托车轮毂的生产线，在绍兴市下属的山区县——新昌县城建好了新厂房，稳定了生产。从工业的角度看，万丰奥特在 1998 年其实刚刚达到了量产规模，而在 1998 年之前，万丰奥特的铝合金车轮生产只是租用了县城里一家倒闭的国有企业的厂房。

　　从外界看，无论是汽车行业还是摩托车行业，国内此时都处于市场的快速上升期。但万丰奥特所从事的摩托车轮毂制造，竞争也是非常激烈的，算上各种类型的公司，万丰奥特总共有 112 家竞争对手。而我们在后面将会看到，万丰奥特是这些企业当中背景最小的一家，这样一家新企业要承办修订标准的国际性会议，不禁让我们对其领头人陈爱莲有些刮目相看。

1998 年万丰奥特承办 IOS 8644 标准修订会议，陈爱莲（左三）与国际委员会主席握手

　　改革开放之后，中国走的是一条以开放促自主的道路。在汽车摩托车行业，主机厂当时已经兴起了一股合资热潮。跨国公司纷纷在中国市场投下重注，与国内很多大型国企进行合资，市场上销售的大都是这些合资企业的产品。

　　因此，就万丰奥特这家新生的零部件企业来说，想对整个产业进行了解和熟知，赞助这样的会议当然是一个好路径。如果没有对行业内其他企业能力的认识，没有在这些企业当中建立起熟悉的人脉，想要形成与它们的合作关系，是非常困难的。从这个意义上来说，万丰奥特承办会议是一条高风险、高收益的路径。

　　1998 年 9 月 15 日，ISO 8644 国际标准修订会议在溪口镇的中信花园大酒店 2003 室正式召开。从事后留存的档案看，这间会议室是一个当时少见的平行讨论的布局。会场里没有布置主席台，只是用会议桌围成了一个长方形的格局。另外，在接近入口处设了一个讲话席。

会议先由东道主王教授和承办方万丰奥特的总经理陈爱莲致欢迎辞。

令所有参会者多少有点意外的是，代表东道主万丰奥特致辞的陈爱莲，是一位时髦的年轻女性，高挑个儿——身高有 1.70 米左右，一头大波浪短卷发，穿一身青灰色的中长袖连衣裙，笑容灿烂，讲起话来非常流畅与豪爽，与传统中国女性含蓄、内向、羞涩的形象大相径庭，这令到场的国外专家们多少有点惊讶。

陈爱莲的欢迎辞非常简短，总共也就 5 句话。她首先欢迎各国专家们的远道而来，接着介绍了万丰奥特是一家创业 4 年的摩托车轮毂企业，不过公司非常重视技术累积，愿意向各国专家们交流学习，最后祝与会者在中国期间工作愉快。

之后，另有一位政府官员向大会表示祝贺，这便是当地主管工业与科技的县长。在东方文化当中，这说明万丰奥特在当地是有不小的影响力的。

陈爱莲的出现之所以令人惊讶，是因为摩托车轮毂的生产，其关键工序是铸造，而这个专业很少能见到女性。

铸造是机械之母，任何机械类产品的源头都是铸造工艺。在国内，20 世纪 90 年代几乎是现代铸造技术发展的开始。稍早一点，国内的铸造所采取的工艺都是砂模成型，然后是金属液浇注，现场又脏又热是肯定的。所以通常情况下，女性很少选择这个行业，更何况是爱好时髦、开朗阳光的陈爱莲。

这也从另一个侧面表明，万丰奥特这家企业，并不简单。

说这家新入行的企业不简单的原因，在这次会议上还有很多体现。比如，陈爱莲简短讲完话、请专家们吃了一顿饭之后，就离开了会议现场。直到会议进入后期参观的时候，她才又露面，给专家们做了一些陪同工作。看起来，她并不像当时很多国企同行的领导者那么悠闲，倒是个很忙的角色。

　　再比如，作为东道主，万丰奥特参与这次会议的人不少，有公司副总经理吕国庆、总工程师朱训明、办公室主任夏越璋，还有三个会务人员。有趣的是，会议名单当中有一位叫雷铭君的专家，本来是代表佛山市中南铝车轮制造有限公司参加会议的，在后来的会议资料里，他的单位改成了万丰奥特。这样一来，万丰奥特倒有7个管理者参与会议了。

万丰奥特东道主参会人员（从左至右：夏越璋、吕国庆、陈爱莲、朱训明）

　　派出如此多的技术人员参加会议，是万丰奥特作为东道主的要求，目的是为技术人员开辟快捷通道，让他们获得与国际主流企业的工程师交流的机会。万丰奥特作为一家新生的民营企业，从一开始就非常注重与同行的交流，几年间，陈爱莲带领团队一有机会就去走访同行。因此这样一次国际会议，万丰奥特有这么多人参与，其实也很正常。

　　虽然只到会了一天多时间，但细心的陈爱莲还是发现，会议的女主持人，上午和下午穿的衣服不一样。因此两个女人很快就穿衣服这件事私下探讨起来，到现在她都记得很清楚，对方告诉她，像这种顶尖级的会议，女性穿得端庄而美丽，体现的是对其他参会者的尊重，女性就应该像鲜花一样漂亮，让人赏心悦目才好。

陈爱莲悄悄地记下了这个细节。

ISO 8644 标准修订会议的总方向，是试图统一摩托车车轮作为一种产品的检测方式，至少使全球的同行业在对产品评价方面有个统一的标准。但由于各国在摩托车轮的生产领域差异很大，各个企业的组织方式也不相同，对产品的检测方式也有不同，所以这次会议遇到的矛盾和争论也很多。历时两天的会议就技术的细节一个一个地进行讨论，每个细节都要花费很长时间。

总体来说，统一标准的讨论中，遇到来自日本企业的阻碍比较大。

就检测来说，全球统一标准考虑的是检测的科学性与合理性。发达国家对摩托车的定位仅仅是交通工具或者说成人玩具，道路条件较好，摩托车的使用环境相对稳定和安全，而在发展中国家，老百姓都把摩托车作为生产和生活两用的"赚钱机器"，往往会超载，道路条件也相对恶劣。

由于不同市场区域对摩托车的需求存在细微的不同，造成生产厂家对于技术要求也不同，进而体现为对检测试验的安全关注度不同。同时，并不是所有车轮生产企业都能对检测手段有大规模投入，因而用比较简单的方法，加一个较大的安全系数来做标准，是通用做法。而日本企业由于规模大，产业成熟，加之其对安全的重视程度高，对于检测手段的投入较大，设备也很完整，所以和当时比较通用的摩托车车轮检测方式及欧洲企业的认知差异较大。

比如，车轮耐受冲击力的试验，国际通用的标准是把车轮在试验的台架上固定，用设备给车轮一个外力，测试车轮的最大耐受外力值，这个值高过了标准当中的规定，车轮就算合格。

耐受外力这个值，反映了金属轮体在加工过程中微观形成的晶体状态；在使用过程中，由金属晶体状态确定的这个耐受外力值的大小，决定了车轮的使用时间长度和行驶过程当中的稳定程度。

但日本标准就要细化得多，它要求把外来冲击力分解成几种，分别做更为精准的检测试验，同时设立几项要求。

在技术领域，朱训明是当时万丰奥特的代表人物。对于深入的技术环节和此次会议的进程，他有十分清晰的了解。多年之后，朱训明还是对当时的争论持有自己的看法：日本企业的这种做法，肯定是对的和更为先进的，但他们就很少考虑其他国家和企业的条件，要推行他们的做法，本身就存在问题。

各国的社会发展阶段不同，对于车轮的安全性要求自然也不一样。强行在国际标准当中推行这样的做法，其实是抬高了整个行业的进入门槛。国际标准作为一个在全球通用的标准，一定要考虑其他因素。比如说，有些企业达不到日本的这个标准，怎么办？不让它再做这行了吗？这一点，日本的专家们考虑得比较少。在此次会议上，中方因初次参与会议，表现得比较中立，而日系和欧美系的企业及研究机构的代表则针锋相对。也是因此，在奉化的这次会议上，专家们并没有形成共识，标准的修订工作也没能进行下去。因此1998年的标准修订会议后来还召开了好几次，最后在江门的会议上才达成了相对的共识。

对于现在万丰奥特的技术人员，尤其是朱训明来说，与全球顶尖企业的交流当然已经习以为常，但对当时的万丰奥特来说却很珍贵。一开始，万丰奥特的技术人员并不清楚会议上为什么有如此激烈的争论，到后来，以朱训明为代表的年青一代终于明白，争论其实争的是国际主导权。万丰奥特在21世纪前后的一些记录档案当中，有员工记下了这种国际水平对于自己的震动：万丰奥特与日本一家同行公司交流，发现自己想象当中的铝水连续处理工艺，日本的同行已经做到了；在铝水浇铸的过程当中，一台设备的操作，万丰奥特要配置4个员工，日本的那家企业只要一个人就可以了；而从设备耗材的使用情况来看，日本的那家企业只是万丰奥特的六分之一。

以上种种，不难看出万丰奥特为什么愿意承办这样的国际会议——除了朱训明讲到的了解前沿技术问题外，几乎在每个环节上，万丰奥特的技术人员都可以从同行那里有所收获。

陈爱莲的雄心

因为要形成统一的国际标准，所以在中国浙江召开的这一次 ISO 8644 标准修订会议，报名参会的技术人员不少。美国、英国、捷克、比利时的企业都派出了代表。作为摩托车生产大国，日本本田公司来了三个人，而且会议的主席也是日本本田公司朝霞技术研究所（简称 HGA）的工程师。

在某种程度上，这其实是摩托车生产重心从欧美向亚洲转移的象征。对于这种标准修订会议，除有关的学术单位之外，大部分企业都更愿意搭顺风车——在标准制定了之后，企业遵照执行即可。

而承办方万丰奥特的出现，在某种程度上代表着中国在摩托车领域里崛起的态势。本来这次会议上，中国出席的只有两个人，除了本次会议的组织者王颂秦教授外，只有国家定点的南昌飞机公司摩托车检测所的所长钱仲明。而万丰奥特的加入，一下子使得中国成为参会人数最多的国家。

陈爱莲在万丰奥特创立 20 周年时，对当年承办 ISO 8644 标准修订会议一事，也有过评价："一流企业卖品牌、卖标准，二流企业卖专利、卖技术，三流企业卖原材料、卖劳动力，说到底，品牌和标准就是定价权、话语权。1998 年的那次会议，万丰奥特的主要目的是要进入全球摩托车车轮制造商的话语权圈子，搞清楚全球的产业布局和最优秀的工程师们在想什么、做什么。客观上，它对我们万丰奥特的地位起到了一个提升的作用。万丰奥特在铝轮上做到规模最大，在很大程度上是因为做到了快速从外行到内行的跨越而实现的。而且那次会议起到了提高公司骨干的认知作用。"

确实，此次会议万丰奥特派出的骨干人物，覆盖了当时万丰奥特正在兴起的两大业务线。

朱训明当时大学毕业才 6 年，是位年轻的技术负责人。在万丰奥特的管理者当中，他是在创业期就加入的为数不多的大学毕业生之一，一直负责万丰奥特摩托车轮毂的研发工作。到 1997 年之后，他又参与了万丰奥特汽车轮毂的研发设计。这个年轻人个子不高，一双剑眉为他增添了不少英气，脾气却比较急躁。

而夏越璋的性格则与朱训明截然相反，是个绵和的人。他家学渊源深厚，早年在国家机械部重点企业干了20个年头，长期从事技术工作和企业管理工作，在机械领域有很好的人脉和丰富的经验，后来还成为中国机械工程学会的资深理事以及中国汽车工业协会政策研究会的特约分析师。

万丰奥特派出参与这次会议的另外一位技术人员，是国内轮毂行业当中的一位重量级人物——雷铭君，彼时他刚刚从当时国内一家大型著名轮毂生产的厂家辞职加盟万丰奥特不久。他在铝轮毂行业长期从事生产技术工作，是一位留美海归的资深专家，对铝轮毂制造十分精通，他是国内摩托车车轮标准的起草人。在万丰奥特汽车轮毂项目上马并开始生产之后，陈爱莲聘请雷铭君来主持万丰奥特汽车轮毂业务线的整体工作。

乍听起来，万丰奥特开始的两大业务线——摩托车轮毂和汽车轮毂的制造，似乎没有多大关系，实际上它们的工业过程是非常相似的。不过，相对于摩托车行业来说，国内汽车业当时正处发展早期，一些大型跨国公司与国企合作的汽车企业抢占先机，瓜分了主流市场，规模要求大，门槛高，因此万丰奥特想要踏入汽车制造的零部件企业行列，是一件非常不容易的事情。

正是因此，雷铭君加盟万丰奥特，是其历史上浓墨重彩的一笔。在万丰被尊称为"雷工"的雷铭君，在国内轮毂制造业工作的历史与国内这个行业的历史几乎一样长。

对于同为技术人员的朱训明和雷铭君，陈爱莲也是有安排的。在溪口镇上，朱训明是万丰奥特自己培养起来的技术骨干，而负责汽车轮毂制造的雷铭君，在技术上已是行业的精英了。作为国家摩托车车轮试验方法的起草人，其他国家的专家也很尊重他的意见。这种新老搭配的人员安排，也体现了万丰奥特的实际情况。他们虽然雄心勃勃，不过确实处在起步点上。

中国奇迹

与其他工作会议一样，热情的中国东道主总会在会议之后安排一些余兴节目。ISO 8644 标准修订会议之后，万丰奥特安排参会代表游览溪口当地的风景名胜，在万丰奥特的档案里，我们看到了当时与会者游览雪窦山的照片。

当然，客人们还应万丰奥特之邀，参观了刚刚建完的部分万丰工业园，这也是新生的万丰奥特在业内人士面前亮相的重要一环。

万丰奥特所在的新昌是一个位于浙江东部的小县城，在浙江，它是为数不多的几个山区县之一，它的境内有一座名山——天姥山，因为李白的一首诗——《梦游天姥吟留别》而名扬天下。"天姥连天向天横，势拔五岳掩赤城。天台四万八千丈，对此欲倒东南倾。"新昌差不多有半个县都在天姥山周围，而扎根于新昌的万丰奥特，也与天姥山有着千丝万缕的联系。

万丰所在的新昌县城有一座建于南北朝齐梁年间的江南第一大佛

与东部沿海地区的其他山区一样，天姥山海拔不算太高（不足一千米），却是一座很秀丽的山，山上植被丰茂，流水潺潺。新昌县城不大，通常人们知道它，是因为当地有一座大佛寺，寺内有建于南北朝齐梁年间的江南第一

（石窟）的佛像，香火很旺。当地人非常勤劳，新昌历届县委县政府又非常支持工业经济的发展，只要企业有需要，常常是主动赶到企业解决问题。所以新昌虽是山区，但工业经济发展水平在省内名列前茅。刚刚建完的万丰工业园，位于新昌县城的城郊。从大佛寺向新昌的西北方向走，很快就进入了工业区。万丰工业园就建在当时刚通车没多久的上三线高速路边上，下了高速拐两个弯就到了。

1998 年，万丰工业园还只是完成了它第一期的建设工程。不过从它对地址的选择上可以看得出，万丰工业园在新昌县所受的重视程度还是非常高的。因为万丰奥特所要运输的轮毂产品数量大，重量也不轻，所以它的位置交通非常方便。

当时万丰奥特的厂区，大概只有它全部建成后 1 000 亩的三分之一面积。厂房都是一层楼，办公楼在其中一幢厂房的前部，大概占了整幢厂房的三分之一。

在这个办公区，十多米高的厂房被分成了两层，底下的一层除了沿墙的地方被隔成了办公室之外，中间还设置了会客区和产品展示区。楼上一个 20 多人的大办公室后面，就是陈爱莲的办公室了。

工业园最大的特色，是工作区与生活区非常近。顺着万丰工业园向后走，就是万丰的生活区。一大批员工和管理者，包括陈爱莲自己也都住在这里面。这种布局，非常具有中国特色。它的最大特点是工作和生活几乎就在一块儿，有着典型的创业味道。

轮毂的生产，在 1998 年的万丰奥特，条件还是艰苦的。

当年，万丰奥特刚刚开始使用重力铸造机制造轮毂——在厂房的一角，原料铝锭被万丰奥特自制的熔炉在 700 多度的高温下熔化之后，变成铝水，之后被浇铸进重力铸造机型腔四壁留出的汤口。经过几分钟的凝固，铸件就可以出炉了。

因为铸造机型腔内的模具，已经被事先设计成为所铸造的轮毂形状，所以铝水凝固的铸件，从一出炉就已经基本具备了轮毂的形状。

这个看似简单的过程，包含有 36 道复杂的工艺流程。由于铝液的熔化和凝固过程决定了轮毂的硬度、强度、韧性和形状，同时还涉及操作的环境和简便程度，所以它是铸造工艺的核心部分。在机械工业的发展历史当中，人们发明了多种铸造工艺来匹配不同的铸件的不同要求。最原始的当然是砂模铸造和浇注定型，后来又逐步出现了重力铸造、压力铸造、锻造、液态模锻、真空铸造、离心铸造等多种形式。这些工艺的差别，主要在于铝液的凝固速度不同，以及操作上的便利性不同。

从铸造机里出炉的铸件还只能被称为"毛坯"。通常情况下，因为凝固的速度很快，所以出炉的铸件，还隐隐带着铝水留下的暗红色，但它很快就会变得美观起来。

接下来的工序是机加工。冷凝完毕，有了硬度的车轮毛坯被送到机加工区域，去掉成型过程当中的浇口、毛刺，按设计要求精密加工，就完成了机加工工序。

然后是涂装工艺，在生产区域的另一边，有一个半封闭的涂装间。机加工完毕的车轮被悬挂起来，成批地通过传送带进入涂装间，进行喷涂作业。等它们出涂装间之后，摩托车车轮就正式加工完毕，进入包装流程了。

机加工完毕时，铝制轮毂就开始变得锃亮发光。等到涂装完成之后，它已经光可鉴人。再加上大部分轮毂的设计都经过细致的美学考量，所以此时它们已经十分漂亮。

在万丰奥特的生产线进一步升级成自动化之后，由于采用了更为先进的设备，从铝的熔炉到铸造机，再到铸件出炉进入机加工环节，可以完全被密封起来，车间的温度因此可以控制。而在 1998 年的生产条件下，由于铝水因为要暴露于空气当中被浇入重力铸造机，所以整个车间的温度是相当高的。

当时，万丰奥特的铝制轮毂生产规模不大，生产一线只有 5 个车间，拥有两条摩托车轮毂的生产线和一条汽车轮毂生产线。

这仅仅是一家刚刚形成规模生产的摩托车车轮制造厂,.它的很多工艺还有待提高。如果要实现陈爱莲的构想——这家厂要成为正在快速发展中的中国车辆制造舞台上的明星,还有非常大的距离。

首先,它的生产必须形成自动的流水化作业,只有那样,生产成本才会随着效率的提升而下降。而工程师们都知道,要形成自动流水作业,就意味着工厂要有足够的订单,否则高投入的物流设施得不到有效利用,意味着生产能力放空。

其次,车轮还可以进一步提高质量,比如涂装应该要密闭,除尘生产才好。半封闭的涂装状态,涂装间内的空气微粒可能会与涂料一起覆盖在产品表面,造成未来使用过程当中涂料的剥落。

最后,从经济性上说,规模的扩大还意味着原料批量的增大,这同样可以提高工厂的经济效益。

万丰工业园

因此,去参观的专家一看就明白,这是一家创业初期的企业。而且,它必须"自己找饭吃",按订单生产,因此不存在从起步之初就规模化的可能。也正是因为这样,它才会呈现出当下这种状态。

不过,当时现场再细听一下的话,也许他们会肃然起敬。因为万丰奥特彼时距离陈爱莲用50万元贷款起步才刚刚4年。而在这家公司背后,是中国拥有十几亿人口的市场。

当时参加了ISO 8644标准修订会议的一名韩国工程师,2014年受邀再一次到万丰奥特的新昌工业园来参观。

相隔 16 年之后，万丰新昌工业园已经完全不一样了，不仅占地比他1998 年来的时候扩大了三四倍，而且发生了一些根本性的变化。

从高速公路转到那条万丰奥特的主干道上，人们就可以发现，现在的万丰工业园已经建起了一幢宏伟的门楼，有内卫监察室在执勤。

进门之后，首先出现的是工业园内的广场。在宽阔的广场南北两头，北边是一个宽宏的露天大舞台，南边则是一幢欧式的办公大楼。整个园区绿树成荫、郁郁葱葱，是典型的花园式园区。除了新昌这个工业园之外，万丰奥特旗下已经有 36 家子公司，这幢办公楼是整个万丰奥特控股集团的总部。

万丰奥特新昌总部的生产基地位于广场西侧。这个生产基地，仍然包括摩轮和汽轮两大业务板块，从属于万丰奥特旗下的两个事业部。另外，因为万丰奥特有自行开发的智能化装备方向，又开辟出了独立的工业机器人园区。

1998 年 ISO 8644 标准修订会议时，被工程师们参观的摩轮生产线并没有被淘汰，还在正常地生产，现在已经使用了工业机器人作为铝水浇铸的手段，汽轮制造的铸造环节也采取了密闭生产，条件大有改观。

中国制造万丰轮毂生产现场

而从规模上，万丰奥特旗下的摩轮和汽轮业务，都已经是全球最大的生产商。在上海、山东、广东、重庆、宁波、吉林、印度等上游原材料提供区和下游市场区域，万丰奥特都设立了大型的生产基地。

出现在 1998 年宁波溪口镇上的那个高挑时髦的陈爱莲，是这一切变化的背后推动者。她的办公室，在那幢欧式办公大楼的二楼。

从 20 世纪 80 年代开始，中国进入了改革开放的时代，西方人把这 30 多年当中中国发生的变化称为"中国奇迹"，指的就是中国发生变化的速度。

在这些"中国奇迹"里，我们看到的万丰奥特所发生的变化，依然令人注目。1998 年的万丰奥特在轮毂制造领域仅仅是个刚进门的新手，甚至未来它能不能在市场上成为一个够分量的竞争对手都是个未知数；而 2014 年的万丰奥特，其年产 4000 万套的规模足以说明，这已经是一个世界级的行业领导者。如此规模的一家企业，足以供应至少一个世界性大国所有的摩托车和汽车所需要的轮毂，就算在中国这样一个人口超级大国，也至少能供应一半以上市场需求。而民营企业的出身，又使得万丰奥特不可能放空生产能力，因此它必然是一个全球化的大型专业制造集团。

从 1994 年创立至今仅仅 22 年，万丰奥特从一个行业的追随者迅速跃升为行业强有力的领导者，陈爱莲是怎么带领万丰奥特做到的呢？

万丰奥特原则

　　ISO 8644 标准修订会议对于万丰奥特 22 年进程来说，只是沧海一粟。在本书的各个章节当中，我们都可以看到，陈爱莲领导下的万丰奥特虽然只是一家浙江的民营企业，却十分注重把自己放在全球一流的平台上进行交流和学习。承办国际标准修订会议，把自己的技术负责人和工程师送到顶级的技术平台上，是万丰奥特高明的经营方式和一贯作风的体现。

　　正是因为万丰奥特这种不断地投入，使员工获得不断成长，这家企业才能从新昌一隅成长为国际化控股集团。

Chapter 1
Debut

Revision to ISO 8644

CITIC Xikou Garden Hotel enjoyed the name of a leading hotel around 1998 for its short distance to the most renowned scenic spot — former residence of Chiang Kai-shek, the former President of the Republic of China.

Even today, this hotel remains evidence of some fashionable elements: the adoption of blue glass curtain wall in its facade decoration back in the mid 1990s, the high ceiling lobby, the winding corridors in its courtyard, which well conveys the style of exquisite gardens of southern China. Besides its prestigious location on East Wulin Road, the main street of Xikou, its modern and distinctive flavor earned it such reputation as "living in the hotel to stay in the scenery".

In addition to the hotel itself, Xikou located in Fenghua, Zhejiang is a pleasant and comfortable resort to dwell in. A myriad of people do know Xikou as President Chiang Kai-shek's ancestral home, but only those who have been there appreciate it as a mixture of tradition and modernism.

Xikou is blessed with magical landscapes like splendid waterfalls and pretty southern-China-style hills. Thanks to Chiang's family, it was once the political center of China and enjoyed the completion of modern infrastructure as well as buildings with profound Chinese culture.

However, despite the unique resources, Xikou remains isolated for some political reasons until mid 1990s when mainland China is opened-up enough and its relationship with Taiwan is improved. Xikou becomes a popular scenic area to welcome thousands of western visitors.

That is why, on September 14, 1998, the newly funded Wanfeng Auto Holding Group Co., Ltd. (Wanfeng Auto for short) finally chose the hotel as the venue to host the International Organization for Standardization for its revision to ISO 8644.

The revision convention was a landmark for China as a newly-opened up country and a novice in international communication, especially in standardization conference. Participants at the conference were from enterprises with high-profile names including Honda, TOYOTA, Halley, etc. from countries like Germany, Japan, Italy and so on. Manufacturers scrambled to send their representatives for new international industry standards would be produced at conference.

To learn the scope of ISO 8644 will help us understand the presence of European major manufacturers at the conference. The full name of ISO 8644 is "Standard Test Methods of Light-alloy wheels for motorcycles and mopeds ", equivalent to the national standard GB/T22435-2008 of China, which refers to "Light-alloy wheels for motorcycles and mopeds".

The ISO 8644 standard revision conference was just a normal work meeting for International Standardization Organization (ISO for short) to amend the test standards in motorcycle wheel production.

However, the background for holding ISO 8644 meeting in China is actually not so simple.

First of all, ISO for Motorcycle thought highly of China's great potential.

The conference held in Xikou, Fenghua was sponsored by Songqin Wang, a female Ph.D supervisor and expert at Research Institute of Motorcycle at Tianjin University. The Institute was founded in 1958 by Professor Shi Shaoxi, the former President of Tianjin University, Academician of Chinese Academy of Sciences, specialized in Internal Combustion Engine.

The reason why the conference was sponsored by Professor Wang and hosted by China was partially due to the influential role of Tianjin University and Professor Wang in China's motorcycle production and testing standards. More importantly, there are two reasons.

For one thing, China is becoming the largest motorcycle market globally "with an annual sales volume of 8 million and an estimated 20 million in the next two years, an undeniable market to all host plants", quoted the President of Motorcycle Standard Organization.

Such a huge market coupled with competitive prices made the motorcycle manufacturers in China very active, with a large number of enterprises and parts makers becoming competitive. That was a considerable force even in the global perspective. Despite the fact that China's domestic manufacturers were not large in their scales and their parts makers were only newly founded. The great market potentials and the ambition of Chinese entrepreneurs were attracting cooperators worldwide.

Most importantly, in 1998, there arose a "going-to-China" craze in the global scope among enterprises, non-governmental organizations and even governments. After years of efforts, WTO had basically opened its door to China. Thus ISO for motorcycle wheels also cherished the opportunity to expand its influence in China.

Globalization was a rising tide in 1998. The so-called globalization refers to the allocation of manufacturers' resources, producing, supplying to the market in a global scope. The end of 1990s witnessed a shift of the traditional industry from western world to Asia. The entire industry found that Asian countries benefited most from globalization compared with the traditional western countries, for Asia was on the one hand a concentrated up-rising market and on the other hand blessed with advantageous resources.

Manufactures of automobiles and motorcycles could be considered the biggest winner for they were highly standardized. The standardization benefited the large enterprises most, to whom the Asian market, especially China was important.

Large multi-nationals normally complete their vehicle design domestically and release it universally. While their production plants will be distributed in all the sales area. This is the result of a pursuit to the lowest cost – only the nearest plants can make the fastest reaction to the market.

Since the host makers in the industry (also known as the host plant) had been globalized, there followed the globalization of parts markers. This trend started spreading in 1998, represented by the manufacturing of motorcycles, when major manufacturers like Halley of US, BMW of Germany and Honda, Suzuki, Kawasaki of Japan had been producing globally and their accessories were supplied both globally and locally, according to the importance of the parts in the procurement system of host plants. While wheels are of a medium importance to host plants, the production of wheels can be either distributive or focused. Thus there are a lot of wheel manufacturers scattering around the world.

A considerable concentration of the host plants and scattering of wheel factories thus led to a great need for a universal standard instead of respective national standards. And that was why ISO organization worked actively in manufacturers internationally.

To offer the opportunity of hosting the conference to China could lend international major enterprises an insight into China and its motorcycle industry, and vice versa. The organizers of ISO 8644 working conference made a really intentioned decision.

Host

It was a newly founded Zhejiang private enterprise, who "caught the ball" as hosting ISO 8644 conference. It was the hero of this book, Wanfeng Auto, a wheel hub manufacturer. It was a big challenge for Wanfeng Auto then to hold an international conference considering its small scale.

Strictly speaking, Wanfeng Auto was an industrial enterprise just starting its mass production after scaling test. In 1998, Wanfeng just decided the new site for its first motorcycle wheel hub factory. Its second project — automobile wheel hub had just entered its test stage. Wanfeng was only four years old then, its name newly decided.

But as for the influence in the industry, Wanfeng Auto was already a big name. In a marketing competitiveness survey co-organized in 1997 by China Automotive Engineering Society, China Automobile Circulation Association, Chinese Brand Promotion Association, motorcycle wheel hubs of Wanfeng Auto swoop four champions in "brand market share rate, quality brand satisfaction rate, customer purchase rate preferred, and the synthesized competitiveness of the brand". However, it was still unexpected to let Wanfeng be the host, considering its sales volume and business scale. Generally, in 1990s, large state-owned enterprises would represent China in most cases. Wanfeng Auto surprised all with a background of neither state-owned enterprise, nor large scale in motorcycle. How did it manage to win the host right?

It was Xia Yuezhang, the General Director of Office first brought the news to Wanfeng. Mr. Xia was responsible for brand planning, familiar with enterprises in the field and the rule of the game in the international practice. When hearing the news from Motorcycle Section, Automotive Division of China Ministry of Machinery that the Motorcycle Research Institute at Tianjin University had received an inquiry for hosting the ISO 8644 conference.

Hosting major international conference was certainly a chance for the Research Institute of Motorcycles at Tianjin University. However, unlike western universities, the funding of Chinese universities was taken in charged by the government. Therefore, the Institute had to find an enterprise to fund and co-host the conference. Problems were that large-scale domestic motorcycle wheel enterprises were state-owned, while private enterprises were cautious in funding such projects. Scholars in Tianjin University with strong self-esteem were less willing to ask for help. The dilemma had created a blank period when the Institute was looking for its co-hosting partner.

Wanfeng Auto was keen to seize the opportunity.

Mr. Xia reported immediately to Ailian who totally agreed that Wanfeng Auto should seize the opportunity.

Ailian believed that learning should be the most important thing for Wanfeng as a newly-founded business: ISO 8644 standard revision conference would surely be a chance for this ascent enterprise and its technical staff to learn and a quick access to the global network of industry professionals. Wanfeng Auto in 1998, although small, was run by a standardized corporate management system. Ailian immediately referred the discussion to a board meeting.

After obtaining the approval from the Board of Directors, Xia Yuezhang made a special visit to Professor Wang at the motorcycle Institute, offering to host the conference.

The conference showed its significance later when we reviewed Wanfeng's 22 years history. Before hosting the conference, Wanfeng was more or less alone in its exploration in the industry; while after that, Wanfeng found an access to the full range of global industry and became more conscious in global layout of its producing capacity. In addition, Wanfeng made a perfect debut at the conference in front of the world famous manufacturers.

Therefore, the conference sponsored by the Motorcycle Research Institute and hosted by Wanfeng Auto was a win-win choice. Of course, from the historical perspective, Wanfeng Auto was the party benefiting more when first entering the field of motorcycle.

"First entering" was no more than appropriate to describe its status in 1998. Wanfeng had just put up several production lines of motorcycle wheel hub and built new factories in Xinchang County, a mountainous subsidiary county of Shaoxing City. Stable mass production had just started, while before which, Wanfeng only rented a plant from a bankrupted state-owned enterprise producing aluminum alloy wheels.

China was experiencing a taking-off in automotive industry and motorcycle industry. But motorcycle wheel manufacturing was an fiercely-competitive industry. Wanfeng had a total of 112 competitors of different types. That is why we could not help wondering how Chen Ailian and Wanfeng bid for the hosting of the conference as a new enterprise.

In1998, when Wanfeng Auto hosted the IOS 8644 Standard Revision Conference, Chen Ailian (third from left) shook hands with the president of the ISO Committee.

With the reform and opening-up policy, China was taking on an approach to promote autonomy with opening-up. In the automotive and motorcycle industry, there was a prevailing trend for host plants to form joint ventures. Multi-nationals invested heavily to form joint ventures with many of the large state-owned enterprises in China, and Chinese market was full of their products.

Hosting such a conference was a smart choice for Wanfeng Auto to get familiarized with the industry; otherwise, it would be difficult to enter into business relationships with other enterprises in the field. In this sense, the conference was a path with high risk and high return.

On September 15, 1998, ISO 8644 Standard Revision Conference was officially held in Room 2003 at CITIC Garden Hotel in Xikou town. The archives show that the conference hall was in a rare parallel discussion layout. There was no podium, with tables laid out in a rectangular pattern and a presenter's chair set at the entrance of the hall.

As the host of the conference, Professor Wang and Chen Ailian, General Manager of Wanfeng Auto first delivered their welcoming speeches.

Somehow to the participants' surprise, Ailian was a fashionable young woman, tall, a height of 1.70 meters, in a blue gray long-sleeved dress, wearing big wave short curly hair and bright smile. Her speech was fluent and straightforward, with a contrast to the traditional Chinese women's subtle, introverted and shy style.

Ailian made a brief welcoming speech, composed of only 5 sentences, i.e. expressing welcome to the participants; introducing Wanfeng Auto as a 4-year-old new enterprise of motorcycle wheel production; promising that the company would attach great importance to technology accumulation and be willing to learn from all the experts; and finally wishing the participants a pleasant trip in China.

Next, the local Country Officer in charge of industry and technology expressed his congratulations to the conference. In Chinese culture, his showing up indicated Wanfeng's influential impact locally.

Ailian's appearance surprised the participants also because the key process of motorcycle wheel production is casting, in which field professionals are rarely women.

Casting is the mother of machinery, the source of any mechanical products. China's modern casting industry only started in 1990s, while a little earlier, sand mold casting and then metal liquid casting were prevailing in the domestic foundry, which stand for dirty and hot working environment. Thus it is by no means an ideal occupation for women, not to mention fashionable young ladies like Ailian.

It shows from another side that Wanfeng Auto is special.

During the conference, this new enterprise showed its specialty in many ways: For example, Ailian left the meeting hall after her welcoming speech and a brief meal with the experts, and did not return until the later phrase to show the experts around. She seemed to have a tight schedule, unlike some leaders from typical Chinese state-owned enterprises.

For another example, Wanfeng, as the host, sent 6 participants including Lv Guoqing, the Deputy General Manager; ZHU Xun Ming, the Chief Engineer; Xia Yuezhang, Director General of Office and three conference staff. Interestingly, an expert called Lei Mingjun who represented Zhongnan, Foshan Aluminum Wheel Manufacturing Co., Ltd. later joined Wanfeng, whose delegation numbered 7 finally.

Wanfeng's participants at the conference (from left to right: Xia Yuezhang, Lv Guoqing, Chen Ailian, Zhu Xunming)

It was Wanfeng's request as the host to send more technical personnel only for the purpose to give them a quick access to the international mainstream companies. Wanfeng Auto has always been attaching great importance to exchanges with counterparts as a new private enterprise. Ailian has taken every chance to lead her team to visit their counterparts ever since their founding. No wonder Wanfeng would send such a big team to the conference.

Being at the conference for the second day, Ailian found that the hostess of the conference wore different clothes in the morning and afternoon. The two ladies soon started a private conversation on dressing code. Ailian still remembers that the hostess told her, a lady should dress decently and gorgeously to show her manners and respect to other participants at such a top meeting.Ailian slipped down the tips.

The general purpose of the ISO 8644 Standard Revision Conference was to work out a universal testing standard or at least a unified evaluation standard for motorcycle wheels. However, because of the differences in the field of motorcycle wheel production in various countries and the varied management of different enterprises, the testing methods were very different. So the conference was hindered with contradiction and disputes. During the two days' meeting, discussions were made on every technical detail and time passed soon.

The greatest rejections came from Japanese companies.

A global unified standard would have to consider the validity and reasonability. In developed countries, motorcycles are positioned only as a means of transport or entertainment machines for adults. There are better road conditions and the riding environment is more stable and safe. While in developing countries, people take motorcycle as a "money-making machine", where overloading often occurs and the road conditions are relatively poor.

Due to the different requirements of motorcycles in different markets, the manufacturers have varied requirements for the technology, which was also reflected in their emphasis of safety in testing. At the same time, not all wheel production enterprises could have a large investment in the detection method. A common practice was to adopt simple methods with a larger safety value. While Japanese companies maintain higher standards than European business in testing due to their large scale, industry maturity, and emphasis on security, large investment in testing equipments.For example, the international common standard for the impact testing of wheels was to fix the wheels on the test bench, exert an external force to the wheels with equipment and test the maximum tolerance of the wheel. If the value exceeds the standards, the wheels are qualified.

This value of external force tolerance reflects the crystal state of the metal wheel in the process of processing, and in the process of use, the tolerance values determined by the metal crystal state determine the wheels' length of use and the stability in the running process.

However, the Japanese standard was much more refined, dividing the impact of external forece into several types and doing more accurate detection tests respectively to meet several requirements.

Zhu Xunming was the representative of Wanfeng Auto in technology,. He had a whole picture of the technical details and the procedures of the conference. Many years later, Zhu Xunming still held his own views on the dispute then: the testing approach of Japanese companies was certainly right and more advanced, but they rarely considered the reality of other countries and enterprises. Thus there would be a problem to implement their practice.

Different countries had different requirements over safety of the wheel for they were at different stages of social development. To force an implement of a higher international standard would surely raise the threshold for the entire industry.

Universal international standards must consider problems such as how to deal with those companies who could not reach the standard of Japan. Drive them out of the business? Japanese experts seemed not to have considered this. Chinese representatives stood relatively neutral as new participants at the conference, while Japan stood tit for tat with European countries and the United States, which resulted in the failure of a consensus. The amendments to the standards did not go smoothly down. Several meetings were held subsequently in 1998 before an agreement was finally reached at the conference in Jiangmen City.

International communication with the world's leading enterprises are no longer new to Wanfeng's technicians especially Zhu Xunming nowadays. At that time, however, such exchanges were quite precious to Wanfeng. At first, Wanfeng's technicians did not understand why such fierce debate occurred. But Zhu Xunming and his team soon realized that the focus of the dispute was international dominance. From the archive of Wanfeng around 2000, we found some interesting records made by a staff member, recalling his shock: in our communication with a Japanese enterprise, we found that aluminum continuous water treatment process, which still remains an imaginary technique in our mind, has already been brought into practice in Japan. Thus one worker in Japan could manage the operation of that has to be fulfilled by four in Wanfeng, with only one sixth of Wanfeng's equipment supplies instead.

Now Wanfeng's motivation in hosting such international conference seems obvious — in addition to Zhu Xunming's preference in learning about leading-edge technology, in almost every aspect, Wanfeng's technicians could benefit from their peers.

Chen Ailian's Ambition

In order to decide on a unified international standard, a herd of nations sent off their participants, including United States, United Kingdom, Czech, Belgium, and so on. Among them, Honda from Japan, as the major motorcycle producing country, sent three representatives. The chairman of the meeting was also from Honda Asaka Technology Research Institute (HGA).

hat was a symbol of the shift of focus from Europe and America to Asia. Most enterprises would prefer to take a ride, i.e. to follow the standards rather than take a lead at such standard revision conference, unlike academic institutes.But the presence of Wanfeng somehow represented the rise of China in the field of motorcycle. Originally, China planned to send only two participants, Professor Wang Songqin, organizers of this conference, and Qian Zhongming, Director of Motorcycle Testing Institute at Nanchang Aircraft Company, a national key enterprise. Later with the presence of Wanfeng Auto, China became a nation sending the largest delegation.

At the 20th anniversary Wanfeng Auto, Ailian made the following comments on Wanfeng's hosting the conference:" The first-class enterprises sell their brands and standards. The second-class enterprises sell patents and technology. While the third rate enterprises sell raw materials and labors. Brand and standard is the right to price and speak. To present at the conference in 1998, Wanfeng's main purpose was to show up before the world motorcycle wheel manufacturers and utter our voice, to learn the global layout of the industry and what the best engineers wanted and what they were doing. It was definitely a quick promotion to our position in the field which brought Wanfeng from a layman to an expert and finally made us No. 1 in aluminum wheel producing. That conference also promoted the cognition of our backbone."

That is true, since the representatives Wanfeng sent were its backbones covering the two rising business lines.

Zhu Xunming only graduated 6 years before from the university. He was a young technician, responsible for researching and developing of motorcycle wheel hub since he joined Wanfeng as one of the few university graduates at her starting period. He began to research and develop automobile wheels in 1997. Zhu was not tall, a pair of sharp eyebrows adding to his masculine, a little hot-tempered.

In contrast, Xia Yuezhang's personality is mild. He has a profound family origin and had been working for a key enterprise of national Ministry of Machinery for 20 years, engaged in technical and management work, experienced in mechanical field, and later became senior member of Chinese Mechanical Engineering Society and the contributing analyst of China Association of Automobile Industry Policy Research.

Another participant Wanfeng Auto sent to the conference was Lei Mingjun, a heavyweight figure in China's hub industry, who had just resigned from a large-scale enterprise to join Wanfeng. He has been engaged in the production technology of the aluminum wheel industry, a senior expert receiving education in the U.S., having a very good command of the aluminum wheel producing technology. He drafted the standard of motorcycle wheel producing in China.

At first glance, the two business lines started by Wanfeng auto — motorcycle wheel hub and automobile hub had nothing to do with each other. In fact, their industrial process was very similar. However, comparing with the motorcycle industry, the domestic auto industry was at its infant stage. Some large multinationals and state-owned enterprises had cooperated to seize the initiative, carve up the most market share in the mainstream market, and set high threshold for those newcomers. Thus it was not an easy task for Wanfeng to enter into the market as an automotive parts enterprise.

Therefore, Lei Mingjun's joining was remarkable in Wanfeng's history. In Wanfeng, Lei Mingjun was respected by all for his experience in this field was almost as long as the domestic hub manufacturing history.

Ailian purposefully sent Zhu Xunming and Lei Mingjun as a team for Zhu Xunming was the local technical backbone trained by Wanfeng, while Lei Mingjun was already the elite of the industry. As the drafter of the national motorcycle wheel test method, he was respected by experts from other countries. Such a team of new and senior personnel also reflected the actual situation of Wanfeng. They were ambitious, but at the starting point.

The Chinese Miracle

It's a Chinese custom for the host to arrange some refreshing cabaret after a working conference. Wanfeng arranged for a sightseeing tour to the local scenic spots, in Wanfeng's file, we found photos taken when the participants visited Xuedou Mountain.

The guests were also shown around part of the newly completed Wanfeng Industrial Park. In this way, Wanfeng made a perfect debut in front of the professionals.

Xinchang County, where Wanfeng is located, is small mountainous county in the eastern Zhejiang Province. In its territory there locates a mountain called Tianmu, which is known to the world because of a poetry entitled "Tianmu Mountain Ascended in a Dream" by Li Bai, famous poet of Tang Dynasty. The lines in his poem read "The Heavenly Mother touches the sky and across her mountains range, her imposing manner rivals the five eminent peaks and eclipses Mount Crimson Gate. The Sky Terrace Mountains may be a hundred miles high, yet it seems it may topple over in the south-eastern corner any day." Xinchang was embraced by the Tianmu Mountain and Wanfeng was also tightly related to the mountain.

Tianmu Mountain, with an altitude not too high (less than 1 km), is a beautiful mountain, covered with giant trees and gurgling creeks. Xinchang County is known for a local Buddhist Temple with the first giant Buddha carved in Qi and Liang during North and South Dynasty years. The local people are very industrious and the local government is very supportive of industrial development. Therefore, Xinchang is ahead of the average level of industrial and economic development in Zhejiang Province. The newly-completed Wanfeng Industrial Park was located in the suburbs of Xinchang County, northwest to the Buddhist Temple. The Industrial Park is close to the latest Upper three Line Express Highway, two turns off the road.

In 1998, Wanfeng Industrial Park had just completed its first phase of construction projects. From the choice of its location, a convenient traffic hub for transporting products, we can judge that Wanfeng Industrial Park enjoys an important role in Xinchang County.

Wanfeng then covered only 1/3 of its full size of 1000 area. Factories buildings are all one-stored structure, offices locating in the front, covering about 1/3 of the whole building.

In this zone, the 10-meter-high factory building is divided into two floors, the offices are set along the wall downstairs and reception area and product display area are in the middle. Upstairs, behind a 20 people's big office, lies Chen Ailian's office.

The Industrial Park features the short distance between the working area and living area. The living area of Wanfeng locates just behind the industrial area, where many employees and managers, including Chen Ailian live. Such layout is very Chinese: working and living together, a typical entrepreneurial style.

The working condition of producing wheel hub was harsh in 1998.

Wanfeng had just started to use gravity casting machines in manufacturing hub. At a corner of the factory, after the raw material — aluminum ingot — melted into liquid in the homemade furnace under a high temperature of more than 700 degree centigrade, it was poured into the gravity casting machine through soup mouth on cavity walls. A few minutes later, the casting can be removed from the mold.

The mold in the cavity has been designed to in the shape of the wheel hub so that the cast liquid aluminum would take basic form of a wheel hub.

This seemingly simple flow is actually composed of 36 complex processes. The melting and solidification of liquid aluminum determines the hardness, strength, flexibility and shape of a wheel hub; and is also involved in the condition and simplicity of operation, thus it is considered the core part of casting. In the development of machinery industry, people have invented many casting technology to match the different requirements of different casting. The most original ones are sand mold casting and pouring casting, which are gradually taken place by gravity casting, pressure casting, forging, liquid mold forging, vacuum casting, centrifugal casting and other techniques. The difference of these techniques mainly lies in the solidification rate of the liquid aluminum and the simplicity of operation.

Castings taken from the casting machine can only be called as the "blanks". Usually, because the solidification is very fast, new castings, bear a dull red of liquid aluminum, but they will soon become beautiful.

The next step is machining. After the completion of the condensation, the blanks with basic hardness blanks are sent to machining area, where the gate, burr in the molding process will be removed according to the design requirements of precise machining.

Next comes the coatinging step. In the other side of production area, there is a semi-closed coating room, where the wheels are suspended after machining and transmitted into the coating room in bulk and painted. The motorcycle wheels are then officially completed and could be packed.

Aluminum wheels shiny after machining are even sparkling after the completion of coating. Coupled with the fine design of aesthetic considerations, by the time they are completed they are beautiful.

Nowadays, Wanfeng's new production lines are upgraded to become automatic and advanced equipments are furnished to form a completely sealed casting process, the temperature in the workshop can thus be controlled. But back in 1998, the production conditions decided liquid aluminum had to be exposed to the air before being poured into the gravity casting machine, so the whole workshop is at a rather high temperature.

Wanfeng had only five workshops with two motorcycle wheel productions line and one automobile wheel production line then.

Techniques remained to be improved. There was a long way to go to achieve Ailian's ambition — to become the superstar at China's stage of vehicle manufacturing, which was experiencing a rapid development.

To realize Ailian's dream, Wanfeng must first fulfill automatic producing flow, only then, the production cost could be reduced with the increase of efficiency. As is known to all engineers, automatic producing line means that the factory must have enough orders, otherwise high investment in logistics facilities could not be used effectively and the production capacity would be wasted.

Secondly, the quality of wheels could be further improved, such as the coating process should be closed. Dust-free production had better to be adopted because Semi-closed coating condition may cause potential peeling of the coat due to the air particles' covering the wheels during the coating.

Finally, the expansion of scale also means the increase of raw materials and cost per unit, which can surely add to the benefits.

Wanfeng Industrial Park Located next to Line Three Express Highway

Therefore, experts visiting Wanfeng found it a business at start-up stage which still had to "hunting" for and producing according to the orders. Mass production was almost impossible at the beginning.

However, they could not help showing respect to Wanfeng since Wanfeng was only four years old, starting with a loan of only 500 thousand RMB and most importantly there was a market of over one billion population to back up the company.

A Korean engineer who attended the ISO 8644 Cnference was invited to visit Xinchang again in 2014. And he was amazed by the great changes of the Industrial Park, which covers an area 3 to 4 times larger than that in 1998.

As soon as we turned to Wanfeng from the highway, a grandiose gatehouse was revealed before us, the internal security on duty in the monitoring room.

A square was in the front of the industrial park with a large open-air stage on the North and a European style office building on the south. The whole industrial park was covered with trees, typical garden flavored. In addition to the Xinchang Industrial Park, Wanfeng Auto owns 36 subsidiaries now. The headquarters of Wanfeng Auto Holding Group lies in this office building.

The production base of the headquarters in Xinchang is located in the west side of the square. The production base still covers motorcycle wheels and automobile wheels, belong respectively to two major business divisions of Wanfeng Auto. Besides that, Wanfeng Auto has developed intelligent equipment, and has an independent robot industrial park.

The production line shown to the visitors in 1998 is still in use today, with industrial robots as operators of aluminum liquid pouring and automobile manufacturing casting process done in a much improved, sealed conditions.

Production site of China-made Wanfeng wheel hub

In terms of producing scale, Wanfeng Auto has become the world's largest manufacturer of motorcycle and automobile wheel. In both upstream raw materials providing areas and downstream market, such as Shanghai, Shandong, Guangdong, Chongqing, Ningbo, Jilin, India, Wanfeng has set up large-scale production bases.

Chen Ailian is the one who makes the change, her office on the second floor of the European style office building.

China has entered the era of reform and opening up since the beginning of 1980s. Westerners refer to the 30 years of high-speed development as the "Chinese miracle".

In the "Chinese miracle", the changes took place to Wanfeng Auto are most impressive. According to the Korean engineer, in 1998 Wanfeng was just a novice in the manufacturing field of wheel hubs. He even questioned its future to become competitive. In 2014, However, Wanfeng auto had achieved an annual production capacity of 4000 million units, a world leader in the industry. Such capacity is sufficient to supply at least one of the world's major powers with all its need of motorcycle and automotive wheels. For even China with such a huge population, at least half the market demand can be fulfilled. As a private enterprise, it is impossible for Wanfeng to waste its production capacity, so it must have developed into a large global-based professional manufacturer.

It is only 22 years ago since Wanfeng was founded in 1994. Wanfeng has completed a shift from a follower to a leader. How did Chen Ailian lead Wanfeng to achieve this?

Wanfeng Auto principle

ISO 8644 Standard Revision Conference was only a drop in the bucket in Wanfeng Auto's 22 years journey. In every chapter of this book, we can read stories of Wanfeng as just a Zhejiang-based private enterprise, attaching great importance to exchange and learning on the first-class global platform. Hosting international standard revision conference, provide its technicians and engineers with top technology platform reflected its consistent operation style and explained how Wanfeng can be superior to its rivals.

Wanfeng Auto constantly invests into the continuous growth of its employees, which helps the company in turn grows from a small local company to an International Holdings.

第二章

万丰创业梦

创业梦萌芽

ISO 8644 标准修订会议上的专家们没有想到的是，眼前这个高挑、爽朗的中国女性，虽然生长在中国山区的小城，却是一个"出挑姑娘"，未来还将成为一家跨国集团的掌舵者。

事实上，到 1998 年的时候，陈爱莲和万丰创业，已经过去了四年。此时，万丰已经渡过最艰难的时期。

陈爱莲的创业起点，发生在 1993 年。当时她已经是一家乡镇企业的厂长，当时在厂里负责技术的朱训明清楚地记得，他突然被陈爱莲叫到家里。陈爱莲让他带人把自己的摩托车拆了，看看铝合金管厂能不能生产其中的轮毂。

朱训明很清楚地记得那辆摩托车是本田摩托，是当时新昌县唯一的一辆高档进口摩托车。陈爱莲平时很喜欢，上下班也一直骑着它。

这就是万丰奥特的起步点：一直在琢磨自己能做什么项目的陈爱莲，在骑这辆摩托车一段时间之后，突然发现这个车的轮子跟国产车都不一样，是铝制轮毂。

这个发现在陈爱莲脑海中擦出了火花。她很快去观察了很多辆当时的国产摩托车，和她原来模糊的记忆一样，这些国产车绝大多数使用钢丝轮。

陈爱莲发现的这个现象，是有很深的历史原因的。一方面，在国内，钢的产量要远大于铝，所以钢铁制品在早年要比铝制品便宜得多，因此国产摩托车采用钢丝轮主要是从成本出发的考虑；而另一方面，陈爱莲当时还没有想到的是，当时摩托车生产厂都是大型的国企，这些企业普遍追求大而全的企业规模，因此轮毂生产当时都是摩托车生产厂的一个部门。

对于市场相当敏感的陈爱莲一发现这个情况，就开始考虑自己所在的工厂能不能做这个产品。因此就有了她让铝合金管厂的技术团队拆自己摩托车的举动。就个人而言，陈爱莲看中摩托车轮毂制造项目，主要原因还是她个人的经历。正是因为陈爱莲知道摩托车和汽车可以给社会带来极大的便利和提高效率，所以她预感摩托车和汽车产品会在国内有很大的发展。

陈爱莲估计得没错，而后来市场表现出来的事实远远要比她的想象大得多。万丰奥特企业起步之时，其实是切入了一个急剧上升的交通工具市场。20世纪90年代初期的中国，进入了经济起飞前的准备时期。

所谓的经济起飞期，从市场的角度看，是人们的活动范围大大增加，因此急需交通工具。不过，当时当地的人民并不富裕，对交通工具最大的诉求就是便宜，同时还要能装载货物。因此在众多可以成为交通工具的产品当中，摩托车最可以满足个人的需求，几乎是一个国家进入经济起飞期时人民必选的交通工具和赚钱机器。

这就形成了一个巨大的需求市场。我们将会在后面看到，在陈爱莲主导下的万丰奥特摩轮工厂在开发印度市场的时候，几乎是完整地把公司上世纪90年代在中国的历程重新走了一遍。

在新兴市场国家，交通工具构成巨大的需求，这当然是事物发展过程中新的一面。人们常用"太阳每天都是新的"来形容这一面，而与之相对应的，有句话叫作"太阳底下无新事"——作为发展中国家的中国经历的这个经济起飞期，西方国家早在20世纪之初就经历过了。摩托车这一商品，在西方已经度过了它的兴盛期，进入了平稳发展阶段，因此到 90 年代后期，市场的增量开始向拥有后发优势的亚洲转移。

陈爱莲的这个判断，与政府在 90 年代之初的宏观决策是一致的。进入 90 年代，国有企业在政府的指导下，采取了"大规模引进"的快速战略来满足需求。在政府的安排下，一大批军工企业转向民用市场，它们大多选择进入摩托车制造领域，政府为这些企业制订的基本战略是"先引进技术，然后逐步国产化"。

这个路径是精心设计过的：由于中国国内市场潜力巨大，当时又正从计划经济向市场经济转型，消费者需要高度统一，也就是说，当时人们的收入水平都差不多，当收入水平到了某种程度，并开始需要摩托车的时候，市场需求总量常常是爆发式地增长，不像其他经济自然发展的国家有一个逐步的普及过程。

在国内摩托车生产厂蜂拥而起、争先恐后地引进国外技术的同时，有一大批原来的军工企业由于世界新军事变革的潮流倒逼，不得不削减常规兵器生产，从而需要通过"军品转民品"另找出路，纷纷投产摩托车，重庆嘉陵、洛阳北易就是其中转型成功的典型案例。一时间，国内摩托车生产厂家出现了国有、军工、航空航天、民营资本各种"成分"百花齐放、大干快上的局面，使市场瞬间的需求很快得到满足，不至于出现大规模黑市、高价的现象。

而在市场需求逐步得到满足的情况下，各企业"逐步国产化"，这就是企业自主积极性发挥的过程了。由于当时国内的资源和劳动力价格都非常便宜，所以配件国产化对摩托车生产是有很大好处的。可以想象，市场上的摩托车价格都是既定的，如果主机厂能寻找到相应的配件厂，其产品在品质满足要求的情况下，价格低于进口配件，那主机厂在销售整车的时候，利润空间就会增大。

在这个战略之下，当时在政府指导下的国企表现出了非常强的活力。80 年代末，《人民日报》报道，天津一家国企为了争取市场机会，从欧洲引进一整条生产线，从考察、决策到采购，总共只花了 22 天时间，创造了一个速度上的奇迹。

而从方式上，当时的国企采取的策略也是多种多样，有财力的企业采取的是引进整条生产线的方式；实力弱一些的企业采用合资的方式，引进国外的资本；更小一点的企业采取横向联合的方式，与国有大企业合作。国内的主机生产，很快就铺展开了。

陈爱莲带领团队在进入摩托车轮毂制造行业的时候，正是摩托车主机制造厂开始深度拓展、实现国外技术引进之后的国产化时期。

而从技术角度看，铝制摩托车轮毂的研发，也并不算很困难。在陈爱莲所在的工厂技术团队成员盛晓方、俞利民、吴兴忠等，通过对陈爱莲那辆铃木摩托上的铝轮毂进行测绘，很顺利地完成了初步的图纸设计，同时进一步深入地解析了铝轮毂产品的加工工艺，利用铝合金管厂的工艺设备，进行了产品的研制。

陈爱莲的创业梦有了第一个要素——产品有了，共同奋斗的创业团队也有了。万丰奥特的铝轮梦，萌芽了。

创业梦（一）

江南路是一条不长的道路，位于新昌的母亲河新昌江畔。陈爱莲所在的工厂在这条路的 50 号。厂地正好占了一个街区，两边是两条巷子，沿着江南路，建了一堵围墙。

在 1994 年，没有多少人会料到，这座小厂房的两条夹道里，会酝酿出一家日后在全球数一数二的国际化集团公司来。

为什么会选在夹道里开张呢？

陈爱莲团队开始创业的时候，并没能得到多少支持。与她所在的工厂相熟的政府官员告诉他们：从总体上看，项目登记为"轮毂制造"的国内企业已经有112家，摩托车铝轮市场供大于求，属于当时国家产业限制之列，有重复建设的嫌疑。她所在的民营企业在原来的运营当中没有留下多少资源，现在对这个市场又不熟悉，政府建议他们不要轻易进入这个行业。

更为困难的是，之前的很多轮毂制造企业都从属于主机厂，这个新项目凭什么与这些企业争夺市场呢？

这种定论一下，陈爱莲的铝轮项目在工厂内部的地位，也随之碰到了问题。

政府官员们的劝告当然是出于好心，但纯粹基于数据的这种劝告，客观上是存在一些漏洞的。

原因就在于，当时的112家轮毂厂，虽然在体制和投资上都有优势，但在竞争力和市场观念上，却大有问题。

之所以出现如此之多的摩托车轮毂厂，是因为当时的国有企业在政府的指导下快速上马摩托车项目时，通常也不会落下配套件生产。由于国企有政府资金投资，所以通常喜欢在配件生产上搞"大而全"——自己投资配件项目。

但由于当时的国企对员工和管理层缺乏激励，对配件生产的重视程度也不高，因此出现的结果是国有企业内部的配件厂图方便，眼睛几乎全都盯着自己内部的订单。而现成的订单反而阻碍了这些企业的市场意识，使得作为摩托车生产当中相当核心的轮毂件资源，在整个市场上匹配非常不均衡。计划经济体系看的是总量，就全国而言，虽然轮毂生产的总能力与主机生产的总量比较吻合，微观上看却是漏洞百出。大而全的国企配件厂目光只盯着内部需求，没有生产配套轮毂的主机厂却常常要低三下四求人，才能建立配套关系，而且在价格上也受到歧视。

这在陈爱莲最初的一系列调研动作上，可以清晰地得到印证。陈爱莲把自己的摩托车轮子拆下，让负责技术的朱训明带领团队仿制并开始研究的同时，她自己也开始对这个市场进行调研。初步的结果是，当时相当一部分主机厂从市场上采购轮毂并不容易，其中最为重要的表现是，市场上的轮毂售价远高于生产成本，有很大的利润空间。这其中的原因就在于，大型国企为摩托车生产建立了配套轮毂厂，但它们并不在意对外的市场销售，导致轮毂的市场价格奇高。

她更进一步发现，在这种体制下的轮毂制造企业，完全缺乏创新意识。一旦形成生产能力，很多年都不会有所改进。这就是为什么陈爱莲明明看到日本的进口摩托车已经开始普遍采用美观大方的铝制轮毂，国产的摩托车还在使用钢丝轮的原因。

陈爱莲会怎么做呢？

年轻时，陈爱莲就有不达目的誓不罢休的性格，此时，这种个性在她身上表现得更为明显了。虽然不能说出一套完整的理论，但在工厂的不同岗位上从事过相当长时间的管理工作、同时更为广泛地接触了市场之后的她已经知道，90年代的国企，其实竞争力非常弱。一个项目，只要企业整个团队认真做，是很快能在业内做出成绩来的。这种来自于实践的自信，使得陈爱莲并不畏惧轮毂市场当时的形势。

但她要起步，还得从企业内部先把项目的架构搭建完整才行。

她首先要搭建的，是一个完整的团队。只有在起步时让骨干团队看到这个项目的希望，项目才可能像一个雪球一样滚起来。

陈爱莲通过谈话一个一个地把团队成员都拉进了自己的铝轮项目组，万丰奥特的公司历程，就这样开始了。

万丰奥特铝轮项目起步时的创业团队总共有15个人。陈爱莲是项目总负责人，朱训明负责试制，张锡康和袁林刚负责销售，盛晓方和吴少英负责铸造，杨旭勇负责金工，俞利民和章益丹负责机模，吴兴忠负责技术，吕永新负责设备，顾鑫灿负责采购，王慧琴负责质量，蔡竹妃负责财务，夏越璋负责办公室管理，这样一个团队就把整个项目的架构搭了起来。

这是一支非常年轻的团队，平均年龄不到30岁。

一支如此年轻的团队，加上陈爱莲从来不知道畏惧的个性，自然是什么都可能会出现。然而他们要去完成的创业计划，实在更令人惊叹。

对所有民营工业企业来说，创业要迈过的第一道门槛，永远是如何形成生产能力。形成生产能力需要包括资金、场地、配套、设备等在内的诸多要素，而万丰奥特起步时，可以说是"一无资金、二无装备、三无厂房"。

从资金来看，当时的陈爱莲所在企业此时并无多少资本，自然无法为摩托车铝轮的开发、研制以及批量生产提供资金支持。董事会定下上马摩托车铝轮项目的时候，就在决议中明确提出："该项目按年产2.5万套规模投资，所需设备投资100万元和流动资金50万元，由铝轮项目自行筹措，利息自负。"因此，在陈爱莲向银行贷款50万元作为流动资金后，设备采购所需要的100万元，则是当时最难攻克的难题。

其实，在拆解陈爱莲的摩托车轮毂的同时，创业团队已经看好了轮毂的生产设备。当时国内的摩托车轮毂生产厂家都采用的是挤压铸造工艺，团队通过查找，选中了天津一家设备厂家生产的压铸式铸造机。但陈爱莲接下来找当时这家厂的厂长商谈的，却是能不能用赊销的方式先把设备拿到手。

这种创业的经历，无疑令人瞠目结舌。铸造机是轮毂制造厂的主要设备。即便创业者"胆大包天"，核心设备赊销，是很难去想象的。况且，对方怎么可能让她赊销呢？

陈爱莲是被逼出来的。正是因为摩托车轮毂生产项目在工厂内部并不看好，优先级不是很高，所以她可支配的资金，少之又少。

但陈爱莲赊销主要的生产设备压铸机，却是有自己另外的打算的。此时，她已经发现轮毂产品市场需求量不小。因此她的盘算是，先拿到一部分生产设备，再拿到足够的订单。而后，用现实在运转的公司和利润，建立银行对自己的信任，拿到部分银行贷款，再把设备的赊销还上。

另外，陈爱莲深谙银行贷款之道，银行之所以不太愿意给企业贷款，关键是银行都是"晴天送伞，雨天收伞"的。如果新项目团队没有运转起来，银行当然不会再给贷款，但只要项目进入了运转状态，银行是非常愿意放贷的。

后来陈爱莲和创业团队一起用实践证明了，这个计划虽然看起来胆大包天，却是有可能实现的。

可能性的根本源泉，仍然来自于摩托车市场正在快速上升的基本现实。1994年，摩托车市场仍然处于供不应求的状态，一是消费者很难买到摩托车，二是摩托车的定价都很贵，生产企业的利润也很高，因此市场规模还在不断扩大。同时，由于摩托车很受欢迎，所以当时还有大量的企业进入这一市场。摩托车的生产厂家之间，已经开始出现了竞争。

主机厂之间的竞争，对于万丰奥特铝轮项目来说，其实是非常有利的局面。这使得他们想做的价廉物美的铝制轮毂产品，更受主机厂的欢迎。

当时摩托车车轮的主要轮型是钢丝轮，到现在，我们还能在街面上的电动车轮当中发现它的踪影。钢丝轮廉价、便宜，造型简单，但不如铝合金车轮美观、豪华、个性化、吸引人们的眼球。

铝轮比钢丝轮轻巧而美观，装配非常容易，强度不亚于钢丝轮，而且能为摩托车提升档次加分。

铝轮毂的出现，对于当时摩托车市场来说是一股新潮。一辆铝轮毂的摩托车，很容易引起消费者的注意。因此采用铝轮毂，有相当的可能来帮助主机厂卖出产品。摩托车本来就处于市场充分竞争的状态，而如果铝制轮毂能帮助当时主机厂实现销售卖点，那么生产摩托车铝轮的前景，也就不言而喻了。

陈爱莲赊销设备计划的第一步，实现得很顺利。

天津那家设备生产厂的厂长，虽然初听陈爱莲提出赊销想法之时，几乎把头摇成了拨浪鼓。但陈爱莲的解释却让他慢慢接受这位年轻女性的想法。陈爱莲给他的解释是，公司只是上了多个项目，资金周转上有点问题，所以想要拖一点时间付款。总体来说，对于压铸机生产厂只是收款时间上迟一点的事，这在当时国有企业三角债遍行的大环境当中，其实是司空见惯的。

除此之外，陈爱莲在压铸机的价格上做了一些让步。这样，4台万丰奥特创业的主要设备——压铸机，就赊了回来。

这些赊来的设备放在哪里好呢？当时场地其实也是非常紧张的。在整个厂里可以集中放下 4 台挤压铸造机的地方，也就是两幢厂房之间那条夹道了。因此万丰奥特创业者们在这条夹道上方做了个简易棚，确保里面的设备和员工不会被风吹雨淋。

这就是后来年销售超百亿，成为全球最大铝轮毂生产企业的万丰奥特的最初模样。

创业梦（二）

陈爱莲和创业团队赊销设备是有时间限制的，他们必须在一年之内，把订单拿到手，进而办理银行贷款，还上设备款。而在这个过程当中，万丰奥特的创业团队在市场和产品上的优势，就可以得到充分发挥了。

虽然人员少，但陈爱莲这支团队相较于市场上 112 家竞争对手，是有优势的。因为万丰奥特铝轮项目是民营的，所以团队当中的每个人都很清楚，如果没有市场，没有主机厂采用这个团队的铝轮，那么他们就没有生存的空间。因此，与所有的竞争对手不一样的是，除了生产人员之外，陈爱莲团队的其他人，都有过上门向主机厂销售的经历。

这在 1994 年，可以说是所有民营企业核心的市场优势。

除了这种市场优势之外，万丰奥特铝轮项目用铝轮切入市场，比竞争对手领先了一大步。由于大批企业进入了摩托车生产领域，因此主机市场的竞争也非常激烈。进口车、合资车和本土车在市场上厮杀得不可开交。万丰奥特能以国产的价格提供与进口车一样的配件，成为主机厂赢得市场份额的手段，当然会受到欢迎。

不过，这还是理论上的优势。对于万丰奥特这个团队来说，要把这种理论上的优势变成现实的订单，要跨越三大鸿沟：首先他们要做出精美的样品，给顾客以信心——他们企业虽然小，但是能做出优质的摩托车轮毂来的；其次是要快速地把生产规模化，使主机厂顾客来考察企业的时候，能看到一家像模像样的配件生产企业；最后更为重要的是，要有款型设计，使摩托车生产厂有选择的余地，从而相信与万丰奥特合作能使得顾客更多地选择自己企业的摩托车整车，提高自己的份额。

陈爱莲的团队，在第一步上就做出了创新。

第一个创新出在样品形式上———一般而言，轮毂厂要取得主机厂的信任，要么给主机厂的管理者们看实物轮毂，要么是给他们看设计图纸，而万丰奥特的创业团队的办法是，给顾客先看木模。

这种变革，出发点就在于万丰奥特铝轮团队的市场意识。陈爱莲和她的同事们要到主机厂上门销售自己的轮毂，显然不能只带图纸去，而因为当时的生产能力很小，所以带着实物轮毂去现场，也不是太现实。因为实物轮毂都是针对订单要求生产的，对于新的顾客，常常是不配套的。除了说明万丰奥特铝轮能做轮毂之外，没有更多意义。

当然，更为重要的是，陈爱莲团队的资金十分紧张，现实要求他们提高上门销售的成功率——他们没有多少经费来反复出差游说同一位顾客。

出路很显然就在对顾客需要的研究上。为提高销售的成功率，在出差之前，陈爱莲和同事们就开始研究对应主机厂的摩托车款式，此时若能做出适合主机厂摩托车款式的轮毂样品，会大幅度提高销售成功率。

新昌作为山区县，本地多的是木匠。因此新昌纺织器材厂里的员工中也多得是好手艺的木匠，要他们按图样做几只木制的轮子来，根本不是问题。更为重要的，这种样品大大降低成本了，而且也非常轻巧。这就是木模样品作为一个市场创新的来源。

而当万丰奥特的销售人员把模型带到主机厂时，木制轮模也备受欢迎。因为这种轮子可以做到高度仿真，所以主机厂的技术人员可以当场把这种轮子模型装在成品摩托车上，看看万丰奥特的铝制轮型是否真的美观、易装配。

　　1994 年是决定性的一年，创业团队当中的每个人都很清楚，闯过去，他们就能把这个项目做起来，否则这个项目从此就不会再有机会，因此每个人都拼了。

　　整个万丰奥特铝轮项目团队最初做营销的，只有陈爱莲和袁林刚两个人。他们最初的销售方式非常简单，就是背着木制轮毂模型坐火车跑主机厂，摸清整个市场的基本情况。

　　不过，机敏的陈爱莲很快发现，单纯的销售人员上门，所起到的作用只能是摸清主机厂的基本情况，把合作的线搭起来。要真正与主机厂建立稳定的合作关系，必须是作为配件生产的轮毂厂中包括技术、营销、生产，以及决策层的人员一起出场，才能让主机厂决策层明白万丰奥特非常重视这一合作项目，进而加速成功销售的进程。

　　一旦明白了这个市场规律，雄心勃勃的陈爱莲就开始自我加压，大胆地提出了万丰奥特铝轮项目团队要争取给国内一流的主机厂供应配件的市场战略定位。

万丰奥特原则

从陈爱莲的早年经历和万丰奥特的创业历程当中，我们可以看到这家企业的一个清晰特征：早年的经历决定了陈爱莲是一个非常有战略思维、敏锐眼光和强烈目标感的人。在万丰奥特创业的过程中，为达到创业的总目标，公司的创业元老们也表现出了强大的韧性。正是因为这种追逐创业目标绝不放手的韧劲，才形成了企业运营当中一系列的创新。

在某种意义上，本书之所以叫"追梦者"，正是对于陈爱莲领导下的万丰奥特内在这种强大的目标感的体现。陈爱莲认为，万丰奥特就是这样一个追梦者，把企业一个个美好的梦想转变成灿烂的现实，从而实现管理层和员工的梦想。

我们在后面可以看到，万丰奥特早期，创业团队的这种目标感，在万丰奥特的发展历程中逐步地变成一种常态，而且得到了加强。这对万丰奥特的企业实践，起到了巨大的作用。

如果说万丰奥特铝轮项目的创业过程有什么传奇性的话，首先要归因于陈爱莲的早年经历，让她选择了摩托车这个大市场。创业之初的万丰奥特，就进入了一个充分竞争的市场，但从小就喜欢挑战的陈爱莲大胆提出了"一览众山小，再览众山无"的市场战略定位，选择前十大高端品牌主机厂作为自己的战略合作伙伴，从而使万丰奥特一开始就占据了高起点、高定位，获得了超常规发展。

充分竞争锤炼了万丰奥特，造就了万丰奥特，大浪淘沙，激流勇进，使得万丰奥特的追梦人们锲而不舍，勇往直前，直奔光辉的彼岸。

Chapter 2
Wanfeng's Entrepreneurial Dream

Budding of Wanfeng's Entrepreneurial Dream

To the surprise of the experts at the ISO 8644 standard revision conference, the tall and cheerful Chinese lady was "an outstanding girl" who would become a manager of a transnational group in the future, though born in a small town in a Chinese mountainous area.

By 1998, fours years had passed since Ailian started to run Wanfeng and brought it through its hardest time.

Ailian's entrepreneurial experience started in 1993 when she was already a director of a private aluminum alloy tube factory. Zhu Xunming, who was in charge of technology then in the factory, still remembers the day when he was suddenly called to Chen Ailian's house to tell apart her motorcycle. She wanted to make sure whether the factory could produce its wheel hub.

Zhu Xunming still remembers that Chen Ailian's Honda motorcycle was the only high-end imported motorcycle in Xinchang County, Ailian's favorite commuting vehicle.

That was Wanfeng Auto's starting point: Ailian was pondering on what they could start with when she suddenly found the aluminum wheels of her motorcycle different from those China-made.

The discovery inspired Ailian who then made a brief research on the domestic motorcycle market which ensured her memory — the vast majority of domestic wheels were made of steel.

There were historical reasons for Ailian's discovery. On the one hand, in China, the output of steel was much larger and the price much lower than that of aluminum products used to be much cheaper than aluminum. The domestic motorcycle mainly adopted steel wheels out of the cost consideration. On the other hand, the domestic motorcycle manufacturers were all large state-owned enterprises who pursued comprehensive production, in which wheel hub production was only a small section.

Chen Ailian was sensitive and began to consider the possibility of developing the aluminum alloy wheel hubs. That was why she asked the technology team to dismantle her own motorcycle. Personally, Ailian's experience as tractor and driver also counted in her choice of the project. She was well-aware of the convenience and efficiency motorcycles and automobiles would bring and their great potential in China.

The market later proved to be even better than Chen Ailian's estimation. Wanfen was lucky to have entered into the transportation market that was taking off in China in the early 1990s.

In a booming market, there would be a tremendous increase in the scope of people's activities which must be supported by an urgent need in transportation. However, at that time, the local people were not rich, their greatest demand for transportation vehicle being its low price and loading capacity. Therefore motorcycles excelled among many other vehicles as they could meet the individual needs and make money as well.

This constituted a huge demand market. Later we can see Wanfeng experienced almost the same story when it expanded to the Indian market.

Transportation vehicles forecast huge demand in an emerging market, which is of course the positive side of the development. Every day is a new day but everything is not new. What China was experiencing then as a developing country had already been experienced by the western countries in the early 20th Century. Motorcycle had passed its booming stage and entered a period of steady development, so in the late 1990s, its incremental margin began to transfer to the Asian market.

Chen Ailian's judgment was in accordance with the government macro policy in the early 1990s when the state-owned enterprises were taking a "large-scale introduction" approach to meet the increasing demand. A large number of military enterprises shifted to the civilian market under the guidance of Chinese government, and most of them chose to enter the field of motorcycle manufacturing. Their basic strategy was to introduce the technology first and then gradually localize.

This approach was delicately designed for the huge potential of Chinese market in its transformation from planned economy to the market economy with consumers need highly unified and people's income levels being similar. When people's income level developed to some extent and their need for motorcycles arose, the market demand would expect to grow explosively, very different from a gradual growth in other countries with natural economic development.

While the domestic motorcycle manufacturing plants swarmed into the field and scrambled to introduce foreign technology, a herd of former military enterprises had to cut down on their production in conventional weapons and refer to the civilian market. Chongqing Jialing and Luoyang Beiyi were successful cases in such transformation. The domestic motorcycle market was suddenly full of enterprises of various types — stated owned, military, aerospace and private — to satisfy the explosive demands and maintain a stable market.

The process of "gradual localization" was one that each enterprise could bring its role into full play for during which, the domestic resources and labor prices were much cheaper so that the localization of parts plants would undoubtedly reduce the costs and increase the profit margin if only the quality requirements of the host plants were met.

Under the guidance of such strategy, the state-owned enterprises showed strong vitality. In the late 1980s, "People's Daily" reported on a state-owned enterprise in Tianjin for it created a time miracle in introducing a whole production line from Europe. In order to win market opportunities it spent only 22 days completing the whole process of making research, decision and purchase.

In terms of approaches, the state-owned enterprises were creative—financially-strong enterprises introduced entire production lines; medium enterprises invited foreign capitals in the form of joint ventures; even smaller enterprises took horizontal joint approach and cooperated with large SOEs. The localization of host plants soon spread up in China.

The time when Chen Ailian led her team into the motorcycle wheel hub manufacturing was just the time when host plants of motorcycles began to localize.

The development of aluminum motorcycle wheel hubs was not very difficult to the team. By mapping Ailian's motorcycle, Zhu Xunming soon completed the preliminary design together with his team members including Sheng Xiaofang, Yu Limin, Wu Xingzhong, etc. In the mean time, they analyzed the processing technique of the wheel hubs and tried to develop their own wheels with the equipment of the aluminum alloy tube factory. Ailian was one step further to her dream then — she had the product and the entrepreneurial team. Wanfeng's dream of making aluminum wheels thus budded.

Ailian's Entrepreneurial Dream I

The Factory, where Ailian started her entrepreneurship was located at No. 50, Jiangnan Road, a short road on the bank of Xinchang River, the mother river of Xinchang County. The factory covered a whole block between two lanes and along Jiangnan Road, they built a wall.

In 1994, few would expect that the future of a top international group would rise in the passage of this small plant.

Why did they choose to start their production in the passage then?

In her early days, Ailian did not get much support. A government official, Ailian's acquaintance, was kind to warn her that "hub production" were already redundant in China with another 112 domestic enterprise that Ailian not enter into an unfamiliar field since aluminum alloy wheels for motorcycle have already been oversupplied and restricted.

In addition, a lot of wheel hub manufacturing enterprises were subordinated to a host plant. How could a new comer compete for market share?

To make things worse, Chen Ailian's position in the factory was even questioned with such the the negative prediction.

The advice of the government officials was of course out of good, but purely based on the data, which should be further discussed.

The 112 existing wheel hub manufacturers certainly had advantages in their company types and investment. But as far as their competitiveness and market awareness, some of them were in trouble.

The reason why there were so many motorcycle wheel manufacturers was that the state-owned enterprises started their project under the government's guidance too promptly. These government-funded enterprises normally would like to engage in an all-embracing mode and invest in their own parts production as well However, due to the lack of incentive for the employees and management, these state-owned enterprises looked down upon the parts production. As a result, their eyes were only fixed on their internal orders which in turn hindered the development of their market awareness, making the production of wheel hubs rather unbalanced to match the real market demand. To be more specific, minor host companies without their own-made wheel hubs were often ignored since their demands were humble and the prices they offered were not attractive enough. Statistics in a planned economy failed to show the problem for only figures such as annual output at a macro layer instead a micro one were collected.

This was demonstrated after a preliminary research conducted by Chen Ailian. While she asked Zhu Xunming and his team to imitate and began to study, she also began to conduct a research on the market. The results were that a considerable number of host plants found it hard to purchase wheel hubs from the market. The market price of wheel hubs was much higher than their cost, leaving a great profit margin. The reason behind the fact was that those large state-owned enterprises were not caring about the external market, resulting in a high market price of wheel hubs.

Further research showed that wheel hub manufacturers in planned economy were out of innovative awareness. Once they formed a production capacity, they would remain unchanged and unimproved for many years. No wonder motorcycles from Japan had already begun a wide use of beautiful and generous aluminum wheels, while steel wheel hubs were still prevailing in China.

What would Chen Ailian do?

Ailian had a determined personality since she was young. At that time, such determination was well performed. Without a complete set of theory, but with rich management experience in different positions at the factory, she had extensive exposure to the market and a thorough understanding of the weakness of those state-owned enterprises in 1990s. As long as the entire team was committed to do a project, they could make it in a short time. Such confidence from practice gave Ailian enough courage to meet the challenges in the wheel hub market.

Of course, she needed to complete the internal construction of management within the factory before starting the project.

First of all, a complete team was a must. Only when she showed the twilight to the backbones, could the team be built up like rolling a snowball.

Chen Ailian talked those backbones into joining the team for developing aluminum wheel hubs. And that was how Wanfeng started its business.

The team had 15 members with Ailian as the leader: Zhu Xunming, responsible for the developing; Zhang Xikang and Yuan Lingang, responsible for sales; Sheng Xiaofang and Wu Shaoying, responsible for casting; Yang Xuyong, responsible for metalworking; Zhang Yidan and Yu Limin, responsible for molding machine; Wu Xingzhong, responsible for technology; Lv Yongxin, responsible for equipment; Gu Xincan, responsible for purchasing; Wang Huiqin, responsible for quality control; Cai Zhufei, responsible for financing; and Xia Yuezhang, responsible for office management. Thus a scheme for management and developing was completed.

This was a young team, with the average age of its members less than 30.

Such a young team, led by Chen Ailian who feared of nothing may encounter anything, but their business plan was more than amazing.

The first threshold for private industrial enterprises always lay in how to form a production capacity. To form its production capacity, Wanfeng needed to conquer a lot of difficulties, including the lack of capital, sites, facilities, equipment, etc.

The factory was not able to provide for any capital and it was decided at the board meeting that the annual output of the new project should be 25 thousand sets, the investment in equipment be 1 million yuan and circulating fund be 500 thousand yuan accordingly, which should all be financed by the project itself and interest be born on the project also. Chen Ailian managed to make a loan of 500 thousand yuan from the bank. But the investment for equipment seemed a mission impossible.

Actually, early when they dismantled Ailian's motorcycle, they had a intention as to purchase squeezing casting machines from a Tianjin factory. But Ailian was thinking of purchasing on credit due to lack of fund.

Such experience in starting business was astonishing since casting machine was the main equipment of a hub manufacturer. Even though the entrepreneurs were bold enough, it was still unimaginable to buy them on credit. The problem was, how could Ailian manage to persuade the seller?

Chen Ailian was forced on the edge. The factory did not think highly of her project, nor did it give the project a high priority, thus Ailian hadn't got much capital in disposal.

Ailian had her own plan. She had already researched on the considerable market demand for wheel products. So her plan was to get a part of the production equipment first, and then get enough orders. A company in operation would win her both profits and bank trust, which would then naturally bring bank loans to pay for the equipment.

Meanwhile Ailian was familiar with the principles of bank loaning. Banks are more willing to save those who can save themselves. If the new project was not in operation, the bank would not be likely to give a loan, but as long as the project entered the operating state, the bank was very willing to lend.

Later Chen Ailian and her team proved with their practice that the heaven-daring plan was able to realize.

The possibility was out of the fact that the motorcycle market was rapidly developing. In1994, the market was still in short supply and it was difficult for the consumers to buy a motorcycle. The market scale was still expanding with prices being high and so were the profits. At the same time, motorcycles were popular and more enterprises were entering the market, and competition between manufacturers was fierce.

The competition between the host plants was good news to Wanfeng's project, for Wanfeng was committed to produce quality aluminum wheel hubs with lower prices.

The steel wheel hubs popular then can still find trace in today's electric bicycles. Steel wheels are cheaper, simpler in shaping but not as good as the aluminum alloy wheels which look more luxurious, personalized and eye-catching.

Aluminum wheels are lighter and more beautiful, easier to assemble and as strong as steel wheels. They can upgrade a motorcycle.

The emergence of aluminum wheels was a new fashion in the motorcycle market. A motorcycle with aluminum wheels was more likely to attract the consumers' attention and became the selling star of the host plant. Thus the prospect of aluminum wheels was out of question within the motorcycle market full of competition.

The first step of Chen Ailian's plan — to purchase equipment on credit — was implemented smoothly.

Despite his denial at first, Ailian finally persuaded the Director of the equipment manufacturer at Tianjian to sell on credit. Ailian's explanation was that the factory just had a temporary problem in cash flow so there would only a delay in payment. That was actually not uncommon in China then with a background of triangle debt among state-owned enterprises.

To broker the agreement, Chen Ailian made some concessions at the price and finally purchased the main equipment — 4 squeezing casting machines—on credit.

Where would the machines be placed then? The only place that could accommodate them were passages between the two factory buildings. Therefore Wanfeng's entrepreneurs built a simple shed above the passageway to shield the machines and employees from wind and rain.

That was the initial appearance of Wanfeng Auto, the top enterprise in aluminum wheel hub production with an annual sales volume of over ten billion.

Ailian's Entrepreneurial Dream II

The time limit for Chen Ailian's team to pay the debt for the equipment was a year. They must get orders so that they could make bank loans to pay for the debts. And during this process, Wanfeng's entrepreneurial team gave full play to their advantages in both market and product.

Despite the small size, Ailian's team had the obvious advantages compared with its 112 competitors: they were more crisis-conscious since Wanfeng was private-funded. All of the team members except for the producing staff had experience of selling in person for they were fully aware that marketing was the only way for them to survive.

That could be considered as the core market advantage of all private enterprises in 1994.

Besides that, Wanfeng took a faster leap than its competitors with aluminum wheel project when entering the market. A large number of enterprises entered the field of motorcycle production. Motorcycles from imported manufacturers, joint ventures and local plants were competing fiercely. If Wanfeng could offer parts with imported quality at domestic prices to help those host plants out in winning market shares, it would surely be welcomed.

Still, this was a theoretical advantage. To put it into reality, Wanfeng had three barriers to conquer: First of all, they must make fine samples to assure it consumers that despite a small business, it was capable enough to make quality products. Second, it must quickly put on mass production so that the host plants could see a decent parts production enterprise in operation when making market research. Finally and more importantly, they must have their own design and leave the host plants room for choice so that they would trust Wanfeng in its capability to attract more consumers and improve their share.

Chen Ailian's team made an initiative in the first step.

Normally wheel factories would show samples or design drawings to the managers of host plants. Wanfeng's team, however, showed its potential customers wood models instead.

That was rather creative. Obviously, it was sufficient and persuasive for Ailian and her colleagues to take drawings only. But due to Wanfeng's small production capacity, it was almost impossible to take physical samples to the scene, because samples generally did not fit for a new customer. There was no point in bringing real sample except for showing their ability to make aluminum wheel hubs.

Another critical reason was their shortage of capital. They had to improve their success rate in sales for they could not afford to travel repeatedly to lobby the same customer.

The way out was to make a thorough research on customer needs. In order to improve their success rate, Chen Ailian and her colleagues would work out specific motorcycle models for the particular host plant before a business trip. It would greatly improve the success rate if they could take the specific sample with them.

There were many outstanding carpenters in Xinchang as a mountainous county. Some staff members of Xinchang Textile Equipment Factory were good at carving, to whom, making a few wooden wheels were nothing. In addition, such wooden samples were low in costs and portable. That was how wooden samples were applied as an innovation.

Interestingly, the wooden samples were welcomed by the host plants for they could achieve a high degree of simulation, so the technical staff of the host plant could try them on a finished motor and see how it looked and whether it was easy to assemble.

The year 1994 was decisive. Everyone in the team knew it as their only chance: going through the year and they would be successful. Everyone was risking it all.

There were only two members in the team who originally specialized in marketing — Chen Ailian and Yuan Lingang. Their initial sales approach was very simple, that is, carrying a wooden wheel model to the host plant in person and finding out the basic situation of the entire market.

However, Chen Ailian soon found that to show Wanfeng's sincerity and to establish a stable cooperative relationship with the host plant, it must be the whole team working together including technology, marketing, production, and management.

Once she understand the market rules, ambitious Ailian proposed the strategic market positioning of Wanfeng as to supply accessories for the first-class domestic host plants.

The benefits of achieving this goal were obvious. The first-class host plants were all SOEs with abundant capital. With their orders, Wanfeng would not be stuck with receivable accounts dilemma. Furthermore, those state-owned enterprises all adopted foreign technology and their product quality were very close to the international advanced level even if they had just put into operation. So their products were popular in the market. There was no need to worry about the orders.

Such prosperity was when the motorcycle market just started booming. Later, however, these state-owned enterprises began to decay because of their unclear property rights, lack of responsibility which resulted in their outdated products, slow-down market moves which lead to their doomed fate. That is another story.

Of course, the threshold in front of Ailian's team was not low to enter the state-owned enterprises.

After she found out the market rule, Ailian created legendary market breakthrough on a single business tour with her team in 1994.

The biggest challenge facing Wanfeng in 1994 was to run up the entire project, while the key was to let the casting equipment operate in full production so as to get bank loans. As long as they got bank loans, the debts could be paid and the project would survive. To put the 4 casting into full production, the team needed a monthly order of 2000 sets.

Unless the order being met, the equipment would be laid idle and the whole plan was likely to fail.

Chen Ailian selected some host plants including a state-owned enterprise at Taizhou City, Jincheng Motorcycle from Nanjing City and Qianjiang Motorcycle from Zhejiang Province. Nanjing Jincheng Motorcycle and Zhejiang Qianjiang

Motorcycle later became big names in this field.

They won the order from the manufacturer at Taizhou easily. Ailian was not contented with the order for it was a small plant still worrying about its supporting suppliers. Cooperation with Qianjiang Motorcycle was most likely due to its former cooperation with Wanfeng and both their origin in Zhengjiang Province. Ailian was confident in winning the order.

Thus the key to Wanfeng's full production lay in the order from Jincheng Motorcycle Group (Jincheng for short).

Several trips around had revealed it to Chen Ailian that to a large extent, the host plants would judge the sincerity and the strength of the parts plants by looking at the visiting team and how they acted. So Ailian borrowed a traveling coach, which was rather rare then, and took all the core members in her team particularly for this marketing campaign. Such practice was already proved to be successful in her previous negotiation t in Taizhou.

Still she felt uneasy when the team arrived in Nanjing where Jincheng Motorcycle was based.

Jincheng used to be a military enterprise shifting from aerospace field to civilian areas. Its large scale and state-owned investment was admired by Ailian and her team – Jincheng was more like a university with fine internal. In the traditional planned economy system, its administrative level was quite high. Such external form was rather overwhelming.

Chen Ailian had known beforehand that they would have a meeting with a Deputy General Manager of Jincheng responsible for motorcycle pipe supplying. When they arrived, the Deputy General Manager was at meeting several executives of Jincheng motorcycle in a conference room. A staff member from Supply Management Office told them the exact position and they waited outside.

About two hours later, the Deputy General Manager only came out of for the bathroom once at the interval and the conference continued. Ailian and her colleagues could only present their business card after two hours of waiting..

Ailian recalled her experience and said her determined personally since her childhood played a key supporting role in that trip. The larger Jincheng's was and the more demanding its management was, the more desired she wanted to win the order. The only thought in Ailian's mind then was to win!

Chen Ailian and her colleagues waited at the door for more than three hours, until the end of the meeting, before they were asked to show their samples to the management of Jincheng Motorcycle.

Wanfeng's team won their first key point.

Jincheng's managers were insightful enough to pick up Wanfeng as its partner at the initial stage of localization. They found the visitors really confident of their technology and had selling points in their new products.

After a brief communication, Jincheng's executives immediately finalize their intention to talk further. Ailian's team studied Jincheng's motorcycle models and develop corresponding wooden wheel samples prior to the meeting. Such preparation counted a lot for the success. Then all they needed was to take the samples to Jincheng's showroom and try assembling and that spoke much louder than words.

The next step went on smoothly with the Deputy General Manager of Jincheng proposed to meet Chen Ailian and her team at their hotel for detailed cooperation.

Overjoyed, Chen Ailian immediately promised that she would meet Jincheng's executives in person the next day and take them to Jinling Hotel for further discussion.

The team actually lived in a small hotel in Nanjing, but they were afraid that

Jincheng's executives would question their strength if they met in a humble hotel.

In desperation, Chen Ailian made the meeting place Jinling Hotel, the most prestigious one in Nanjing. That's why she would pick up the top executives in persona.

Everything seemed well handled, but Ailian and his colleagues still wanted to save fund. So they booked only one room the next day's meeting at Jinling Hotel. Ailian also bought a pack of first-class cigarette branded "Ashima" especially for Zhu Xunming out of her own fund, because Zhu was the only one smoked in the team and he would be responsible for passing cigarettes to the guests the next day.

Many years after when Zhu Xunming recalled the experience, he would still find the detail impressive. People in Wanfeng make it the story of "a pack of 'Ashima' in exchange for a big market".

That night, Chen Ailian and her team checked in Jinling Hotel and crowded in one suite. The next morning, Chen Ailian drove her car to fetch the Jincheng managers. They had breakfast together at the hotel and held a meeting in the suite. Finally, they achieved the order of Jincheng Motorcycle.

Plus the order from the third host plant they visitted, Zhejiang Qianjiang Motorcycle Co., Ltd. (Qianjiang Motorcycle for short), Chen Ailian and her team all together swoop down orders of 2000 sets of wheels, an exciting success for Wanfeng Auto in its first step and the market had been established!

Winning the first battle, Chen Ailian called for a meeting the right evening when she returned to Xinchang.

Ailian made a passionate speech with confidence at the meeting: "From now on, we can set our goal as No. one in the market! We are to conquer every obstacle and difficulty, and to seize every minute and second to win all of the top ten motorcycle factories in China with the fastest speed. Don't have a single moment of fear. Market shows no mercy to the weak. We are to borrow the prestige of large-scale factories. Only when we carry out this marketing strategy steadily, can we remain invincible. we need to understand that we are creating an unprecedented market in china!"

Her words boosted the morale greatly and every salesman at present was deeply encouraged.

Luoyang Northern EK Chor Motorcycle Co. Ltd (Northern Ek Chor for short) was located in the Central Plains area of China, a market for which all parts companies spared no effort to compete. Zhang Xikang promised Chen Ailian to enter Northern Ek Chor's market with integrity and win-win concept within six months. First, he established a rapport with the Director office of Northern Ek Chor, and expressed his willing to meet their General Manager. Hard work paid off, one afternoon, the General Manager agreed to meet Zhang Xikang. When they met, Zhang Xikang only stated his views on the development trend of the motorcycle market in the future. He did not talk about selling products, which surprised the General Manager. Impressed by Zhang's sincerity and his vivid and accurate analysis to the market, the Manager immediately signed the first contract.

In the meantime Yuan Lingang, responsible for Jiangsu section swoop down the orders of Chunlan Motorcycle and Wanfeng Auto became its main supplier.

Enough orders were the second setp to the success of Chen Ailian's entrepreneurial dream. Now there only left the final step — get a bank loan to the pay the debt for the casting machines.

Much to her surprise, the local bank refused to give a loan to the new project. Hardly had Chen Ailian entered the office of a local state-owned bank President, did the President learned her intention and immediately got to his feet, picking up his briefcase and said: "Sorry but I have to something important to handle now.

Could you please come with appointment next time? "

Ailian did not seem frustrated with such decline. She gave a generous friend-like response: "That's fine, Sir. Don't be nervous. I just want to invite you to guide our work in our factory. Could you come another time at your convenience please?" Ailian was confident that with the customer orders, as long as the bank had an understanding of their situation, he would surely make the loan.

Appropriate words and clever response made the President a little bit awkward. So not before long, the President visited the company. After he saw the busy producing scene, he immediately approved a loan of 2 million yuan, a fairly large loan at the time.

The president was cautious in his investigation and proved to be wise to give the loan. Despite the order, Wanfeng's project was still a small one.

On October 19, 1994, Wanfeng's first patch of products were officially completed and was loaded for delivery to Nanjing Jincheng Motorcycle. The entire factory staff were sending off at the passageway, trucks' front faces covered with red ribbons, fireworks set off for to celebrate the formal birth of Wanfeng Auto Holding Group Co., Ltd.

Wanfeng Auto principle

From Chen Ailian's early experience and Wanfeng Auto start-up process, we can see that the enterprise features a very strategic thinking, insightful and sensitive leader. In achieving its business objectives, the company's founders also showed a strong perseverance. It is because of their pursuit of business objectives and the tenacity never to let go, the enterprise created a series of innovation.

In a sense, that's why this book is entitled "Dreamer" to convey the objective of Wanfeng under the leadership of Chen Ailian. In Ailian's eyes, Wanfeng Auto is such a dreamer trying to turn every dream of the enterprise and that of its management and staff into reality.

Later we will see the sense of objective had become a regular state of Wanfeng Auto at its early stage and was continually reinforced with time going, which played a huge role in Wanfeng's success.

The legend of Wanfeng's entrepreneurial process owes to Chen Ailian's early experience and her choice in motorcycle market. Wanfeng Auto started up from a fully competitive market, but welcomed the challenge with the positioning of market leader by forming strategic partnership with top ten high-end host plant brands. That is how Wanfeng Auto achieved an unconventional development speed by starting high and positioning high.

Fully competitive market tempered Wanfeng Auto, created it, and made its dreamers a group of tide-players with perseverance and courage to ride to glory.

第三章
起步摩轮

用 60 万换来的品质标准

万丰奥特铝轮项目的技术负责人朱训明在 20 世纪 90 年代的时候，还只是个 20 多岁的大学毕业生。在他眼里，万丰奥特铝轮项目的启动，其实就是 30 多岁的陈爱莲带着一批不知天高地厚的毛头小伙子试图干一番事业。

所以 1995 年春节，陈爱莲要把一批价值 60 多万元的市场急需的待发产品报废的时候，朱训明的脑袋"嗡"的一下子懵了。

当时，陈爱莲描绘了"万里之行，始于轮下；丰功伟业，基在创新"的创业蓝图，万丰奥特的第一个梦想就开始上路了。不过就在 1995 年春节，这个第一步看起来很顺利的梦，就遇上了质量问题。

1995 年的正月初八，陈爱莲站在厂房的假山喷泉旁边召集铝轮项目的管理者和员工开会。春节假期铝轮项目全体工作人员都在加班，所以人们还以为陈爱莲有什么喜事要说。没想到她告诉大家，从大年三十到正月初七，杨旭勇车间主任带领团队生产出来的轮毂，有相当数量存在瑕疵。原因在于铸造加工中的熔融过程不稳定，所以做出来的产品强度虽然达到了行业的标准，但离万丰奥特自己定的要求有差距。

当时的场面，可以用悲壮来形容。在工厂的喷泉边上，堆满了这 8 天生产的产品。万丰奥特铝轮项目的创建者们对这个痛苦的教训当中到底有多少个轮毂已经记不清了，只记得涉及的产品总金额是 60 多万元，多达几万套，印象当中喷泉边上全都被轮毂堆得满满的。

此时离陈爱莲这支创业团队拿足订单开工不过几个月时间。在此之前摩托车生产企业使用铝轮的产品在市场上受到了顾客的喜欢，非常畅销，所以铝轮项目在其新生的第一个春节，就要全面加班。只是没想到，生产任务的饱满使得员工普遍求快，加之春节期间的检验没有到位，大批量的产品出现了瑕疵。

当时负责精加工车间的杨旭勇认为："订单量大求快是一个原因，另一个原因就在于当时我们采用的是挤压铸造工艺，铝液流入模具腔体并挤压成型，这就有点像倒啤酒，速率一旦掌握不好，倒快了，铝液当中就容易混入气泡，形成缩松，轮毂的强度就会下降。"

堆得像小山一样的轮毂边上，是一脸严肃的陈爱莲，以及铝轮项目的所有员工。她一字一句地对大家说："品质是铝轮项目的生命，没有品质，我们绝对不可能生存下去！这 8 天的产品，存在着安全隐患，因此必须全部报废，拉去重新回炉！"

为什么要把新的轮毂重新回炉呢？因为这家新生的公司，面临着品质与速度的关键性选择，而陈爱莲的决定是干脆的。在这次现场质量会上，全体加班人员非但没有受到奖励，很多干部反而还被处罚了。产品的重新回炉，是为了实现未来万丰奥特对于品质的高度自我要求。

从这个场景里，我们不难看出的是，由于一系列的创新，刚刚创建的万丰奥特到了 1995 年的时候，外部的订单已经没有太大问题。由于采取了精密铸造，万丰奥特的铝轮产品外观漂亮且重量又轻，对比当时大部分摩托车配件商所提供的钢丝轮产品已经胜出了，这使得主机厂的订单更快地集中到这家新生企业当中来。正是因为这个原因，仅仅开工几个月，万丰奥特员工就要在 1995 年春节加班，8 天时间就生产了几万套轮毂产品。

1995 年，南昌摩托车行业组长叶奕康视察万丰研发的中空结构摩托车铝轮，该产品填补了国内空白。背后的假山喷泉旁边，是当年重新回炉 60 万元产品的地方

在外部订单饱满，但产能上又存在瓶颈的情况下，这家新生的企业能走多远？问题直接就以"大批量不合格品如何处理"这种形式摆在陈爱莲面前。

而当我们深入了解了陈爱莲的内心世界之后，对她在这一幕当中的表现的动机就能一目了然：本来，她的创业就是经历了千辛万苦的成果，而且对眼前的这家企业，她还抱有更大的梦想，怎么可能让产品品质上的问题挡住了创业团队的步伐呢？

重新回炉 60 多万元有瑕疵的轮毂，使得万丰奥特从起步时期就建立了一个品质原则，走上了建立万丰奥特控股集团的第一个台阶。在万丰奥特，这个原则至今仍非常清晰，那就是——品质是不容动摇高于一切的立身之本。陈爱莲的这个动作，使得万丰奥特从一开始就摆脱了初次创业企业在"企业自身追逐利润"与"满足市场当中顾客的要求"这两个相互矛盾的目标之间的摇摆，坚定地走向了一条可持续发展的企业道路。

为了提高产品品质，让万丰奥特的产品逐步在市场上赢得口碑，陈爱莲还采用了出人意料的做法，出资数万元作为活动和奖励基金，由当时具有影响力的《摩托车信息》杂志发起，搞了一次"万丰奥特铝轮杯"有奖征文活动，主题是"中国摩托车——发展与研讨"。这家媒体上与政府主管部门，下与摩托车行业内各大企业，都有很深的交集。

在一家企业里，试图对行业建言的人，不是企业的精英，也会是一些非常有想法的人。所以这样征文活动，其实就是多赢之道。从各大企业的参与者来说，它给企业内部的人一个展示自己想法的舞台，也给领导们发现人才提供了机会；而从媒体的角度来看，《摩托车信息》能联系上这批企业内部人士，其实是加强了杂志与企业之间的联系。

当然，在无形中，收获比较多的是刚刚成形的万丰奥特。创业团队不仅可以从征文的文章里清晰地了解到各大企业的动态和它们当时要解决的问题，同时还能了解到具体的每一个人在这些主机厂里的位置和作用。

更为重要的是，在"万丰奥特铝轮杯"有奖征文比赛之后，《摩托车信息》杂志举行了一个隆重的颁奖仪式，陈爱莲和万丰奥特的创业团队作为赞助商出席了这个仪式并给获奖者颁奖。因此万丰奥特这支创业团队，给业内留下了非常好的印象，而且也认识了一大批摩托车主机厂的管理者。这为未来的营销，尤其是为万丰奥特未来在摩轮车轮毂项目中能选择更多的优秀主机厂合作，打下了一个很好的基础。

成型

万丰奥特铝轮项目 1994 年 10 月在中宝工棚试制成功后，1995 年就开始另起炉灶，租用一家倒闭的地方国营造纸厂厂房，借船出海了。

因为中宝给万丰奥特的只有两条夹道的场地，来自摩托车生产企业的订单一多，不仅万丰奥特本身的生产空间不够，而且如果主机厂要来人考察，这种情况也不像家正规的企业。

这家地方国营造纸厂是在"文革"期间大办"五小工业"时贸然上马的，

但工艺落后，污染严重，属于淘汰之列。到 1995 年，企业早已停产，厂房成了"烂尾工程"，一些车间徒有四壁，没有屋顶，地面杂草齐胸，一片衰败景象。

陈爱莲看中了这个地方，就与对方协商，用很低的价格把这其中的两幢厂房租了下来。万丰奥特铝轮项目的铸造基地就在那儿应运而生，解决了当时没有铸造场地的燃眉之急。

浙江万丰摩轮有限公司创立大会

租下厂房后，团队中的年轻人打扫场地、改造厂房、加盖屋顶、整修地面、安装调试设备，最后正式投产。这两幢原本只会更破败的厂房，就这样成为万丰奥特摩轮产业的第一个关键突破。

当时，大家的热情都非常高涨。制造部门里俞红莲、梅仁安、张惠成、陆仕平等几位负责人，经常是天不亮就赶到车间，一天忙碌下来，回家吃完晚饭，又都自发地赶到车间。当上夜班的员工来了，为了鼓舞员工们的干劲，他们还常常把自己的工资拿出来，买馒头作为夜宵送到车间给员工吃。大家每天都精神饱满、斗志昂扬、浑身有使不完的劲。

在这次搬迁的背后，从 1995 年到 1997 年这三年中，摩托车轮毂市场的扩大，以及万丰奥特铝轮项目创业时的几个创新点，都有力地推动着这家年轻公司向前进。

1994年进入摩托车轮毂市场，万丰奥特创业团队赶上了好时候。我们在第一章当中已经知道，1997年的中国已经是一个摩托车生产大国，年产摩托车800万辆，到2000前后，这个数据达到了2 000万辆，但是倒推5年，1993年中国的摩托车生产总量只有300万辆。从1993年年产300万辆摩托车，到1997年年产800万辆，这个过程，正是中国摩托车行业分工细化、配套完善的过程。

当然，产品上的创新，更是这家新生的公司去争取市场份额的关键。

在摩托车轮毂项目搬迁投产之后，创业团队发现，当时的摩托车轮毂，正在发生一次新的变革，新型更为安全的碟刹车型正在替代传统的毂刹，这种变化造成了轮毂形状的很大变化。而铝轮在适配碟刹车型方面，更是拥有很大的优势。由此，万丰奥特很快对自己生产的摩托车轮毂进行了设计改型，并全面铺开了碟刹轮毂的生产，使得其摩托车铝轮更受主机厂认可。

产品上的创新，使得万丰奥特铝轮项目在市场上走得很顺。1995年之后，万丰奥特的铝轮已经成为国家级重点产品。而同时，万丰奥特的摩托车轮毂业务开始为一批优质主机厂配套。

之后一年，万丰奥特的创业团队，又开始走出了新的一步。在摸清了国内市场的动向之后，这个团队率先进入了观念国际化的过程。

这是有契机的。1996年万丰奥特的摩轮参加广州国际摩托车展，这是一个重要的转折点。

在最初上门营销进入市场之后，由于内部的一系列改进，万丰奥特的铝轮项目虽然规模不大，产品却已经走到了同行前列。所以到1996年，创业团队认为万丰奥特铝轮的市场营销应该有一个新的方式，在摸清了整个摩托车行业的国内格局后，他们试图走到更大的天地中去，刚刚成立不久的万丰奥特于是参加了1996年的广东国际摩托车展。

万丰奥特这一次在广州行业展览上的亮相，引起了业内很大的反响。当时国际上三家大型摩托车生产巨头：日本本田、意大利比亚乔和法国标致，都开始尝试与万丰奥特接触。

　　巨头企业们之所以跟万丰奥特接触，当然是因为它们此时已经开始重视中国市场。通常情况下，国外的摩托车生产企业要进入中国市场，有三种方式：第一种是产品进入，也就是在华销售；更看好中国市场的企业会采取合资方式与中国企业一起生产，此乃第二种；另外，90年代后期，由于国外企业已经对中国市场越来越熟悉，中国政府的政策也开始开放，所以当时一部分企业也有独资的可能性，此乃第三种方式。

　　只要这些国际上的主机生产企业试图以合资和独资生产的方式进入中国市场，与万丰奥特这样的配件企业接触就是必要的。因为通过供应链的整合，就地寻找配套企业是摩托车销售降低成本的重要因素。万丰奥特虽然初创，而且规模很小，但因为产权明晰，管理体制顺畅，机制灵活，所以更受国外摩托车生产企业的青睐。

陈爱莲带领团队去欧美和日本对摩托车主机厂和轮毂厂进行考察

　　这种接触和合作，本来只会让万丰奥特在规模上扩大，不过，因为陈爱莲的学习精神，它就变成了万丰奥特这家小企业进一步领先的机会，想要有机会为国外大型生产企业配套生产，万丰奥特就要进一步提升自己，向国际水平靠拢。

因此在 1996 年之后，陈爱莲带着朱训明、王文林、俞利民等骨干团队，多次去欧美和日本，对从事摩托车生产的主机厂和轮毂厂进行了考察。

创业团队的这种做法，对于月产只有三万多套轮毂的企业来说，未免有些奢侈。在 90 年代的后期，万丰奥特团队当中的一大批骨干，先是去日本，后到欧洲，再到美国，几乎把全球轮毂生产企业都考察了个遍。

在相当程度上，国际考察使他们迅速打开了视野，并决定了未来万丰奥特在规模扩展之后采取的路径；而同时，通过与国外同行的交流，万丰奥特的管理层认识到了，处于黄金阶段的中国市场将对万丰奥特的业务起到什么样的作用，从而大大增强了这支团队的自信。

实际上，只有有了与巨头企业的合作，万丰奥特团队才有了去国外考察的机会。因为万丰奥特的这种考察非常细致，不但要看国外企业的生产现场，而且要与这些企业的管理者进行交流。考察完一家企业之后，常常还伴有万丰奥特团队成员的讨论，所以只有在与国外的主机厂和配件企业形成了合作关系之后，万丰奥特的骨干团队才能通过合作形成的网络去国外进行考察。

万丰奥特这种学习型的企业文化的形成，推动力在于陈爱莲是一个乐于分享的人。在她创业的年代，国内崛起的企业大多由管理风格上属于老虎型的企业家执掌，而她在管理风格上却属于孔雀型。她一直认为企业的领导者就是公司整体利益的代表。万丰奥特作为一家企业，管理团队的成员要一起到市场最前线获得最直接的体会，只有骨干成员都有了统一的认识和一致的行动，企业才能有高效率。

正是因此，万丰奥特在崛起的过程当中的正确做法中，除了确立"品质第一"的公司原则之外，去观察学习国外同行的运营经营，也是关键。从 1996 年开始，万丰奥特在国内外同行当中参观学习的时间长达两三年，把公司的骨干团队关于一流企业的认识，统一在了国外的优秀公司身上。

陈爱莲的这种个性和国际化视野，也正是为什么她会资助1998年ISO 8644标准修订会议的原因。她觉得技术人员只有与最优秀的工程师交流，到最好的工厂当中去实地看，才能真正快速地把企业做成世界一流。

从某种意义上，新昌境内的这家轮毂工厂，从一开始就把利润投入到了正确的方向上——此时的铝轮项目团队最好的投资方向就是创业团队自身。作为一批刚刚入行的创业者，他们最需要的，就是用"最高的标准"来要求自己的企业。

这种交流的最直接结果，就是使万丰奥特的骨干团队都意识到了，万丰奥特作为一家轮毂生产企业，运营当中的最大问题，就是投资能力不足。

投资能力不足其实是那一代创业者共有的问题。如果再晚10年，像万丰奥特这样的企业，无疑是资本市场上的宠儿。有黄金般的产品市场、管理团队有足够的创新意识、领导者在市场上有长远的眼光，为项目找到投资应该是不成问题的。但在90年代，由于国内资本市场没有发育，所以万丰奥特的创业团队必须用自身滚动发展的方式来解决资金问题。

没有足够的投资，造成的问题就是在设备选型上没法自如选择。在万丰奥特严格了品质标准之后，铝轮项目的产能成了最大的瓶颈。

我们已经知道，这其中相当一部分原因，是因为创业团队选择设备的时候，还不够内行。他们选择的压力铸造设备操作并不容易，在如此前提下，万丰奥特又把产品标准提得很高，铝轮项目的产能就出现了困难。

这当然是令人觉得极其无奈的。当时万丰奥特团队看着巨大的市场却毫无办法，因为品质好，客户需求量每月达到几十万套，但万丰奥特就是生产不出来，每月只能生产三万多套。

事后看，万丰奥特最初在租用造纸厂厂房的两年多的时间里，实际上是要从试制性质逐步孵化成大规模项目。就万丰奥特而言，这两年其实是成长的阵痛时期。因为要逐步地到大规模生产，中间就涉及大量的工艺提升问题。

而陈爱莲的两个实践，奠定了万丰奥特未来两个重要的产业基础：首先是通过报废 60 多万元产品的举措，使得这家新公司有了严格的品质意识，从散漫的新企业变身成为纪律严格的创业团队；而接下来陈爱莲倡导的对全球同行企业的不断考察，则为这支团队注入了不断学习的基因。

对国外同行们的考察，使得万丰奥特的创业团队能用国际的眼光来看待自己的企业。而这一轮考察的直接效果，是改变了万丰奥特的设备采购走向。

万丰奥特在开始起步时之所以采购了压力铸造项目，是因为当时国内普遍的轮毂生产厂都采用的是挤压铸造设备，因此万丰奥特也随大流采购了这种设备。

但创业团队的考察队伍到国外同行企业当中一参观，就发现了：国外的摩轮车轮毂厂在铸造成型这一关键工序上，主流工艺用的都是相对更成熟的重力铸造设备来生产，这与国内主要采用挤压铸造的方式大相径庭。

这中间的差异，使得万丰奥特团队受到很大启发。重力铸造又称金属型浇注，指的是让金属液体沿铸造模具型腔壁逐步注入，以大浇冒口来保证铸件的成型和内在品质，而后冷凝成型的铸造方式。相对于压力铸造，这种铸造方式因为内部的气孔和缩松要少得多，所以强度和稳定性都要更好，尤其适用于像轮毂这样的安全配件的生产。

但因为没有多少资金，所以万丰奥特不得不采用滚动投入的方式来逐步做大。好在摩托车轮毂在 90 年代中后期都是黄金市场，所以万丰奥特可以边生产、边学习、边投入。而创业团队在设备上达成的共识，使得滚动扩大当中的铝轮团队开始在采购上转向，从压力铸造逐步转向到了重力铸造。这个过程，经过了两三年工夫。后来由技术总负责人朱训明出任厂长，进行了工艺上的彻底改革。

到 1997 年，万丰奥特征用了 1 000 亩土地建设属于自己的新工业园，1998 年部分厂房建设完成，万丰奥特搬进了新建的工业园，整个公司迅速走上了规模扩张的道路。

在国外考察时，万丰奥特的企业团队发现，在全球的轮毂生产同行当中，大规模是必备的共同特征。

以现在的眼光看，我们非常容易理解为什么轮毂生产企业作为摩托车和汽车的配件企业，必须要有规模优势。这其中，轮毂作为主机厂需要的一个重要零部件，产品本身的标准化程度很高，保证了轮毂工厂可以规模化；而更为重要的是，规模化会使得轮毂生产企业获得各方面的议价权，从而有效地降低成本，吸引主机厂将更多订单集中于具有规模优势的轮毂厂，使得轮毂企业强者恒强，最后在竞争中胜出。

面向全球采购设备（右一陈爱莲）

当时，万丰奥特的创业团队抢先认识到这一点，一方面让这支团队意识到了竞争当中的残酷性，同时，这也激发出了整个团队强大的动力：这无疑是一场漫长的赛跑，但只有在中国这个黄金市场上，万丰奥特才有可能获得这种规模优势。而这一切对他们所有人来说，都无疑是一次巨大的机会。

当时负责设备采购的吕永新对万丰奥特在这期间不停地扩张深有感触。在他看来，万丰奥特之所以日后能在摩托车轮毂行业内脱颖而出，与创业期陈爱莲想把企业做到全球最大，是有着紧密关系的。

陈爱莲带着公司骨干在全球考察之后，万丰奥特在最初的摩轮生产中几乎从来没有停止过设备上的扩张。资金除了支付正常的原料款之外，最大的用途就是不停地采购设备和建设厂房。

为此，吕永新的一个重要工作，就是跑北京和上海——当时重力铸造设备有很多是进口的，他去北京和上海，一是要与生产这些设备的厂家驻国内办事处谈判，敲定设备采购合同，另外就是要跑政府部门，把相关手续办下来。

但这种扩张使得万丰奥特的财务负责人蔡竹妃无时无刻不感到巨大的压力。因为要不断进行扩张，所以当期的利润对万丰奥特来说，似乎根本无足轻重。在整个90年代，万丰奥特的资产负债率一直要求控制在70%左右，因此蔡竹妃的核心工作就是跑贷款，收货款。

这是一项很有难度的工作。企业不断获得贷款的前提，就是要准确地还清每一笔到期的银行贷款。因此陈爱莲高度支持财务部门的权威性，蔡竹妃的工作经常是直接指挥到市场部门的每位营销人员，去把应收账款收回来，以支付银行到期的贷款。

在这个过程当中，国内银行业的一个变革，对万丰奥特的扩张起到了巨大的帮助作用。90年代后期，国内开始出现了股份制银行。

相对于国有大银行严格的等级制度，刚刚成立的股份制银行更为灵活，它们必须在国内刚刚成形的新兴民营企业当中，寻找有希望的工业项目开展贷款业务。因此这些股份银行能打破严格按中央、省、地市、县级别分配贷款的比例，还能灵活地根据企业的要求派生贷款种类，放贷速度也比较快。

敏感地发现了这个动向后，万丰奥特开始把银企合作的重点转向了当时最为活跃的股份制银行深圳发展银行。陈爱莲想得很清楚，万丰奥特必须要快，要赶在时间的前头，在国内产业黄金期同步扩张。

质量万里行

在万丰奥特的历史上，1999 年是一个重要的转折点。从这一年开始起，万丰奥特的摩托车轮毂业务，开始全面走向领导者地位。

万丰奥特在摩托车轮毂领域的这种势头，在 1998 年已经显山露水。我们在第一章当中已经看到，到 1997 年，创业短短三年的万丰奥特已经获得了多个业内"品质第一"的奖项。而在这些奖项背后，这家新生的企业，已经获得了国内多家摩托车主机厂的青睐。

但对于万丰奥特来说，此时的优势，还仅仅建立在其对于品质的重视上。产业真正的优势，也就是规模效应，还没有到来。

就总的经济形势而言，1999 年实际上是国内经济发展的一个低点。1998 年，东南亚金融危机使得中国经济的发展处于考验之中，那两年，人们对中国经济最关注的是还能不能保住 8% 的 GDP 增长率。而在摩托车行业，拐点的因素更为明显，因为经过 90 年代的黄金时代，到 20 世纪末的时候，摩托车行业面临三大变局。

第一个变局是，摩托车市场从井喷式增长，开始逐步向平稳增长过渡。世纪之交的摩托车市场，一方面碰到了部分家庭从摩托车向汽车升级的需求变化，另一方面部分城市已经开始实施"禁摩"政策，此后市场需求从百万辆到千万量级的快速突破，逐步回落到理性增长。

第二个变局是，市场总格局的变化，以及消费者对摩托车这个产品的认知更为清晰，使得摩托车生产企业从竞争初期时群雄并起的格局，向大企业集中的市场转化。市场的各方面门槛都在提高，所以总量虽然还在增长，但生产企业却已经是苦乐不均，出现了强者恒强的局面。

第三个变局是，1999 年之后，对摩托车主机厂而言，"只要形成生产能力就能赚钱"的日子过去了。消费者的需求向两个方向发展，一个方向是摩托车作为交通工具向下的进一步普及，越来越多国内的普通消费者开始进入这个市场，在这个方向上，以重庆民营的摩托车生产企业为代表，在市场上掀起了价格战，加速了摩托车向农村和乡镇消费者的普及；而在另一个方向上，一部分合资企业和国内企业，开始向消费者需求价值方向转进，逐步地成为精品摩托车的生产者。

在这种市场情况下，陈爱莲提出的"一览众山小、再览众山无"，一定要选择"一流主机厂成为自己的战略合作伙伴"的市场战略定位，开始发挥巨大的作用。

在摩托车这样的竞争性市场当中，一流的主机厂意味着持续的增长，而给这样的企业配套，像万丰奥特这样的轮毂生产企业，在市场上自然也得到了增长。

但这一战略构想要落实，对万丰奥特提出了两点挑战。

第一个挑战是发现，这个挑战的难度在于营销部门不仅要对当下的市场热点进行判断，紧跟主流市场，使得万丰奥特始终与摩轮车和汽车生产企业当中的强者结成战略联盟，更要保证对未来市场可能产生的变化做出判断，使得万丰奥特始终与强者站在一起；

第二个挑战，也是更为重要的，是要与一流主机厂配套，还不能仅仅是有品质意识，一流主机厂的要求不仅在于品质，更在于此时它们在配件采购领域常常有很多选择，万丰奥特要提升规模上的优势，进而转变为价格优势，这点在它与主机厂的双向选择上，更为重要。

在这样的宗旨指导下，这家新生的公司把合作的重点放在了对零部件厂要求极为严格的广东大长江集体有限公司（以下简称大长江）身上。

其实早在 1997 年，负责广东片区的营销员张静就体会出这家摩托车生产企业的与众不同。大部分摩托车生产企业对于轮毂的关注和检测，除了外形之外，主要以安全性为主，检测体系和指标要素，都围绕着轮毂的安全性。而大长江对于轮毂配件的关注点有四个，除了安全性，外观当然也要符合要求，另外，它对于轮毂件的尺寸和涂装，也有非常严格的要求。

这种严格要求的方式，对于很多轮毂生产企业而言，常常被理解为负担。而在万丰奥特，却引起了陈爱莲和时任铝轮销售经理张锡康的注意。

在创业起步之初，万丰奥特的配套重点是国有大企业和中外合资企业。因为摩托车刚刚兴起的时候，消费者无法辨识谁是真正优秀的产品，此时国有大企业和中外合资企业因为投资充分，所以能很快地打广告，消费者主要靠广告来选择产品，另外地域性也是一个重要选项。此时做配套企业的就比较复杂，因为要不断跟踪市场，而当时市场中的热点比较多。

但到90年代后期，真正的市场选择力量开始出现。像重庆"摩帮"这类企业，主要是靠价格战来争夺市场。[1]因为它们的生产效率比国企和外企要高，因此打得起价格战。

此时万丰奥特已经形成了"保持跟进但不占领顶峰"的策略。万丰奥特发现，大长江的做法与很多民企不太一样，它主要是做顾客价值，不太参与价格战，有一段时间内，国内的摩托车价格跌到了两千元人民币。但大长江的整车价格始终保持在六七千元，它的产品质量做得很好，对品质和市场渠道始终管控得非常严格。比如，万丰奥特的轮毂在进入大长江的供应体系之时，就反复了相当多的次数。

这引起了万丰奥特团队的注意。张锡康和张静随即就去了解了大长江的背景，发现这家公司的领导人是北方一家研究所的技术人员出身，到广东创业之后，与日本铃木公司合作创办这家摩托车生产企业，而后逐步独立成为一家民营公司。

由此，陈爱莲大胆决定，把万丰奥特的技术资源投入到加大与大长江的战略合作当中去。她觉得，坚持品质的主机厂，一定是有未来的。

到1999年，万丰奥特开始脱颖而出，具备了在硬件生产上达到业内一流

---

① "摩帮"这个词为中国摩托车制造人士用来形容摩托车制造带的名词。中国制造业的"军转民"这个突破口，成就了在重庆"摩帮"这个名字很响、江湖味很浓的摩托制造群体，成为重庆的一纸重要名片，也造就出伊明善、左宗申等一批"摩帮"名字。——编者注

的水平。在几年当中，由于万丰奥特把所有的公司盈利都投入到设备的扩产上去，在设计研发、工艺装备、现场管理、质量体系上都与国际接轨，而且从规模上，已经达到了100万件的生产能力。在2000年前后，从硬件上率先达到国际先进水平。

此时的陈爱莲格外清醒。她很清楚，新昌本是个浙江最典型的农业县，因此万丰奥特的员工队伍，最初其实更多来自于本地农村。要把这支队伍带成一支训练有素的工业企业团队，不是只靠重新回炉60多万元不合格产品那么简单。

当时，万丰奥特已经有了100万件的产能规模，比起国内同行来说，品质已经达到了一定的水平。在性价比上，顾客很喜欢选择万丰奥特的产品。只是比起国外的产品来说，还有一定的距离。尤其是在品质控制细节问题上，万丰奥特还不能做到非常完美。但对于"做得更好"，公司管理层内部也有一些分歧，因为要把品质做到更高水平，管理上是有难度的，而且成本也会上升。

陈爱莲为推动品质提升想出来的办法是，从顾客的角度入手。1999年夏天，她独自带领一支团队，对国内万丰奥特配套的所有摩托车主机厂做了一次回访。

质量万里行活动

　　到 1999 年，"质量万里行"在国内已经不是一个新鲜名词，这个词最早由媒体发明，主要是指政府机构和传媒在销售机构内对企业产品实行监督。而由企业老总带着自己的管理小组请下游公司为自己找毛病的，其实是万丰奥特在经营管理与营销模式上的创新。

　　万丰奥特的"质量万里行"，是十足的万里行，行程 12 000 公里，总共走了江苏、山东、河南、四川、广东 5 个省，走访了南京金城、金城铃木、江苏春兰、轻骑铃木、北方易初、重庆建设、中国嘉陵、重庆隆鑫、从化天马和大长江 10 个主机生产厂。

　　正因为是创新，所以万丰奥特管理小组的收获是相当大的。

　　从"质量万里行"的出发点上看，万丰奥特要达到的目的是相互矛盾的两个方面。一方面，针对摩托车生产企业的管理层，"万里行"小组要让主机厂的管理者们明白，万丰奥特是一家非常重视品质的企业，产品的品质在国内也是领先水平，进而稳固万丰奥特的产品在摩托车生产企业当中的地位。

　　另一方面，"质量万里行"小组要在客户的基层，也就是摩托车生产组装车间员工当中，去仔细听取他们的意见，把万丰奥特的摩托车轮毂因为生产概率上发生的事故找出来，并进行系统性分析，从而找出在生产上可能存在的问题。

　　他们达到了这个目的。在团队带回来的报告当中，很多万丰奥特瑕疵性的问题都被下游企业的员工反映出来。比如，批次当中漏包装、加工有毛刺未清干净等。

　　学过工程的读者一看就知道，这些问题，在大规模生产当中其实是一个概率问题。但也正好印证了万丰奥特当时还存在"品质控制细节"的问题，万丰奥特为此开了一个全公司的"质量万里行"报告大会，陈爱莲专门在会议上做了讲话，当时主管摩轮产销的朱训明、张锡康也做了发言，检讨摩轮工厂在实施重力铸造一年之后存在的系统性问题。

　　万丰奥特在 1999 年启动"质量万里行"，其实并不是一件容易的事情。

在早期回炉 60 万元产品，质量警钟常敲长鸣之后，万丰奥特的铝轮已经达到了一个比国内同行的品质相对要领先的水平上。要再一次提高品质标准，其实要提高的已经是企业的管理水平和人员素质了。

就在"质量万里行"的报告会上，陈爱莲开始明确提出，万丰奥特的摩托车轮毂，三年内要在规模上做到亚洲第一，世界第二。

"亚洲第一，世界第二"的目标，并不是一个简单激励人的口号。因为万丰奥特此时已经知道了第一是什么样的企业。当时已经正式加盟万丰奥特汽车配件生产线的雷铭君专门撰文介绍了全球最好的摩托车轮毂工厂。他认为，意大利的格里米卡公司就是万丰奥特的未来。

格里米卡公司的年产能是 900 万只，除了规模世界第一之外，它的铸造线实现了全部机械化，而且是连续生产，铸造机是无人操作的，全部实现了计算机系统控制，批量化生产。这样，人为因素对产品质量的影响就基本被消除了。

万丰奥特当时已经实现了低压铸造、数控加工、三坐标测量、X 光探伤和粉末涂装，但是在物流、模具、三维设计、过程控制、在线检测和自动化程度上，还有待提高。

所以接下来，万丰奥特快速进行从人开始的又一轮提升。一方面，把相当一批技术和管理人员送出国门去培训；另外一方面，万丰奥特开始建立自己的培训中心，进一步提高全体员工的综合素质。

此时，因为在市场上已经立住了脚，所以机会开始敲响这家实际年龄只有 5 岁的年轻公司的门了。

扩张的尝试

在万丰奥特创业早期，陈爱莲觉得真正需要勇气的瞬间，发生在 1999 年万丰奥特收购上海二守合金有限公司（以下简称二守合金）与镇政府官员进行实质性谈判的时候。如果那天她不主动离开，这场谈判，以及后面的收购，就攻不下来。

这确实是一场艰苦的谈判，原因就在于万丰奥特谈判小组给出的价格触及了对方的底线。他们代表万丰奥特对二守合金的出价，只有原始投入的三分之一。

二守合金是90年代中韩合资的产物，是当年上海市领导去韩国招商引资的成果。当时，上海易初有限公司（其生产的摩托车是中国最早的名牌摩托车之一，以下简称易初）有一个在浦东新建100万辆高档摩托车基地的雄心勃勃的规划，韩国二守集团闻风而动，与浦东合庆镇政府合资用500万美元，注册成立了上海二守合金有限公司，计划为上海易初的幸福牌摩托车进行配套。

但事与愿违，就在二守合金建成之机，亚洲金融危机汹涌而至，韩国二守集团自身出现了资金问题，陷入困局。更为要命的是，易初也在上海市产业调整中出局。

因此，刚刚建好厂房、调试好设备的二守合金，就陷入没市场、缺技术的困境无法生存，不得不由上海合庆镇政府出面，在同行当中寻求被并购的机会。时任上海浦东合庆工业发展公司的总经理胡伟康通过行业协会找到万丰奥特，认为只有万丰奥特才能救活二守合金。

当陈伟军、俞林、吕永新、楼震宇等工作组成员受邀到二守合金的现场深入考察之后，发现这家企业就资产而言，状态非常好，有很好的区位优势。而万丰奥特当时已经给十多家大型的摩托车生产厂家配套，就市场而言，二守合金所能生产的摩托车轮毂正是万丰奥特供不应求的产品。对于这家年轻企业来说，当时最为苦恼的就是投资不足，产能不够。

不过，要实现万丰奥特的目标，关键在于能否以较低的价格盘活二守合金的这笔资产。如果价格较高，对于整个企业来说，并购就存在较大风险，因为此时万丰奥特现金流并不宽松，而且发起并购也并无必要。因为总体来说，当时新昌的土地、人力资源等要素的成本都比二守合金所处的浦东要低。

因此，万丰奥特对二守合金的资产出价，确实不高。

从账面资产看，二守合金的净资产在 5000 万以上。中方占比 45%，而外方由于违约，须承担赔偿责任，已表明愿意放弃权益，换取中方不追究索赔的立场。中方投资人作为二守合金的股东，它出手这笔资产，引进万丰奥特这个专业厂商，可以寄希望于未来，也就是万丰奥特开始正常运作之后产生的税收。这对于它来说，是源源不断的收入来源。与其守着一批没有运转起来的资产，让它一天天地贬值，不如把它交给一个优秀的合作者，让它产生税收。这也是万丰奥特在谈判当中最大的优势。

因为这样的出价，1999 年 6 月，陈爱莲和谈判小组一起去镇政府进行最后的谈判时，并没有受到欢迎。

她走进镇政府的会议室，发现二守合金的厂长和镇政府管理工业的办公室工作人员都在。但他们都不怎么说话，只是应付式地跟万丰奥特的谈判小组成员谈，迟迟没有一个最后的结果。

陈爱莲等了很长时间，但始终没有等到她要的"就这么定了"的答复。她知道，这是最后的出价，她的谈判对手们希望她在最后时刻让步。因此在等了两个小时也没有等到最后结果时，她站了起来。"如果今天我们谈不出结果的话，那么就改天吧，我们双方都想一想，有了确定的答案之后，再坐下来谈。"陈爱莲说着，就站起来准备离开。

这就是陈爱莲所说的关键时刻。对于她来说，这是经营当中"小心翼翼地冒险"这一原则的体现。

所谓"小心翼翼"，指的是陈爱莲心里是有底的。从概率上说，她猜因为她的离开，陷入僵局的谈判可能会有变化，但就算她自己，其实也不敢确定变化是否会发生。不过，她心里的底牌是，这次谈判真的不行也没有关系，万丰奥特可以再等一等。

而所谓的"冒险"，指的是陈爱莲说要走，就真的离开了镇政府的会议室。从内心深处，她知道敢不敢放弃，其实是万丰奥特能不能拿下二守合金这家工厂的前提。既然镇政府的领导们要万丰奥特的谈判小组来谈，就证明她对于万丰奥特拿下二守合金的资产的总判断是对的。而她和同事们到现场后发现对方的领导没有来谈，则说明万丰奥特的出价，已经使得谈判对手觉得这个价格成了一块鸡肋，而这反过来证明万丰奥特的出价相当准确。

因此她必须要冒险一搏，很明显的是，二守合金的中方政府投资人也是高手，所有的道理，他们都看得很明白。不过他们还想试探一下万丰奥特是否会因为急于扩张而在价格上略做让步。

收购上海二守合金

心里有底的陈爱莲走出镇政府办公大楼的会议室是很自然的，因此走得也很快。但就在她走到镇政府的大门口时，却听到有人在叫她的名字。

早有准备的陈爱莲回过头来一看，有一个人站在二楼的办公室窗口叫她。谈判小组的同事告诉她，这人就是镇党委书记，叫他们回去再谈谈。陈爱莲心里咯噔了一下，就明白了，这事儿要成。

她回到了二楼镇党委书记的办公室。果然如她所料，之所以前面镇里所有的工作人员都没有与万丰奥特谈判小组进行实质性谈判，是因为作为统管镇里事务的党委书记觉得万丰奥特对二守合金这笔资产出价太低，试图以冷场的方式来让万丰奥特再加价。而陈爱莲真的要走，则使得镇党委书记知道，万丰奥特给出的是真实的最高价，而当地的党委和政府确实在考虑资产价格的同时还在考虑未来税收收益。

之后的谈判，就变得非常顺利，万丰奥特得以用相当低的价格，拿下了二守合金的资产。

当然，谈判时的强势和弱势，其实更多决定于谈判之外。合庆镇政府的领导们与陈爱莲在谈判桌上的博弈，其实无非争的是一个双赢结果当中谁赢得更多一些。双方都清楚，对这宗收购案来说，万丰奥特确实是非常合适的收购者。

原因就在于当时的整个产业格局，以及万丰奥特在这个格局当中的地位。

1999 年在国内的摩托车市场上，分化已经开始了。

这一年，由于汽车已经开始进入国内家庭，摩托车已经从消费的热点产品位置上退了下来，总的市场需求量虽然还在扩张，不过人们已经开始对摩托车产品的厂家有了一些认识，名牌产品已经开始出现了。

这个时候的市场，已不再是只要投入就能销售了。市场演变成了强弱分化的局面，优秀的企业，由于产品稳定，成本控制得当，所以在市场上如鱼得水。而弱势企业的市场就难以开拓，企业的生存发生困难。

上海的二守合金，正是这个市场的后来者，所以一旦原来构想中合作的主机厂出局，它就很难在现有的市场当中再切走一块蛋糕。

而此时，万丰奥特经过 5 年多在市场里的摸爬滚打，其管理层已经把握住了万丰奥特所进入的轮毂制造和汽车、摩托车配件市场的基本规律。

轮毂制造的门槛并不是很高，如果设备得当、检测手段到位，跨越轮毂制造的技术门槛对于一家企业来说，并不困难。

技术门槛不高是万丰奥特进入市场时，业内已经存在多家竞争对手的原因。1994 年万丰奥特进入这个产业，时机选得非常好。因为当时摩托车行业刚刚兴起，所以主机厂才不会对配套厂验厂①，万丰奥特得以白手起家，之后这样的机会就不多了。产业一经兴起，度过了市场的黄金时代，主机厂就意识到，无论是在摩托车，还是万丰奥特后来进入的汽车领域，轮毂是整个产品当中重要的安全件，所以被称为主机厂的摩托车和汽车生产厂家对于轮毂的质量稳定性要求相当高，对于配套轮毂厂进入供应商行列时，会逐步地严格验厂，而且对每批产品的品质也有抽检。因此1994年到1998年，正是陈爱莲领导下的万丰奥特对于生产和检测设备的不断投入，才使得它很快在市场上立住了脚。

站住脚之后，万丰奥特作为一家配套企业，下一个门槛是生产过程中的规模扩张和成本控制。这两个要素对于万丰奥特来说是一个硬币的两面；在万丰奥特，这样的例子比比皆是。以原料采购为例，到1999年，万丰奥特每年只能生产几万个轮毂的时候，它在大部分原料供应商面前都是小型顾客，而当它解决了全部品质和技术问题，市场上的摩托车制造企业纷纷开始与它合作之后，在第一大原料——铝锭上，它就逐步发展成了大主顾，有了与铝厂议价的主导权。

有了良好的产业地位，万丰奥特需要的就是规模化生产。此时主机厂与万丰奥特的合作源源不断。盘活上海二守合金的资产，让它产生利润并不是什么难事。同一块资产，只要按万丰奥特当时对产业的运营方式和市场动作来操作，就会很快运转起来。

这就是陈爱莲在收购上海二守合金资产谈判当中强势姿态的由来。不过，就当时而言，万丰奥特最为短缺的就是现金，因此陈爱莲和万丰奥特的谈判小组对于价格是高度敏感的。

虽然这次谈判过程中充满刀光剑影，但其实陈爱莲和合庆镇政府的几位领导心里都很清楚：谈判越是激烈，意味着双方做事的认真程度也越高。在万丰奥特收购了二守合金的资产之后，新公司仅三个月就实现了原企业三年的产量，

---

① 验厂，即按照一定的标准对工厂进行审核或评估。——编者注

由亏损步入了盈利。因为确实做到了在谈判过程当中的税收承诺，企业与政府之间的关系反而相处得非常融洽。正是因此，后来万丰奥特开启整车项目时，合庆镇政府还给予了很大的支持。

进退重庆

北京化工大学的女毕业生杨慧慧一进入万丰奥特，就知道这是家很有发展前途的企业。因为当时几乎所有国内一流的摩托车厂，都把万丰奥特列入了配套供应商的行列。

21 世纪之初，国内摩托车的生产企业形成了三大区域，分别是江浙、广东和重庆，成为三个国内当时摩托车的主要生产基地。江浙区域包括了万丰奥特最早开拓的钱江、金城、无锡捷达和春兰几大摩托车产商；广东区域内万丰奥特认定了大长江，因为它一直坚持按国际标准在做产品，前景非常好。

不过，理想是要逐步成长的，而 2000 年前后的现实是，摩托车主机市场开始呈现出一个新的动向——价格战。这一轮价格战的主要掀动者，是被称为重庆"摩帮"的一批重庆摩托车生产企业。

重庆"摩帮"的构成成分比较复杂。除了赫赫有名的军工企业嘉陵、建设以外，其中规模比较大的有隆鑫、宗申、力帆和银钢四大家企业，小一点的更是不计其数，从总的市场份额看，在国内摩托车生产厂家里，重庆"摩帮"绝对称得上三分天下有其一。

重庆摩托车主机厂掀起来的这一轮摩托车价格战，有它背后的客观原因。国内摩托车最早的生产企业当中，西南兵工局下属的军工企业是一支非常有力的竞争势力，形成了建设、嘉陵等多家大型企业。而由这批企业形成的技术传播，使得重庆当地出现了大批摩托车民企。

由于重庆当地的人力资源、土地价格较低，因此重庆生产摩托车有一个巨大的优势，那就是成本在国内是比较低的。所以，重庆的摩托车企业在市场竞争当中有一个巨大的利器，那就是低价。它们也由此发动了多起价格战争，一度占据了很高的市场份额，对国内摩托车的普及，做出过很大的贡献。

重庆"摩帮"以成本控制为导向的企业策略，自然会传导到为它生产配件的上游企业当中来。

而万丰奥特在通过并购把企业做成大格局的同时，也在考虑，沿着配套企业的成本控制的方向，如何能做到与主机厂的共赢。而沿着这条思路，万丰奥特的管理层已经在寻找机会，做成本最优化，把万丰奥特的生产基地布局到主机生产厂边上去。

把配件的生产做到与主机厂"门对门"，这是一条后来被万丰奥特管理层共同认可的原则。就轮毂的生产而言，实施这个策略，能与主机厂达到高度双赢。一方面，轮毂作为一个产品，运输的物流成本并不低，实现"门对门"策略，降低了轮毂厂的成本；另一方面，对于主机厂来说，有了"门对门"的零部件厂，无论设计的完成、生产过程中问题的发现和改进，在时间和速度上都会有很大的提高。

机会说来就来，2001 年，重庆隆鑫摩托邀请万丰奥特到重庆投资，双方合作来开设生产基地。在整个投资当中，万丰奥特作为管理方占 70% 的股份，而隆鑫占 30% 的股份。

隆鑫之所以邀请万丰奥特到重庆去投资建设摩托车轮毂厂，是因为它本身对于摩托车轮毂有过小型投资。进入那个领域之后，隆鑫发现，摩托车轮毂到 2000 年前后，已经是一个门槛非常高的行业。轮毂的生产既需要有技术力量来支撑主机厂的要求，又需要规模生产来降低成本。同时，重庆当地有大量的摩托车厂正在进行价格战，试图在国内把摩托车的普及率提到更高的一个水平，所以从数量而言，轮毂生产的市场很大，邀请万丰奥特在当地一起开轮毂厂，应该是有前途的。

隆鑫的这个构想在时任摩轮事业部总经理的张锡康向陈爱莲汇报后，获得了正考虑把轮毂生产与厂商实现"门对门"供应的陈爱莲的认同。经过董事会的讨论，确定了投资可行性方案，而杨慧慧则以总经理的身份，出现在了万丰奥特重庆工厂的新场地上。

但是在投资重庆工厂方面，万丰奥特还是留了一手：重庆工厂采取的是轻资产的策略。在陈爱莲的动议之下，万丰奥特的董事会没有像投资其他地方那样通过拿地来投资工厂，而是采用了租用厂房的方式进入重庆。总体来说，对于重庆工厂的投资，万丰奥特采取的是"试水"的姿态。

当时重庆民营摩托车生产企业为了争取市场空间而大打价格战，当然可以因为摩托车普及率的提高而获得相当的市场份额。不过，所有制造业企业经营者都明白的是，制造业企业要获得顾客的认同，一味地依靠价格战，而不提高顾客价值，是比较困难的。更为重要的是，到 2000 年前后，国内市场上汽车的消费已经开始出现，从市场的动向来看，留给摩托车通过价格战来赢得份额的时间段，也不会太长，所以万丰奥特在投资重庆的轮毂厂上，采取了相当谨慎的策略。

不过，重庆"摩帮"在国内掀起的价格战，在 2000 年前后一段时间内，帮其占据了市场的主要份额。因此对重庆工厂的投资，确实为万丰奥特在规模上攀登全国第一的地位，起到了重要作用。

由于杨慧慧团队努力开拓市场，加上万丰奥特在业内已经具有了轮毂专业生产厂商的品牌形象，因此它的重庆工厂开工之后，除了与隆鑫主机厂很自然形成配套之外，重庆的相当一批摩托车厂都开始寻求与这家新工厂配套。万丰奥特这家叫作重庆新锐的新工厂，取得了非常良好的效益。

事实很快证明万丰奥特在重庆投资走的这步"轻棋"是对的。重庆的摩托车生产企业在市场上发起价格战的原因是他们本地的各方面资源的价格低，与其他地区的摩托车生产企业相比有着价格优势。

但价格战是市场上的一把"双刃剑"，因为它过于简单，所以很难总是掌握在正确的人手里。

合理的价格战，要求生产企业在管理上下功夫，在降低自身成本的情况下使用价格竞争，但始终要保持售价高于成本。可是一旦市场上的价格战开始，常常会有竞争者放弃"售价高于成本"这一原则，一味用低价格来迎合消费者，试图做大规模来降低成本。

在摩托车的市场上，价格战一旦开打，很快就越过了合理的边界。在价格战最为惨烈的 2000 年前后，一辆原来万元左右的摩托车，被重庆的民营摩托车生产企业拉到过每辆最低两三千元。

移师巴蜀，将触角渗透到中国摩托车工业的发祥地重庆

这种惨烈的价格战，造成的效果是多方面的。一方面，在参与价格战的重庆摩托车企业当中，价格战使得企业失去了创新的动力，单纯地成为跟风生产企业，失去了对于技术研发的投入；另一方面，价格战对于重庆整个摩托车生产企业的总体形象并没有带来良性效应，反而使得重庆的摩托车相较于江浙和广东的产品，被烙上了"便宜货"的印记。

另外，价格战也使得位于上游的万丰奥特受到了影响。主机厂之间的价格战，必然压迫着他们寻求更低价的配件。万丰奥特虽然坚守品质底线，但在很多地方还是受到了影响。

重庆"摩帮"的产品主要销往城乡接合地区及农村，由于边远地区对摩托车管理的不规范，导致挣扎的主机厂开始采取一些不规范的操作。

而这将给严守"守法"这条底线的万丰奥特，带来巨大的麻烦。

主机厂不规范的操作，需要得到配套厂家的全力配合，因此这种不规范很快会传导到配套厂家身上。当时，摩轮事业部张锡康总经理向董事会汇报了这个情况，征询碰到这样的情况怎么处理？最后董事会决策：万丰奥特必须走正道。既然重庆市场上的这种竞争已经是个普遍现象，万丰奥特就得考虑退出这个市场了。

不过，经过重庆的实践，配件厂与主机厂"门对门"的这个策略，却已经成为万丰奥特董事会成员的共识。既然重庆市场陷入了价格战，那董事会就决定采纳张锡康的建议，要把重庆的这个轮毂工厂，布局到竞争力最优的企业——大长江门边去。

此时，万丰奥特董事会对市场的总判断已经开始在市场上得到兑现。价格竞争为重庆"摩帮"扩大了市场份额，但也在消费者当中建立了品质较低的形象。而万丰奥特决心要全力配套的大长江，由于该公司在市场上一直有着较高的品质形象，所以它的市场份额开始上升。

这一策略的市场效果比较慢，因为它是在产品做精的基础上，慢慢再追求自然做大的一个结果。然而到了21世纪，它的力量就显示出来了。因为这时候，消费者已经都知道大长江旗下的"豪爵"摩托产品品质优秀，所以选择它的人就多了。因此它的整体销量在2005年之后开始持续增长，跃居国内摩托车生产企业的绝对第一位置。

万丰奥特的决策层觉得，大长江这样的公司，实际上是会在未来的市场竞争当中占有优势的。因为如果摩托车脱离了大众交通工具的市场，那么消费者的选择，在价格和品质之间，会高度倾向于品质而不是价格。而相对于简单的价格竞争来说，品质竞争来自于细节，更代表着企业的竞争力，所以万丰奥特非常看好大长江的未来。

而大长江的决策层也知道，万丰奥特的摩轮产品因为持续地改进品质，在配套企业当中品质是占据上风的，因此很早就向陈爱莲提出要与万丰奥特形成"门对门"的配套关系。

很显然，万丰奥特在众多轮毂生产企业当中的优势，早已显露无遗了。

不过，要从重庆把企业迁到大长江所在的江门，面临着一个挑战。万丰奥特在当地已经植根了五年，员工已本地化，要迁到千里之外的广东江门，这些员工会跟着一起过来吗？

正确的决定总是会得到员工的支持，万丰奥特在重庆的工厂总共有400人，在工厂搬迁之前因为要搬走的消息传来，除了有一部分想留在重庆的员工离开之外，当重庆工厂正式迁址到广东江门时，有300多名员工，都跟着工厂一起到江门来了。原因很简单，因为员工们已经对万丰奥特有了如家一般的归属感，觉得跟着万丰奥特这家公司，未来有前途。

位于江门的广东万丰摩轮有限公司分两期年产量500万套，已成为大长江的核心供应商。

摩轮的新生

通常情况下，每个企业的产品，总是有它的生命周期。万丰奥特的摩托车轮毂自1994年进入市场，到21世纪前后，与差不多所有的主机厂都实现配套，而且在滚动发展过程中达到了数百万套计的生产能力，实际上已经走到了市场的巅峰。

不过，走上了巅峰的另一层意思，常常也就是无论市场怎样发展，企业都可能要走下坡路了。而在摩托车市场上，这种倾向似乎更是如此。2003年，国内汽车产业开始风起云涌，摩托车的大众交通工具角色正在逐步被汽车取代，很多城市的"禁摩"政策也随之而来。因此国内摩托车市场走下坡路的倾向似乎已经成为一种必然。那么万丰奥特的摩轮是不是也会走下坡路？

由此，万丰奥特内部存在一些声音，就是摩托车既然受限，可能未来的发展就存在问题了。不过，一向喜欢听大家意见的陈爱莲，这次却觉得并非如此。在她看来，摩托车作为一个产品，其生命周期关键在于消费者有没有需求，在市场上受到政府的政策限制，其实并不是一个很大的问题。她觉得如果摩托车作为一个交通工具，它的生命是有终点的话，那就一定是因为有了更好的替代品。

21世纪来临后，国内媒体关注到在中国之后崛起的印度，陈爱莲也就把目光投射了过去。

当时，万丰奥特的业务线已经涉足汽车轮毂。因此她抓住了一次印度的塔塔汽车邀请全球供应商在印度开会的契机，专程去了一趟印度。

那一趟印度之行，给她留下的印象极深。印度虽然与中国在各方面都有不小的差距，但塔塔汽车给客人们介绍的印度和企业的情况，给有着早期创业经历的陈爱莲以强烈的印象：印度此时的经济发展与万丰奥特创业时点上的中国高度相似。

通过此次印度之行，陈爱莲认为：当时的印度与90年代的中国，有着高度的相似性。而到了塔塔汽车的车间，无论是塔塔汽车的选型、用料、定价，都一再印证了已经对汽车行业非常熟悉的陈爱莲之前的观感。

经历过20世纪90年代的读者都知道，作为发展中国家的中国，摩托车与汽车是有过相当长的并行时间的。50年代，中国就有了汽车，一直到90年代，人们才开始富裕起来，但还不足以购买汽车，于是摩托车就大行其道。而此时，国内的汽车业高度追求通用性，"老三样"的桑塔纳、夏利和富康，在市场上大行其道。一直到2000年前后，很多家庭都已经具备了汽车的购买能力时，市场上的汽车种类才开始多样化起来。

陈爱莲在参观塔塔汽车时就感受到了印度市场对于汽车通用性的强烈需求。她明白，追求通用性，意味着整个市场在追求低价。而此时，印度市场对于交通工具的需求，很可能是通过摩托车来实现的。

带着这个印象再去观察市场，她发现，街道上确实存在大量摩托车，而且与万丰奥特创业时国内市场情况相似的是，印度的摩托车也是采用钢丝轮的。

她即刻产生了一个念头，要将所观察的结果，变成万丰奥特的行动。回国后，她当即要求张锡康团队避开国内的"红海"之争，加快速度开辟印度市场这个大"蓝海"。

张锡康带领团队在 2003 年去印度时，正是印度经济最初发展的时刻。他很快就摸清楚，当时摩托车在印度市场也正开始旺销，而印度境内总共有四家大型摩托车制造企业，其中有两家分别是与日本的公司合作，另外两家是民族制造企业。与日本合资的本田英雄摩托车公司是印度最大的摩托车生产企业，民族企业百佳吉的市场销量排位第二位，接下来是印度的另一家民族企业TVS摩托车有限公司和日本的本田公司。

张锡康在走访印度的摩托车生产企业的过程中，从数据上进一步确认，印度当时的摩托车采用的主要是钢丝轮。印度摩托车市场的这种格局，对万丰奥特的铝制轮毂非常有利。只要装上铝制轮毂能提高主机厂的销量，这个市场很快就能打开。

而有了在中国的经验，万丰奥特在开发印度市场的时候，就更为老练了。张锡康在走访了印度所有的摩托车主机厂之后，选择了百佳吉作为万丰奥特的摩轮轮毂在印度市场的切入点。

这是有原因的。事实上，印度的摩托车市场，就萌发时间而言，比中国要早得多。

百佳吉这家企业就创办于"二战"后的 1945 年，并早在 1960 年成为一家上市公司。而在 1983 年，本田公司就采取合资的方式进入印度市场，建立了本田英雄摩托车公司，与百佳吉摩托车公司发生了激烈的市场竞争。本田英雄利用自己的技术生产高档的摩托车，主要在印度城市里销售；而百佳吉则采取相应的策略，针对本田在印度的投资有限，不能在印度做深市场的弱点，用小型摩托车开辟农村市场，深入地占领了普及化的一端。

但这并不意味着万丰奥特进入印度市场为时已晚。万丰奥特选择开辟印度市场的 2003 年，正是印度抓住了信息化浪潮实现经济起飞的时候。这里有一个重要的背景是，在 2000 年前后，西方国家在 IT（信息技术）和软件领域所掀起的信息革命浪潮已经波及全球。由于印度政府在国内大力推广软件产业的教育，又加上印度人口普遍有着良好的英语基础，所以此时西方外包的软件服务产业很大一部分落在了印度，印度的经济由此进入了起飞期。

与中国一样，印度市场在这个时期对摩托车的需求大增，因此摩托车厂商纷纷加大投资，扩大生产规模，以期在满足市场的同时发展自身。

选择百佳吉作为万丰奥特进入市场的切入点，张锡康是有着自己专业的判断的。可以说，这是一个经过反复讨论、深思熟虑之后的市场策略。

万丰奥特董事会之所以选择百佳吉作为市场的切入口，正因为这家企业处于印度摩托车产业当中的第二名。百佳吉处于挑战者地位，因此更容易采用变革的姿态。一旦百佳吉的管理者们意识到铝制轮毂被他们采用会带来市场份额上的巨大变化，那么他们无疑会比冠军企业更积极地去推进这个变革，以期改变市场的总格局。

而一旦百佳吉在市场上获得成功，万丰奥特的铝制摩托车轮毂会很快被几家大厂一起采用。

张锡康把万丰奥特在国内推广摩托车铝轮的数据，细致客观地介绍给百佳吉的管理者们。

中国市场的事实证明，采用铝制轮毂，确实让国内的摩托车厂商的销售额迅速上升。铝制轮毂大方美观，而且有利于厂商对摩托车进行造型上的变化。而对于消费者来说，铝制轮毂的个性化程度更大，便于消费者在选购摩托车时呈现自己的个性和喜好。

不过，百佳吉的管理者比较保守。他们还是比较担心新装铝制轮毂，会不会影响它已有的销量。所以万丰奥特在进入印度市场的初期，花了很多时间和精力来说服他们，这个过程是相当折磨人的。

　　从营销一线摸爬滚打出来的张锡康，出了名的有耐心和毅力。其关键在于他真心地觉得，采用铝制摩轮，对于顾客公司来说是非常有利的，因此就一直没有放弃。

　　张锡康是位杰出的营销领导者，他善于从百佳吉的角度来看问题，他觉得对方的迟疑也是有理由的。因为这家企业的生产，当时已经到了非常大的规模。一个车间每月就可以总装 20 万辆摩托车。

开拓印度市场（左三：陈爱莲、左一：张锡康）

　　而且，当时印度市场正处于快速上升期，主机厂的管理者们一方面非常希望改变市场的格局，冲击市场第一的地位；另一方面，也担心万一出现问题，可能会影响百佳吉已有的市场地位。

　　经过反复讨论，百佳吉的管理者接受了万丰奥特的观念，开始与万丰奥特建立供应关系，并在市场上大规模推广铝制轮毂的摩托车。在之后的一段时间，它的销量增长很快，甚至开始往本田英雄占据的高端市场渗透。在

2003 年以及之后的两年中，拥有百佳吉摩托甚至成为印度中产阶层的标志。

百佳吉改变了印度摩托车市场的格局，是因为这家企业的管理者看到了印度的经济变动，采取了一系列动作。除了采用铝制轮毂之外，百佳吉摩托车在价格制订上采取了低于本田和本田英雄的策略，同时在发动机方面也进行了技术改进。

百佳吉的崛起，使得它的产品成为被模仿的对象。从 2005 年起，印度的摩托车厂家纷纷开始向万丰奥特订购铝制轮毂，因为采用万丰奥特铝轮会为其市场规模增长带来很大的提升。万丰奥特在印度大胆的市场行动，结出了丰硕的果实。

万丰奥特在印度摩轮市场的开拓，其实走出了国内产品进军海外的另外一种模式。在万丰奥特开拓出印度市场之后，国内产能过剩的铝制轮毂厂家看到了一片新"蓝海"。

传统意义上，摩托车和汽车的配件厂商要进军海外，通常是依托主机厂商实现的。也正是因此，在万丰奥特之前，国内轮毂，甚至整个汽车、摩托车配件行业，都没有像万丰奥特这样去主动开拓市场。

但是在印度，中国摩轮车厂商行销全世界的脚步，恰恰被印度本土的政治和商业势力挡在了门外。2000 年前后，以廉价著称的国内摩托车厂商也曾把眼光盯在印度市场上，但很快行内大佬们发现，作为一个外国品牌，中国摩托车主机很难进入印度市场。因为印度的摩托车厂商自身竞争力也不差。以百佳吉为首的几大厂商对于本土市场的理解相当深刻，最显著的表现是印度的摩托车油耗非常低。110CC 的摩托车百公里油耗要达到 1.5 升以下，而这一标准构成了一道很高的进入门槛。与此同时，印度厂商看到中国摩托车有进军印度的迹象时，游说印度国会对摩托车进口关税进行了大幅度提高，使得中国摩托车的核心优势——廉价，完全失去竞争力。

正因此，传统的配件商跟随市场战略，在中国摩托车进军印度市场上，失去了效应。

　　随着万丰奥特摩轮进军印度市场并撬动了整个格局，摩托车轮毂的生产企业也开始大幅度跟进这个市场。中印之间的这块产业形成了高度互动的局面，也因此，万丰奥特摩轮开辟印度市场的这个案例，被写入了哈佛大学商学院的案例库。

　　而这个经典案例的执行者张锡康，在万丰奥特的企业史中，他带领余登峰、张建国、陆仕平、梅仁安、江道峰、罗海峰等人组建的团队付出了 10 年的热血、激情与斗志，以执着感动客户，使万丰奥特实现了全球三分天下有其一，确立了行业细分市场的绝对领导地位。

万丰奥特之道

摩托车轮毂作为万丰奥特的起家产品，在发展过程当中奠定了万丰奥特以后发展的两个关键因素。

首先，作为一家民营企业，万丰奥特高度重视品质和信誉，倡导从客户的角度来看待自己的工作。早期陈爱莲毅然重新回炉60多万元有瑕疵的轮毂产品和"质量万里行"这两个案例，都说明这家公司在创业期当中的生存和发展之道——只有顾客满意，公司才能发展。

其次，万丰奥特作为一家民营企业，之所以能快速发展，是因为它把民企的市场能力发挥到了极致。深刻地理解了摩托车主机企业的市场诉求，并积极在市场的变化当中寻找规律。使得万丰奥特能进入市场，并作为一个零部件企业始终与主机企业当中的强者合作。

最后，更进一步地深刻理解一个国家在经济发展当中所呈现出来的规律，是万丰奥特在开辟印度市场当中胜出的关键点。万丰奥特摩轮很快把这条规律总结出来，指导在印度市场之后的国际化。

市场有自己的规律，万丰奥特正是把握了这样的规律，并按市场的规律铸成了自己的优势，所以才能创业成功。

Chapter 3

Starting business with motorcycle wheel production

The Quality Standards Set With ¥600 Thousand

In the 1990s, Zhu Xunming, the leading technician of the Aluminum Wheel Project of Wanfeng Auto, was then only a college graduate in his 20s. In his opinion, Chen Ailian, then in her 30s, was actually attempting to launch her career with a group of fearless young men when she started up the project.

Therefore during the Spring Festival of 1995, Zhu got dumbfounded on hearing that Chen Ailian was going to scrap the new products , worth about 600 thousand Yuan .

Then, Wanfeng Auto started to pursue its first dream with Chen Ailian's blueprint for the company by saying " The long journey starts from the wheel and splendid achievement bases on innovation". Yet right in the Spring Festival of 1995, the dream was confronted with quality problem in its seemingly smooth first step.

On the eighth day of the first lunar month in 1995, Chen Alian had a meeting with the assembled project managers and staff, standing by the rockery and fountain. Working overtime during the whole holiday of the Spring Festival, the staff of the Wheel project took it for granted that Chen was to announce some good news. Unexpectedly, She said there were considerable quality flaws in the wheels newly produced by Workshop Director Yang Xuyong's team during the holiday, from the last day of the last lunar year to the seventh day of the lunar new year. Because of the melting instability during the casting process, the products met the professional standard yet failed to satisfy Wanfeng Auto's own company standards in product strength.

It was a strikingly spectacular scene with all the products newly produced during the past eight days piling high around the fountain. The project creators couldn't tell the total number of the hubs wasted in the painful failure, yet they were deeply impressed by the loss, well worth over 600 thousand yuan with more than 10 thousand hubs stacking around the fountain.

It was only several months after Chen Ailian and her entrepreneur team started to work with the orders they'd received. Before that, the motorcycles from the motorcycle enterprises that had adopted aluminum hubs won immense popularity with the customers in the market. So the all staff of Aluminum Wheel Project needed to work overtime during the first Spring Festival after its establishment. But what's out of their expectation was that the staff fully occupied with producing tasks generally tended to work faster. Additionally, the quality inspection didn't go alongside the production during the Spring Festival, and large numbers of hubs were turned out with defects.

Yang Xuyong, then responsible for the workshop of finish machining, claimed "we worked too fast with the large number of orders at hand, that is one reason for our failure; another reason lies in the squeeze casting process we then adopted by extruding and molding the aluminum liquid that flows into the mold cavity. This is kind of like pouring the beer into a cup: once it goes too fast without proper speed control, the aluminum liquid is liable to have bubbles inside, which leads to shrinkage porosity and decreases the strength of the hubs."

Beside the mountainous hubs stood Chen Ailian with a look of solemnity and all the staff of the aluminum hub project. She said word by word to everyone at present: " Quality is the life of the aluminum hub project, so our company can't survive without good quality. Since the defective products of the past eight days may contribute to safety hazard, all of them should be scrapped and remelted."

Why should the new hubs be remelted? For a new company faced with decisive choice between quality and efficiency, Chen Ailian's decision was promptly crucial. At the on-site quality meeting, none of the staff that worked overtime was rewarded, yet many leaders were punished instead. To make the company highly self-disciplined in product quality in the near future, the new products went melted down again. From the incident, it's not difficult for us to notice the external orders were then not a big problem in 1995 for Wanfeng Auto, the newly built company, owing to a series of innovative approaches it had taken. With precision casting, the aluminum hubs, physically light and beautiful, of Wanfeng Auto were far superior to their counterparts made of the steel wires offered by most motorcycle component vendors, which quickly attracted orders from the motorcycle manufacturers to assemble to the new company. As a result, the staff of Wanfeng Auto had to work overtime during the Spring Festival holiday in 1995 just several months after its start-up, turning out more than tens of thousand of sets of hubs within eight days.

In 1995, Nanchang motorcycle industry leader Ye Yikang inspected the hollow-structured motorcycle aluminum hubs developed by Wanfeng which had filled the gap in domestic market. It was beside the rockeries and fountain behind that once stacked the remelted products worth 600 thousand yuan.

When the full external orders met with the company's bottleneck in producing capacity, how far could the newly-built company go? The question how to deal with the large quantities of substandard products came directly to Chen Ailian.

After we thoroughly understand what Chen Ailian thought in her inner world, we will be fully aware of the motive for her action: truly the business was the reward of all efforts and hardships she had made and experienced, and she had greater anticipation of the enterprise in front. How could she allow her entrepreneurial team to be trapped and blocked by the product quality problem?

Remelting the defective hubs ,well worth over 600 thousand yuan, has enabled Wanfeng Auto to set its own quality standards on the threshold of its business and move a step further to the establishment of Wanfeng Auto Holding Group. In Wanfeng Auto, the principle is still crystal clear that quality unshakably comes first as the solid basis of the company. Chen Ailian's action enabled Wanfeng Auto to avoid the swings, since its early start-up, between the two conflicting goals — the pursuit of profits and the requirement to meet the customers' demand, and firmly led the company to a sustainable way development.

To improve the product quality , Chen Ailian took unusually measures to help Wanfeng Auto gradually win good reputation with its products in market. With more than ten thousand yuan as the activity and incentive funds, she engaged as the program sponsor in the prize essay contest of Wanfeng Auto Aluminum Wheel Cup initiated by the then influential magazine Motorcycle Information with the theme of China's Motorcycle — Development and Research, for the media has quite good interactions with both the responsible government departments and the companies of motorcycle industry.

In an enterprise, those who attempt to give advice are either the elites or people with unique thoughts. Thus it's actually a win-win activity to hold the prize essay contest. To the enterprises that participated in it, the program had provided the staff with stage to display their thoughts , and offered the company leaders an opportunity to identify talents as well; while as for the media, the program had connected Motorcycle Information with a batch of insiders from the industry, which virtually strengthened the link between the magazine and the enterprises.

Certainly, Wanfeng Auto·, the new company, reaped more rewards, though invisible, in the activity, since the entrepreneurial team could not only keep abreast of the latest development in each motorcycle company and their issues to be resolved, but also inform themselves of the participants' specific positions and roles in the motorcycle manufacturers.

More importantly, as the sponsor, Chen Ailian and her entrepreneurial team of Wanfeng Auto attended the grand prize-giving ceremony held by the magazine Motorcycle Information after the program , and awarded prizes to the prize winners. The entrepreneurial team of Wanfeng Auto thus had left a good impression on the motorcycle industry, and furthermore, they also got to know a lot of administrators from the motorcycle manufacturers, which laid a good foundation for Wanfeng Auto's future sales and , especially, the cooperation with outstanding motorcycle manufacturers in the project of motorcycle wheel hubs.

Formation of the Company

After the successful trial in the workshop of Zhongbao in October of 1994, the Aluminum Wheel Project of Wanfeng Auto started the business by batch manufacturing the wheels in the workshop rented from a bankrupt local state-owned paper mill. It seemed that Wanfeng Auto was then starting its voyage only with a borrowed ship.

Because Zhongbao only provided Wanfeng Auto two narrow lanes as its work place, with the increasing orders from the motorcycle manufacturers, Wanfeng Auto wouldn't have enough spacious factory floor for production. Moreover, it made Wanfeng Auto far from a formal company to produce its own products in such situation, especially when it was time for the motorcycle manufacturer to visit to ensure the possible cooperation between each other.

The local state-owned paper mill was rashly established during the Culture Revolution when the five small scale industries were warmly encouraged to be built. Owing to its backward technology and serious pollution, the paper mill had been in line for elimination. By 1995, the mill had been shut down and the factory floor soon became an unfinished project in a scene of sheer decay, with some roofless empty workshops full of chest-high lush weed.

Satisfied with the place, Chen Ailian rented two of the factory buildings at a favorably low price after negotiation. There the manufacturing base of Wanfeng Auto's aluminum wheel project thus was founded in time, which eased the urgent cry for a casting field the new company had at that time.

After renting the workshop, the young people in the team started to clear up the field, renovate the factory buildings, repair the roofs, mend the floor ,and install and debugged the equipment. After the preparation, Wanfeng Auto went into production with its first vital breakthrough in the two originally decayed factory buildings.

During that period, everyone was highly enthusiastic. Yu Honglian, Mei Ren'an, Zhang Huicheng Lu Shiping, directors of the manufacturing sector, often arrived at the workshop before dawn in the morning, and in the evening after a day's work, they used to hurry back to the workshop spontaneously after supper at home. They always prepare steamed bread at their own expense for the employees on night shift as night snacks so as to motivate them. Everyone was high in spirit full of energy and courage each day.

After the move, Wanfeng Auto, the young company, was greatly propelled forward by the expansion in the market of motorcycle wheel hubs from 1995 to 1997 and the innovative aspects of the aluminum wheel project in its early business.

When entering the motorcycle hub market in 1994, the entrepreneurial team of Wanfeng Auto were confronted with good times. As we've mentioned in the first chapter, China had already become a country of motorcycle production, with an annual output of 8 million motorcycles, in 1997, and the figure increased to 20 million around year 2000. Yet just five years ago, the total output of China's motorcycles was only 3 million each year. From 1993 to 1997, the motorcycle industry in China had undergone the process of specified division and systematic refinement, with the yearly output growing from 3 million to 8 million.

Of course, innovative products are the key to bigger market shares for the new company in competition.

After the motorcycle wheel hub project went into production, the entrepreneurial team noticed the motorcycle hubs were then under a new reform — the safer new disc brakes were replacing the traditional drum brakes, leading to a great transformation in the shape of wheel hubs. Aluminum wheels obviously had greater advantage in adjusting to motorcycles with disc brakes. So, Wanfeng Auto promptly improved the design of its own hubs and fully started to produce hubs suitable for disc brakes , turning its aluminum wheels more popular among motorcycle manufacturers. Product innovation paved a smooth path for the aluminum wheel project of Wanfeng Auto in the market. After 1995, Wanfeng Auto's aluminum wheels became the national key products. Meanwhile, Wanfeng

Auto began to produce motorcycle wheel hubs only for a batch of excellent motorcycle makers. One year later, Wanfeng Auto's team made a new step further — clearly informed of the development of domestic market, the team took the lead in the process of internationalization in concept.

There was an opportunity. It was an important turning point when Wanfeng Auto participated in Guangzhou International Motorcycle Show with its motorcycle wheel hubs in 1996. After the initial door-to-door marketing, with a series of inner improvement, Wanfeng Auto took the lead in the market with its products, though the aluminum wheel project was then in small-scale production. As a result, in 1996, the team ,holding that a new marketing device should be adopted, were trying to explore in a bigger world , and the newly-founded company attended the International Motorcycle Show in Guangzhou that year.

In the show, Wanfeng Auto quickly aroused great attention with its first appearance. The three major international motorcycle manufacturing giants, Honda of Japan, Piaggio of Italy and Peugeot of France, at that time all started to contact Wanfeng Auto.

The reason why the giants contacted Wanfeng Auto was that they had begun to attach much importance to the market in China. Generally, foreign motorcycle manufacturers could enter Chinese market in the following three methods: by introducing its products to China, ie, selling their motorcycles in China; by establishing joint ventures with Chinese companies — usually preferable to foreign companies that were more optimistic about Chinese market; or by opening single-invested enterprises in China. In the late 1990s, since foreign enterprises became more and more familiar with the market in China due to the opening-up policy, some of them were likely to build single-invested companies here in China at that time.

As long as the international motorcycle manufacturers attempted to enter Chinese market either in the form of joint ventures or the form of single-invested enterprises, it is necessary for them to associate with such motorcycle part maker as Wanfeng Auto. For it was the key factor for motorcycle makers to decrease the cost in sales by cooperating with suitable component providers after the whole chain of supply was integrated. Newly-founded and small-scaled as it was, Wanfeng Auto more appealed to foreign motorcycle makers because of its apparent property right, sensible management, and flexible mechanism.

Chen Ailian leading her team visited the motorcycle manufacturers and hub factories in Europe, America and Japan.

But for Chen Ailian's learning spirit ,such association and cooperation with foreign companies would only have led to Wanfeng Auto's expansion in scale, and now it turned into an opportunity to send the small enterprise well ahead of others. To have chance to produce parts for the foreign giant manufacturers, Wanfeng Auto should have more self-improvement so as to draw close to the international standard.

Therefore, after 1996, Chen Ailian, together with Zhu Xunming, Wang Wenlin, Yu Limin, the backbones of the team, had been to Europe, America and Japan for many times to visit the motorcycle factories and hub factories

To an enterprise that could only produce 30 thousand sets of hubs, what the entrepreneurial team did is somewhat a kind of luxury. In the late 1990s, a batch of backbones of Wanfeng Auto's team went fist to Japan, then to Europe and then to the United States, having visited almost all the hub enterprises in the world.

To a great degree, the international investigations quickly widened their horizons and decided the path they would take when Wanfeng Auto expanded in scale in the near future. Meanwhile, through the communications with their foreign counterparts, the management had realized the effect of Chinese market on Wanfeng Auto's business in the golden period, which greatly enhanced the team's self-confidence.

In fact, only in the cooperation with giant enterprises could the team of Wanfeng Auto have the opportunities to study abroad, for they had very careful and comprehensive studies. During the visits, not only had they investigated the production sites of the foreign enterprises, but they also had communicated with the administrators. The team members used to have discussions after visiting each enterprise. Therefore, only after they worked with foreign motorcycle makers and component enterprises could the backbones in Wanfeng Auto's team study abroad through the network established during the cooperation.

The enterprise culture — learning — of Wanfeng Auto was formed with Chen Ailian's sharing character, the driving force for their corporate culture. During the time when she started her business, most enterprises thriving then were managed by tiger entrepreneurs, while she can be regarded as a peacock boss, ie, a liberal in management. She believes the leader is the representative of the interests of the whole company. As an enterprise, Wanfeng Auto can be highly efficient only when its core members reach a consensus about the business and act in unison in daily work, which can't be realized unless members of the management go and experience directly in the market themselves.

Therefore, besides the company principle that quality comes first, studying abroad and learning from their foreign counterparts is another importantly wise measure they took during Wanfeng Auto's rise. Since 1996, it had lasted for two years for Wanfeng Auto to learn from the domestic and abroad counterparts, and thus the backbone team in the company had reached a consensus about their understanding of such enterprises of the first rank as the outstanding foreign companies.

Chen Ailian's character and her international vision explained why she would finance the conference on the revision of ISO 8644 standards in 1998. In her opinion, only by communicating with excellent engineers and by visiting the best factories in person can the technical personnel truly lead an enterprise to the world-class one quickly.

In a sense, the hub factory in Xinchang wisely invested their profits at the very beginning on its own entrepreneurial team, the best field for the team of aluminum hub project to invest at that time. To a group of new entrepreneurs, what they needed most was to manage their own business with the highest standards.

The direct result of the such exchanges was to get the core team of Wanfeng Auto aware that , the biggest issue of the hub enterprise in its operation was the insufficient investment .

Lack of investment is actually the common problem to the entrepreneurs of that time. Had it been ten years later, such an enterprise as Wanfeng Auto would undoubtedly have been the favorite of the capital market. With the golden market, the innovative management team and the far-sighted leader, it wouldn't have been a problem to attract enough investment for projects. Yet in the 1990s, the domestic capital market being undeveloped, the entrepreneurial team of Wanfeng Auto had to develop their business at a progressive speed so as to solve the capital issue.

Insufficient investment restricted the free choice of producing equipment. After Wanfeng Auto had set its own rigorous quality standards, the capacity of the aluminum wheel project became the greatest bottleneck.

We now know that's partly due to the fact that they were then inexperienced in choosing proper equipment. The pressure casting machines they had purchased were hard to operate, yet Wanfeng Auto had set very high quality standards for its products. In this case, the capacity of the aluminum wheel project was caught in trouble.

It is of course frustrating. The team of Wanfeng Auto were helpless in front of the huge market. Because of the good product quality, the customers needed more than 100 thousand sets of hubs each month. However, Wanfeng Auto couldn't satisfy the demand with its monthly capacity of over 30 thousand sets.

Viewed later on, Wanfeng Auto , during the initial two years in the rented workshop of the paper mill, in fact was progressively nurturing its trial production into a large-scale project. To Wanfeng Auto, it was kind of the growing pain during those two years, because it would definitely involve a lot of problems in the advancement of technology when the company gradually mass-produced its products.

Chen Ailian's practice laid two important foundations for Wanfeng Auto's business. Firstly, she aroused the awareness of rigorous quality standards throughout the new company by scrapping the products that were worth more than 600 thousand yuan, which turned a slack new enterprise into a disciplined entrepreneurial team. Then the continual visit to global enterprises of the same trade advocated by Chen Ailian had endowed the team with endless learning habit.

Studying from the foreign counterparts enabled Wanfeng Auto's entrepreneurial team to view their own company with the international perspective. And the direct effect the round of visit was the change in equipment procurement in Wanfeng Auto.

The reason why Wanfeng Auto bought the pressure casting equipment was that it was widely used by all the domestic hub enterprises at that time , and Wanfeng Auto just followed the tide.

However, as soon as the team visited the foreign enterprises, they found the gravity casting machines, comparatively maturer than the pressure casting types, were widely used in casting, the key technological process, in most abroad hub factories, which was greatly different from the squeeze casting technology adopted in domestic factories.

Wanfeng Auto's team was greatly enlightened by the differences. Gravity casting, also known as metal mold casting, is to gradually inject metal liquid into the casting mold cavity with large riser to ensure the shaping of casting and its inner quality, and then shape the casting with condensation. Compared with pressure die casting, this casting technology can increase the strength and stability of the products with much fewer blowholes and less dispersed shrinkage inside, and as a result, it can be especially applied to the production of such safety parts as the hubs.

Yet without enough capital, Wanfeng Auto had to develop its business by injecting investment at a progressive speed. Thanks to the golden market for motorcycle hubs in the middle and late 1990s, Wanfeng Auto could produce hubs ,meanwhile learn from others and simultaneously invest its business. The consensus about equipment among the pioneering team prompted the progressively growing team of aluminum wheel project to shift in equipment purchase, from die casting machines gradually to gravity casting ones. The process lasted for about 2 to 3 years. Later on the casting technology was thoroughly reformed after Zhu Xunming, the technical chief , worked as the factory manager.

In 1997, Wanfeng Auto requisitioned land of 1000 mu and built the new industrial park of its own, and moved there in 1998 after some workshops were built. From then on, the company quickly led to expansion in scale.

The pioneering team of Wanfeng Auto noticed during their abroad visits that large scale was the essential common feature of all the hub factories throughout the world.

From today's viewpoint, we easily understand why, as motorcycle and automobile component providers, hub enterprises must have advantage in production scale. Among all the components , the wheel hub , an importantly indispensable part that all motor vehicle makers need,had been highly standardized in production, which ensured the mass production of the hub factories. More importantly, large-scale production enabled hub enterprises to have the bargaining power , so as to reduce the costs and attract more orders of the motor vehicle makers to the hub enterprises with advantageous scale, making the strong in the hub industry even stronger till its final victory in the competition.

Purchasing equipment globally (Chen Ailian on the right)

At that time, the pioneering team of Wanfeng Auto had foreseen such situation, and it made them aware of the cruel competition and meanwhile greatly motivated them. No wonder, in the long race, only in the Chinese golden market was Wanfeng Auto likely to have the advantageous scale. To all of them, it was undoubtedly a great opportunity.

Lv Yongxin, then responsible for equipment procurement, had a deep impression about Wanfeng Auto's continual expansion at that time. As far as he is concerned, the reason why Wanfeng Auto could later on stand out in the motorcycle hub industry is closely attached to Chen Ailian's attempt to develop the company into the world's biggest at the start-up period.

After Chen Ailian's global visit with her core members, Wanfeng Auto nearly never stopped the growth in equipment during its early hub production. Besides the normal payment for raw material, funds were mostly spent on the procurement of equipment and the construction of the workshops. Therefore, one important task of Lv Yongxin was to frequently travel to Beijing and Shanghai, for most of the gravity casting machines then were imported from abroad. He traveled to Beijing and Shanghai, for one thing, to negotiate with the offices of the device makers in China and then sign the purchase contract, and for another to visit the government agencies to go through the related formalities.

But the expansion made Cai Zhufei, Wanfeng Auto's financial director, greatly stressed all the time. Because of the constant expansion, the current profits seemed insignificant to Wanfeng Auto. Throughout the 1990s, Wanfeng Auto's asset-liability ratio was required to be controlled at about 70%, so Cai's major task was to take out loans and to collect the payment for goods.

This was a tough job. To an enterprise, the precondition for constant loans from the bank is to repay each loan at the due time completely and accurately. So with Chen Ailian's strong support for the finance sector's authority, Cai Zhufei always directed each of the sales staff in the marketing department to get back accounts receivable in order to pay the bank loan at due time.

During that period, a change in domestic banking industry greatly helped Wanfeng Auto with its expansion. In the late 90's, the joint-stock banks began to emerge in China.

Compared with the state-owned banks in strict hierarchy, the newly-founded joint-stock banks were more flexible in business, for they had to target the promising industrial projects among the booming private enterprises, freshly-formed, to start their loan businesses. As a result, these joint-stock banks could break the strict limit on the proportion of loan allocation in accordance with the central , provincial, city and county levels. Also, they could flexibly derive loan types according to the enterprises' requirements with relatively faster lending rate.

Sensitively alert to the trend, Wanfeng Auto started to shift mainly to Shenzhen Development Bank, the most active joint stock bank during that time ,for cooperation. Chen Ailian was quite clear that Wanfeng Auto must go promptly ahead of time to expand together in step with the golden period of domestic industries.

Quality Survey Odyssey

In Wanfeng Auto's history, the important turning point came in 1999, for it started to take the lead comprehensively in motorcycle hub business right since the year.

In 1998, there had been already enough signs of Wanfeng Auto's lead in the motorcycle hub industry. As what we can see from Chapter One, by 1997, Wanfeng Auto had already won the Best Quality Award in the industry for many times during three short pioneering years. And the new enterprise , behind these awards, had gained the favor of many domestic motorcycle makers.

But to Wanfeng Auto, this advantage was only based on its great attention to the product quality, while its real industrial advantage, the scale effect, was yet to come.

In terms of the overall economic situation, the domestic economic development actually hit a low in 1999. In 1998, China's economic development, against the Southeast Asian financial crisis, was under test, so whether China could keep the growth rate of GDP with 8% was the major public concern during those two years. However, the inflection point had even more obvious effects on motorcycle industry, for after the golden times in the 90's, it was now confronted with three major changes at the end of the 20th century.

The first change was that the motorcycle business started to transform gradually from the growth spurt to steady increase. At the turn of the century, the motorcycle market encountered , for one thing, some households that were now having demands for automobiles instead of motorcycles, and for another the ban on motorcycles imposed in some cities. Thereafter, the market demands progressively fell back to rational increase from the explosive growth with millions of to ten millions of motorcycles in demand.

Since the general pattern of the market transformed and the consumers had clearer understanding of motorcycles, the motorcycle industry originally with all the enterprises in the marketplace became largely enterprise-centered. All aspects of the market requirements improved, the motorcycle manufacturers, though still growing in total number, were faced with unbalanced development, and the strong ones turned even stronger. That was the second change.

The third change was that the time ,when all the motorcycle makers could make money as long as the they had production ability , had passed after 1999. The consumers' demands developed in two directions. One on hand, the motorcycle won increasing popularity as transportation among common consumers in growing number, and in this condition the motorcycle makers, with the private motorcycle enterprises in Chongqing as the preventatives, launched the price war, accelerating the popularization of motorcycles in the town and the country. On the other hand, some joint ventures and domestic enterprises began to satisfy consumers' demands for the good value of motorcycles and gradually became manufacturers of premium motorcycles.

Under this market circumstance, the market strategy, proposed by Chen Ailian, to cooperate with the first-class motorcycle makers started to take great effect. She then compared it to mountain climbing — Mountains appear small once you stand on the highest of them, and no mountains around can block your sight once you stand on the summit of the highest one,

In the marketplace of the motorcycle, the first-class motor vehicle maker means sustainable growth, and the hub enterprise, like Wanfeng Auto , can also naturally increase its market share by working with the former as the motorcycle part plant.

It put forward two challenges on Wanfeng Auto to implement the strategy.

The first one was to discover. The marketing department had to not only make judgments on the hot market issues and closely follow the mainstream of the market so as to ensure the strategic alliance between Wanfeng Auto and the strong ones of the motor vehicle makers all the way, but also forecast the possible market changes in the future to make sure that Wanfeng Auto could always go along with the strong. That was what made the challenge so difficult.

The second challenge, the more important one, lied in the cooperation with the first-class motor vehicle makers. In component procurement, not only do these enterprises demand for products of high quality, but they usually have many options. So it was not enough for Wanfeng Auto to merely have quality awareness in the cooperation with them. Wanfeng Auto thus should improve its scale advantage and then transform that into its price advantage, which was more significant in the tow-way choice between Wanfeng Auto and the motor vehicle makers.

With such principles, the new company focused mainly on Guangdong Dachangjiang Group Co., Ltd (Dachangjiang for short), which was very strict with it component providers, for cooperation.

In fact, as early as in 1997, Zhang Jing, the sales representative responsible for the market of Guangdong Province, had noticed the difference between this motorcycle maker and the other ones. Most motorcycle manufacturers mainly paid attention to the safety of the wheel hubs in addition to the product appearance, and their testing systems and index elements were centered on hub safety. Yet

Dachangjiang focused on four aspects of the hubs — both the hub safety and shapes should meet its demand, and besides, there were demanding requirements for the size and the coating of the hub. In many hub enterprises , such strict requirements were usually viewed as a kind of burden, while in Wanfeng Auto, the requirements attracted the attention from Chen Ailian and Zhang Xikang, the sales manager of aluminum wheels at that time.

At the very beginning , as a component factory, Wanfeng Auto focused its business on large state-owned enterprises and sino-foreign joint ventures that could quickly advertise their products because of their sufficient investment. During the time when motorcycle started to be popular, for lack of knowledge to distinguish between motorcycles of really good quality and the common ones, the consumers mainly relied on the advertisements to make choices in purchase , and the region where they lived was another important factor to their purchase choices. Meanwhile, the situation was quite complicated for the component enterprises, for they had to constantly track the market which was then with a lot of hot spots.

But in the late 90's, the real market forces began to emerge. Enterprises, like Mobang, earned their market share mainly through the price war. With higher productivity than the state-owned and foreign enterprises, they could afford the price war.

Now Wanfeng Auto had developed the strategy of just keeping pace with the market but not taking the lead. Wanfeng Auto found Dachangjiang ,different from many private enterprises, focused mainly on customer value, with little interest in the price war. During the time when the domestic price of the motorcycle decreased to 2000 yuan, Dachangjiang still kept its motorcycle price at 6-7 thousand yuan. With high quality products, Dachangjiang had very strict control and management of its product quality and the market channels. For example, before being admitted to Dachangjiang's supply system, Wanfeng Auto's hubs had been refused by it for many times.

This aroused the attention of Wanfeng Auto's team. Zhang Xinkang and Zhang Jing immediately started to investigate the background of Dachangjiang and found out that its leader , once a technician of a research institute in North China, founded the motorcycle enterprise in cooperation with Japanese Suzuki Company after he started up his business in Guangdong Province. Thereafter,it developed into an independent private company step by step.

As a result, Chen Ailian made an audacious decision to invest Wanfeng Auto's technical resources into the strategic cooperation with Dachangjiang so as to improve the cooperation between them. She believed the motorcycle maker that adhered to good quality in production was sure to be a promising one.

By 1999, Wanfeng Auto had started to stand out, with the first-class hardware manufacturing in the industry. Within the past few years, all the profits invested on the expansion of equipment, Wanfeng Auto had brought its design and development, technological equipment, field management and quality system in line with the international standards. It had had the capacity of a million in production scale. Around 2000, Wanfeng Auto had been the first to reach an international advanced level in hardware

Chen Ailian was especially sober-headed at this time. She was fully aware that Xinchang was one of the most typical agricultural counties in Zhejiang Province, and most of Wanfeng Auto's initial employees were actually from the local countryside. It was not an easy job to turn the team into a well-trained team of an industrial enterprise, nor could it be simply realized by remelting a batch of substandard products worth more than 600 thousand yuan.

At that time, Wanfeng Auto had had the production scale of a million pieces, and compared with the domestic counterparts, its quality had reach a certain level. Viewed from the competitive price, Wanfeng Auto's products were more popular among customers, yet when these products were compared with foreign ones, there was still a gap between in between. Wanfeng Auto was then unable to perfect its products especially in the details of quality control. But even among the company administrators, there were different viewpoints on the issue of doing better. Because there would be difficulty in management, as well as the relevant cost increase, for Wanfeng Auto to improve the product quality to a higher level,

Chen Ailian's approach to improve the quality was to start from the perspective of customers. During the summer of 1999, she alone led a team making the return visit to all the domestic motorcycle manufacturers that were cooperating with Wanfeng Auto.

By 1999, Quality Survey Odyssey had been no more a fresh term in China. The term was initially invented by the media to refer to the quality supervision of the goods in market from the government agencies and the media. When the company chief together her management team invited the downstream enterprises to find fault with her own company, it was in fact Wanfeng Auto's innovation in its management and marketing.

Wanfeng Auto's Quality Survey Odyssey was a real long march of 12000 kilometers, covering five provinces, Jiangsu, Shandong, Henan, Sichuan, and Guandong. During the journey, they visited Nanjing Jincheng, Jincheng Suzuki, Jiangsu Chunlan, Qingqi Suzuki, Beifang Chuyi, Chongqing Jianshe, China Jialing, Chongqing Longxin, Conghua Tianma and Dachangjiang, totally ten motorcycle makers.

Because of this innovative approach, the management team of Wanfeng Auto reaped a lot.

Viewed from the motive its Quality Survey Odyssey, Wanfeng wanted to achieve two conflicting goals. On the one hand, targeting the management of the motorcycle makers, the team of Quality Survey Odyssey attempted to make them understand that Wanfeng Auto attached great importance to its product quality, and thereby Wanfeng Auto's products had already took the lead in quality within the country. In this way, the team stabilized the position of Wanfeng Auto's products in the motorcycle production enterprises.

On the other hand, the team visited the workers on the assembly line , the customer basis, in the motorcycle enterprises, and carefully heeded their opinions. After finding out the occurrences of accidents caused by Wanfeng Auto's hubs in production, the team systematically analyzed the the data so as to identify the possible problems in their production.

They attained the goal. In the report the team brought back, many defects of Wanfeng Auto's products had been listed by the staff of the downstream enterprises, for example, some products in the same batch were delivered without package, and the veining was not cleared in the process.

To readers who have learned engineering science, these questions, easily understandable, are in fact the problem of probability in mass production, yet it also verified that there were problems in the details of Wanfeng Auto's quality control. The enterprise, therefore, held a meeting to report its Quality Survey Odyssey to all the staff. On the meeting, Chen Ailian especially gave a lecture, and Zhu Xunming and Zhang Xikang, then in charge of the marketing of the motorcycle hubs, made self-criticism for the systematic problems within a year after the adoption of gravity casting technology in the motorcycle hub factory.

Actually, it was not easy for Wanfeng Auto to launch the Quality Survey Odyssey in 1999. The 600-thousand-yuan hubs remelted in its early business had been working as a constant reminder of the product quality, and after that, Wanfeng Auto had been leading the way in the quality of aluminum hubs, compared with its domestic counterparts. To improve the quality standards to a even higher level was in fact to improve the management quality and staff quality of the enterprise. In the report meeting of Quality Survey Odyssey, Chen Ailian clearly put forward the goal that Wanfeng Auto's production scale of motorcycle hubs should be the largest in Asian and the second largest in the world within three years.

The goal of being the largest in Asia and the second largest in the world was in no sense only an inspiring slogan, since wanfeng Auto then had already known what the enterprise with the world's largest production scale look like. At that time, Lei Mingjun, who had formally joined Wanfeng Auto and worked on its assembly lines of auto components, wrote an article on the world's best motorcycle maker in particular. He believed Italian Gerry Make (?) would be what Wanfeng Auto was like in the future. Gerry Make (?) had the world largest production scale with the annual capacity of 9 million pieces, and besides, it had realized mass production with fully-mechanized casting lines that could work continually with automatic casting machines operated by computer system. In this way, the impact of human factors on the product quality had been basically eliminated.

Wanfeng Auto then had adopted low pressure casting, CNC machining, three-dimensional coordinate measurement, X-ray flaw detection and powder coating, but in logistics, molds, 3-D design, process control, online detection and automation degree it still needed to be improved.

Therefore, Wanfeng Auto quickly started its self-improvement for the second time, firstly from its personnel. For one thing, it sent a considerable number of technical and management personnel abroad to get trained; and for another, Wanfeng Auto established its own training center to further improve the overall quality of its staff.

Right at this time, with a foothold in the market, the young company of only 5 years welcomed the opportunity now .

The Attempt to Expand

In Wanfeng Auto's early business, the moment that really called for courage in Chen Ailian's opinion came during the acquisition of Ershou Alloy Co.,Ltd (Ershou Alloy in brief in the following parts)in 1999 when Wanfeng Auto had the substantive negotiation with the government officials of the town. If she had not left on her initiative that day, the negotiation as well as the acquisition that followed would have resulted in nothing but failure.

This was indeed a tough negotiation, because the bid that Wanfeng Auto's negotiating group offered for Ershou Alloy was only one-third of its original investment, which was the bottom line of the other party.

Ershou, the joint venture of China and South Korea in the 90's, was founded with the investments that the leaders of Shanghai City attracted from South Korea . At that time, Shanghai Echu Co., Ltd (The motorcycle produced by the compay was one the earliest Chinese brand. Echu in brief in the following parts) had an ambitious plan to establish a one-million-high-end motorcycle base in Pudong. Hearing the news, Ershou Group of South Korea quickly cooperated with the local government of Heqing Town in Pudong and founded the joint venture — Shanghai Ershou Alloy Co, Ltd — with five million US dollars to produce components for the motorcycles with the brand name of Xingfu produced by Shanghai Echu.

Yet unfortunately, the Asian financial crisis took place right during the time when Ershou Alloy was established, and Ershou Group of South Korea was stuck in funding issues itself. Even worse, Echu was knocked out of the market during the industry adjustment in Shanghai City.

Therefore, Ershou Alloy ,though with newly-built factory buildings and debugged equipment , was caught in dire straits with little chance to survive, for lack of market and technology. The government of Heqing Town had to shoulder the responsibility of seeking opportunities to be merged and acquired among the company's counterparts. Hu Weikang, who was then the general manager of Pudong Heqing Industrial Development Company, contacted Wanfeng Auto with the help of the Industry Association, believing Ershou Alloy could only be saved by Wanfeng Auto.

When Chen Weijun, Lv Yongxin, and Lou Zhenyu,together with their team members, made a thorough field investigation of Ershou Alloy with invitation, they found that in terms of its assets, the company was in quite good state , coupled with the advantage of a good location. Wanfeng Auto at that time had supplied more than ten large-scaled motorcycle makers with its products, so as far as the market was concerned, the hubs to be produced in Ershou Alloy would be the products of Wanfeng Auto that was now in short supply in the market. But to a newly-founded enterprise, the great headache of Wanfeng Auto was the insufficient investment and its inadequate capacity.

However, to achieve Wanfeng Auto's goal, the key lied in whether they could revitalize the assets of Ershou Alloy at a comparatively low cost. If the price was too high, the acquisition would be a great risk to the whole enterprise, since , for lack of inadequate circulating funds, it was not necessary for Wanfeng Auto to make the acquisition. After all, the land and labor costs in Xinchang were far less than those in Pudong where Ershou Alloy was located.

Therefore, Wanfeng Auto's bid for Ershou Alloy was indeed not high.

From the book assets, the net asset value of Ershou Alloy was above 50 million yuan. Of the entire value, China held 45% and the the foreign party took the rest part. Liable for its default, the foreign party had declared to give up all its rights in exchange for the compensation claim from China. As the shareholder of Ershou Alloy, Heqing Town government, the Chinese investor, wanted to sell the assets to Wanfeng Auto, the professional producer, in hope of being rewarded by the tax revenue, the source of its endless income, after Wanfeng Auto's normal operation. The local government would provide the assets to an excellent partner so that they could generate taxes rather than keeping the assets devalued day by day without being properly used. And that was also Wanfeng Auto's biggest advantage in the negotiation.

Because of their low bid, Chen Ailian and her negotiating team were not welcomed in the last round negotiation with the town's government officials in July, 1999.

She walked into the conference room of town government, and found that both the director of Ershou Alloy and the government office workers responsible for the industry management of the town were there. Yet they didn't talk much but just had perfunctory exchanges with Wanfeng Auto's negotiation members, delaying their final decisions. A long time as she waited for, Chen Ailian didn't receive their replay "The deal is done" as she had expected. She knew it was the final bid and the negotiating rivals wished her to make a concession at the last moment. So she got to her feet after two hours' fruitless wait. "If we can't achieve an agreement today, let's put it off to some other time. We both parties will reflect on it and then continue the talk after we all have the definite final answers."Said Chen Alian, standing up ready to leave.

This was the critical moment as Chen Ailian had said. To her, this manifested the business principle of taking risks carefully in management.

The word "carefully" actually indicated that Chen Ailian was certain of the result in her heart. Even though in terms of probability, she guessed that her departure could probably bring changes to the negotiation at a deadlock, she herself was not sure of the changes. However, she treated it as the last resort in her heart that it didn't matter if the negotiation failed and Wanfeng Auto could wait.

As to "taking risks", it was true that Chen Ailian really left the government conference room of the town once she said so. In her inner world, she was clearly aware that to give up or not decided whether Wanfeng Auto could acquire Ershou Alloy. Since the town leaders invited Wanfeng Auto to have the negotiation, it indicated that she made a generally sound judgment on Wanfeng Auto's chances to take over Ershou Alloy. After she and her colleagues arrived, they found the leaders of their counterpart didn't come to negotiation, which revealed Wanfeng Auto's takeover bid became something like a chicken rib — something that one is hesitant to discard in spite of its little value — to their counterpart. And this in turn proved Wanfeng Auto's accurate bid.

So she had to take a risk. Obviously, the Chinese government investors of Ershou Alloy were highly experienced, with all the situations fully understood. But they still wanted to test whether Wanfeng Auto would slightly make any concession on the bid due to its eager desire to expand.

Chen Ailian, confident of the final negotiation result, went naturally out of the government conference room in the office building and she walked very fast. But just as she approached the entrance of the town's office buildings, she heard someone calling her from behind.

Already prepared for the change, Chen Ailian turned around and found a man standing by the window of the office on the second floor was calling her. Her colleagues in the negotiation team told her this was the Secretary of the Town Party Committee who asked them to go back to continue the talk. Chen Ailian , silently shouting Yeah in her heart, quickly understood it would be done.

She returned to the office of the Secretary of the Town Party Committee on the second floor. As she had expected, the reason why the all the office workers of the town didn't have virtual negotiation with Wanfeng Auto's negotiation team was that the Secretary of the Town Party Committee, in charge of the general business of the town, regarded Wanfeng Auto's bid for Ershou Alloy too low and tried to make the buyer raise the takeover bid with deliberate silence on the negotiation. Seeing Chen Ailian really left, the Secretary of the Town Party Committee realized Wanfeng's bid was indeed the highest one they could offer. And the local party committee and government did think about the asset price while considering the future tax revenue.

The following negotiation went on smoothly, in which Wanfeng Auto acquired Ershou Alloy at a very low takeover bid. Actually, it was the factors outside the negotiation that more distinguished the strong party from the weak one during the negotiation .In the negotiation between Chen Ailian and the government leaders of Heqing Town, both parties were trying to gain more from the win-win result. And both parties were clearly aware that Wanfeng Auto was the most suitable buyer of the takeover.

That was because of the entire industry situation as well as Wanfeng Auto's status against the background at that time.

In 1999, the split in domestic motorcycle market took place.

During the year, the motorcycle retreated from the position of hot consumer goods, with the car entering the domestic household. Though the overall demands were still growing in the market, the consumers had had some knowledge of the motorcycle manufacturers and motorcycles of famous brand started to appear.

At this time, the market was no longer the place where one could sell his products as long as he had invested. The market then had evolved into the place separating the weak from the strong — the distinguished enterprise competed in the market like a duck to water, owing to its stable production and proper cost control, while the weak enterprise was struggling to survive with its market hardly developed.

As a new-comer to the market, Shanghai Ershou Alloy could hardly take a piece of pie in the current market, once its formal cooperation partner, the motorcycle manufacturer, was knocked out of the market.

Meanwhile, Wanfeng Auto had competed in the market for more than five years, the company's management had grasped the basic market rules of hub production and those of the motor vehicle components.

The hub manufacturing is not technically demanding. With proper equipment and standardized testing measures, it is not difficult for an enterprise to cross the technical threshold of hub production.

Just because of the comparatively low technical bar, there had been many competitors in the industry of hub manufacturing when Wanfeng Auto joined in the field. It was a good chance when Wanfeng Auto entered the industry in 1994, because during during the time when the motorcycle industry was newly started, motor manufacturers didn't inspect the component suppliers' factories. So Wanfeng Auto could start from scratch, but there were not such times later on. Once the motorcycle industry became prosperous after the market's golden period, motorcycle makers began to realize that be it in the motorcycle industry or the auto industry which Wanfeng Auto later entered in, the wheel hub is the most important safety part of the whole vehicle. Therefore, the motorcycle and auto makers , known as OEM, made enormous demands on the stable quality of wheel hubs. They would gradually have strict factory inspection after a supporting hub maker became one of their component suppliers, and moreover they would sample each batch of the supplier's products so as to check the product quality. So from 1994 to 1998, it was because Wanfeng Auto under Chen Ailian's leadership continually invested in manufacturing and testing equipment that the company quickly gained a steady foothold in the market.

After Wanfeng Auto got a footing in the market as a supporting enterprise, the scale expansion and the costs control during the production set the next bar for it to cross. The two factors , to Wanfeng Auto, were the two faces of the same coin, and in the company, there were numerous such examples. Take the procurement of raw materials for example, till 1999 with a yearly output of only several ten thousand hubs, Wanfeng Auto had been only a small customer to most of the raw material suppliers. Yet after it solved all quality and technical problems, more and more motorcycle makers in the market started to cooperate with it; Wanfeng Auto then gradually became a big customer in aluminum ingots, the first major raw material and started to play a dominant role when bargaining with the aluminum plants.

After achieving a high status in the industry, Wanfeng Auto needed to produce in large scale. Now that motor vehicle manufacturers in growing number turned to cooperate with Wanfeng Auto, it was not a hard job to make profits by revitalizing Shanghai Ershou Alloy's assets. The same assets would work out right once operated with Wanfeng Auto's mode of management and marketing.

That was why Chen Ailian held strong attitude in the negotiation when taking over Shanghai Ershou Alloy. However, at that time, Wanfeng Auto was in acute shortage of cash, so Chen Ailian and her negotiation team were highly sensitive to the price.

Though the negotiation was filled with serious conflicts, both Chen Ailian and the government leaders of Heqing Town were quite clear that the more furious the bargaining was, the more seriously both parties took the negotiation. After Ershou Alloy was taken over by Wanfeng Auto, it took the new company only three months to make profits from its initial deficit, with a yield amounting to three years' total output of the original enterprise. Wanfeng Auto did live up to the promise of tax payment made during the negotiation, so the enterprise and the government went on very well with each other. For this reason, the government of Heqing Town later on gave great support to Wanfeng Auto when it started up the vehicle project.

Entering into and retreating from Chongqing

Yang Huihui, a graduate of Beijing University of Chemical Technology, knew that this was a promising enterprise as soon as she entered Wanfeng Auto as an employee, for almost all the first-class domestic motorcycle manufacturers then kept Wanfeng Auto as one their supporting suppliers.

At the beginning of the 21st century, there were three major manufacturing regions of domestic motorcycle industry , Jiangsu & Zhejiang, Guangdong and Chongqing, where the three main production bases of domestic motorcycles were located. In Jiangsu & Zhejiang region, the major motorcycle makers included Qianjiang, Jincheng, Wuxi Jetta and Chunlan, which were the earliest markets of Wanfeng Auto. Among the motorcycle makers in Guangdong region, Wanfeng Auto set its cooperation goal on Dachangjiang, a company of good prospects due to its long time adherence to international standards in production.

However, the dream needs to be fulfilled gradually, while the fact around the year 2000 was that a new trend — the price war — appeared in motorcycle market. The initiators of the price war in this round were a batch of Chongqing motorcycle makers, known as Chongqing Mobang.

Chongqing Mobang, with complicated composition, included four large-scale motorcycle makers, Longxin, Zongshen, Lifang and Yingang, and numerous smaller ones, besides the well-known military enterprises Jialing and Jianshe. Viewed from the market share of the domestic motorcycle makers, Chongqing Mobang accounted for one third of the market.

There was an objective reason for the price war of motorcycle started by Chongqing motorcycle makers. Among the early domestic motorcycle manufacturers, the strongly competitive military enterprises subordinate to Southwest Munitions Bureau built up several large-scale motorcycle manufacturing companies , like Jianshe and Jialing. The technology transmitted from these enterprises led to the establishment of a large batch of private motorcycle businesses. Because of the local labor resources and the low costs of land , motorcycle enterprises in Chongqing had greater advantage over other domestic competitors in costs — their costs were comparatively lower than their counterparts'. As a result, they launched several rounds of price wars and even had taken a very big share of the market for a time, making a great contribution to the popularity of motorcycles in China.

The enterprise strategy centered on costs control in Chongqing Mobang naturally influenced the upstream enterprises, the component suppliers. When Wanfeng Auto expanded its scale by acquisition, it considered how to achieve a win-win situation with the motorcycle makers while developing as a supporting enterprise with its costs controlled. With the ideology, the management of Wanfeng Auto had started to seek chances to optimize its costs by locating its production bases alongside the motorcycle manufacturers.

It was later commonly recognized as a principle among Wanfeng Auto's management to locate the component production factory on the doorstep of the motor vehicle maker. In terms of the hub production, the strategy, if carried out , enabled Wanfeng Auto and the vehicle makers to achieve a win-win situation . For one thing, As products, the hubs had to be delivered with considerable logistics costs. So the strategy of having the motor vehicle manufacturer on the doorstep decreased the costs of the hub factory . For another, to the motor vehicle maker, with the component factory on the doorstep,not only could the designing process be greatly shorter in time, but also the problem detecting and solving during the production process could be much faster in speed.

The chance came quickly. In 2001, Chongqing Longxin Motorcycle invited Wanfeng Auto to invest in Chongqing and the two companies even cooperated in building up a production base. Of the entire investment, Wanfeng Auto, as the management, held 70% of the stock shares of the new company, while Longxin 30%.

The reason why Longxin invited Wanfeng Auto to invest in a new motorcycle hub factory in Chongqing was that it once had had small investment in motorcycle hubs. After entering the field, Longxin found that the motorcycle hub industry had been technically highly demanding around the year 2000. The hub production needed not only technical forces to fulfill the motorcycle manufacturer's demands but also mass production to reduce costs. Meanwhile, many local motorcycle makers in Chongqing were competing in the price war, trying to promote the popularity of motorcycles to a even higher level in the country. As far as the quantity was concerned, there was a large market for hub production, so for Longxin, it would be promising to invest in a hub factory together with Wanfeng Auto

When Zhang Xikang, the general manager in the department of hub affairs at that time, reported Longxin's idea to Chen Ailian, who was considering the plan to locate Wanfeng Auto's hub production next door to the motorcycle maker, Chen surely approved of the idea. After the discussion at the board level, the feasible investment plan was settled, and Yang Huihui appeared as the general manager in Wanfeng Auto's new factory in Chongqing .

But in the investment of the new factory in Chongqing, Wanfeng Auto kept a card up its sleeve: the new factory in Chongqing was operated with the asset-light strategy. With Chen Ailian's proposal, the board directors of Wanfeng Auto didn't invest in the new factory through land purchase as they did in other places; well, instead, they start the business in Chongqing with rented factory buildings. Generally speaking, Wanfeng Auto took the tentative steps while investing in the factory of Chongqing.

At that time, the private motorcycle manufacturers in Chongqing , launching the price wars to compete for market share , could of course earn considerable shares in market when the motorcycles were more and more popularized. However, all the manufacturing enterprises understand it is hard for them to attract customers only by launching price wars rather than by improving customer value. More importantly, when it was around 2000, autos began to be consumed by common customers in domestic market. Considering the market trend, it wouldn't last long for the motorcycles to win more popularity in the market through price wars. Therefore, Wanfeng Auto took a very careful strategy when investing in the hub factory of Chongqing.

However, the domestic price wars in motorcycles launched by Chongqing Mobang did enable them to gain a bigger part of the market share. In this case,

Wanfeng Auto's investment in Chongqing actually played an important role in its way to be the largest in scale throughout the country.

Because of the efforts made by Yang Huihui's team to open up the market, as well as its brand image that Wanfeng Auto already had inside the industry as a professional hub manufacturer, a considerable number of motorcycle manufacturers started to seek for cooperation with the new factory that was naturally the supporting component factory of the motorcycle maker Longxin after it went into production. Wanfeng Auto's new factory, known as Xinrui, in Chongqing had made healthy profits.

It quickly proved that the asset-light strategy Wanfeng Auto took in its investment in Chongqing was wisely correct. It was because of the local low costs in all the resources that the motorcycle makers in Chongqing started price wars in market. They had advantage over their competitors of other regions in price.

But the price war is a double-edged sword in market. Being too simple, it usually can hardly be kept in the right people's hand. In rational price war, the producer should put more effort into the management and he should always keep the selling price higher than the cost price when competing in the price war with the costs reduced. But in the market, once the price war starts, there will always be competitors giving up the principle of keeping the selling price higher than the cost price. To cut the costs by expanding in scale, they always cater to the consumers by low prices

In motorcycle market, once beginning, the price war soon crossed the rational boundary. During the harshest price wars around 2000, the motorcycle initially worth 10 thousand yuan was sold at a price as low as 2 to 3 thousand yuan by the private motorcycles in Chongqing.

Transferring to Bashu (ie, areas in Sichuan province and Chongqing City) with tentacles penetrated in Chongqing, the birthplace of Chinese motorcycle industry

The effect of the harsh price wars was multi-faceted. For one thing, the enterprises engaged in the price wars lost their innovation motives, and instead, with no more investments in technical research and development, they just simply followed the tide. For another, the price wars didn't contribute to good overall image of all the motorcycle enterprises in Chongqing, but rather they made the motorcycles produced in Chongqing branded as bargains when compared with those produced in Jiangsu & Zhejiang and Guangdong.

Furthermore, Wanfeng Auto was also influenced by the price wars though it is in the upper reaches of the industry. The price wars among them inevitably forced the motorcycle makers to seek cheaper components. Though adhering to its bottom line of quality, Wanfeng Auto was still affected in many aspects.

The products of Chongqing Mobang were mainly sold in the suburban and rural areas. Owing to the substandard management of motorcycles in remote areas, the motorcycle makers that were struggling in the competition started to adopt some substandard operations.

And that brought about great troubles to Wanfeng Auto that was seriously sticking to the bottom line to be law-abiding.

Since the substandard operations of the motorcycle maker need all-out cooperation of its supporting factories, the latter will soon be negatively influenced. At that time, Zhang Xikang, the general manager in the department of hub affairs, reported the situation to the board directors, inquiring about the solutions. Finally, the board made the decision that Wanfeng Auto must follow the respectable path. Now that such unhealthy competition was the common sight of the market in Chongqing, Wanfeng Auto had to consider retreating from the market.

Yet after the practice in Chongqing, the strategy to arrange the component factory next door to the motorcycle makers had become the consensus among the board of Wanfeng Auto. Since the market of Chongqing had been stuck in price wars, the board followed Zhang Xikang's advice to relocate the hub factory in Chongqing to the doorstep of Dachangjiang, the most competitive enterprise.

At this point, the overall judgment that Wanfeng Auto's board made about the market started to be proved correct by the market. The price wars enabled Chongqing Mobang to enlarge the market share but meanwhile gave their products an image of low quality among the consumers.Wanfeng Auto was determined to be the supporting component maker of Dachangjiang with all its efforts. As Dachangjiang had always enjoyed a good image for its product quality in the market, its market share started to rise.

The market effect of Dachangjiang's strategy came quite slowly, since, based on fine products, it was the natural result of the progressive growth in scale. In the 21sth century, however, the market effect appeared obvious. Because at this time, the consumers had already known that the motorcycle with the brand name Haojue produced in Dachangjiang was superior in quality, many people turned to it in motorcycle purchase. As a result, with its overall sales continually increasing after 2005, Dachangjiang held the first position in domestic motorcycle industry.

Wanfeng Auto's decision-makers believed the company Dachangjiang would acturally have superiority in market competition in the future. If the motorcycle was no more the public transport in the market, between the price and the quality, the consumer's choice would be highly quality-oriented rather than price-oriented. Compared with the simple price competition, the quality competition, based on details, could more stand for an enterprise' competitiveness. Wanfeng Auto was so very optimistic about Dachangjaing's future.

Well, Dachangjiang's decision-makers were also aware that Wanfeng Auto, with its hub products constantly improved in quality, had gone into the lead in product quality among the supporting component enterprises. Therefore they had recommended Chen Ailian early before to make Wanfeng Auto their supporting component supplier with its hub production next door to them. Apparently, Wanfeng Auto was far superior to all other hub manufacturing enterprises.

However, to relocate the Chongqing factory to Jiangmen where Dachangjiang was located, they were faced with a challenge. Wanfeng Auto had operated the factory in Chongqing for 5 years with all local employees. So would these employees tranfer to Jiangmen Guangdong, thousand miles away from Chongqing, together with the factory.

Correct decisions can always win the staff's approval. There were 400 employees working in Wanfeng Auto's factory in Chongqing. When the word came that the factory would be relocated , only a part of the employees wanting to stay in Chongqing chose to leave the factory. When the factory in Chongqing was formally relocated in Jiangmen Guangdong, 300 employees moved to Jiangmen together with the factory. That was simply because the employees had felt a sense of belonging here in Wanfeng Auto as if it were the home, and they believed in the promising future by following the company Wanfeng Auto.

Wanfeng Motorcycle Hub Co., Ltd, loacted in Jiangmen Guangdong Province and established in two phases, became the core component supplier of Dachagnjaing with a yearly output of 5 million sets of hubs.

The New Life of Motorcycle Wheel Hubs

Year 2000. Usually, the product of each enterprise has its life span. Wanfeng

Auto's motorcycle hubs, entering into the market in 1994, had been the matching components for almost all the motorcycle makers around the beginning the the 21th century. During its progressive development, Wanfeng Auto acturall had reached the summit of its business in the market with the capacity of millions of sets of hubs.

However, reaching the summit has another meaning — usually no matter how the market develops, the enterprise on its business summit is likely to face a downturn in development. And so was it in the motorcycle market. In 2003, the domestic auto industry developed dramatically, while the motorcycle was gradually replaced by the the automobile as the public transport, which was followed by the ban on motorcycles in many cities. Thereby, the domestic motorcycles seemed to be doomed to take the downturn in the market. Then would Wanfeng Auto's motorcycle hubs also fall into a decline?

Therefore, different opinions rose inside Wanfeng Auto that future development of the company would be in trouble due to the restriction of motorcycles. But this time Chen Ailian, who usually likes to listen to others' opinions, thought differently. In her view, to the motorcycle, also a product, its life span is closely linked to the consumers' demands for it. Actually it wouldn't be a big problem when it was restricted by the government policy in the market. She held that as a transportation vehicle, the motorcycle may die out only when there is a better alternative.

When it was in the 21st century, the domestic media focused on India which was rising after China, and Chen Ailian also paid attention to the country. At that time, Wanfeng Auto had opened up business in auto wheel hubs. So she seized the opportunity to make a special trip to India when Indian Tata Auto invited all its suppliers throughout the world to have a meeting in Inda.

The visit to India gave her a deep impression. Though there were wide gaps between India and China in each aspect, according to the information that Tata Auto introduced to its guests about India and its enterprises, Chen Ailian, who had entrepreneurial experiences early in her business, had the strong impression that the economic development in India was highly similar to that of China during Wanfeng Auto's pioneering days.

From this trip to India, Chen Ailian believed that India at this point was highly similar to China in the 90's. In the workshops of Tata Auto, all the vehicle model , producing materials and pricing repeatedly confirmed Chen Ailian's initial judgment about Indian economy. She was now very familiar with the auto industry.

As is known to all the readers that had experienced the days in the 90's of the 20th century, in such a developing country as China, it had been quite a long time when motorcycles and cars developed in parallel. China produced cars in the 50's, yet the people couldn't afford the cars even until the 90's when they became financially well off. During that period, the motorcycle industry was booming, while meanwhile the domestic auto industry highly focused on universality of the cars with three common models — Santana, Xiali and Fukang — greatly popular in the market. It was not until the time around 2000 that cars became very diverse in the market , since many households could afford the cars then.

When visiting Tata Auto, Chen Ailian could feel the great demand in Indian market for the general purpose of the cars. She understood that the pursuit of universality of the product indicated that the whole market were pursuing low price. Meanwhile, the demand for transport vehicles in Indian market were most likely to be met with motorcycles.

Observing the Indian market with such thought, she discovered that there were lots of motorcycles on the street. And what was similar to the situation in domestic market when Wanfeng Auto started its business was that Indian motorcycles also had wire wheels.

It immediately came to her that what she had observed here should be turned into action in Wanfeng Auto. As soon as she returned, she asked Zhang Xikang's team to avoid the competition in domestic Red Sea, but speed up the development of the giant Blue Sea in Indian market

Zhang Xikang led his team to India in 2003, the early time of Indian initial economic development. Quickly he figured it out that motorcycles sold very well in Indian market. Inside the country, there were four large-scaled motorcycle manufacturers, two of which cooperated with Japan respectively and the other two of which were national manufacturing enterprises. Hero Honda, a Japanese joint venture, was the largest Indian motorcycle maker, Bajaj,the national enterprise, ranked the second in sales in India, the third one was an Indian national enterprise, TVS Motorcycle Co.,Ltd, and the fourth Japan's Honda.

During Zhang Xikang's visits to the Indian motorcycle manufacturers, he confirmed from the data that there mainly were wire wheels in Indian motorcycles then. The pattern of Indian motorcycle market was quite favorable to Wanfeng Auto's aluminum hubs. Once the motorcycle makers could increase their sales with aluminum hubs in their motorcycles, the market here could be quickly opened up.

With the experiences gotten in China, Wanfeng Auto was more sophisticated when developing Indian market. After visiting all the motorcycle makers in India, Zhang Xikang Chose Bajaj as the opening for Wanfeng Auto's motorcycle wheel hubs to enter into Indian market. There was cause for him to do so. Actually, in terms of the budding period, Indian motorcycle market started much earlier than that of China.

Bajaj was established in 1945 after World War II, and became a listed company early in 1960. In 1983, Honda entered into Indian market with the joint venture, Hero Honda, and started fierce competition with Bajaj Motorcycle Company in the market. Hero Honda, producing upmarket motorcycles with its technical advantage, made its sale mainly in Indian cities; while Bajaj took advantage of Honda's inability to widen the market in India because of its limited investment to open up the market in rural areas with scooters. With this competing strategy, Bajaj firmly held its market share by popularizing the motorcycles.

But it didn't mean that Wanfeng Auto was too late for Indian market. When Wanfeng Auto started to open up its Indian market in 2003, Indian economy started to boom in the wave of Information Technology. An important background of that time was that the telecommunications revolution in IT and software of western countries had spread throughout the world around 2000. Since Indian government did much to popularize the education in software industry throughout the country, and additionally Indians in general have a quite good language foundation in English, western countries outsourced most of their software service industry to India. And thus Indian economy started to take off.

The same as it was in China, there were increasing demands for motorcycles at this time in India. The motorcycle manufacturers thus started increasing the investment, expanding the producing scale in order to satisfy the demands in market and to develop themselves as well.

Zhang Xikang had his own professional judgement about why to take the cooperation with Bajaj as the opening for Wanfeng Auto's participation in Indian market. Actually, the market strategy was made after repeated discussion and careful consideration.

The reason why Wanfeng Auto's board of directors took Bajaj as the entrance to

Indian market was that this company held the second place in Indian motorcycle industry. As a challenger, Bajaj was more likely to take reform steps. Once Bajaj's management realized that their adoption of aluminum hubs could lead to dramatic increase in their market share, they would be undoubtedly more active than the champion enterprise in advancing the reform so as to change the overall pattern of the market.

Once Bajaj succeeded in the market, Wanfeng Auto's motorcycle aluminum hubs would be quickly adopted by several large-scaled manufacturers. Zhang Xikang objectively introduced in detail Wanfeng Auto's domestic data on the promotion of its motorcycle hubs to Bajaj's management. The facts in Chinese market proved that domestic motorcycle manufacturers did have their sales rapidly increases with aluminum wheel hubs in their products.The aluminum hubs, handsome and elegant, could work to the manufacturers' advantage to change the motorcycle shapes. While to consumers, aluminum hubs, more personalized, were more favorable for them to demonstrate their personalities and tastes.

However, Bajaj's administrators , quite conservative, were concerned that adoption of the aluminum hubs might have negative influence on the sales they already had. So during the early period Indian market, it took Wanfeng Auto a long time and energy to persuade them. It was quite a torturing process.

Zhang Xikang, having experienced a lot in the front line of marketing, was well-known for his patience and perseverance. He truly believed that it was rewarding for the customer company to adopt aluminum hubs and that was the key point why he didn't give up along.

Opening up Indian Market (Chen Ailian , the third one on the left; Zhang Xikang, the first one on the left)

Zhang Xikang, a distinguished marketing leader, was good at analyzing the question from Bajaj's perspective and believed Bajaj's hesitation was justified. This enterprise had had a very large production scale, with 200 thousand motorcycles produced monthly in each of its workshop.

Furthermore, Indian market was then rapidly growing. The management of Bajaj Motorcycle were ,on one hand, looking forward to the changes in the market pattern so as to challenge its opponent that held the largest market share, while on the other hand, worried that Bajaj's market position would be influenced in case of the problem. After repeated discussion, Bajaj's administrators accepted Wanfeng Auto's idea and popularize motorcycles with aluminum wheel hubs in large scale in the market, after establishing the supply-and-demand relationship with Wanfeng Auto. During the following period of time, Bajaj quickly increased its sales and even started to penetrate the upscale market dominated by Hero Honda. In 2003 and the two years that followed, it even became a symbol of Indian middle class to have the motorcycle produced by Bajaj.

Bajaj changed the motorcycle market pattern in India, for its management had noticed the transformation in Indian economy and thereafter had taken a series of steps. Besides adopting aluminum wheel hubs, Bajaj priced its motorcycles lower than Hero Honda's , and meanwhile improve the technology in the engine.

With Bajaj's rise, its products became the targets to be imitated. From 2005, Indian motorcycle makers began ordering aluminum wheel hubs from Wanfeng Auto, since they could greatly increase their market share by adopting Wanfeng Auto's aluminum hubs in their motorcycles. Wanfeng Auto's audacious operation in India rewarded it with fruits.

Wanfeng Auto's development in Indian motorcycle market actually initiated another pattern for domestic products to enter overseas countries. After Wanfeng Auto had opened up Indian market, home aluminum wheel hub makers with overcapacity saw the new Blue Sea.

Traditionally, auto and motorcycle component manufacturers usually depended on the motor vehicle makers to enter the overseas countries. Because of this, before Wanfneng Auto , no hub company and even none of the entire auto and motorcycle component industry, had ever been so active as Wanfeng Auto in opening up the market

But in India, the local political and commercial forces shut the door to Chinese motorcycle manufacturers that were setting foot in the international market. Around 2000, the domestic motorcycle makers, well-known for their low prices, once fixed their eyes on the Indian market, yet quickly, these biggies of the industry found that , as foreign brands, Chinese motorcycles could hardly enter Indian market. For Indian motorcycle makers were also very competitive. Some big manufacturers headed by Bajaj had though understanding of their local market, and the most noticeable indication of it was that Indian motorcycles had very low fuel consumption. The oil consumption of a 100 CC-sized motorcycle was no more than 1.5 liters / hundred kilometers, and this standard became a very high threshold. At the same time, noticing the signs that Chinese motorcycles would advance towards India, Indian motorcycle manufacturers persuaded their National Congress into increasing the motorcycle import tariffs greatly, turning Chinese motorcycles' core advantage — low prices — useless in competition.

As a result, the traditional component enterprises that followed the market strategy had no effect on Chinese motorcycle makers' efforts to enter Indian market. As Wanfeng Auto entered and changed the whole pattern of Indian market, other motorcycle hub manufacturing enterprises force also followed the former into the Indian market. There formed a situation with high interaction between China and India in the industry. Therefore, Wanfeng Auto's case of opening up its

追梦人

market in India had been recorded in the case base by Harvard Business School.

Zhang Xikang, the executive of the classic case, led his team, composed of Yu Dengfeng, Zhang Jianguo, Lu Shiping, Mei Anren, Jiang Daofeng and Luo Haifeng, and worked for ten years with their enthusiasm, passion and strong will. They moved the customers with their persistence and enabled Wanfeng Auto to enjoy one third of the world market with the absolute leadership in segment market of the industry.

Wanfeng Auto's Principle

During developing process, motorcycle wheel hubs, as Wanfeng Auto's start-up products, contributed two key factors to the company's later development.

First of all, as a private enterprise, Wanfeng Auto attaches great importance to quality and credibility and advocates treating its own business from the customer's perspective. Both the case that Chen Ailian resolutely remelted the defective hub products worth more than 60 thousand yuan in the company's early stage and the case of Quality Survey Odyssey demonstrate the company's way to survive and develop during its pioneering period that only when customers are satisfied can the company grow.

Secondly, it is because Wanfeng Auto has taken full advantage of its marketing ability that the private enterprise can develop so rapidly. It is the thorough understanding of motorcycle makers' market demands as well as the active research for the laws of market changes that has led Wanfeng Auto to the market and enabled the component enterprise to always cooperate with the stronger ones of the motor vehicle makers.

Finally, the key to Wanfeng Auto's success in opening up the Indian market is its thorough understanding of the laws appearing in a nation's economic development. The laws that were quickly summarized by Wanfeng Auto in its overseas marketing of motorcycle wheel hubs have been guiding the enterprise' internationalization after the establishment of Indian market.

The market has its own laws. It is just because Wanfeng Auto has grasped the laws and formed its own strength according to the laws of the market that the enterprise has succeeded in establishing its business.

第四章

激战汽轮

起步

从万丰奥特 22 年的创业历程当中，可以清晰地看出，作为创始者的陈爱莲，虽然是位女性，却是一个心胸宽广、进取心很强的人。

不过，她的进取心比我们已经看到的还要大。

1996 年 6 月，万丰奥特的摩托车轮毂业务刚刚走上康庄大道，一直在负责摩托车轮毂项目开发的技术负责人朱训明跟随陈爱莲赴美国进行了为期 10 天的考察。考察回来后，陈爱莲亲自动笔撰写了一份内容非常全面详尽的《赴美国考察调研报告》。

她在报告中详细分析了美国轿车轮毂的年总需求量在 700 万只左右，其缺口约 200 万只需依赖国外进口；美国四大汽车厂总生产量中约有 30% 的汽车配套为铝合金车轮，每年铝轮的增长率为 5%；汽车经销商在销售时把原有铁轮毂换成铝轮毂的用量，每年估计占 8%；美国目前是世界上汽车拥有量最多的国家，对年轻人来说，让私家车装上铝轮就觉得像穿上名牌衣服一样时髦，所以市场上一旦有新款式的铝轮上市，就把旧款式的铝轮换掉，这部分的用量也相当可观。考察中，陈爱莲已与美国一家汽车铝轮经销商赖雷·安德先生进行洽谈，他与万丰奥特合作达成意向，每年包销 20 万只以上汽车铝轮。

赴美考察，坚定了陈爱莲上马汽车轮毂项目的决心

经过这次赴美考察，陈爱莲强烈地感受到世界变化之快真是令人难以置信，特别是国外汽车零部件的先进程度更是让她惊叹不已，也更加坚定了她要上马汽车铝轮项目的决心。

在某种意义上，从事了摩托车轮毂的生产，再进入汽车轮毂领域，是规模扩大的另一个方向。这是因为就轮毂制造工艺而言，除了核心工序铸造环节不一样，汽车轮毂和摩托车轮毂的基本工艺都相同，因此把铝轮项目扩展到汽车轮毂，对万丰奥特而言是一个新的提升。

1996 年的万丰奥特，正处于高速扩张期，各方面都非常紧张，因此对汽车轮毂研制的投入并不大。不过，公司还是建立了一支以朱训明、俞林、俞利民、吕永新、顾新灿、楼震宇等人为主要成员的试制小组，在一个 10 多个平方米的房间里，开始为公司的下一个方向做准备。

20 世纪 90 年代后期还没有计算机辅助设计系统，对于汽车轮毂的设计，技术人员有一个熟悉的过程，在这个过程里，他们的工作就是测绘，用现在时髦的术语来说，叫"逆向工程"。说白了就是把已有轮毂样品用测绘的方式画成图纸，以此来熟悉这个产品，再根据未来顾客的定制要求进行集成创新，设计出新的款式获得客户的认可，再进行工艺准备和送样，在客户检验合格达到设计要求后组织生产。

除了成立汽车轮毂科研小组之外，此时，陈爱莲还在做另外一件事情。有了摩托车轮毂的生产经历，万丰奥特想要达到的国际化水平的要求，陈爱莲心中也早已经有了直观的感受。在汽轮项目上，她和整个创业团队都希望能有一个系统性总体技术框架搭建者来为万丰奥特的汽车轮毂生产打基础，使得万丰奥特的汽车轮毂生产从一开始就能达到国际先进的标准。

这就是我们在第一章当中看到的万丰奥特总工程师雷铭君的来历。

万丰奥特董事会最后选定雷铭君来主持万丰奥特汽轮的技术工作，是因为经历摩托车轮毂的三年生产之后，万丰奥特已经对整个铝轮行业的状态非常了解。在轮毂生产企业当中，把品质标准提得很高，同时已经开始达产的万丰奥特，已经在 112 家同行当中走到了第一方阵。但汽车轮毂的生产要求更高，因此必须要坚持高起点的定位，而聘请一位有丰富体系经验的总工来搭建万丰奥特汽轮的生产是十分必要的。

要去哪里找这样的人，陈爱莲心里也有了方向。国内汽车轮毂生产企业实力顶尖的是北方一家大型国有企业和华南的一家合资企业。

陈爱莲看中的正是合资企业出身的南方那家铝合金轮毂公司的副总工程师雷铭君。为了让万丰奥特尽早达到国际化水准的体系，1996 年年底，万丰奥特决定以百万年薪总额，聘请雷铭君、蒋性芳等 4 人组建技术团队，来保障万丰奥特汽车轮毂制造的技术体系化。

不过，雷铭君和蒋性芳并不是那么好请的，他们负责着华南这家大型轮毂制造企业的技术体系，而且雷铭君还是"车轮试验方法国家标准"的起草人。陈爱莲最初南下广东去邀请他们加盟的时候，虽然以高薪相邀，却并没有得到回应。因为当时的万丰奥特还处于创业阶段，这个企业能做成什么样，雷铭君和蒋性芳心里并没有底。

　　然而，此时的陈爱莲已经走出去看到过国际化的轮毂制造企业的状态，她知道，一个优秀的企业，不仅仅需要几位尖端的技术人员，更需要建立一个完整的技术体系。而雷工和蒋工，正是万丰奥特所需要的技术体系的领军人物。

　　所以，陈爱莲"三顾茅庐"，解决了雷铭君和蒋性芳工作上、生活上的很多后顾之忧。他们被陈爱莲的真诚所感动，开始对这个看起来时髦、漂亮，却非常执着于自己的目标的浙江女性有了更深的了解，知道她言出必行、重情重义，所以就放心地来到新昌，再次创业。

　　雷铭君、蒋性芳等专家团队入驻万丰奥特三个月，就研发出了与欧洲同等水平的汽车铝轮，而且还培养出了李伟锋、童胜坤、钱志芳等一批万丰奥特自己的专家型人才。

　　陈爱莲之所以执着地带着刚刚成形的万丰奥特接连开拓市场，是因为她看到了未来的市场变化。

陈爱莲三顾茅庐聘请雷铭君（左三）、蒋性芳（左二）等专家

万丰二十周年庆典上陈爱莲授予蒋工、雷工功勋奖章

相比起摩托车产业，汽车产业显然是一块更大、更有未来的市场。入行两年之后，陈爱莲很清楚地认识到，如果说摩托车产业的兴起是一个国家经济起飞期的先声的话，那么汽车产业的兴起则是一个国家经济腾飞的象征。

此时的关键，在于汽车市场开始崛起。一个国家的人均国内生产总值（GDP）达到 3 000 美元之时，在这个关键时间点上，该国将会开始出现私人拥有汽车的起步点。而当人均GDP达到 6 000 美元的时候，轿车开始大规模进入家庭，汽车业迎来它的黄金时期。

中国在 1997 年国内生产总值为 7.9 万亿，如果计算人均国内生产总值，在 750 美元左右。看起来似乎与 3 000 美元的距离还远，不过因为国内的城乡差距很大，人均国内生产总值达到 3 000 美元的城市数量，已经不少。

我们可以清晰地看到这其中的变化：如果说陈爱莲在 1994 年带领团队进入摩托车轮毂的生产领域是因为中宝主观要转型的话，那么在 1996 年年底进入汽车轮毂制造领域，则是创业团队试图要为未来去取得争先的机会。

在轮毂制造范围内，只有赢得规模，才是赢得市场的最初先机。万丰奥特要做到一流，这是一个巨大的门槛，进入汽车轮毂制造，只是这其中的第一步。

而接下来的准备工作，同样不容易，首先要做的就是设备引进。万丰奥特在汽轮项目上从一开始的目标就是要达到国际先进水平。经过反复论证，刚刚成形的创业团队把设备采购的目光盯准了国际上一流企业通用的低压铸造机。

因为有了摩托车轮毂的盈利支持，这次万丰奥特可以不先找米再买锅了。在设备选型上，陈爱莲巧妙地用全球招标方式，把欧、美、日等设备供应商请上门来，让他们比性能、比价格、比服务，打起擂台。"鹬蚌相争，渔翁得利"，万丰奥特从容地拿到了性价比最好的产品，而废标的厂商也心服口服，并希望未来还有合作的机会。经过招标选择，创业团队选中了美国一家叫作"帝国设备"的供应商，这是一家老牌的低压铸造机生产企业，全球主要轮毂生产商的设备，不少都是由这家企业供应的。

当时，美国的这家帝国设备公司在中国国内处于市场的顶端。本身它生产的低压铸造机就是业内最为先进的设备，而且在中国，当时风起云涌的汽车零部件厂，无论是生产轮毂的，还是生产其他铸件配件的，在设备选型上几乎都不约而同地采用了帝国设备公司的低压铸造机。由此我们可以想见，帝国设备公司在中国市场上，必然是拥有很大的价格话语权的。

但这家公司没有想到的是，在万丰奥特，他们面临的是一场非常艰苦的谈判。

帝国设备公司的设备确属顶尖，但价格也是高得令人难以接受。相较于市场上每套少则10多万美元，多则二三十万美元的设备价格，帝国设备公司的低压铸造机一台的标价就高达30多万美元。当时负责万丰奥特设备采购的吕永新记得折合人民币报价，这种低压铸造机要208万元。

万丰奥特当时没有多少预算。虽然决心要让公司拥有达到国际一流水平的装备，但也不能让项目从一开始就背上沉重的包袱。因此万丰奥特团队决定，要在 150 万元之内拿下首批汽车轮毂的试生产设备。

双方对价格有如此之大的分歧，这场谈判当然艰苦。

1997 年年底，陈爱莲、朱训明、夏越璋和吕永新 4 人，在新昌一家叫作白云山庄的宾馆里，就进口帝国设备公司的低压铸造机，与帝国设备公司谈判团队的谈判整整进行了一个通宵。

万丰奥特团队之所以执意要把采购价格谈到自己可接受的范围内，是因为他们很清楚，帝国设备公司的设备先进性，其实与它的制造成本并无多少关系。它在国内市场上的强势地位，主要是由于国内有相当一批政府投资的企业采购而造成的。帝国设备公司的内部人员应该非常清楚，他们面临的竞争同样激烈，中国作为一个大国，在汽车需求快速增长的背景下，很快会有企业进入低压铸造机的生产，届时他们将失去这个市场。

一个通宵之后，最终帝国设备公司的谈判团队妥协了，万丰奥特采购的低压铸造机单价，落实在万丰奥特的期望值上。

人、财、物都聚集起来之后，万丰奥特工业园一开园，汽车轮毂项目的头一批设备就进入园区，开始形成生产能力。当然，要说此时万丰奥特在汽车轮毂领域里已经有很大的进展，其实倒还不是。在最初，由于帝国设备公司的低压铸造机价格确实过高，所以万丰奥特只能购买 5 台低压铸造机，但在当地，已经是破天荒的一项巨额投资了。与此同时，在万丰奥特最初进入汽车轮毂制造的时候，还采用了部分重力铸造设备。

两个支点撬动的市场

1998 年年初，美国的拉斯维加斯机场来了几位中国客人。不过，他们受到的可不是欢迎，而是美国海关人员由于对中国人的不信任而进行的严格盘查。

追梦人

　　陈爱莲之所以要带领团队到美国拉斯维加斯参观车展，是为了拓展万丰奥特的汽车轮毂业务。历经了千辛万苦的筹备期之后，万丰奥特在进入国内市场时遇上了巨大的障碍。

　　于 1996 年看到汽车市场的巨大前景的，在中国国内，并不只有陈爱莲一个人。20 世纪 80 年代，只要到过西方国家的中国人，都会注意到，这些国家的主要交通工具是汽车。不过，所有与万丰奥特一样试图把这个前景转化为商业机会的企业，都会遇上一个巨大的壁垒。原因就在于国内的汽车制造，在 90 年代还没有完全走出计划经济体系。

　　90 年代，由于汽车的市场需求已经快速上升，很多人都看到了满街进口车的现实，所以"要大力发展汽车工业"成为全国上下的共识。不过当时政府制定的路线，还是带有很浓厚的计划经济色彩。

　　当时政府在汽车工业上的主要策略是，以国内一汽、二汽和上汽在内的"三大"，以及北汽、天汽和南汽在内的"三小"为主构成国内汽车工业的骨架，以它们为主来寻求与国外汽车公司的合资。

　　这样的产业路线，使得国有大型的汽车厂快速上马，用合资产品满足市场，同时企业也获得了比较好的利润。但同时形成了一个封闭的市场体系，使得像万丰奥特这样的企业很难进入国内的主流汽车厂的供应体系——当时合资企业都有自己的配套体系。在 90 年代中期，这个封闭的体系完全能自给自足，不需要外来的配件供应。

　　这个体系甚至影响了 90 年代之后的市场格局。到了 21 世纪之后，国内主流汽车厂垄断汽车市场的局面最终被打破。但在汽车配件的供应上，众多供应商的规模都很小，品质也不稳定，因此在很长一段时间内，民营汽车的配件品质无法与主流汽车厂竞争。

　　万丰奥特在 90 年代进入汽车轮毂产业，最终使得企业在汽车的主机市场开放之后，无论在规模与品质上，都处于领先者的地位。但在 90 年代起步初期，万丰奥特尚需克服巨大的困难才能使自己存活下来。问题就在于，有了产能之后，没有市场，像万丰奥特这样的民企怎么能活下来呢？

　　这就是万丰奥特团队去著名的拉斯维加斯汽车展参会的原因，他们要在美国寻找市场。

陈爱莲带队参观美国拉斯维加斯车展，拓展汽车铝轮业务

　　万丰奥特进入摩轮市场之后的局面，大大地激励了万丰奥特团队。他们都坚信，万丰奥特既然能在摩托车轮毂市场上站住脚并快速打开局面，那就一定也能在汽车轮毂市场上站住。令陈爱莲感动的是，每一年万丰奥特团队去拉斯维加斯，年轻的小伙子们总是忙于寻找客户，没有一个人去近在咫尺的赌场和景点游玩。

　　万丰奥特成功了。

　　到90年代后期，中国制造的能力，在世界范围内是有目共睹的。因为中国是全球范围内最大的发展中国家，而同时，中国制造产品物美价廉，所以只要中国厂商能提供的产品，常常是在世界范围内的低价。

　　因此，美国汽车售后市场的经营者们，也正在寻找着来自中国的汽车配件。就轮毂而言，这个产品在美国汽车的售后市场上，有着很广泛的消费者。

在全球，美国素以"轮子上的国家"而闻名，不过人们较少了解的是，它还是个改装车的市场大国。崇尚自由与个性化的美国消费者买到汽车之后，常常委托汽车售后服务商对汽车进行有特色、个性鲜明的改装，而换一套"时装化"的漂亮轮毂是一个重要选项。因此来自中国的轮毂制造商万丰奥特，受到了美国售后服务商的欢迎。

就轮毂制造的正规厂商而言，美国的售后市场并不是一个非常适合大规模制造的市场。所谓个性化制造，是美国售后市场的服务商们与消费者协商之后，确定轮毂所需要的轮型，以它已形成市场品牌影响的商标委托万丰奥特进行贴牌生产。

来自美国的售后市场轮毂订单，对于正规的轮毂制造大厂来说，并不是好选择。这个市场的特点是，它的单品利润率较高，要求也不如给汽车主机厂做配套高。但它的核心问题是批量很小，甚至常常是几个轮毂就要做一个批次，所以轮毂加工企业需要为此不断更新模具。但对于刚刚起步的万丰奥特来说，这样的订单却提供了一个重要的起步点，它撬开了万丰奥特通向汽车轮毂产业的大门，使得万丰奥特可以在民营汽车配件供应商还没有成规模的时候，率先在市场上抢跑了。

如果说美国售后市场作为第一个支点让万丰奥特的汽车轮毂项目活了下来，那么在一两年之后，万丰奥特就迎来了第二个机会，开始从国外的边缘市场，切入国内市场。2000 年前后，汽车市场巨大的前景像一块磁石一样吸引着国内的民营资本，国有主机厂垄断市场的状况，首先在边缘得到了突破。

政府关于国内汽车市场由"三大"和"三小"汽车制造厂构成骨干企业的构想，确实在很长时间内成为主流。不过，由于经济发展过程当中，解决交通问题的市场需求很大，而且市场的热点也不只国有汽车厂生产的轿车一个领域，因此很快这个格局被打破了。

此时进入这个市场的个体，各式各样。有相当大的一批是由各个地方政府投资的汽车厂，还有各种合资经营的汽车厂，而部分看到了市场先机的民营资本，也以合资、买断许可证等方式，进入了这个市场。

主机市场一旦多样化，万丰奥特团队的远见就开始得到市场的回应：此时有了轮毂生产经验的万丰奥特，成了主机厂在轮毂配件的优选供应商。万丰奥特的生产能力很快在这些厂家那里得到了释放，汽车轮毂业务也开始上台阶了。

不过，在 2000 年左右开始激增的主机厂订单，使万丰奥特又碰上产能瓶颈。因为机会总是一起出现的，1999 年，万丰奥特出资收购了上海二守合金，以一元钱的代价买了五元钱的资产，尝到了低成本扩张的甜头。纵使利润很好，而且银行非常支持，但要再次扩张汽车轮毂产能，万丰奥特资金实力依然不足。

因此迈上这一台阶的过程，充分体现了万丰奥特的企业个性和陈爱莲的企业家精神。

要产能上台阶，铸造设备当然是核心。通过采购美国制造商帝国设备公司的低压铸造机，万丰奥特谈判小组对国际贸易业务已经相当精通，不仅成功地说服了制造商降价，还在贸易合同中充分保障了万丰奥特的权益，以非常老到的方式在付款条件与分期时点等方面最大限度地规避了风险，如支付条件，万丰奥特否定了离岸价、到岸价、成本加保险等传统方式，而始终坚持到采购商使用地点验收合格付清全款的原则，也由于这一条件，使得后续的合作并不愉快，供应商帝国设备公司出现了大麻烦，构成了严重违约。而万丰奥特据理力争，挽回了损失。

在万丰奥特和帝国谈判商定采购低压铸造机的合同当中，双方约定分期付款，最后一笔尾款要到用户安装调试完毕，验收合格才支付，其实，这完全符合国际惯例。但是由于帝国设备公司对中国的出口程序不熟悉，也没有在中国的办事机构，拿不到中国政府的准许进口批文，只能委托香港一家公司代理这一单业务。但是香港公司在操作这单业务的过程当中，因为试图将利润最大化，采取的是灰色入关。结果在国内运输过程当中被海关查扣，耽误了合同约定到万丰奥特的时间，而且一耽误就长达几个月。所以万丰奥特的汽车轮毂业务并没有如期开工，它也就按合同约定顺理成章地扣下了10%的货款作为违约金。

这本来是美方公司的错，但这家美国公司因为觉得技术在手，因此对万丰奥特扣下尾款的举措非常不满，单方面采取了行动。在它的低压铸造机控制程序当中，设置了含有远程控制的锁机程序。帝国设备公司的行动就是启动了远程锁机程序，把万丰奥特采购的几台低压铸造机全部锁定，不能启动，变成了中看不中用的摆设，无法正常使用。经过再三谈判，双方陷入互不相让的僵局，怎么办？万丰奥特的技术人员硬是用集体的智慧，破解了技术难关，自行编写出了控制软件，而且对设备电脑人机界面实现了汉化，变得更加好使，在万丰奥特人面前，坏事变成了好事。

正因此，万丰奥特的一批技术人员决心要自行研发低压铸造机，这个想法一经提出，陈爱莲立即拨款80万元予以大力支持，经过与国内科研院所的联合攻关，产自万丰奥特的低压铸造机还真就成功研制了出来，在万丰奥特已经与美国帝国设备公司经反复谈判而达成的每台120万元基础上，万丰奥特的自制低压机又降价一半，每台成本当时下降到60多万元。

这个过程造就了万丰奥特的智能化产业，我们将在下一章当中有机会去了解。而在这里，我们还得看万丰奥特汽车轮毂扩张的下一步。

要大规模投资汽车铝轮的产能，除了低压铸造机之外，当然还需要多种配套设备。当时在万丰奥特担任总会计师的俞林算了一笔账，发现起码需要投资一亿左右。陈爱莲在深思熟虑之后，决定再次大胆出击。

90年代末，国内的民营企业刚刚开始在设备采购上使用招标制。经过反复考虑之后的万丰奥特团队，向设备制造厂家给出了设备招标方通告。在一系列评标和议标之后，万丰奥特向设备厂家开会提出，可以在价格上让步，条件是设备厂家提供财务支持，对万丰奥特在账期内提供类似融资租赁的分期付款方式。

这就是陈爱莲要反复计算的原因。她仔细地比对了万丰奥特现有的汽车轮毂订单利润率，发现万丰奥特一旦投入生产，利润可以支持逐步偿还设备的分期付款本息。再加上万丰奥特摩轮已经形成的资产规模和利润支持，相信设备厂商会同意万丰奥特的做法。

万丰奥特以零首付的方式引进了最关键的汽车铝轮设备
（从左至右：陈爱莲、朱训明、吕永新）

果然，如万丰奥特团队所料，通过一轮轮机智的谈判，万丰奥特硬是从国际设备供应商那里获得了1亿元的信用额度，以零首付的方式引进了最关键的汽车铝轮生产设备。设备厂商之所以会同意这样的做法，就是因为万丰奥特当时率先一步在摩轮业务上实现了规模化，拥有了产业领导者的无形资产，因此万丰奥特能说到做到。而万丰奥特的成功，就在于一直以来，它也确实能说到做到。

万丰奥特第一步的汽轮规模扩张，再一次上了一个台阶。

挖潜

工业企业的利润，一方面来自于下游为顾客创造价值，另外一方面来自于规模化生产形成的挖潜。既然有了摩轮和汽轮两大业务线的市场保底，而同时又使用了较高的财务杠杆率，那么，万丰奥特接下来要向管理要利润了。

万丰奥特的第一步挖潜，来自于大宗原料铝锭的采购。

陈爱莲首先把万丰奥特的创业干将盛晓方调到了采购经理职位上。

在创业之初，盛晓方一直是在车间担当负责人，为人非常忠诚，脚踏实地、任劳任怨。一开始他觉得调任采购经理，应该是离开生产一线比较轻松的工作。不过陈爱莲一布置工作，他就知道这块骨头难啃。

陈爱莲的要求很明确，也非常高。她认为采购如果仅仅做到把原料买来，那就没有必要设采购经理这个岗位。万丰奥特设采购经理，就是要懂得经营和理顺供应链，并和供应商建立互惠双赢、长期合作的伙伴关系。这起码要做到三点：首先是采购成本要领先于公司采购规模的扩大而逐步下降；其次，采购要给公司的现金流减轻压力，在大宗物资的采购上逐步做到有账期；另外，在谈判的过程当中，要了解采购物料的制造成本，由此万丰奥特可以了解原料产品的利润，在公司考虑扩张的时候，可以优先采用内部化生产的手段。

盛晓方在这三个原则的指导下，确实是动足了脑筋。

铝制轮毂的制造，大宗原料当然是铝锭。不过，20世纪80年代国内的铝锭生产厂商都是国有大厂。当时的万丰奥特，无论就企业规模还是采购量，对于国有铝厂来说，都只是一个无足轻重的客户，几乎是不可能做到在铝锭原料价格上有议价权的。

但盛晓方做了一段时间的采购之后，很快就发现，像万丰奥特这样需求逐渐增长的铝加工企业，要取得采购上的主动权，首先是要选择适合自己的电解铝生产厂。一般做采购，总是希望合作者是大厂。与大厂合作有很多好处，总体就是一句话，做采购的不用操心，不过问题在于他们不太在意万丰奥特这样的顾客，企业也就拿不到采购谈判当中的话语权。

盛晓方给采购部门想出的办法是，尽可能地把采购渠道合理化和最优化，不能吊死在一棵树上，或被某家供应商牵着鼻子走，以此来提升在原料采购谈判当中的主动权。

因为万丰奥特所用的铝锭，在整个铝冶炼行业来说是比较普遍的一种工艺。生产厂家很多，因此盛晓方就选择一些中等规模以下的企业来做采购。一方面，万丰奥特的采购部门所涉及的生产厂家很多，这样视野会宽阔一点，有时候就可以向对方提一些特殊要求，帮助生产厂家提高。而另一方面，万丰奥特规模增长的速度非常快，在采购量迅速上升的过程当中，生产厂家会很快感到万丰奥特是一家有前途的企业，因此在采购上的谈判筹码就加大。

在把多渠道做到极致时，接替盛晓方的下一任采购负责人梁品松甚至把目光放到了90年代一度进入中国市场的俄罗斯铝材上。

那种铝锭，就品质而言是符合万丰奥特要求的。因为俄罗斯资源丰富，但这些年加工工业和汽车制造业的发展滞后于中国，铝材需求远低于中国，所以俄罗斯境内的铝价是很低的。在90年代初期，俄罗斯的出口比较混乱，因此铝锭并没有形成对中国的有序出口，只是在中俄边境上形成了一个类似于自由市场的场外市场。这种市场的缺陷是只认现金交易。

一心想为公司省钱的梁品松，怀揣着大笔的现金来到中俄边境，在他一接触到这个秩序混乱、毫无保障的黑市后，就开始后悔了。

因为没有保障，一切都只能听当地几个俄罗斯人的指挥。

铝锭运到中国境内之后，就在露天堆放着。买主只能远远地向货场瞄一眼，就得定下来买不买，那几个俄罗斯人根本不理买家，接下来就是交钱。交完钱之后，他们负责给客人装上车，采购方只能在货到站之后才能接收。

买不买呢？当时梁品松到了指定地点之后，已经觉得这不是可以长期稳定采购的。如果不买，那他不是白来一趟了吗？因此他决定，还是要买一批，至少要把自己的差旅费给赚回来，他心里明白，其实万丰奥特生产铝轮时，成形的铝锭是要重熔的，所以只要铝锭的元素牌号符合标准，就能满足公司的生产条件。

在交出了半数的货款后，梁品松的神经就绷紧了。老是在琢磨如果货不到怎么办，数量上有出入怎么办，杂质含量非常高又怎么办？所以眼看着货物被装上了车，他就赶紧赶回浙江，赶在了货物到达之前先到了新昌。一直到亲眼看着所有铝锭全部收货、计量、入库都完成了，心才放了下来。

陈爱莲带队开拓日本市场、考察日本设备（左起：俞开红、吕永新、陈爱莲、俞素兰、盛晓方、张惠成）

这批货并没有出差错。不过，梁品松却再也不敢采购第二批俄罗斯铝材了。因为那实在是过于冒险了。

采购俄罗斯铝锭，只是以盛晓方、梁品松为主的万丰奥特采购部门在原材料渠道来源多样化上的一个极端尝试。除此之外，多样化采购铝材，使得万丰奥特在与上游企业采购谈判中拥有了巨大的主动权。感到了压力的上游厂家，纷纷向万丰奥特给出了一定时间的账期。

而对于当时资金不足的万丰奥特来说，每月使用数万吨的铝锭上出现这种账期，在一定程度上给自己留下了资金上巨大的腾挪空间。

万丰奥特的进一步的挖潜，依然来自于奥特采购团队对上游的进一步了解。他们发现，传统铝制品铸造，使用的是标号为A356的铝锭。原因在于这种铝锭的成分当中含有一定比例的硅、锰、稀土元素，比较适用于重力和低压铸造。

采购小组发现，当时市场上的A356牌号铝锭，与一般纯铝铝锭相比，存在一定的价差现象。这主要是因为市场上对A356铝锭的需求大，而国有铝厂没有跟上市场的需求，生产量比较小。这种不平衡的供求关系，导致了A356铝锭比纯铝铝锭的价格要高不少。

经过仔细核算，采购小组得出结论：公司完全可以把由铝厂完成的A356铝锭加工环节，纳入到万丰奥特的生产工艺当中。这是因为万丰奥特在使用铝锭进行铸造时，本身是要升温将铝锭熔融的。因此在这个环节当中，万丰奥特自行组织在纯铝铝锭中加入硅、镁、稀土元素，就可以得到适合铸造环节加工的铝锭。

这种技术改革，从根本上就是把铝厂的加工环节省却了一步，大量节约了成本。

万丰奥特的这种挖潜，从根本上使得这家年轻的企业有了更强的市场适应能力，可以适应更多下游主机厂的要求。

并购山东都瑞

如果说1999年万丰奥特为了摩轮业务并购上海二守合金，是它对中外合资企业第一次进行扩张并购的话。那么2001年万丰奥特为了汽轮业务再次并购山东铝业和韩国都瑞集团在山东威海合资设立的山东都瑞轮毂有限公司，则是亚洲金融危机给万丰奥特送来的又一次重要机会。

都瑞集团是韩国在亚洲金融风暴来袭之后受到了不少影响的一家大企业。

在 1997 年之前，它是韩国的第一大轮毂生产企业，在全球知名度也很高。都瑞集团的社长名叫金乙泰，是韩国汽配产业的知名人物。在韩国，都瑞集团有三个生产基地，它在中国无锡和沈阳分别也投资了合资合作项目，山东都瑞轮毂有限公司集团是金乙泰引以为荣的样板生产线，陈爱莲正是在寻访全球优秀同行的时候，认识了都瑞集团的社长金乙泰。

都瑞集团的兴起，是韩国经济在 20 世纪 80 年代成为"亚洲四小龙"之一的真正写照。如果说 1998 年万丰奥特承办 ISO 8644 标准修订会议是中国经济崛起的例子的话，那么，日本和韩国的汽车业其实兴起得更早。早在 70 年代晚期，日韩系汽车以"精益制造"，以及节能省油的小车型，杀进了原本汽车业极为发达的美国市场，导致美国三大汽车公司陷入危机。而沿着经济实用的车型标志，在 80 年代后期，日韩两国的汽车更是在全球都成为新一代汽车的后起之秀。

因此，当陈爱莲带领团队在全球走访的时候，都瑞集团成为她一个重要的关注对象。而都瑞集团社长金乙泰，此时也正领导着都瑞集团处于全面扩张时期。金乙泰是具有全球眼光的，他在全球战略布局当中，把重点放在了中国，分别在东北的沈阳、沿海的山东威海和华东的无锡，布下了三家工厂。

这三家工厂，其实都是有战略意图的。以山东威海的山东都瑞轮毂有限公司为例，当时都瑞集团在这里设点，一方面是韩国的大宇汽车公司准备在山东投资建厂，而它是都瑞集团长期的合作伙伴，所以都瑞集团在威海设厂，就有了基本订单。另一方面，都瑞集团在设厂的资本结构设置里，邀请中国铝业股份有限公司（以下简称中铝）山东分公司（原山东铝业公司）入股 45%，这样就寻求到了原料上的优势。另外，90 年代，山东的汽车工业开始进入发展阶段，所以都瑞集团的布局，颇见功力。

不过，由于韩国特有的政商关系紧密的特点，韩国汽车企业在海外扩张采取的是赶超战略。由于政商关系密切，当时韩国的大量汽车企业在亚洲金融危机之前，纷纷利用大额银行贷款，采取非常高的杠杆率来加速自己在全球设厂的动作，这在经济高速发展的时候，不会有什么大的问题。但是，当暴风骤雨般的亚洲金融危机来袭之时，400%的资产负债率，就成了套在金乙泰脖子上的绞索。

韩国的经济腾飞，是全球产业向亚洲转移的产物，这就意味着韩国的政商两界对经济收缩都没有深刻的认识。因此1997年爆发亚洲金融危机之时，韩国大批企业同时受到海外市场不振，以及银行对未来的预期下降开始紧缩放贷的压力，相当一批企业陷于倒闭状态。而其中，都瑞集团的长期合作者，大宇汽车公司就是首当其冲的一家大型汽车生产企业。2000年，大宇汽车公司受亚洲金融危机的影响而被迫倒闭。

汽车业是个分工细密、协作程度很高的行业。在采取高杠杆率的发展速度之下，则更是如此，大宇汽车公司的倒闭，极大地缩减了它的主要配套厂商都瑞集团的订单来源。雄心勃勃的都瑞集团也因此受到巨大现金压力，在大宇汽车公司倒闭之后，尽力扩张的都瑞集团不得不收缩资产，以求减轻现金压力。它旗下在中国投资的沈阳都瑞轮毂有限公司、山东都瑞轮毂有限公司等，都出现了难以为继的局面。

山东都瑞轮毂有限公司总投资2.5亿人民币，注册资本1000万美元，其中韩国都瑞集团和山东铝业公司都以现汇出资450万美元，韩国都瑞集团以技术和市场品牌作价100万美元，符合中国中外合资企业相关法规，但山东都瑞轮毂有限公司真正的资本金到位只有900万美元，按当时的汇率估算，也不过7 000多万元人民币，不足以支撑工厂建设总投资，缺口资金如何解决成了一个大难题。当时，通过融资租赁方式由山东铝业公司为担保方解决了价值750万美元（相当于6 000多万元人民币）的进口设备款，而剩下的1亿多元人民币资金缺口，除500万美元（相当于4 000多万元人民币）系向银行借款以外，其余就是项目施工单位的填付资金了。

可以说，山东都瑞项目建成之日，就是它难以化解支付危机之时。韩国大宇汽车公司的社长因躲避债务流亡海外，韩国都瑞集团的金乙泰也因破产危机，受到韩国政府的监管，山东都瑞轮毂有限公司一下子从香饽饽沦落到臭豆腐，债权人忧心忡忡，赶紧向威海法院提交了破产申请，山东都瑞轮毂有限公司被威海法院受理，并依法公告和组织了公开拍卖。当时亚洲金融危机的余波也席卷了中国，现金为王，过冬保命是多数企业的第一选择，有谁还有能力和兴趣到威海接盘？当然，也的确有人想摘这个桃子，这是位于昆山的一家老牌台资企业，但是他们的出价与拍卖的底价差距甚远，威海法院第一次公开拍卖惨遭流拍。

山东都瑞轮毂有限公司总经理早就听闻万丰奥特在市场当中的品牌影响力以及在同行业中的地位，于是专程带领团队从威海赶到新昌，邀请陈爱莲去救活这家企业，至于转让的价格可以谈。在陈爱莲看来，这次收购机会非常好，但在2001年，万丰奥特能不能一口吞下当时都瑞集团在山东投资的轮毂厂，是一次很大的挑战。

要不要拿下山东都瑞轮毂有限公司的资产？拿下它，万丰奥特就能迅速超过国内多数同行，在规模上成为行业领跑者。但对于万丰奥特来说，吞下山东都瑞轮毂有限公司，障碍在于它规模实在太大了，仅仅账面资产就超过2.5亿元。更重要的是，当时国内企业界刚刚度过亚洲金融危机，对中国国内的汽车业发展的市场规模到底有多大，看法多种多样。吞下这笔资产，未来能有那么多的汽车主机厂可供配套吗？

陈爱莲马上带领夏越璋、吕国庆、吕永新4人去实地考察洽谈。刚到威海的那个晚上，陈爱莲做了一个梦，梦见前面一方稻田，一半已经枯萎了，而另一半则绿油油的，很是喜人。第二天吃早餐时，她把这个梦境跟团队一讲，大家都认为这是个吉祥之梦，那绿油油的半边稻田，不正寓意着万丰奥特收购山东都瑞轮毂有限公司以后将迎来勃勃生机吗？

万丰奥特团队到现场考察下来的结果，是喜忧参半。喜的是都瑞集团在威海投资的工厂，其格局相当不错。山东都瑞轮毂有限公司不仅有很好的地址，是一家全新的工厂，厂房、设备都是新的，而且还为未来的发展留下了很大的余地。

但问题在于，这家厂的产品没有市场，虽然有30多人去韩国培训过，但远没有掌握铝车轮的核心技术。而且，韩方原来的派驻人员带走了全部技术资料和工艺文件，扬言不把他们请回来，谁都没法把生产线运转起来。

当然，这些恰恰是万丰奥特的强项。万丰奥特能拿下山东都瑞轮毂有限公司，那就是如虎添翼，如鱼得水。所以，万丰奥特团队当场就一致认为要把这家厂拿下来。

但陈爱莲要求夏越璋团队必须在4 000万元之内拿下这个投资两个多亿元的资产。只有把价格控制在这个投资范围内，万丰奥特并购都瑞轮毂有限公司，才能避开未来市场波动的风险，立于不败的地位。因为在这个投资范围之内，万丰奥特的这家新厂就没有太大的财务压力，只要开工，就有盈利。

同时，陈爱莲认为，对于都瑞集团和山东铝业公司来说，这项投资已经失败，没有办法收回了。因为山东铝业公司是被都瑞集团拉进这个合资案当中的，鉴于国有资产保值增值的要求，如果这家企业进入了拍卖程序，那么它可收回的资产也非常少。所以这次并购谈判并没有多少障碍。

夏越璋下定决心，一定不辱使命，要把这个并购项目做好。他也很快找到了解开并购的钥匙——让山东铝业公司和威海政府明白，万丰奥特是最为合适的并购对象。万丰奥特可以通过山东都瑞轮毂有限公司的重组，使山东铝业作为担保方，把通过融资租赁获取的750万美元进口设备以其名义重新作为资产投入，保留了山东铝业的股份。由万丰奥特接盘拍卖资产（重置评估价为12 500万元人民币），获得除融资租赁资产以外的全部厂房、土地、设备、配套设施的处置权，与山东铝业重新向工商管理机关注册登记设立威海万丰奥特奥威汽轮有限公司，盘活有效存量资产，使这家企业重新运转起来。由此，这个合资案当中的山东铝业公司就可以减少国有资产的损失，开创一个万丰奥特、山东铝业公司、威海当地政府三方多赢的新局面。

为什么说万丰奥特是这笔资产最合适的收购者？万丰奥特团队拿出的理

由合情合理，都瑞集团在威海的投资，都是用于轮毂制造的专业设备。因此只有专业厂家来接手，才有可能将这笔资产正常地运营起来。而只有资产得到正常的运作，山东铝业作为投资者才能得到投资的回报，地方政府才能有税收。因此如果将合资企业的资产拆零拍卖，那样地方政府当然可以收回土地，都瑞集团的合资方也能收回部分投资，但这都是一次性的收回。远比不上经营回报和税收的细水长流。而为什么万丰奥特是这笔资产最合适的运营者呢？因为万丰奥特当时已经在轮毂制造领域建立了竞争优势，配套的摩托车制造企业和汽车制造企业都在不断地增加，正需要不断扩充产能。

并购都瑞，成立威海万丰

　　经过十上山东的反复洽谈，夏越璋代表万丰奥特提出的这个方案，得到了威海当地各方的支持。2001 年 7 月，万丰奥特一举收购了威海法院拍卖的山东都瑞轮毂有限公司的全部资产，山东都瑞轮毂有限公司更名为威海万丰奥威汽轮有限公司。万丰奥特从新昌总部先后分 6 批派出了 108 名将士，其中包括了生产管理、技术研发、市场营销、后勤保障等骨干人员，让这家公司重新开始运转。后来威海万丰奥威汽轮有限公司在万丰奥特的经营下，多次进行了扩建和技术改造，成为业内效益最好的公司，很多年份里，利润分配都达到股权年收益率 100%，在制造业中创造了令人难以置信的奇迹，当然这是后话。

第三个支点：跨入主流

在万丰奥特完成对都瑞集团威海工厂的并购之后，由于这家新企业对浙江万丰奥威汽轮股份有限公司（以下简称万丰奥威）[①]的重要性，一直执掌着万丰奥威汽轮技术和质量工作的雷铭君和蒋性芳两位工程师，被陈爱莲派上了前线。而在万丰奥威汽轮的新昌生产基地，朱训明开始出任汽轮业务的总经理，张锡康出任摩轮业务的总经理。

此时，国内的汽车主机市场已经风云再起，版图突变。

进入 21 世纪之后，由于中国经济高速发展势头一再持续，对汽车业来说，最为关键的一个指标——人均GDP 3 000 美元，此时已经临近。到 2004年，国内的东南沿海地区大部分城市都已经突破这一水平。

人均GDP 3 000 美元这一指标对汽车业之所以重要，是因为一旦国内经济突破这一水平，汽车将进入普及阶段，此时消费者大量购买汽车的需求，将突破政府的政策约束，整个国家汽车业将迈入繁荣期。

当时国内市场的总走向，没有脱离这个大势。

推动这个走向的，有两股力量。一方面，由于中国加入世界贸易组织（WTO）后，国外汽车制造大厂与国内企业的合作大门已经全面打开，因此国外资本与地方政府合作，纷纷投资汽车制造。而另一方面，看到了汽车庞大而快速上升的市场需求，一大批有实力的民营企业也开始投资汽车制造业。

---

① 浙江万丰奥威汽轮股份有限公司系万丰奥特控股集团联合中国汽车技术研究中心等发起设立的股份制公司，拥有浙江新昌、宁波北仑、山东威海三个生产基地，是国际上优秀的汽车铝合金车轮专业供应商。——编者注

这一时期，新建的汽车企业的核心产品都是家用轿车。

这打破了传统国内汽车业"三大"、"三小"汽车厂形成总体供应的格局。随之而来的是中央政府开始因势利导，逐步放开汽车生产管理。最为典型的就是在 2002 年工业与信息化部发布的《汽车生产目录》当中，一直想进入轿车生产领域的国内民营汽车制造公司吉利突然榜上有名了。

万丰奥特团队看到这种情况，非常敏感地意识到，推动万丰奥威汽轮向主流市场转进的时机，应该已经到来了。从 2003 年起，在朱训明、叶驯彪等管理团队的努力下，万丰奥威汽轮就着力推进向后来成为国内汽车主流的轿车工业配套前行。

不过，想要进入到为主流汽车厂的配套序列当中，并不是一件容易的事情，大型汽车制造厂的供应商管理有着一个严格的秩序排列。像万丰奥特这样的零部件企业要进入这个序列，主机厂首先要对其产品进行严格的试验，而后还要在供应商与主机厂之间建立共有的设计和技术平台。一家大型主机厂的流程做下来，通常都要一两年时间。由于万丰奥威汽轮在售后市场和微车市场已经轻车熟路，而现在却要推动整个企业向这个方向转型，并不是那么容易。

对于这个门槛，万丰奥特团队认为一定要迈过去。此时，在摩托车轮毂业务上，万丰奥特已成为顶尖级公司，大大激励了整个管理层，使得这个团队并不觉得汽轮业务"有利润"的现状是令人满意的。他们已经明白，一家企业真正令人满意的状态，是被社会广泛认同而且称道，作为一家汽车业配套的厂商，那就必须要与最优秀的厂商形成战略合作伙伴关系。

到 2005 年，万丰奥威汽轮进军世界主流汽车厂商的成果开始出现：这一年的 4 月，美国福特汽车公司的考评组到达万丰奥威，完成供应商考察项目；7 月，通用汽车的项目组到达万丰奥威，完成供应商考评；紧接着在 10 月，万丰奥威开始配套通用的豪华车庞蒂亚克；同一月份，上海大众公司完成对浙江万丰奥威的考评；年底，法国 PSA 集团完成对威海万丰奥威汽轮有限公司的考察，并将其纳入了自己的供应商体系；2006 年 4 月，万丰奥威进入了德国奥迪公司的供应商序列……

从这一连串的动作，我们不难看出，万丰奥威的管理层为这一转型选择的路径是非常精心的。万丰奥威并没有直接从国内主流的汽车制造厂入手，而是转了一个大弯，与跨国汽车制造公司的总部对接，并开始进入国内主流市场。

这当中，透露出了万丰奥特管理层对于整个汽车产业的理解，我们已经知道，全球汽车业是一个庞大的体系。作为一家汽车配套企业，万丰奥威直接进入全球体系，至少有几个好处：首先是提高了万丰奥特的开放性，避免单个市场的起伏影响业绩；另外，与这些大公司的合作，有力地推动了万丰奥威自身能力的建设。

由于国内汽车业版图上，与国外大型汽车公司合资是主流。所以，已经与国外汽车公司总部形成了配套关系，同时自身能力又得到了很大提高的万丰奥威，进入国内汽车主机厂配件供应体系就显得相当自然。

威海万丰转型记

万丰奥威汽轮向主流市场的转型推进，在新昌大本营进行得十分顺利。但在完成并购同时开始运营的威海万丰奥威汽轮有限公司（以下简称威海万丰）公司，就受到了一定的阻力。

万丰奥特并购了山东都瑞轮毂有限公司之后，在威海的汽轮业务主要以给当时销量相当大的各类微型车配套为主。在 2001 年之后，经过以俞素兰总经理为首的经营团队一年半时间的努力，业务一度非常红火，使得威海万丰的股东——山东铝业公司，以及威海万丰所在地——山东威海高新区政府的领导们非常满意。

业绩上出色的表现，是因为威海万丰拥有优秀的企业文化。2002 年，威海万丰的副总经理王岳军在 8 月 26 日为新品开发连夜试产，27 日早晨又准时上班，陪同当时来检查的高新区环保局领导视察环保技术工程的准备工作。由于王岳军长时间工作，过于疲劳，在上房顶察看环保设施时不幸失足，经抢救无效而献出了年仅 34 岁的生命。

王岳军以自己的宝贵生命塑造了威海万丰文化的不朽灵魂。在悲痛之余，万丰奥特发出了"向杰出青年干部王岳军学习"的口号，肯定其在威海万丰开创时期做出的突出贡献。

不过，一家企业在一个市场方向上挖掘得越深入，常常意味着转型起来就越困难。威海万丰正是在已有业务上取得了巨大进展，所以要向当时看起来还只是一个可能性的轿车轮毂市场转型，显得比较滞后，导致刚投资建立的 60 万件二期工程无法达产。2003 年年底威海万丰走到了历史的最低谷，面临可持续发展的严峻考验。

此时，威海万丰董事会调用了从万丰奥特内部成长起来的另一个重要经理人梁赛南，让这个年轻女将来推动威海万丰的转型。2004 年年初，梁赛南走马上任，接替俞素兰出任威海万丰的总经理。

万丰奥特对梁赛南的培养，由来已久。

2001 年 9 月 12 日，在上海华亭宾馆参加一个政府培训项目的梁赛南因为临上飞机了，所以给陈爱莲打了一个电话汇报自己的行程。

正常培训过程中的梁赛南打来这个电话，其实是正常的一个举动。不过就算在电话里，她也听得出陈爱莲焦急的声音。因为梁赛南参加的是一个封闭培训项目，因此她有很长时间没有与公司联系了。梁赛南不知道，她以为不联系代表她是正常的。可是得不到她消息的陈爱莲，早已经急得团团转了。

因为梁赛南参与的培训项目，是政府发起的高级人才海外培训项目。梁赛南在国内培训结束后，要到美国去开始第二阶段的学习。

当时陈爱莲并不知道梁赛南处于什么状态，是否已经到达了美国。前一天晚上，她看到了美国受袭的新闻报道，第一个念头想到的就是可能已经去了美国的梁赛南。马上给梁赛南打电话，可是因为封闭培训，所以没联系上。因此直到梁赛南主动向公司汇报自己要去美国的第二天上午，陈爱莲已经足足急了大半天了。

接到了梁赛南的电话，陈爱莲还是很高兴的。她对梁赛南说，第一是别怕，正常地完成这次培训是最重要的；第二是每周要给公司来个电话报平安。另外，陈爱莲告诉梁赛南，她已经给梁赛南的账户里打入了足够的美元，让她在美国培训的时候，别太抠着花钱，"该花的地方要挥金如土，不该花的地方要一分不舍"。

威海万丰经营管理团队（前排左六为梁赛南）

万丰奥特的众多经理人当中，梁赛南在起点上，几乎是非常不起眼的。因为她进入万丰奥特时只是个中专毕业生。1996年她到万丰奥特，其实就是看到了报纸上的一则招聘启事，所以来应聘总经理办公室的文员工作。而且进入万丰奥特之后，按公司的规定，所有管理岗位的员工都要到第一线实习，所以她在完成本职工作之余还要到检包车间顶岗。

　　梁赛南做了文员之后，给陈爱莲的第一印象并不优秀。办公室当时急需的，是一个能在内务上全面精通的人。所以梁赛南一到岗，陈爱莲就问她，会打字吗？她说不会。接着问她，懂档案管理吗？她也说不会。陈爱莲对这个新文员，多少有点皱眉头。

　　一看到董事长皱眉头，梁赛南心里其实已经非常着急了。除了加强业务学习之外，梁赛南决心要表现得比别人更好一点。她的办法是，晚上下了班，就在城里学要用的各种技能，除此之外，她决定每天要到得更早一点。

　　每天早上 7 点半，梁赛南第一个就到了办公室。当时的办公室是一个大房间，员工加起来有 20 多人，因此就有 20 多张桌子。她一张一张地擦过去，到了 8 点半所有人都到了的时候，这 20 多张桌子，梁赛南就全擦过一遍了。

　　年轻的文员这么干，多少让陈爱莲觉得有点意外。一开始，她还觉得可能是因为梁赛南想留在她的办公室里，才这么干的。心里想，公司并不需要一个擦桌子的年轻人。但是她很快就发现，工作当中需要的那些技能，梁赛南也很快就熟练起来了。

　　而掌握了所有技能之后，梁赛南并没有因此不擦桌子了，她还是像以前一样，每天都把大办公室里的桌子全部擦一遍。这使得陈爱莲觉得，这个年轻人是个勤奋的人。

　　所以 6 年之后的 2001 年，有一天，梁赛南上班之后就被陈爱莲叫到了办公室里，送了她一份很大的礼物。

　　当时万丰奥特是浙江省重点扶植企业，因此每年企业可以选择一名高级管理者，参加政府联系的海外人才培养项目。这一年，陈爱莲让梁赛南去参加的是美国一所大学的工商管理硕士（MBA）培训。为了让梁赛南够得上这个培养项目的门槛，还给她上报了一个"部长"的职务。虽然政府要求企业派出高级管理者参加培训，但万丰奥特把这个范围扩展了一些，扩展到已经确定要培养的人才身上。

　　2001 年年底，结束了培训的梁赛南回到了公司。此时，万丰奥特已经开始了又一轮的扩张，决定要试水汽车制造业，并在浦东这个中国改革开放的前沿阵地买了一幢写字楼。陈爱莲让梁赛南去主管这幢楼的装修工程。此时梁赛南已经结婚并怀上了孩子，但是她却毫不退缩地答应了下来。她在上海租了间房子。在怀孕的七八个月里，一直主管着办公楼的装修工程，一直到她临产之前，才终于把装修工程做完。

前来检查装修工作的陈爱莲看完之后很感动，她能看出来整个项目梁赛南是精打细算过的，而且装修的风格也非常有特色、有品位，认为梁赛南是在万丰奥特内部成长出来的人才，要更多地培养她。

休完产假，梁赛南被调回新昌，迎接她的是更大的挑战，继续负责新昌总部办公大楼的装修工程。此次装修结束后，她又被派到摩轮生产线上，去全面地了解生产一线的工作。经过了这样反复的考验之后，万丰奥特开始重用梁赛南，派她出任上海二守合金公司的总经理，果然，短短一年时间，梁赛南就不负众望，带领李林君等人组成的团队，经营业绩远超前面四任总经理。

在出任上海万丰奥特铝业公司总经理和之后数个重要经理人职位的过程中，梁赛南对自己的长处和短处有着清醒的认知。这位年轻的女将知道，自己的长项是勤奋，善于与人沟通，能很快地赢得他人的信任；而弱项是她不太懂技术，所以每到一个职位上，她都主动承担市场开拓工作，同时以自己努力的工作来赢得团队中技术人员的信任。

这使得她几乎在每个职位上的业绩都很出色，正如陈爱莲所说的那样，民营企业的最大的强项，就是看准市场的动向，把核心产品的市场做大，去取得与各方面的共赢。梁赛南带领团队取得出色的业绩，也使她得到了万丰奥特高层更多的信任，因此在推动威海万丰的转型时，很自然地想到了她。

站在整个行业的高度上，2004年，威海万丰不向轿车市场转型，公司的业绩必将萎缩。因为轿车占据大众随市场主流的过程，就是这个汽车产品进一步挤压微车市场的过程。当时的国内人均GDP已经向汽车普及的另一个关键转折点——人均GDP 6 000美元迈进，而此时，汽车市场当中，轿车已经要开始淘汰微车了。

这个景象，事后我们可以看得很清楚。在微车最兴盛的时候，很多农村的营运车辆都是微车，甚至相当一部分北方城市的出租车市场也被微车占据。典型的城市如北京，在 21 世纪的头几年当中，微型面包的士车（简称面的）占据了很大一部分市场，受到工薪阶层的欢迎。而以 2004 年为拐点，由于轿车普遍降价，加上政府开始对汽车的尾气排放进行控制，微车很快就从北京消失了。

这样的动向，早在 2003 年已经有表现，不过万丰奥特派出到威海万丰的高管团队，更多专注于生产管理，而对于市场的变化，显然关心得不够。因此，虽然陈爱莲非常赞赏这支团队的工作精神，但还是认为一定要派梁赛南出任新的总经理，把威海万丰的市场方向扭转过来。

要让威海万丰顺利转型，关键在于梁赛南要带领团队在转型的过程当中迅速地做出业绩，使得威海万丰的政府管理部门、股东、管理层和员工满意，只有这样，威海万丰的转型，才能顺利地进行。在梁赛南赴任前，陈爱莲叮嘱她说，威海万丰要力挽狂澜，关键是要与五个大型的轿车生产厂建立合作关系，让它们成为威海万丰的忠实顾客。

这转变，不仅是威海万丰在做，新昌的万丰奥特汽轮生产部门也在做。在家用轿车开始流行的浪潮里，万丰奥特下定决心要把公司的主要市场放到国内来，下定决心要收缩原来万丰奥威的主要客户——美国的售后市场，使它成为辅助市场。

正是因为两头都在做转型，所以梁赛南显然得自谋出路，因为新昌总部此时已经很难再像刚刚并购威海万丰一样，把拿下来的订单转移给它一部分了。

刚一上任，梁赛南就对管理团队许下承诺："给我半年时间，威海万丰的业务，一定会更上一层楼的。"她带领团队开始猛跑市场，往往一出去就是半个月，白天谈业务，晚上赶大巴。有时候往往就跑到半夜十二点多，她就坐在酒店大堂等，因为很多酒店凌晨一点钟以后入住就算当天的住宿费。当时的梁赛南一点都不担忧市场会怎么样，她常常跟团队讲，威海万丰的产品有这么好的品牌优势，当前只是营销模式和客户沟通上还欠火候，只要把营销团队建设抓起来了，威海万丰的明天肯定会很灿烂。

梁赛南的努力方向是正确的，但要收到成效，却需要时间。

不仅是梁赛南领导下的威海万丰，万丰奥特进入汽轮制造的主流供应商行列的过程，都要比它进入摩轮复杂。因为在国内摩托车生产企业兴起之时，政府是有产业保护政策的，国外厂商要进入中国市场，必须要与国内厂家合资生产，而且当时的国有主机生产企业必须占到控股地位。

国内企业的控股地位，保证了它们在配件采购上的自主性。因此，万丰奥特在金城摩托获得了管理层的认可之后，很快就进入了供应商序列。

但是到了 21 世纪，万丰奥威要成为轿车工业的主流供应商时，情况就为之一变。当时的国内轿车工业由于规模很大，而且技术复杂度高，不仅主要采用与国外企业合资的形式，而且外资的汽车公司在合资企业当中是具有很大话语权的。为了保障汽车市场当中的消费者权益，当时主要的合资企业在选择国内配件供应方面，都采取了非常小心翼翼的推进策略。一方面，外资方要考虑他们原有供应商的利益；另一方面，对于国内供应商的产品品质要求，也提高了很多。

这是一个体系。一方面，主机厂要检验像万丰奥特这样的供应商是否有保障供应的能力；另一方面公司要送样给主机厂，产品必须通过他们的整车试验，才能进入供应商的序列。

不过，中国政府在同意轿车的生产厂家以合资方式生产汽车的同时，也有一个主导的倾向，那就是中国市场当中销售的汽车，要尽可能地采用中国企业的产品，所以政府的领导对于国有合资企业的考核当中，"国产化率"（也就是汽车主机采用国产配件的比率）始终是一个重要指标。

而在 2003 年，合资轿车的国产化在关键时刻。此时，由于国内轿车普及率骤然提高，汽车生产企业如果再对国内生产的轿车大量采用进口配件，除了在众多汽车品牌的竞争当中，价格不占优势之外，更为重要的是，配件的数量和供应速度都将成为问题。

万丰奥特正是因为对于这个形势看得非常清楚，所以才会给梁赛南团队下达转型要求，而梁赛南团队跑主机企业的市场的收效也相当之大。

有了如此勤奋的经营团队，威海万丰的转型实施得非常顺利。到 2006 年，万丰奥威整体在国际市场上转型得非常顺利，主攻国内市场主机厂的威海万丰更是得到了各大汽车制造企业的青睐。由于主机厂订单纷至沓来，威海万丰要求公司董事会再给威海工厂增加投资，进一步扩张产能来满足生产要求。到 2010 年，梁赛南担任威海万丰总经理的两届 6 年里，带领叶冬炳、杨春军、徐福孙等人组成的团队创造利税增长 28 倍，打造了行业的样板工程！

万丰奥特之道：怎样打开一个封闭的市场

汽车行业是国内开放得比较晚的市场之一。从最初中央政府规划的"三大"、"三小"汽车厂主导整个国内市场格局，到后来地方国企逐步渗透进入市场，再到像吉利这样的民营企业撞进市场准入的大门。汽车，尤其是轿车行业的发展，从封闭走向开放用了很长时间。

这对于像万丰奥特这样的民营企业并不是很有利。汽车零部件行业的劣势，在于不能直接接触到终端消费者。主机生产企业对于零部件企业的选择关乎到像万丰奥特这样的企业的生死。

而万丰奥特走的，是一条从产业边缘逐步进入主流的道路。万丰奥特一开始选择国外的售后市场和微型汽车市场，进入了产业的边缘地带。进而选择与国外的主机厂合作，带动国内主机厂选择万丰奥特，则是一条曲折的道路。

不过，万丰奥特选择这条道路，适应了国内汽车主机厂逐步从封闭走向开放的国情。尤其是在 2004 年，汽车开始在国内普及之后，因为市场竞争使得主机厂必须选择有竞争力的零部件企业，所以万丰奥特的市场道路开始越走越顺。而我们可以注意到，万丰奥特于 2005 年之后大力推动企业进入为顶尖主机厂提供配件的行列，则是万丰奥特汽车铝轮业务得到发展的关键之举。

从生产和技术的层面看，万丰奥特的汽车轮毂与摩托车轮毂之间，具有高度的相关性。在摩托车轮毂市场上居于领导地位的万丰奥特，试图进入汽车轮毂的生产，是企业相关多元化的顺理成章之举。不过，相似的产业却有不同的市场情况，是万丰奥威历史如此曲折的主要原因。

作为国内的民营企业，万丰奥特在发展历程当中另一可圈可点之处，在于陈爱莲带领着万丰奥特多次抓住时机，完成低成本的产能并购。顺应时代要求，把上海二守合金和山东都瑞轮毂有限公司这样的企业，并入万丰奥特自己的生产序列当中，实现了优势企业产能的规模化。而促成这一切的金融危机，对于万丰奥特来说，着实成为"危中之机"。

Chapter 4
The Wheel Hub War

The Start

The 22-year of business-building history of Wanfeng Auto Holding Group clearly shows Chen Ailian, the founder of the business empire, a female though, she is a broad-minded, aggressive person.

However, she's more ambitious than she actually shows.

Wanfeng Auto's motorcycle wheel hub business had been just on the right track to promising future in June 1996, and Chen Ailian went to the United States for a 10-day business visit, accompanied by Zhu Xunming, technical director of the development of motorcycle wheels project. Upon returning from US, Chen Ailian wrote a very comprehensive and detailed research report in person.

In this report she went into details, finding out the total annual demand of US car wheel hubs was about 7 million, of which about 2 million were supplied by imports; 30 percent of total vehicles produced by four key US auto manufacturers were equipped with aluminum alloy wheels, and the amount increased by 5% every year; it was estimated that about 8% iron wheels were replaced by aluminum alloy wheels when vehicles were sold by car dealers . The United States was now the country with highest levels of car ownership, where young people believed aluminum alloy wheels to their cars was a fashionable dress to them, so once a new style of aluminum alloy wheels was available in market, old ones would be replaced. Therefore, the market share was also quite considerable. During her trip in America, Chen Ailian negotiated with an auto aluminum alloy wheel dealer, Ray Andrew and two parties had reached an intent on cooperation about an exclusive sell of more than 200,000 automotive aluminum alloy wheels every year.

The trip to the United States made Chen Ailian more determined about launching the auto wheel hub project.

After coming back from America, Chen Ailian was strongly amazed by the incredibly rapid change of the world. She was especially marveled by the advanced foreign auto parts, which made her more determined to launch the auto aluminum alloy wheel projects.

In a sense, moving into the field of automotive wheels production after engaging in production of motorcycle wheels is a different direction in business expansion, as in terms of wheel manufacturing, basic technology for car wheels and motorcycle wheels are the same except the core stage of production - casting process. As a result, to Wanfeng Auto, integrating automotive wheels into its production of aluminum alloy wheels was a self-enhancement.

In 1996, Wanfeng Auto was in full and rapid expansion, which meant it hardly made both ends meet. Therefore, the development budget in the automotive wheel was quite limited. However, the company still managed to set up a research team with key members like Zhu Xunming, Yu Lin, Yu Limin, Lv Yongxin, Gu Xincan, Lou Zhenyu, etc. In a room of 10 square meters, they began to do the preparation work for the next direction of the company.

In the late 1990s the computer-aided design system was not available and technical personnel needed time to familiarize themselves with the products. During this process, their job was mechanical drawing by hand. This process is reverse engineering, in current popular term. That is, first, technicians gets familiar with the product by measuring and drawing the sample products, and then makes customized innovations based on requirements of future customers. After the new design is accepted by customers, production preparation will start. Once the sample products delivered to customers passes testing and examining, mass production will kick off.

In addition to the research team, this time, Ailian had been working on something else. With the experience of motorcycle wheel production, Chen Ailian knew exacted what Wanfeng Auto needed to reach the international level. For the automotive wheel hub project, she and the entire research team were hoping to have someone who could build a systematic overall framework of the production technology to pave the way for Wanfeng Auto, so that the automotive wheel production could reach the advanced international level from the very beginning. This is why Lei Mingjun, chief engineer of Wanfeng Auto, who is mentioned in chapter one of this book, was invited to the company

Wanfeng Auto's board of directors finally chose Lei Mingjun to supervise the technical work of automotive wheel production because they had already acquired deepened knowledge about the entire aluminum alloy wheel industry from the three-year motorcycle wheels production. With high quality standards and reaching planned production capacity, Wanfeng Auto, was in the A-list among 112 other competitors in this industry. However, automotive wheel production has higher requirements, and thus a higher starting point is a must-do. it is therefore necessary to have a chief engineer with rich and systematic experience on production.

Where to find someone like this? Chen Ailian already had an ideal candidate in her mind. At that time, two leading domestic automobile wheel production enterprises were a large state-owned enterprise in north China and a joint- venture company in the south.

The perfect candidate was Lei Mingjun, who was working as the deputy chief engineer in company in Southern China. To meet international standards as soon as possible, in the end of 1996, Wanfeng Auto offered four technical experts, including Lei Mingjun, Jiang Xingfang, an annual salary over millions to set up a research team to guarantee the technology system of car wheel production.

However, Lei Mingjun and Jiang Xingfan were not easy to be persuaded. They two took in charge of the technology system of this large wheel manufacturing company in the South China, and Lei Mingjun was the one who drew up the National Standards of Wheel Testing Method. At first, Chen Ailian went South to Guangdong to make offers to them with high salaries, but they didn't give her a positive answer. The main reason was Lei Mingjun and Jiang Xingfan were not quite sure about the future of Wanfeng Auto because this company, in their eyes, was still in the start-up stage.

However, having witnessed the international wheel manufacturing levels in America, Chen ailian knew what an excellent enterprise needed was not only top technicians, but a complete and established technology system. Lei Mingjun and Jiang Xingfang were exactly what Wanfeng Auto craved for, leaders of the technology system.

After Chen Ailian paid repeated visits to the two experts, acted like the famous romance in Chinese history "Three Visits to the Cottage" and eased their concerns about both work and life. They were moved by the sincerity of Chen Ailian and came to understand more about the good-looking, stylish but persistent women from Zhejiang. Knowing her as a person who was sympathetic, righteous and equal of her words, they finally joined her in Xinchang with all trust and started up again.

Three months after arrival of the expert team headed by Lei Mingjun and Jiang Xingfan, the automotive aluminum alloy wheels which could compete with its European counterparts were successfully developed. Meanwhile, technical personnel of Wanfeng Auto were cultivated and a group of young talents like Li Weifeng, Tong Shengkun, and Qian Zhifang came to the fore.

The young Wanfeng Auto led by Chen Ailian persisted in market expansion, for she had foreseen the future changes in the market.

"Three Visits to the Cottage" performed by Chen Ailian in order to invite Lei Mingjun (left), Jiang Xingfang (second from left) and other experts

Compared with the motorcycle industry, the auto industry has a bigger market with brighter future. Two years after entering into this industry, Chen Ailian clearly recognized that, if the rise of the motorcycle industry is a prelude of the country's economic take-off, then the rise of the automobile industry is a symbol of a country's economic boom.

The key was that the auto market began to rise. When a country's GDP per capita reaches US $ 3,000, a crucial point, it is the starting point for owning private cars.

When reaching $ 6,000, the auto industry will celebrate its golden age when a large number of families will buy their own cars.

China's GDP was 7.9 trillion in 1997, that is to say, in the terms of per capita GDP, it was around $ 750. The number seemed far below $ 3000, but given the great unbalance of development between urban and rural areas, GDP per capita in a number of cities had exceeded US $ 3000.

The difference between the transformation and the previous one was very obvious. In 1994, Chen Ailian and her team stepped into the motorcycle wheel production industry was resulted from Zhongbao's initiatives to make a transition; whereas at the end of 1996 the team marching into the automotive wheel manufacturing market was due to the fact that the team itself was to seize the opportunity to gain the competitive edge in the future.

In the wheel hub manufacturing industry, scale of production is the key to dominating market. This is the threshold for Wanfeng Auto to be a first-class company and it is only the first step toward the automotive wheel manufacturing industry.

The following preparatory work was very tough as well. The first step was the introduction of equipment. From the beginning, Wanfeng Auto aluminum alloy wheel project had set the international advanced standard as the ultimate goal, the newly-formed team decided to purchase low pressure casting machines commonly employed by those international first-class enterprises after repeated discussions.

With the profit from motorcycle wheels production, this time Wanfeng Auto could start the project slowly and patiently. Chen Ailian made equipment purchase a global bidding process which attracted suppliers from Europe, America, Japan and other areas, and had them compete against each other in equipment performance, prices and service. "When shepherds quarrel, the wolf has a winning game," Wanfeng Auto was not a wolf but it did win the best offer, best value for the price. The winner of the bidding war was an American company called Imperial Equipment. It was a veteran manufacturer of low-pressure casting machines and the supplier of many of the world's major wheel manufacturer. Even those who lost in the bidding had nothing to complain and still hoped for opportunities for future cooperation.

At the time, this American supplier was at the top of the domestic market in

China. The low-pressure casting machines it produced were the most advanced equipment in wheel hub production industry. Besides, all the leading domestic manufacturers of auto parts, wheel hubs and casting fittings were loyal customers of the low pressure casting machine equipment of this company. Thus, it was not hard to imagine who had the louder voice in pricing in Chinese market.

But what the American company did not expect was an arduous negotiation with Wanfeng Auto.

The equipment Imperial Equipment provided was of top quality, but the price was too high to be acceptable by Wanfeng. The market prices for one low pressure casting machine ranged from over $100,000 to about $200,000 or $300,000, but the same machine was priced as high as more than $300,000 by Imperial Equipment. Lv Yongxin, who was responsible for the procurement of equipment for Wanfeng Auto clearly remembered the quoted price was 2,080,000 RMB

The budget was limited. While the team determined to own equipment of world-class quality, the heavy financial burden from the outset was the least they wanted for the project. Therefore, Wanfeng Auto team decided to cut the price down under 1,500,000 RMB for the first batch of equipment for production trial run.

The differences in price were so huge that the negotiations went on toughly.

At the end of 1997, in a hotel named Baiyun Hills in Xinchang, the intense bargaining between the four people of Wanfeng Auto (Chen Ailian, Zhu Xunming, Xia Yuezhang and Lv Yongxin) and the delegations of the Imperial Equipment went through all the night.

Why did Wanfeng Auto team have the determination to keep the purchase price in an acceptable range? Because they knew very well that the cutting-edge equipment made by Imperial Equipment had little to do with its manufacturing cost. The strong position it held in Chinese market was attributed mainly to the equipment purchasing of a considerable number of domestic government invested enterprises. Imperial equipment company's staff knew clearly about the fierce competition they would be facing. In a big country like China, with the rapid growing demand for cars, it wouldn't be long before businesses started to take up the low-pressure casting machine production. When that day came, they would lose the control over this market.

At the end of one night negotiation, the Imperial Equipment team compromised. Wanfeng Auto finally acquired the purchase price for one low-pressure casting machine as it had expected. Now everything was ready. The moment Wanfeng Auto Industrial Park opened, the first patch of automobile hub production equipment was sent there and the production began. Of course, it was too dramatic to say that Wanfeng Auto had made much progress in automotive wheels industry. At the beginning, due to high prices of low-pressure casting machines, Wanfeng Auto could only afford five machines. In the local area, this was already a huge investment though. At the same time, at the early stage of production, some gravity die casting equipment was also adopted.

The Market moved by Two Fulcrums

At the start of 1998, a couple of Chinese passengers arrived at the international airport in Las Vegas, America. Instead of receiving a warm welcome, they were carefully questioned by local Customs officers who had doubts about Chinese people.

Chen Ailian came to the international auto show in Las Vegas with her team for the purpose of expanding auto wheel business. A huge barrier had arose when Wanfeng Auto started the exploration of domestic market after the long preparation phase filled of twists and turns.

Wanfeng Auto was not the only one which had foreseen the opportunity. Those who ever travelled to Western countries in the 1980s couldn't help noticing that cars were the major means of transportation in those nations. Unfortunately, all the other companies who shared the same way of thinking with Wanfeng Auto, attempting to turn the prospect into business opportunities, found them facing a huge obstacle: the Chinese auto-making industry was still under the government policy control of planned economy in the 90s.

The 1990s witnessed the surging demand for cars and many imported cars in streets. There was an agreement throughout China on developing Chinese own auto industry , but the government's guidelines of auto industry were still strongly planned-economy-oriented.

The strategy employed by the government was seeking for cooperation with foreign auto manufacturers on the basis of the framework constructed by "Big Three" (FAW, SAIC, DFAC) and three "Small Three" (BAIC, TJFAW, NAC), Such guidelines led to a quick start to production project by the large manufacturers and their foreign partners.

In this way the market was fed with products by joint ventures and those Chinese auto-makers gained satisfied profits as well. The problem was this caused the closure of market system, shutting auto parts providers like Wanfeng Auto out of the market of supplying the major auto-producers with auto part and accessories. In fact, at that time, those joint ventures had their exclusive supplying systems which operated well in the mid-1990s, denying those out of the system any business chances

The system had a far-reaching influence on the market pattern even beyond the 1990s. It was not until the advent of 21 century that the control over auto industry maintained by major car-makers monopolies was challenged. In auto parts sector, most private-operated companies which were small-scale and also unable to provide products with guaranteed quality found it hard to compete against the major suppliers for a long period of time.

Chen Ailian and her team on the international auto show in Las Vegas for business expansion

By entering the wheel hub market in the 90s, Wanfeng Auto had been taking the lead in the latest opened automobile market on either scale or quality. In the start-up stage, however, Wanfeng Auto had to overcome a lot of difficulties to survive. How could a private company like Wangfeng Auto handle the challenge of having capacity but no customers?

This is why the Wangfeng Auto team appeared on the famous auto show in Las Vegas, looking for opportunities in American market.

The achievements in the motorcycle wheel industry had encouraged the Wangfeng Auto team. Now that they had managed to get a foothold and make a significant breakthrough shortly afterwards in the motorcycle wheel market, they had strong confidence to succeed in the auto wheel market. Chen Ailian felt very touched when she saw the young team members had been busy searching for customers rather than visiting casinos and tourist sites very close by on their every visit to Las Vegas.

And Wanfeng Auto finally made it.

In the late 1990s, the production capacity of China was acknowledged by the whole world. As China is the biggest developing country on the globe, and "made-in-China" meant quality products with reasonable prices. Back at that time, China was the home of producers who usually offered products with comparatively low prices.

American auto aftermarket suppliers, therefore, were also looking for Chinese business partners. There had been a good market for auto wheels in America, as it is well known that this is a country on wheels, but it is less known that the country has been keen on car tuning. Those American customers who valued individuality and freedom tended to ask car dealers to make personalized modifications to their cars once the deal was done; one common demand was "a fashionable dress"— a set of new wheels, which made the auto wheel maker, Wanfeng Auto, increasingly popular in American market.

But an auto wheel manufacturer should be clear that what would please American auto aftermarket was not mass production, but tailor-made products. That is, after customers and suppliers made an agreement on specifications of wheels, Wanfeng Auto would get orders from a leading brand in auto wheels for OEM processing.

Orders from American aftermarket, for a large auto wheel producer, were not the best choice. The benefit was for every single wheel, profit margin was good and it was less demanding in technology compared with the orders from auto manufacturers. The downside was also obvious: size of orders. Sometimes, one order had only a couple of wheels, causing the frequent change of moulds for foundry. However, these orders were the first step for Wangfeng Auto which just set off for the long journey, helping it open the door to auto wheel industry and gave it a head start over other small competitors in the market.

It was the American market which could be called"the first fulcrum"that helped auto wheel project to survive, and the"the second fulcrum"was the super opportunity Wanfeng Auto encountered one or two years later; focus started shifting from overseas market to domestic market. In the year of 2000, the prospect of auto market was attracted private capital like a huge magnet in China.

The breakdown of monopoly of major domestic auto producers began from the auto parts market.

For years, government's idea of "Big Three" factories and "Small Three" ones as pillar producers was the mainstream guidelines. With the rapid economic development, supplies had lagged behind demands in market and the demands were far more than the cars made by state-owned auto factories, so the old market pattern was soon broken.

A range of companies flooded in, numerous of which were factories invested by local governments. Joint ventures of different kinds also stepped into the market. Some private companies seized the opportunity for market access by forming joint ventures or buying out production license.

Once the auto industry became diversified, Wanfeng Auto started to get the rewards of its vision in market: its prior experience in auto wheel production made it stay on the top of the list for main engine providers when they searched for wheel hub producers. Its production capacity was now fully utilized and certainly the project was making progress

Opportunities came in pairs. In 2000, production capacity hit a bottleneck as orders from auto factories had rocketed. One year ago, Wanfeng Auto purchased a China-Korea joint venture, Shanghai Ershou Alloy Company; it, for the first time, got benefit from low-cost expansion by acquiring an asset worth five times as much as the takeover payment. This was a good bargain and supported by banks, but the financial strength was now not strong enough for expanding wheel production capacity again.

How Wanfeng Auto managed to reach a new level through capacity expansion embodied the company personality of Wanfeng Auto and the entrepreneurship of Chen Ailian.

Casting equipment was, of course, the key to further development. Wanfeng Auto team has learnt a lot from the negotiation with Imperial Equipment, and with it's rich experience in international trade, the team not only persuaded the supplier to cut price, but had its own rights and interests fully guaranteed in contracts. The practiced team did the utmost in risk aversion in many aspects; take pay terms for instance, refusing the common payment terms like FOB, CIF, CFR, Wanfeng Auto insisted on paying off after equipment was delivered to designated location and passed quality inspection. However, it was the pay terms that caused trouble to cooperation. Imperial Equipment made a big mistake and breached the comtract. Wanfeng Auto argued on the grounds of contract terms and recovered losses successfully.

Progressive payment was accepted and written in the contract of purchasing low pressure casting machines, and the payment of balance would be made after completing the installment, test and inspection of machines, which was a practice adopted worldwide. Without full understanding of the import and export process of China and branch offices in mainland, Imperial Equipment found it impossible to get import permit issued by Chinese government. It had to commission a Hong Kong company to finish the contract. In order to obtain the maximum profit, the Hong Kong company didn't properly follow the regulations on administration of import goods, leading to the customs seizure of the equipment during transportation in China and a late delivery. Without the equipment which was supposed arrived a few months earlier, Wanfeng Auto could do nothing but missed the agreed date of production, which was used by Wanfeng as an excuse to take 10% payment for goods as penalty for breach of agreement.

It was obvious that Imperial Equipment should take the responsibility for what had happened, but as the provider of key techniques, it was very unhappy for not getting the balance payment, so it took some measures. By activating the remote lock function integrated in the low pressure casting machines control programs, Imperial Equipment turned the expensive machines into several pieces of junk which could not get started and be used. Despite rounds of negotiation, both sides reached a deadlock. Was there another way? Technicians of Wanfeng Auto worked together and cracked the control system with collective wisdom. They wrote the control program by themselves, and they even created the human-machine interface in simplified Chinese, which made the machine easier to operate. That was what Wanfeng Auto was capable of: making an unpleasant incident end up well.

After this, some technicians felt determined to produce the low pressure casting machine by themselves. Chen Ailian was very supportive of the project and as soon as hearing the idea, she offered a grant of 800,000 RMB. The technicians cooperated with domestic institutions and succeeded. Each low pressure casting machine purchased from Imperial Equipment after tough negotiation was worth 1,200,000 RMB, but the same product made by Wanfeng Auto was only half the price, 600,000 RMB.

The research and development of home-made equipment made contributions to the "intelligent industry" of Wanfen Auto, which will be discussed in the next chapter. Now, what's the next step of auto wheel production expansion plan?

Funds should be poured into a variety of supporting equipment in addition to low pressure casting machines to realize the expansion of production capacity. According to Yu Lin, who was the Chief Accountant, the estimated number was about 100 million RMB. Chen Ailian decided to gave it a try after thinking the plan over.

In the late 90s, it was new for private companies to put out equipment purchase to tenders. With careful consideration, Wanfeng Auto published the tender notice. After a series of discussion and evaluation, Wanfeng Auto held a meeting, promising the equipment suppliers with more attractive prices; in return, suppliers were supposed to offer favorable payment terms --- the installment payment of equipment leasing in credit term should be granted .

Such requirement was based on careful thoughts. By analyzing the current profit margin ratio of auto wheel production, Chen Ailian discovered that the production expansion would bring enough profit cover the principal plus interests of installments. Considering the profitability and scale of assets of motorcycle wheel business owned by Wanfeng Auto, she believed that those equipment producers would accept her proposals.

Wanfeng Auto introducing the key aluminum auto wheel production equipment with zero down payment.

Unsurprisingly, witty and tactful in rounds of negotiation, Wanfeng Auto earned a credit line of 100 million RMB from international equipment suppliers and introduced the key aluminum auto wheel production equipment with zero down payment. Since Wanfeng Auto had took the lead in scaling up motorcycle wheel production which made it a leader of this industry, Wanfen Auto was able to keep its word. The key to Wanfeng Auto's success lies in that it has always kept its promises.

Wanfeng Auto went further on a new level on auto wheel business expansion.

Tapping Potentials

One source of profits for industrial companies is the value created for the downstream customers, and the other is potential tapping on the basis of mass production. Being backed up by both the motorcycle wheels and auto wheels markets, coupled with deployment of high financial leverage ratio, Wanfeng Auto was then to improve chances of more profit by material purchase management.

The first thing to do was about the bulk orders of the raw material- aluminum ingots.

Chen Ailian appointed Sheng Xiaofang, a most valuable member of the startup team, as the procurement manager.

Sheng Xiaofang had been the director of workshops at early stage of the startup of Wanfeng Auto. He was loyal, down to earth and hard-working. He thought things would be easier since he was now away from production lines. But when Chen Ailian told him his responsibilities, he came to realize how challenging his job was.

Chen Ailian was clear about her expectations and was very demanding, because she believed what a procurement manager should do was far more than raw material purchasing , otherwise, it was not necessary to employ one. The procurement manager of Wanfeng Auto should be knowledgeable in management, be familiar with supply chains, and be able to establish a long-term relation which was mutual beneficial. There are three requirements for achieving this: first, the purchase cost was supposed to decrease faster than the increasing amount of purchase; next, trying to relieve the pressure on cash flows by gradually earning credit term for bulk commodity purchase; finally, getting to know the manufacturing cost of raw materials in negotiation so that the Wanfeng Auto would know the profit of raw material products. In this way, when the company planned an expansion later, it would give preference to producing material commodities by itself.

Following these three guidelines Sheng Xiaofang racked his brains to figure out new ideas of potential tapping.

The essential raw material for producing aluminum alloy wheels is, of course, aluminum ingots. However, the major domestic aluminum ingot producers were state-owned factories in the 1980s, to which, Wanfeng Auto was an insignificant client, in terms of the size of the company or the procurement. Consequently, it was impossible to have much bargaining power in purchase.

After engaging in procurement for a while, Sheng Xiaofang soon discovered for Wanfeng Auto, an company with an increasing demand in aluminum processing, it was necessary to choose a proper electrolytic aluminum producer if it wanted its voice to be heard in procurement. Normally, procurement directors were more willing to purchase from large factories, which had many benefits; first and foremost, in doing so, the procurement staff had little to worry about. But the problem was large producers gave little attention to clients like Wanfeng Auto, leading to its inferior position in the bargaining of procurement.

The solution Sheng Xiaofang came up with was try their utmost rationalize and optimize the sources of procurement. Without putting all the eggs in one basket and being controlled by one supplier, they could fight for more dominance in the bargaining.

The processing technology of the aluminum ingots used by Wanfeng Auto was a quite common in aluminum smelting industry, so there were many capable suppliers, among which, Sheng Xiaofang chose those under medium-sized factories. By dealing with a diversity of suppliers, Wanfeng Auto broadened their horizon and made special requirements which could help the producers to make improvement. On the other hand, Wanfeng Auto had been experiencing fast expansion; when suppliers sensed the rapid increase of purchase, they would realize the huge potential of this client which offered an edge in the negotiation of procurement.

In perfecting the diversity of procurement, Liang Pinsong, the new director of procurement sector, successor of Sheng Xiaofang, even noticed the aluminum ingots imported from Russia in the 90s.

In terms of quality, those Russian products were suitable for Wanfeng Auto. Russia was a country with abundant resources, but its processing industry and auto-making industry developed far more slowly than China, which resulted in the extremely low price due to the very low demand for aluminum material. In the 90s, Russian export was lack of efficient administration, and the aluminum export was also not well regulated , creating a unusual market like a free market along the border between China and Russia. The only defect was the only accepted payment in the market was cash only.

Being obsessed with saving money for the company, Liang Pinsong arrived at the China-Russia border carrying a huge amount of cash. He started to regret the moment he stepped into the chaotic black market with nothing guaranteed.

Thus, all he had no choice but to do as told by the Russians.

The aluminum ingots were piled up in an open area after being transported into China, the clients had to make decisions by only took a glance from a distance. The Russians cared little about clients' worries. After receiving the cash, the Russians would be responsible for loading up the goods and the buyers couldn't take a close look at the goods before reaching the designated place.

To buy or not to buy? When Liang Pinsong stood besides the loading bay, he was quite sure this was not a long term and stable source of purchase. However, if he gave up, he came all the way in vain. So he decided to purchase a batch of ingot, at least he had to earn his travel expenses. As he knew all the ingots would be remelted before being used for the wheels production, there would be no problem for production as long as the metal grades met the requirements.

Liang Pinsong became nervous after making half payment of the goods. He couldn't help keeping wondering nervously: what if the transportation went wrong? What if there were discrepancy in the volume of the ingots? What if the ingots had a too much impurity content? The second the loading of goods ended, he hurried back to Zhengjiang province and managed to reach Xinchang before the arrival of goods. He didn't feel relieved until he witnessed those aluminum ingots being received, accounted ,measured and sending into warehouses all the way.

Everything went well with those Russian aluminum ingots, but Ling Pinsong never bought Russian goods again because that was too risky.

Purchasing Russian ingots was an extreme experiment carried out by the procurement sector directed by Sheng Xiaofang and Liang Pinsong in their efforts to diversify the purchase sources. The diversity of procurement sources enable Wanfeng Auto to have more control when negotiating with upstream suppliers; therefore, those suppliers who were under great pressure offered certain periods of credit term.

Wanfeng Auto was cash-starved at that time and had a monthly demand for tens of thousands of aluminum ingots, so such credit term, long or short, contributed to tremendous opportunities for capital turnover to some extent.

Another way of potential tapping was to dig deeper and understand more about upstream enterprises. Wanfeng Auto found out A356 aluminum ingots was used for production of traditional aluminum products, for the proportion of the elements of silicon, manganese, selenium of such ingots was proper for gravity casting and low pressure casting.

The procurement team identified the difference in market prices between aluminum ingots A356 and normal pure aluminum ingots, mainly because A356 aluminum ingots had been high demand in the market whereas domestic aluminum factories who had insufficient productivity to fulfill the demands. As supply and demand remained unbalanced, A356 aluminum ingots was priced much higher.

With careful analysis and double check, the procurement team drew a conclusion that Wanfeng Auto could integrate the processing of A356 aluminum ingots which was the job of aluminum factories part into their own production line. Those purchased A356 aluminum ingots had to be melt again by high heat for casting, thus Wanfeng Auto could purchase the low-priced pure aluminum ingots and add elements of silicon, manganese, selenium in the remelting stage to obtain what required for casting.

This reform in technology was substantially cost-saving for it completely removed the processing of aluminum factories.

By taking different measurements like this for potential tapping, Wanfeng Auto, the young enterprise, fundamentally made itself more adaptable in market, having an edge to cope with requirement from more auto manufacturing companies.

Acquisition of Shandong Dooray

In 1999, Wanfeng Auto made its first expansion through the takeover of a joint venture, Shanghai Ershou, for its motorcycle wheels business. In 2001, another opportunity came up, a gift from the Asian financial crisis. Wanfeng Auto made the acquisition of Shangdong Dooray Auto Wheel Co. Ltd. (hereinafter referred to as Shandong Dooray), a joint venture built in Weihai, Shandong province, invested by Shangdong Aluminum Industry and Dooray Group of South Korea.

Dooray Group was a big South Korean enterprise badly hurt in the Asian financial crisis. Before 1997, it had been the largest wheel-maker in South Korea and enjoyed a global fame. The president of Dooray Group was Kim Er Tae, a key figure in auto part business in South Korea. Apart from three domestic production bases, Dooray Group also had joint venture projects in Wuxi and Shenyang in China. Shandong Dooray was a prototype of the production line that Kim Tae Er felt proud of. Chen Ailian got to know Mr. Kim Er Tae in her global trips to visit excellent foreign counterparts.

The rise of Dooray Group vividly mirrored the rapid growth of South Korea as one of the Four Asian Dragons in the1980s. If the conference on the Revision of ISO8644 hosted by Wanfeng Auto in 1998 reflected the rise of Chinese economy, the auto industry in Japan and South Korea had developed much earlier. Back in the late 70s, with their Lean Production system and small fuel-saving products Japanese and South Korean cars made their way into the highly developed auto market of America, getting the Big Three U. S. Automakers scratched their heads. With the small economy car models, cars produced in Japan and South Korea had been the up-and-coming stars in the world market in the late 80s.

That was why Dooray Group won special attention of Chen Ailian and her team during her trip around the world. At this time, Kim Er Tae was leading Dooray Group on its way to make worldwide expansions. With global insights, Kim Tae Er put emphasis on China in his global strategic layout by establishing three factories in Shenyang, Weihai and Wuxi, which were located in Northeast of China, a coastal city in Shandong and East China respectively.

There were strategic intents behind the three factories, of course. Take Shandong Dooray in Weihai, for example, Dooray chose Shandong because it had known that Daewoo Motors, an auto maker of South Korea, which was its long term partner also, had an investment plan in Shandong; as a result, it didn't have to worry much about receiving first orders. Besides, in its capital structure, Shandong Branch of

Aluminum Corporation of China (hereinafter referred to as CHALCO) was invited to hold 45% share, which guaranteed its advantage in raw material procurement. What's more, auto industry in Shandong started to take off in the 90s. Obviously this layout demonstrated the foresight of Dooray.

However, thanks to the particular government-business relation in South Korea, auto makers of South Korea usually employed the forging ahead strategy in their aggressive expansion overseas. Due to the close government-business relation at that time, numerous auto corporations made use of huge amount bank loans, i.e. a very high leverage ratio, to speed up the moves in factory building all over the world before the advent of financial crisis. This might not cause big trouble when economy enjoyed high growth rate, but when the Asian financial storm stroke, the 400% debt-to-asset ratio, for Kim Er Tae, became a noose around his neck then.

The economic boom of South Korea was a result of the shift of manufacturing industry towards Asia, which showed a lack of profound knowledge of economic contraction. In the wake of the financial crisis in 1997, a large number of South Korean businesses were affected by the shrinking overseas market; meanwhile, they were stressed by the credit squeeze which caused by the banks' lack of confidence in the future, contributing to many corporate bankruptcies. Daewoo Motors, a long term partner of Dooray, was one of those who had to bear the brunt of the crisis and it was forced to go bankrupt in 2000.

Auto industry involved specified division of work and highly interdependent collaborations. It was more so in terms of such high leverage ratios. The close-down of Daewoo Motors dramatically cut down orders of Dooray as its accessory manufacturer. The ambitious Dooray Group now was suffering enormous financial stresses. After the shutdown of Daewoo Motors, it had to give up the expansion plan and start reducing its assets instead in order to ease the great pressure of cash shortage. Meanwhile, two joint ventures it invested in Shenyang and Shandong also found it hard to survive.

The total investment in Shandong Dooray Limited would reach 200 million RMB and its registered capital was 10 million US dollars. Both Shandong Branch of CHALCO and Dooray Group contributed their own share of capital which was worth 4.5 million US dollars in the form of cash. Dooray also contributed its market brand and technology which was worth 1 million US dollars, which was in accordance with the relevant law and regulations concerning joint venture business in China. However, the paid-in capital were 9 million US dollars, which according to the exchange rate at the time, was only worth about 70 million RMB and was not enough to complete the factory construction. One difficult problem was how to make up the shortfall in funding. Shandong Branch of CHALCO who acted as guarantor already paid 7.5 million US dollars (about 60million RMB) for the imported equipment by financial leasing. Of the shortfall of more than 100 million RMB, 5 million US dollars (about 40 million RMB) was borrowed from banks, the rest was prepaid by the construction unit of the project.

It would be fair to say the day Shandong Dooray project was completed would be the day it had to face the payment trouble. The president of Daewoo Motors was now living in exile to avoid creditor and Kim Er Tae, meanwhile, was monitored by South Korean government for his company was at the risk of bankruptcy. Shandong Dooray suddenly became so unwelcome that creditors with deep concerns filed bankruptcy petition to local people's court of Weihai in haste. The petition was accepted by the court and it later made announcement and put it up for a public auction. Though less affected, China still suffered in the crisis. Who had the capability and interest in bidding on a bankrupted company when most businesses found cash was the king and keeping cash to survive the storm was the first option? Someone did have some interest. It was a long-established corporation of Taiwan, but the takeover bid it made was much lower than the reserve price, so Shandong Dooray remained unsold after the first auction.

The general manager of Shandong Dooray and his team traveled all the way from Weihai to Xinchang to see Chen Ailian as he had heard so much about Wanfeng Auto and known it well for its brand influence and good reputation. He begged Chen Ailian to save his company. The price of takeover was open to discussion. Chen Ailian saw it as a good chance, but in 2001, it was a great challenge for Wanfeng Auto to complete the acquisition of the joint venture in Shandong invested by Dooray Group .

To be or not to be? With the asset buyout of Shandong Dooray, Wanfeng Auto would immediately surpass the majority of domestic counterparts, and become the industry leader in terms of scale. But for Wanfeng Auto, the obstacle to the takeover was the huge scale of Dooray; it had a more than 250 million US dollars' worth of book assets. More importantly, since the domestic business community had just struggled through the Asian financial crisis, views varied on how great the market scale of China's domestic auto industry would be. If Wanfeng Auto did swallow this huge asset, would there be the high demands from the automotive manufacturer in the future?

Chen Ailian immediately went to Weihai with Zhang Xiayue , Lv Guoqing, Lv Yongxin for on-the-spot investigate and negotiation. The night of her arrival at Weihai, Chen dreamed about a huge rice field, half of which withered, while the other half was vigorously green. The next day, she shared the dream with her team over breakfast. Everyone agreed it was an auspice. Wasn't the half green rice field just a good omen of the prosperous future of Wanfeng Auto after the acquisition of Shandong Dooray?

The investigation result was mingled hope with fear. The team was happy to see that the factories Dooray invested in was quite good conditions. Shandong Dooray not only enjoyed a good location, but was a brand new factory with new workshops and equipment. In addition, it had rooms for future development.

But the problem was this factory's products were not accepted by the market. Although more than 30 employees had been trained in Korea, but it was far from mastering the key technology of aluminum wheels. Moreover, the Korean team had left with all the technical materials, and claimed that no one could not get the production line running unless they were invited to come back.

Technology was exactly the Wanfeng Auto's strength. If the acquisition was successful, Wanfeng Auto's competitive power in the market would be greatly strengthened. There and then, the team made the unanimous decision that Wanfeng should make the deal.

But Chen Ailian asked Zhang Xiayue's team to acquire that 2 billion asset at the cost of less than 40 million. Only with that price, the merger could avoid the risk caused by future market fluctuations. Because in this way, this new factory would not suffer much financial pressure. As long as it started running, the profit would be gained.

Meanwhile, Chen believed that, for Dooray Group and Shandong Branch of CHALCO, the investment had failed, and there was no way to save the sinking ship. Shandong Branch of CHALCO was invited to participate in the joint venture project by Dooray Group, and given the requirements of value preserving and increasing of state-owned assets, if the joint venture had been put up for auction, little assets could be retrieved, so this merger agreement could be reached with ease.

Zhang Xiayue was determined to accomplish this mission. He quickly found the

追梦人

key to the mergers and acquisitions — making Shandong Branch of CHALCO and Weihai government understand Wanfeng Auto was the most suitable one for the acquisition. With assets reorganization of Shandong Dooray, Shandong Branch of CHALCO, the guarantor, would retain its shares using 7.5 million US dollars'worth of imported equipment via financial leasing as an asset re-investment. Then, through auction, Wanfeng Auto obtained disposal rights of all assets (whose replacement price was 125 million RMB) including workshops, land, equipment and supporting facilities other than financial leasing assets. Finally, together with Shandong Branch of CHALCO Wanfeng Auto would register with industry and commerce administration authorities and established a new enterprise — Wanfeng Auto Aowei Auto Wheel Co. Ltd. .

Thus, by liquidizing current remnant assets the company could go back on the right track, and state assets of Shandong Branch of CHALCO would suffer less loss in this joint acquisition project, a win-for-all situation among Wanfeng Auto, Shandong Branch of CHALCO and Weihai government could be achieved.

Wanfeng Auto was the most suitable suitor because Wanfeng Auto team came up with a reasonable plan. All Dooray Group's investment in Weihai was put into the specialized equipment for wheel manufacturing. Therefore, only being taken over by professional manufacturers, these assets could be operated properly. This was the only possible choice for Shandong Branch of CHALCO, as an investor, to get the return on investment. And in turn, local governments could obtain taxes. If the joint venture's assets was auctioned detachedly, the local governments could get the land back, and Dooray group's partner was also able to recover part of the investment, but this was one-time deal which was much less lucrative than gaining continued and steady profit and tax return. In addition, Wanfeng Auto had already established a competitive advantage in wheel manufacturing industry, and the number of motorcycle and auto makers were constantly increasing, showing an urgent need for Wanfeng to expand capacity. Hence, Wanfeng Auto was the most appropriate enterprise to operate this acquisition.

Merging Shandong Dooray & founding Weihai Wanfeng

After ten rounds negotiations in Shandong, the proposal put forward by Xia Yuezhang on behalf of Wanfeng Auto gained the support from all parties in Weihai. In July, 2001, Wanfeng Auto purchased all the assets of Shangdong Dooray Ltd. at the auction held by Weihai people's court, and it was renamed Weihai Wanfeng Aowei Auto Wheel Co., Ltd. From Xinchang Wanfeng Auto headquarters, Wanfeng Auto dispatched 108 key staff in 6 groups responsible for production management, technology development, marketing, and logistics to help the company operate again. Later, under the management of Wanfeng Auto, Weihai Wanfeng Aowei Auto Wheel Co., Ltd. became the industry's most profitable company through repeated expansions and technical innovations. In many years afterwards, the rate of return on common stockholders' equity reached 100%, which was a miracle in the manufacturing industry. Of course, that was several years after the takeover.

The Third Fulcrum: Going Mainstream

Considering the significance of Shandong Dooray, two key engineers, Lei Mingjun and Jiang Xingfang, who had been in charge of the wheel technology and quality control, were sent there by Chen Ailian right after the acquisition was completed At the wheel production base in Xinchang, Zhu Xunming took the position as general manager of auto wheel business, and Zhang Xikang was appointed as the general manager of motorcycle wheel business.

At this time, the domestic automobile market was undergoing major changes.

Entering the 21st century, China experienced sustained rapid economic growth, and GDP per capita was approaching $ 3,000, which was one of the most critical indicators for auto industry. By the year of 2004, in most cities of Chinese southeast coastal area, GDP Per capita had already exceeded this level.

For auto industry the importance of the $3000 per capita GDP lied in the fact that once the domestic economy reached this level, cars would be popular across China. People's demand for owning cars would break the restraint of government's policy, and the whole automobile industry of China would flourish.

The domestic market development was consistent with this trend.

There were two forces behind this process. On the one hand, since China had joined the World Trade Organization (WTO), foreign auto giants saw the opportunities of cooperating with domestic enterprises and then started to invest in auto manufacturing with local governments. On the other hand, noticing the fast increasing demand, a large number of competent private enterprises started to engage in the investment in car-making industry as well.

During this period, family cars were the core products of new auto companies.

This broke the traditional Big-Three plus Small-Three supply-demand pattern of domestic auto manufacturing industry. In the light of the trend, the central government gradually relaxed the control over auto production. The case in point was in 2002, Geely, a domestic private auto maker which was eager to get access to car production popped up in the Automobile Production Catalogue issued by Ministry of Industry and Information Technology.

Wanfeng Auto team instantly sensed this was the right timing for Wanfeng Auto to enter the mainstream market. Since 2003, with the efforts of the management team directed by Zhu Mingjun and Ye xunbiao, Wanfeng Auto focused on becoming a major supplier of aluminum alloy wheels for domestic automobile car producers.

However, being qualified for a mainstream automobile supplier was not easy job at all. A large auto manufacturer had a strictly controlled sequence of its supplier management. To enter this sequence, an auto part enterprise like Wanfeng Auto must first receive rigorous testing on its products, and then established a mutual design and technology platform between Wanfeng Auto and OEMs; the whole process usually took one or two years. Since Wanfeng Wheel had done well in aftermarket and micro-vehicle market, it was quite difficult to carry out such a big transformation.

Wanfeng Auto team believed this was the obstacle they must overcome. Wanfeng Auto had now become a top-class in the motorcycle wheel industry, so the greatly inspired management did not consider it satisfactory that the auto wheel business was just "profitable". To them, what could be called satisfactory was becoming an enterprise widely recognized and appreciated by the society. As an auto part manufacturer, it is essential to form a strategic partnership with the best auto makers.

In 2005, Wanfeng Aowei's marching into the worldwide mainstream market saw significant achievements: In April, Ford Motor Company's evaluation group arrived at Wanfeng Aowei and finished their supplier inspection project; in July, the project team sent by GM reached to complete the evaluation work; Then in October, Wanfeng started supplying products for GM luxury model Pontiac; in the same month, Shanghai Volkswagen Company completed evaluating Zhejiang Wanfeng Aowei; at the end of this year, the French PSA Group integrated Wanfeng into their supplier system after v the investigation on Wanfeng Aowei, and; in April, 2006, Wanfeng qualified for the German Audi's suppliers sequence .

From a series of events above, it can be easily seen that the management chose the path of transformation with great care. Wanfeng Auto did not start the transformation with seeking cooperation with the mainstream domestic automobile factory directly. Without taking the conventional way, they cooperated with overseas auto manufacturers before entering the domestic market.

This revealed deep insights the management had into the entire automotive industry. The global auto industry is a huge system. As an auto parts supplier, Wanfeng Auto benefited a lot from its integration into the global system: first, it improved the openness of Wanfeng Auto and avoided fluctuation caused by domestic market only; finally, the cooperation with these big companies was a strong impetus to its own capacity Wanfeng Auto.

Establishing joint venture with major foreign auto makers was the mainstream in Chinese automobile industry. Hence, having built a cooperative relationship with foreign auto companies, and with its capacity greatly improved, it is quite natural for Wanfeng Auto to enter the domestic auto parts supply system.

The Transition of Weihai Wanfeng

Wanfeng Aowei Auto Wheel's transition was carried out smoothly at the headquarter in Xinchang. But Weihai Wanfeng Aowei Auto Wheels Co. Ltd. (hereinafter referred to as the Weihai Wanfeng) which started to operate after the acquisition came across some difficulties.

After Wanfeng Auto acquired Shandong Dooray Co. Ltd., the major business was supplying parts for various micro cars which had great demand in the market. After 2001, the business was once very successful with industrious one and half years' efforts made by the team led by General Manager Yu Sulan, which pleased the shareholder of Weihai Wanfeng — Shandong Branch of CHALCO and local government leaders of the High Tech Zone where Weihai Wanfeng is located.

The brilliant performance in business can be attributed to the excellent enterprise culture of Weihai Wanfeng. On August 26, 2002, the vice general manager Wang Yuejun stayed up late to inspect new products pilot production. The next morning, he still went to work on time and accompanied leaders from Environment Protection Bureau of High Tech Zone to inspect the preparation work for the environment protection project. When examining the environment protection facilities, he accidently fell down from the roof due to the fatigue after longtime work, and devoted his life to the company's prosperity at the age of 34.

Wang Yuejun created the immortal spirit of culture in Weihai Wanfeng with his valuable life. Being in great grief, Wanfeng Auto called on all employees to learn from Wang Yuejun — The Outstanding Young Leader — and praised highly about his incomparable contribution in the pioneering stage of the Weihai Wanfeng.

However, the more professional a company was in one specific market, the harder it would find to shift its focus of production. Due to the great progress in its motorcycle wheel production, Weihai Wanfeng lagged behind in auto wheels market which was just a market of possibility at that time. The newly built second phrase project which was supposed to produce 600,000 wheels failed to meet its designed capacity. Weihai Wanfeng's business hit the historically low in 2003 and was facing the great challenge of sustainable development.

At this critical moment, the board of Weihai Wanfeng borrowed Liang sainan, an excellent manager grown up in Wanfeng Auto, hoping the young woman could promote the market transformation. Early in 2004, she took the place of Yu Sulan as the General manager of Weihai Wanfeng.

Liang Sainan had been trained in Wanfeng Auto for long.

On September 12, 2001, Liang Sainan who was attending a government-organized training project called Chen Ailian to report her itinerary in Shanghai Huating Hotel before starting the air journey.

It was quite normal for Liang Sainan to make a phone call during the regular training. However, she could sense the anxiety through the voice of Chen Ailian.

Liang Sainan had not made contact with the company for a while because the training was behind the closed doors. She thought if she didn't contact the company, then it represented everything was fine with her. However, she didn't know how concerned Chen Ailian was for having not heard from her for so long.

The overseas training program for advanced talents Liang Sainan participated in was organized by the government. Liang Sainan was about to receive the second phrase training in US after finishing the training sessions in China.

Meanwhile, Chen didn't know where Liang Sainan was and whether she had arrived in US. The night before that day, Chen saw the news report about 911 terrorist attack and the first idea jumped up in her mind was Liang Sainan who might have just gone to America. She called Liang in no time. But she could not contact her because the training was the behind the closed doors traning. Chen had been worried for almost whole day when she got the phone call from Liang Sainan in the next morning.

The management team of Weihai Wanfeng (Liang Sainan, the sixth from the left, front row)

When Chen Ailian received the call from Liang Sainan, she was very glad and told her not to be afraid. Chen Ailian said the priority was to finish the training and the second important thing was Liang Sainan should call the company every week to make her well informed about Liang's stituation. She also said that money had been deposited into Liang Sainan's account and she didn't have to be stingy with money as long as she could make every penny count.

Liang Sainan was very unnoticeable among the managers of Wanfeng Auto at the start, because she was only a graduate of secondary school when she was employed. In 1996, seeing the want ads in newspapers, she applied for a post of clerk in the general manager's office. After she was recruited, she had to work in packaging inspection workshop besides finishing her office work, because all newly recruited management staff were required to finish internship in the front line, according to the regulations of the company.

Liang Sainan failed to make a good first impression on Chen Ailian when she started her secretary work. At that time, the office was in bad need of a person can effectively handle the internal management of the company. As soon as Liang Sainan arrived, Chen Ailian asked if she could type. The answer was no. Then Chen Ailian asked if she knew something about file management. She shook her head again. Chen frowned upon the new clerk because it seemed that Liang Sainan was not the right person for the office.

Seeing the board chairman's unpleased expression, Liang Sainan was very anxious. Consequently, she learned diligently, and determined to perform better than other staff. After work, she studied hard on skills needed in office work. And she decided to arrive at the office earlier in the morning.

Liang Sainan would arrive at the office at seven thirty every morning, always the first one to get there. More than 20 employees worked in this big office then, and there were over 20 desks in the room. When everyone else started their work at eight thirty, Liang Sainan had cleaned every desk in the office.

Chen Ailian was a little surprised about her hard work. At the beginning she thought the new clerk did so simply because she wanted to secure her job in the office. And the company didn't need a young woman who could clean desks. But she soon noticed that Liang Sainan was becoming proficient in the required skills in work in a very short time.

After Liang Sainan had been competent in her work in the office, she still persisted in cleaning all the desks in the office as usual. At this time,Chen Ailian realized Liang Sainan was a diligent young woman.

Six year later, one day, when Liang Sainan just arrived at the company she was asked to meet Chen Ailian in her office who offered Liang Sainan a great gift.

Wanfeng Auto was one of enterprises specially assisted by government in Zhejiang. Therefore, the company was entitled to choose a senior manager to participate in an oversea talent training program hosted by the government. In that year, Liang Sainan was sent to a MBA project held in an American university. Chen Ailian gave Liang Sainan title of director so she could be qualified for the program. Though the government required for the high rank management of companies to attend the training, Wanfeng Auto had offered chances to talented candidates.

When Liang Sainan returned from her training in the end of 2011, the company just commenced its new round of expansion, targeting on car-making industry and purchased an office building in Pudong which is the forefront of Chinese reform and opening up. Chen Ailian commissioned Liang Sainan to take charge of the decoration project of this new building. Although Liang Sainan was newly married and expecting a baby, she accepted this job without any hesitation. She rented an apartment in Shanghai and was in charge during the first 8 months of her pregnancy and finally finished all decoration work just before the delivery.

Chen Ailian was deeply moved after she inspected the decoration project. She knew that Liang Sainan did carefully budget for this project and the decoration style was tasteful and distinctive. Now she firmly believed Liang Sainan was a great talent who grew up in Wanfeng Auto and was qualified to bear more responsibility in the company.

When her maternity leave was over, Liang Sainan was transferred to Xinchang to rise to a bigger challenge — taking charge of decoration project of the headquarter building in Xinchang. After that, she was sent to the assembly line of motorcycle wheels to obtain a full knowledge of the front line production work. After a series of tests, Liang Sainan was put in a more important position in the company, the general manager of Shanghai Ershou Alloy company. Liang Sainan didn't let everybody down. She led the team including Li Linjun achieved much better performance than four previous managers.

Then Liang Sainan took up the position of general manager in Shanghai Wanfeng Aluminum Company and held several other important managing posts afterwards. Soon she become well aware of her strengths and weaknesses. Her strengths are diligence, excellent skills of communication and the ability of winning trust. However, she didn't know much about technology. For this reason, she actively undertook market exploring work and earned the trust from technical personnel in the team with her efforts as soon as she came to a new post.

Therefore, she did well in every position. Just as Chen Ailian once said, private enterprise's strength lies in being sensitive to the market, focusing on expanding market of knockout products and achieving win-win situation.

The outstanding performance of Liang Sainan and her team earned more trust of Wanfeng Auto's senior executives. It is not surprising for the management to regard her as the right person for the transformation of Weihai Wanfeng.

From the perspective of industry development, Wanfeng's profit was bound to shrink if it did not shift its focus to sedan market. With sedans taking the major auto market shares the market shares of micro cars suffered correspondent declining. The per capita GDP of China at the time was close to $6000, another critical turning point of car popularization. The sedans were ready to take the place of mirco car in auto industry.

Today we can see clearly that in the golden days of micro cars, many cars used in countryside were miro cars, and they even dominated the taxi market in many northern cities in China. In Beijing, the most common taxies were mini passenger vans which were very popular among wage-earners in the first several years of 21th century. But in 2004, sedans became less expensive, coupled with exhaust control advocated by the government, the micro car vanished quickly in Beijing.

This trend appeared in 2003 already, but the management team of Weihai Auto sent by Wanfeng Auto focused too much on the production management and didn't pay enough attention to the market change. As a result, though Chen Ailian spoke highly of the diligent work of the team, she insisted in appointing Liang Sainan as the new manager could turn Weihai Wanfeng into right direction of market.

The key to Weihai Wanfeng's successful transformation was that Liang Sainan and her team must make achivements very quickly to satisfy the government, shareholders, management and workers. Only in this way, could the transformation be done smoothly. Before Liang Sainan left for Weihai Wanfeng, Chen Ailian told her the only way to save the day was to establish cooperative relationship with five large car manufacturers and make them become loyal customers of Weihai Wanfeng.

Not only Weihai Wanfeng, but the auto wheel production sector in Xinchang was carrying out the transformation as well. Seeing sedan gaining popularity, Wanfeng Auto decided to shift the focus back onto the domestic market and to turn its major clients — aftermarket in US into secondary market.

For this reason, the headquarter in Xinchang could no longer share some orders with Weihai Wanfeng as it did at the start of the merger. Evidently, Lang Sainan had to stand on her own two feet.

Liang Sainan made a promise to her management team as soon as she arrived, "Give me six months, we can do better." She and her team then to devoted to the market exploration. Usually, she would travel for about half a month for business. She would negotiate with potential partner at day, and rush to catch buses at night. When she went back to hotel late at night she would always sit at the lobby instead of checking in until it was after 1 o'clock, which could save one day accommodation fee. She never worried about the market. She kept telling her team that Weihai Wanfeng had a good reputation for its products and its brand, and the problems lied in marketing mode and communication with clients. As long as the marketing team could do better, the company surely had a brilliant future.

Liang Sainan was correct about her judgements. However, it took time to see the results of the efforts.

Becoming a major supplier of auto wheels was more complicated than becoming that of motor cycle wheel, even for Wanfeng Auto, let alone for Weihai Wanfeng run by Liangsainan. This was because when domestic motorcycle producers started to thrive, they were blessed with protective policies made by the government; that is to say, foreign manufacturers had to cooperate with Chinese producers if they wanted to enter Chinese market, and Chinese companies must be the controlling shareholders in the joint ventures.

The status of controlling shareholders entitled domestic motorcycle producers the right of choosing suppliers by their own. Thus, Wanfeng Auto became one of Jincheng's suppliers shortly after gaining the acknowledgement of Jincheng Motor's management.

When it came to becoming a major supplier of the sedans industry in the 21th century, things were quite different. Due to the large scale of domestic auto industry and high complexity of technology, most domestic manufacturers had to choose the form of joint venture to cooperate with foreign producers and foreign companies had great say in decision making in the joint venture. For the sake the right and interest of consumers, the prominent joint ventures were always careful with their choices of domestic spare parts suppliers.

On the one hand, foreign partners had to consider the interest of their original suppliers. On the other hand, the quality requirements for domestic suppliers were raised dramatically. Therefore, in this system, the car makers must be sure suppliers like Wanfeng Auto had the competent capacity. Furthermore, suppliers must send some sample products for testing. They could actually get into the sequence of suppliers after the sample products passed the vehicle performance test. However, though Chinese government permitted producing sedans by means of joint ventures, it also indicated a guideline saying that the products intending for domestic market should use as many Chinese auto parts as possible. Consequently, the localization rate, namely, the ratio of home-made parts in the whole vehicle had always been a important indicator in the evaluation of state-run joint ventures.

The year of 2003 was critical for home-made sedans by joint ventures. Due to the sudden popularity of sedans in domestic market, if the car makers kept using a large number of imported parts, the prices couldn't be competitive. What's worse, both the amount and the supply speed of imported products could be troublesome in this competitive market.

That's why Wanfeng Auto ordered Liang Sainan to implement the transformation. It was very clear of the situation and Liang Sainan made remarkable achievements in expanding market.

With this hardworking management team, the transformation of Weihai Wanfeng went on very well. In 2006, Wanfeng Auto transformed successfully in

International market. Meanwhile, Weihai Wanfeng who had focused on domestic auto market was popular with major car manufacturers in China. Resulted from rapidly growing orders, Weihai Wanfeng applied to the board for the more investment in its factories to meet the need of bigger capacity. By 2010, Liang Sainan had been in the position of general manager for 2 terms, namely, 6 years in Weihai Wanfeng. She and her team which included Ye Dongbing, Yang Chunjun, Xu Fusun etc. increased the profit by 28 times and become the model of the industry.

The key to the road of Wanfeng's success: icebreaking in a locked market

Car industry was one of the latest markets which were opened up in China. Initially, the central government planned a market dominated by "Big Three" and "Small Three" manufacturers. However, local state-owned enterprises intended to compete in this field soon. Finally private enterprises e.g. Geely Auto, gained permission from the government to produce automobiles.

This market change was not good for private companies like Wanfeng. The vulnerability of auto parts industry lies in the fact that the parts producer cannot contact the terminal consumers directly. Therefore, the auto manufacturer's choice is decisive to the enterprises like Wanfeng.

The road Wanfeng Auto chose was marching from the edge to the central part of auto industry. At the beginning, Wnfeng Auto concentrated on foreign aftermarket and micro vehicle aftermarket which are secondary in the industry. Then, it determined to collaborate with domestic auto manufacturers and in turn, persuaded other domestic manufacturers chose the products of Wanfeng. This road was long and tough.

Nevertheless, this road complied with the development trend of auto industry in China. In 2004, after sedan cars became popular with Chinese people, Wanfeng strode on a road to great success, because auto manufacturers had to selec parts producers as their partners. Evidently, the key to the rapid development of Weihai Auto's car aluminum alloy wheel business is being qualified for supplying spare parts of top auto producers.

In terms of production and technology, The car wheel production is highly relevant to motorcycle wheel production. As a top motorcycle wheel producer, it is reasonable for Weihai Auto to enter the car wheel market and realize the diversification of its products. However, the different market of similar industry was the twist and turn in this tough road toward success.

As a domestic private-owned enterprise, Wanfeng Auto another worthy effort in the course of development was that under the leadership of Chen Ailian, Wanfeng Auto seized the opportunities repeatedly to complete the acquisition of new production capacity at a low-cost. Moreover, Conforming to the requirements of the times, Wanfeng Auto merged enterprises like Shanghai Ershou Alloy company and Shandong Dooray Wheel Co., Ltd. and fulfilled large scale production in competent factories. And all this can be attributed to the financial crisis. For Wanfeng Auto, indeed, it is a "bliss in the storm."

第五章

从低压机到机器人

"争气机"

2001 年 4 月的一天，万丰奥特技师陈国栋像几天来他常常做的一样，站在美国那家帝国设备公司制造的低压铸造机面前。一段时间以来，他每天都跑到这台庞然大物面前琢磨。不过这一天有点不一样的是，他感觉到有人推了他一把。

这是他的一个同事加朋友，开玩笑式地问他："你老是到这里来看这台低压铸造机，是不是想有一天把它也造出来？"

这句问话是有来历的，因为陈国栋在万丰奥特是个技术能手。他的学历不高，只有高中文凭，不过从小对于电气和机械方面有着狂热的兴趣。30 多岁的他，几乎没有落下过电气领域的每一个浪潮，从最早的组装收音机，到后来的电视机，再到工业计算机控制、计算机编程，他都有所涉及，并渐渐由入门到精通。

陈国栋的这种个人爱好，在万丰奥特得到了鼓励。万丰奥特有个技术迷的小圈子，在生产基地边上有一个地方，是陈国栋这拨技术迷们非常爱去聚会的地方，他们经常在那里交流技术的新动向。

有了这个基础，再加上万丰奥特与帝国设备公司之间关于低压铸造机的纷争，使得陈国栋有空就跑到低压铸造机面前去琢磨它的机械原理和控制程序，因此就有了这个玩笑式的动议。

陈国栋多少听出点这问话里的戏谑意思，就说："也未免就一定造不出来吧？"他观察这台铸造机确实很长时间了。觉得它的机械结构对于万丰奥特这样的机械类公司来说，并没有什么真正的困难之处，关键在于机械的整个动作由被称为"PLC（可编程逻辑控制器）"的工业单片机控制。显然设计者对于轮毂制造流程十分熟悉，每个动作的流程都恰到好处。

心里有了底，陈国栋就说了点稍稍过头的话。这个玩笑式的动议，就这样一步步地成真了。陈国栋和万丰奥特的这拨技术迷们，把这个动议汇报给当时汽车轮毂的技术负责人俞利民，这就有了公司会议决定拨款80万元试验费支持这个技术小组的事。

万丰奥特自主研发低压机五人小组
（从左至右：陈国栋、曹方永、俞利民、张水勇、赵增光）

从万丰奥特进入轮毂行业的一开始，我们就知道，这是个创新点子从来就受到很高赞誉的公司。1997年陈爱莲就提出了"科技创新是企业发展的永恒主题"的文化理念，并把这句理念刻在了公司的宣传墙上。正是因为如此，万丰奥特从来就不给技术人员和员工在创新上设置任何障碍，这个公司才会生生不息，不断开拓出新的天地。万丰奥特当然会对俞利民的这个技术小组给予有力的支持——如果突破了低压铸造机的制造"瓶颈"，万丰奥特将迎来的是一个完全全新的汽车轮毂竞争状态。

为收集资料，借鉴同行经验，俞利民、陈国栋、曹方永、张水勇、赵增光等5人团队先后考察了意大利LPM公司、美国帝国设备公司、日本富助公司及国内几家铸造设备厂。5人小组中，除了张水勇是大专学历外，其他人都是清一色的高中文凭。

通过对国外进口机技术资料的充分探讨、分析，不知修改了多少套方案，试了又试；不知画了多少张图纸，画了又撕；不知又有多少个不眠之夜，大家牺牲了所有休息时间。所有项目小组成员的脑海里除了低压铸造机，还是低压铸造机！

万丰奥特研发成功国内第一台低压铸造机，一举打破国外技术垄断，
填补了国内的技术空白

2001 年 7 月 18 日，经过 100 天时间的研发，这个技术狂热者的组合还真研发成功了国内第一台自主开发的低压铸造机。它一经面世，不仅一举打破了国外的技术垄断，填补了国内的技术空白，后来还成为国家的替代进口设备。

然而创新在万丰奥特远远还没有结束。

从传统的思维而言，一家轮毂制造企业拥有低压机的制造技术，构成了这家企业的一项竞争力。万丰奥特管理层应该对这项技术进行保密，使这项竞争力长久地留在企业里，至少也应该留得越长久越好。

不过，万丰奥特团队在铸造行业内时间久了，深知我国是铸造大国，但并不是铸造强国，铸造的工作环境差、技术落后、产品低端化等是这个行业发展的瓶颈。而低压铸造机之所以卖得贵，相当一部分原因是因为它的自动化程度高、材料利用率高、不合格品率低，还大大改善了铸造一线工人的工作条件和降低了他们的劳动强度。

这是由低压铸造机的原理决定的。从工艺上说，低压铸造机较之原来的压铸、重力铸造等生产方式，最大的差异在于它用连通管原理，把铸造环节前端工厂熔化的金属液体与铸造过程当中铸造机的成型的型腔连接了起来，而后采用差压的方式，使金属液体充满型腔。这样的工艺方式，改变了传统的需要用人工来传递高温金属液体的方式，使得铸造车间的高温作业状态大大改善。

对于这台具有核心技术的设备，公司要不要面向市场去销售？万丰奥特内部是有争议的。因为万丰奥特的低压铸造机的高性价比，较国外的设备有很大的竞争力，所以打开市场是非常容易的。不过一旦万丰奥特低压铸造机的市场打开了，同时也意味着万丰奥特的铝轮制造现有的一部分竞争力就消失了。也就是说，一些潜在的对手会被自己培育出来。

不过，陈爱莲并不认为万丰奥特的竞争力由低压铸造机构成。她的眼界更为开阔，当时她觉得从技术的角度来看，低压铸造机的市场应用远远超过了万丰奥特所从事的轮毂制造，更是涉及了众多铝制产品铸造，有着广泛的前景。如果万丰奥特因为惧怕削弱核心竞争力而排斥铸造机进入市场，那肯定是不对的。因为万丰奥特的铸造机不向市场推广，迟早也会有专业公司做出来推向市场，国产低压铸造机在轮毂甚至于金属铸造类产品当中普及，是迟早的事。

当然，更为重要的是陈爱莲认为公司的核心竞争力来自企业文化，万丰奥特有一种氛围，在其中的每一个人都努力上进，兢兢业业地做到最好，而由此，企业就能衍生出各种各样的竞争优势，这才是万丰奥特的核心竞争力。

在她的坚持下，万丰奥特低压铸造机研发成功之后，很快就开始向市场进行推广。这种开放的态度，使得万丰奥特的低压铸造机从一个技术小组对国外产品的创新突破，最后成就了一家企业——浙江万丰科技开发有限公司（以下简称万丰科技）。

低压铸造机的市场

2006年的4月18日是两年一度的中国国际铸造展开幕的时候。这一年，铸造展上第一次出现了万丰科技的身影。经过了4年多内部供应和改造的万丰低压铸造机，在这次的铸造展上终于亮相了。

铸造设备是铸造展的重点。本次展会当中，万丰科技的低压铸造机在国产馆位于一个核心位置，在公司总经理江玉华的带领下，万丰科技在参展时做了精心布置，6米高，重达20吨的万丰低压铸造机闪亮登场，力压群雄。因为这套设备的精细化程度，以及万丰奥特在铸造业内的声望，所以万丰科技的低压铸造机一经亮相，就吸引了众多围观者，硬是把国际馆当中的进口设备给比了下去。

万丰奥特低压铸造机应用现场

这是当时一位万丰科技的员工为《万丰报》记录下的现场:"4 天的展出当中,万丰科技展台人流不绝,一共接待了 100 多批次的客户,达成合作意向的有 10 多家,而更多的是铸造设备的专业厂家同行在打量我们。中国铸造协会的老理事长贾成斌、李永圣等领导和专家兴致勃勃,分别带队参观了万丰科技展台,为我们研发的低压铸造机能替代进口机器感到自豪,纷纷询问低压铸造机的客户使用情况,并表示一定会带队到万丰科技考察。"

到了 6 月,万丰科技的低压铸造机又参加了铸造设备的上海展,同样是收获颇丰。而此时离万丰奥特自行研发低压铸造机,时间已过去了 5 年。

万丰科技的低压铸造机一经面世,就得到了国内轮毂业同行的认同。21世纪之初,汽车业的市场扩张使得相当一批民营企业开始上马轮毂制造。万丰科技的低压铸造机在市场上,有两个很明显的优势:其一是它的价格要远低于国外的产品;其二,因为万丰科技是本土企业,所以万丰科技的低压铸造机不仅根据本土市场的状态在做改进,而且因为万丰奥特在轮毂制造领域已经开始取得领导者的地位,所以采购万丰科技的低压铸造机,上马轮毂制造的民营企业还可以得到很多轮毂制造领域的技术服务。

　　这种优势使得万丰科技的低压铸造机面世之后，国外的同行针对中国市场进行了降价，即使这样，最高峰时，万丰科技生产的低压铸造机占据的市场率达到55%以上。

　　而万丰奥特把低压铸造机项目孵育完成，成立单独的科技开发公司之后，成为总工程师的陈国栋，则必然开始站在这家新公司的前景上考虑问题。

　　这就使得万丰科技有了更为广阔的市场。低压铸造从某种意义上说是铸造的一种先进工艺，它的应用范围要远远比轮毂制造这一个领域广泛。在大型和复杂机械部件的成型过程当中，只要标准化程度高、符合低压铸造工艺要求，成批量生产的厂家，都有可能成为低压铸造机的潜在客户。

　　被推向市场的万丰科技其实在2006年之前就开始多样化发展。低压铸造机面对的是一个大市场。除了轮毂制造之外，如果实现了模具的变换，低压铸造机适合的铸件领域非常多。2006年之前，万丰科技就已经突破了万丰奥特的主业，转而为汽车配件当中的复杂铸件如缸盖、发动机的油泵体做上游配套；继而又突破汽车业，转向研制电力行业的复杂铸件设备。

　　万丰科技之所以在市场上表现活跃，与万丰集团内部的经营方式有很大的关系。从开始走向市场之后，万丰科技遵循整个集团一贯以来重视员工积极性的传统，在每个专业方向上试行了专业项目负责人制度，实现了专家领导下的项目小组对产品科研负责的方式来经营这家技术含量高的公司。

　　万丰科技把复杂的铸造机设备分解成机械、电气、液压、气控和保温炉等多个模块，实现价值链的梳理，分项目承包到每个由主力工程师带领的项目小组当中。由专家级的工程技术人员自由选择和匹配项目组人员，进而达到高度的工作效率，而且通过经济效益的连接，把专家的眼光，也同万丰科技的市场推广联结起来。

　　这使得万丰科技形成了两大优势：一方面，万丰科技的技术和研发力量在这种体制之下不断得到加强，形成了人才优势；另一方面，万丰奥特集团作为母体企业，它的超常规发展给万丰科技提供了源源不断的市场和一个科技公司发展最为需要的东西：需求。

下一个方向——机器人

基于对铸造领域的了解，2006年之后，万丰科技规划公司的下一步方向，应该是在条件极其艰苦的轮毂铸造车间里，逐步地应用机器人技术来实现全自动化的工作，进而把机器人技术推广到整个铸造行业当中去。

这个发展方向，显然会得到陈爱莲的支持。每年夏天，万丰奥特的铸造车间里，由于环境温度高，所以坚持生产的一线工人总会有人中暑，因此每年这个时候，也是万丰奥特各级高管到车间一线去慰问送水的时候。

陈爱莲虽然处事刚强，但内心其实非常柔软。万丰奥特的党委副书记徐志良对此印象深刻。他记得有一年，陈爱莲非常严肃地找到他，说公司的后勤工作没有跟上，为中暑员工安排的休息室太小。直到徐志良在员工餐厅附近找到一个更为宽敞的大房间，开辟成输液室，安装好空调，并让她亲自去看过，陈爱莲才放下心来。

这种高温下的作业环境，在国内的铸造行业当中十分普遍，而且除了低压铸造机之外，仍保留有大量重力铸造设备。重力铸造设备操作简单、方便，造价低廉，因此就算有低压铸造机可供采购，但在很多简单铸造领域，重力铸造设备仍然是铸造设备当中的主力。

万丰奥特针对铸造车间的高温现场想过很多办法。最有意思的一个是在车间内开辟送风系统，并在送风系统的出风端口上加注水的遮拦物，使得空气流过遮拦物时温度得到降低，从而定向地给工位上的工人降温。

这确实是一个没有办法的办法。因为铸造现场铝水的熔化温度很高，因此在这个场地上，无法使用空调降温。能给定点工位用冷风来降温，已经是最优的选择了。

而解决现场高温的根本办法，只能是通过自动化的方式，尽可能地减少，或者实现工序上的无人化。

而经过了数年的研发，到 2008 年之后，人们走进万丰奥特的铸造车间，会发现这家公司重力铸造现场的生产方式发生了重大变化。

现在，铝水熔化炉和重力铸造机之间，已经有了一个巨大的半圆形分隔区，而中间固定矗立着一台动作敏捷的工业机器人。它可以"不辞辛苦、任劳任怨"地 24 小时不间断地工作，面对着呈半圆整齐排列的 6 台重力铸造机，按程序加注熔化的合金铝水。这 6 台重力铸造机分别需一名员工看管，在重力铸造机的一个凝固铸造流程完成之后，操作铸造机的员工在铸造机边按下一个操作链，机器人在几秒钟之内飞快地完成"在熔炉当中取铝水——送铝水到重力铸造机注液口——注液"三个程序。而同样的工作，如果由人工来做，一天一夜三个班次需要 18 个身强力壮的年轻劳动力。也就是说，一台工业机器人，24 小时可以减少 15 个劳动用工。这在如今劳动力已经严重短缺的浙江，是多么有意义啊！

而在机器人完成这个过程的时候，铸造机操作员则在机器人送过来的铝水中取出少许铝水，等机器人注液完毕，铝液开始凝固之时，对重力铸造机补充注液——这是因为铝水在凝固过程中会产生体积收缩。

差不多一分钟过后，铸造机内的铝水凝固完成，铸造机顶出已经成型的铝体，一只轮毂毛坯就完成了铸造过程。

这个看似简单的过程，是国内铸造业开始走向国际水平前沿的标志，也是万丰科技的工程师们一年多时间辛苦研制出的结晶。因为机器人能定量取、注铝水，快速响应多台铸造机的要求，以及在操作过程当中每一个动作，都含有复杂的计算程序。

有了机器人参与操作，减少了操作员工与铝水的近距离接触，使得传统铸造高温的现场得到了很大改善。

而对铸造企业来说，好处在于两个方面。其一，当然是可以让高温现场员工人数减少；其二，在于机器人浇注时，关于铝液的稳定性和数量都可以控制，因此对于提高铸造环节的品质大有帮助。

万丰科技总经理吴军对浇注机器人的开发过程印象深刻。他和万丰科技的工程师们在很长时间内都困惑于铝水在重力铸造机凝固之后产生的那个收缩量，按自动化的设计要求，这个收缩量，无疑需要机器人自动补足，但这个过程很难在机器人程序当中完成。

一开始，万丰奥特在摩轮工厂里推广浇注机器人的使用，并没有受到一线员工的欢迎。因为万丰奥特车间里的每个工位都有定额考核，试用机器人工位的员工很担心试用不顺利，会耽误他们的定额完成，影响工资收入。

但是随着时间的推移，机器人设备的优势就体现出来了，由于万丰科技的技术人员在设计上考虑得很周到，因此机器人一经安装完毕所展现出来的工作环境改善和工效提高，使得工位上的工人们可以比较轻松地完成定额，因此他们很快喜欢上了机器人，进而开始帮助工程师想办法解决凝固收缩的问题。

员工们想出来的办法简单而有效。他们让工程师设计机器人取铝水时多取一些，使得机器人倒铝水时，操作员工可以从机器人的坩埚当中直接取出补缩的铝水，用人工补缩，这个方法使得困扰技术人员很久的难题轻松地迎刃而解。

进入机器人产业

如果说低压铸造机让万丰科技无意间进入工业智能化领域的话，那么到工业机器人时期的万丰科技，就开始成规模地进入这个产业了。

工业机器人作为一个产业的发展，在全球的范围内始于 20 世纪 60 年代。由于智能控制和工业计算机的普及，使机器人制造具备了技术可能性。到了七八十年代，由于西方的大规模生产工业非常普及，工业机器人已经开始应用于部分危险工位，最早的应用就出现在汽车制造领域。汽车制造生产流水线当中的焊接等工位，由于工作简单重复，劳动强度大，很早就使用了焊接机器人。由此相继形成了一批具有影响力的、著名的工业机器人公司，其中包括：瑞典的ABB，日本的发那科（FANUC）、安川电机（YASKAWA），德国的库卡(KUKA)，美国的Adept Technology，意大利的柯马（COMAU），这些公司已经成为其所在国家的支柱企业。

　　与世界范围内技术发展相适应，中国出现机器人技术大约在80年代。当时政府启动实施了"高技术研究发展计划（863计划）"，对机器人技术进行

万丰奥特自主研发的工业智能机器人下线

攻关，当时的机械工业部牵头组织了点焊、弧焊、喷漆、搬运、堆垛等型号的工业机器人攻关，其他部委也积极立项支持，形成了中国工业机器人研发的第一次高潮。到90年代，我国相继开发了7种工业机器人系列产品，102种特种机器人，实施了100余项机器人应用工程。到90年代末期，我国建立了9个机器人产业化基地和7个科研基地，包括沈阳自动化研究所的新松机器人公司、哈尔滨工业大学的博实自动化设备有限公司、北京机械工业自动化研究所机器人开发中心等。

不过技术发展只是提供了机器人应用的可能性。真正实现机器人应用的，还是像万丰奥特这样的大规模制造企业。在像重力铸造这样的工位已经成为必须被自动化替代的情况下，大规模制造带来了工位需求，而机器人能明显地提高工业效率，就使得机器人有了被工业企业使用的可能。

而更为重要的是机器人应用当中的细节问题。正如吴军提到的那个铝液补浇流程，如果没有充分的企业实践基础，科研人员是无法在实验室里就把细节考虑得如此清晰的。

在中国成为全球最大的工业化发展国家，同时劳动力价格的上升又为机器人的大规模使用打开了空间之后，机器人产业化所面临的问题就迎刃而解了。

要看清万丰科技在机器人产业当中的运营空间，我们可以来看一篇关于重庆企业机器人产业化的报道：

3月20日，中科院重庆研究院一间40多平方米的实验室。

里面堆放得满满的，全是"高科技"产品——机器人。

"我们已经有6个机器人项目，还在研发很多款不同类型的机器人。"留法博士张祺兴奋地说。

一旁，该院机器人技术研究中心副主任郑彬脸上却露出了愁容。他说："机器人做出来了，但'养在深闺'，还难以走出实验室。"

研究机构"干瞪眼"，机器人产业化"无门"。

一台体型有些庞大的"机器人",不仅"视力好",能够进行高速、高精度光学自动定位,而且"手脚灵活",依靠伺服控制系统能够麻利地完成LED极性分拣、三色混插、剪脚、弯脚等动作。

"这叫作'高速LED插件机器人',目前正在完善中。"郑彬告诉记者,以前LED行业都是手工插件,效率低、易出错,如果用机器人,就能有效地解决这些弊端。"6月份就能出样机,可以替代8~10个工人,但成本却不到国外产品的1/3。"

"这种LED插件机器人填补了西南地区在LED领域自动化设备生产的空白。目前我们正在寻找中试基地,希望与企业进行合作。但遗憾的是,至今还没有一家企业找上门来。"郑彬叹息说。

其实,受到"产业化"困扰的,并不只郑彬一人。

"我们搞机器人已经有20多年的历史了,但一直是有技术没市场,进展十分缓慢。"重庆大学自动化学院教授石为人坦言,申报国家和市级科研项目,都有产业化考核目标,但由于本地企业不接招,研究机构只有"干瞪眼"。

是企业对机器人项目不感兴趣吗?

其实不然。

3月5日下午,市经信委组织召开了机器人产业发展企业座谈会。

原本邀请了20多家企业参会,结果现场来了30多家企业,很多企业还是老总和技术负责人一起来的。不停地加凳子,会议室被挤得满满的。

企业家们之所以如此重视座谈会,是因为企业在做机器人系统集成的过程中,在部分关键技术上存在"瓶颈",希望通过面对面交流,找到相关合作。

郑彬认为,开发机器人产品,并没有很多企业想象的那么难、那么复杂。"深圳一家企业推出的一款扫地机器人,仅去年一年的时间,就销售了60多万台,其中70%~80%出口海外,创造了2亿多元的收入。实际上,扫地机器人的技术含量并不高，但这家企业瞄准市场需求，快速实现了产业化。"

这篇来自重庆的报道，很清晰地讲述了机器人产业化当中的问题。高校的科研人员运用技术可以生产出机器人，不过因为对企业的需求了解得不够清晰，所以机器人的大规模使用，也就是产业化成了问题。这中间的差异在于企业是讲求效益的，机器人的应用，首先要解决企业在运营过程当中出现的困难，才有可能规模化。

而万丰科技由陈国栋、张水勇、章旭霞等人组成的研发团队，正是因为考虑到了铸造企业现场工位高温这样的环节，所以推出的机器人一经使用，就得到了员工的普遍喜爱。在整个机器人产业链当中，万丰科技的管理层采取了开放的态度，他们在技术上积极与哈工大以及国际上著名的机器人应用领先的ABB公司合作，才推出了我们看到的浇注机器人。

梦想

"网络智能制造是中国制造的未来，是走向中国创造的必由之路！"2014年6月13日，在以"重新想象、重新出发"为主题的2014浙商大会移动互联网峰会上，全国人大常委会副委员长、中国科学院原院长路甬祥振聋发聩地说道。

路甬祥认为，网络智能制造是制造文明的新形态，是向中国创造跨越的核心，全球金融危机、产业变革等外部经济形势和日本发展协同机器人与无人工厂，美国重振高端制造业，中国实施智能制造发展规划等大国科技振兴策略，又加快了制造文明的转型，从而推动制造技术与产业向全球网络智能制造转型。他还特别提醒民营经济活跃的浙江省，更应该抓住网络智能制造的发展机遇，依靠创新驱动发展，促进节能减排、减人增效，从而提升浙江制造服务在全国、全球产业链中的地位、价值和竞争力，打造浙江经济的升级版。

作为浙江省人大常委会副主任、浙商发展研究院院长的王永昌在大会上致辞时说，中国正处于爬坡过坎的阶段，需要新的产业支撑点和增长点。浙江是民营经济、市场经济先发之省，目前正在全面推进"三名四换（名企名品名家，腾笼换鸟、机器换人、空间换地、电商换市）等发展战略性举措，浙江有望成为加快转型发展、科学协调发展的先行之省。

万丰科技正是抓住了全球智能制造的发展机遇，进入了"机器换人"这个大产业的应用环节。万丰科技现任董事长倪伟勇和总经理吴军团队，提出了企业的需求，由国际国内领域内专家来形成解决方案，并由万丰科技和科研机构一起来实现。这种公司化运营技术产业的形式，在万丰科技得到了很好的发展。

现在，在新昌工业园区万丰奥特产业园的周边，万丰科技有了自己独立的厂区。这片不大的厂区有四幢独立的厂房，就万丰巨大的产能而言，科技公司的规模不大，但却使得万丰科技在整个机器人产业当中有了自己的优势，它有了很多科研机构所不具备的规模试验条件，加上万丰奥特深厚的产业基础，因此很多科研机构都愿意与万丰科技合作开发新产品。

万丰科技的构想，仍然与铸造业高度相关。在浇注机器人成功投入万丰轮毂产品生产之后，万丰科技已经开始为下一步在铸造现场实现少人化开始努力。现在，万丰的机器人已经实现单台机械手控制6台铸造机进行浇注，打破了国际上单台控制4台铸造机的纪录。

当然，这还仅仅是机器自动化的一个方向。重力铸造现场的少人化，对应的是国内劳动力开始稀缺的现状，机器人的应用正是为了应对国家的这个经济形势变化。随着国家大力推进"机器换人"的装备革命，以及对整个技术的掌握程度更深入，万丰科技快速成长，如今已经跻身全国十大机器人制造商，更是牵头制定行业国家标准的企业之一。

而万丰科技的目标显然并不限于此，用总经理吴军的话说，万丰不只是单纯的提供机器人产品，而是为对方提供整条生产线的设计，运行和维护的全过程服务。

"别的企业一台机器人只能换 2 个工人，我们设计的生产线可以做到一台机器替换 4 到 6 个工人。我们刚刚完成了中国核工业的订单，由于涉及放射性污染，工人不能长时间在生产线上操作。我们提供了整套的无人化生产线，现在完全不用受时间制约。"

万丰科技步入了高速发展通道。

万丰奥特之道：开放塑造公司竞争力

万丰奥特起家时更多地属于传统制造业，因此，万丰奥特进行的低压铸造机和机器人的研制等，实际上都是万丰奥特从传统制造业向先进制造业的转型过程。

传统制造业与先进制造业之间，并不是简单的谁取代谁的关系。这一点，我们可以从万丰奥特智能化产业与零部件产业之间的关系中清晰地看出来。正因为万丰奥特在轮毂制造当中的优势市场地位，使得万丰奥特客观上产生了对低压机和机器人的需求，衍生出了万丰奥特智能化部门的基本市场，而因为万丰奥特对轮毂业务的开放态度，使得万丰奥特智能化部门能在市场上站住脚，并得到壮大。同时，基于万丰奥特本身的需求，万丰奥特的智能化部门在生存的同时，逐步地向外扩张市场有了很好的基础。

公司的运营当中，技术部门能否脱离主业，独立寻找到自己的市场，对于企业的管理者来说是一个重大的考验。通常情况下，能自己制造低压机这样的关键设备，常常会被像轮毂企业视为公司的核心竞争力，因此被企业封锁起来，不对外寻找市场。如果万丰奥特这样做，很可能数年之后，低压机制造部门就会失去竞争力。而正是因为陈爱莲采取开放的态度，让万丰奥特的智能化部门自己在市场上找饭吃，既锻炼了万丰奥特轮毂制造的竞争力，也塑造了智能部门在竞争压力下形成自己的市场优势。

Chapter 5

From Low Pressure Casting
Machine to Robot

The Low Pressure Casting Machine Independently Created by Wanfeng

One day in April 2001, Chen Guodong, the mechanic in Wanfeng Auto, stood in front of the low pressure casting machine produced in Empire Equipment & Supply Co, Inc. of the United States as he did for days. It had been like this for some time that he came and thought in front of the huge machine everyday. But today, it was a little different, he felt pushed by someone.

It was his colleague and friend , and the man joked to him: "Is it because you want to produce one like this by yourself that you always come to see the low pressure casting machine?"

The reason why his friend said so was that Chen Guodong is a technical expert in Wanfeng Auto. Though he has no college degree but only a high school diploma, he has been crazy about electrics and mechanics. The man in his 30's had never missed any great transformations in electrical field. Initially he dabbled in the radio assembly and later the television assembly, and then in industrial computer control and computer programming, and he has gradually become proficient in them.

In Wanfeng Auto, hobbies such as Chen Guodong's had been encouraged. There is a small technical circle for technology fans in the company. The place beside the production base is where Chen Guodong and other technology fans always like to go and have parties to exchanges views about the latest technological development.

In this condition, coupled with the dispute over the low pressure casting machine between Wanfeng Auto and Empire Equipment Company , Chen Guodong went to look at the low pressure casting machine and reflected on its mechanic principles and control program as long as he was free. Thus came his friend's joking proposal accordingly. Noticing his friend's bantering tone, Chen Guodong replied: "Is it not something impossible to be produced?" Having observed the machine for a very long time, he believed that its mechanical structure was really not something difficult to build for the machinery company as Wanfeng Auto, for the whole set of the machine movements was controlled by an industrial Single Chip Microprocessor. Obviously, the designer was so familiar with the hub manufacturing process that the process of each movement was designed just fine

Inwardly confident, Chen Guodong went a little far with such big words. The joking proposal was thus turned a serious one step by step. Chen Guodong and other technology fans in Wanfeng Auto reported the proposal to Yu Limin, the responsible technical director of car wheel hubs at that time. And in this way did the company meeting decide to allocate 800 thousand yuan as the experimenting fund for sporting the technical group.

Since Wanfeng Auto initially entered the hub industry, we know innovative ideas have been highly appreciated here in the company. In 1997, Chen Ailian put forward the enterprise cultural concept — Technological innovation is the permanent theme of the enterprise development — and had it impressed on the propaganda wall of the company. As a result, Wanfeng Auto has never set any bar to its technician and staff's innovation, which has enabled the company to constantly open up new worlds during its ceaseless growth. Wanfeng Auto, of course, would strongly support Yu Limin's technical team, since only if they broke through the bottleneck of manufacturing the low pressure casting machine would Wanfneg Auto welcome a completely new state in the competition of auto wheel hubs.

In order to collect data and learn from other enterprises of the same trade, the five-member team, composed of Yu Limin, Chen Guodong, Cao Fangyong, Zhang Shuiyong and Zhao Zengguang, successively investigated Italian LPM , Empire Equipment & Supply Co, Inc. from US, Fukusuke Kogyo Co.,Ltd from Japan and several domestic casting equipment manufacturers. In the five-member team, except that Zhang Shuiyong had a degree of a three-year college education, all the others just had the same high school diplomas.

With thoroughly full research and analysis of the foreign technical data of the imported machine, they revised the program for numerous times and tried it time and again. They didn't know how many drafts had been drawn and then torn, nor did they know how much rest time had been sacrificed during the numerous sleepless nights. The only thing thought in the minds of all the project members was the low pressure casting machine, nothing but the low pressure casting machine.

On July 18th, 2001, after 100 days' of research and development, the team with a group of crazy technology enthusiasts did succeeded in creating the first domestic self-developed low pressure casting machine. Once produced, it soon broke the foreign technology monopoly , bridged the gap in domestic technology, and later became the national alternative to imported equipment.

However, innovation has in no sense come to an end in Wanfeng Auto.

From the perspective of traditional thought, the manufacturing technology of low pressure casting machines owned by a hub production enterprise constituted its competitiveness. Wanfeng Auto's management should have kept the technology secrete in order to keep the competitiveness in the enterprise forever , or at lest as long as possible.

However, having worked for a long time in the foundry industry, Wanfeng Auto's team were fully aware that China was only a big country but not a strong one in foundry industry, because of the bottleneck, composed of poor working conditions, backward technology and low-end products , in the development of the industry. Well, there was a great reason for the high price of the low pressure casting machine. Because of its high degree of automation, high rate of material utilization, and low rate of substandard products, the low pressure casting machine can greatly improve the working conditions and decrease the labor intensity of the workers in the front line of casting.

This is determined by the working principle of the low pressure casting machine. From the process, the greatest difference between low pressure casting machines and the former pressure casting and gravity casting ones lied in the principle of the communicating vessel applied in their way of processing. Because of the principle, the low pressure casting machine connected the metal liquid melted in the early process of molding with the mold cavity of the casting machine during the process, and then fill up the mold cavity with metal liquid by differential pressure. Such technology changed the traditional manual way of transferring the high temperature metal liquid, greatly improving the working conditions in the casting workshop with high temperature.

Should the company sell the equipment with core technology in the market?

There were different voices inside Wanfeng Auto. Compare with other domestic counterpart equipment, the low pressure casting machine produced by Wanfeng Auto could be more competitive for its high cost performance, so it would be easy for the company to open up the market. Once the market of Wanfeng Auto's low pressure casting machine was developed, it meanwhile meant that part of the company's competitiveness in aluminum wheel hub production would disappear. That is to say, some potential competitors would be nurtured by themselves.

However, Chen Ailian didn't think Wanfeng Auto's competitiveness was constituted by the low pressure casting machine. With wider horizons, she felt that in terms of the technology, the application market of low pressure casting machines was by far bigger than that of the hub manufacturing which Wanfeng Auto was engaged in, for it involved the foundry of many aluminum products and had bright prospects. It was definitely wrong for Wanfeng Auto to restrain its own casting machines from entering the market just for fear that the company's core competitiveness might be weakened. Even if Wanfeng Auto didn't market its casting machines, sooner or later some professional company would manufacture and market them. Of course, more importantly, Chen Ailian believed that a company's core competitiveness derives from its enterprise culture. There is an atmosphere in Wanfeng Auto, in which everyone was diligent and ambitious , and everyone was trying his utmost. Therefore, the enterprise could evolve various kinds of competitive advantages of its own, and this was Wanfeng Auto's key competitiveness.

At her insistence, Wanfeng Auto began to market its own low pressure casting machines soon after the machine had been successfully developed.The opening attitude enabled Wanfeng Auto's low pressure casting machine project to evolve from a technical group's innovative breakthrough in a foreign product into an enterprise — Zhejiang Wanfeng Technology Development Co., Ltd (hereafter referred as Wanfeng Technology in short) — in the end.

The Market of Low Pressure Casting Machines

On April 18th in 2006, it was the time for the opening of the China International Foundry Exhibition held once every two years. In this year, Wanfeng Technology first appeared in the foundry exhibition. Wanfeng's low pressure casting machine were finally unveiled in the foundry exhibition after over four years' internal supply and improvement.

The casting equipment is the focus of a foundry exhibition. In this exhibition, the low pressure casting machine of Wanfeng Technology was exhibited in the center of the hall for home-produced equipment. Under the leadership of Jiang Yuhua, the company's general manager, Wafeng Technology made careful arrangement and full preparation for the exhibition. Wanfeng Technology's low pressure casting machine, 6 meters in height and 20 tuns in weight, beat all the other exhibits with its shining first public appearance. Because of the equipment's fine workmanship and Wanfeng Auto's reputation in foundry industry, Wanfeng Technology's low pressure casting machine attracted lots of viewers as soon as it was unveiled, simply defeating the imported equipment in the international hall.

Wanfeng Auto's Low Pressure Casting Machine on the Application Field

This is the scene that was recorded by an employee of Wanfeng Technology for the newspaper Wanfeng: During the 4 days' exhibition,visitors came to the display booth of Wanfeng Technology in an endless stream. We received more than 100 batches of of customers and reached the cooperation intention with more than ten companies. We were more viewed by our counterparts from the professional foundry equipment makers. Leaders and experts of China Foundry Association , such as the chairmen Jia Chengbin and Li Yongsheng, respectively visited Wanfeng Technology display booth with their teams in high spirits. They, proud that the low pressure casting machines we have developed can take the place of the imported ones, asked the customers about their use of the equipment and said they would lead teams to inspect Wanfeng Technology."

In June of that year, Wanfeng Technology's low pressure casting machine took part in Shanghai's exhibition of the foundry equipment again and also reaped a lot. Till not, it had been already five years since Wanfeng Auto started to research and develop its own low pressure casting machines.

The low pressure casting machine of Wanfeng Technology was recognized by domestic enterprises of the same trade in the hub industry as soon as it was marketed. At the beginning of the 21st century, the growing market of the auto industry attracted a considerable number of private enterprises to the field of hub manufacture. Wanfeng Technology's low pressure casting machine had two obvious advantages in the market. Firstly, it was by far cheaper than the foreign one in price. Secondly, as a native Chinese enterprise, Wanfeng Technology can improve its low pressure casting machines according to changes in domestic market. Additionally, since Wanfeng Auto had held the lead in hub manufacturing, the private enterprises that were to start their own hub production with the low pressure casting machines purchased in Wanfeng Technology could also be offered lots of technical services in the hub manufacture.

Even though foreign enterprises of the same trade ,directing at Chinese market, decreased their product prices, when confronted with the advantages that Wanfeng Technology enjoyed after the production of its low pressure casting machines, Wanfeng Technology accounted for 55% of the market share with its products at the peak time.

After Wanfeng Auto fostered the low pressure casting machine project and developed it into an independent technology development corporation, Chen Guodong who was already the chief engineer, was bound to begin considering the new company's prospects from its perspective.

It provided Wanfeng Technology with a bigger market. In a sense, low pressure casting is a kind of advanced technology with a much wider application range than the field of hub manufacture. During the molding process of the parts for the large and complex machinery, as long as the low pressure casting machine is highly standardized with its quality consistent with the requirements of the low pressure casting process, companies with mass production are likely to the potential customers of the low pressure casting machines.

Actually, Wanfeng Technology had started to diversify its products before it entered the market in 2006. The market that the low pressure casting machine was faced with was a big one. Beside the field of hub production, the low pressure casting machine can be applied to many other fields of casting if the mold can be transformed. Before 2006, Wanfeng Technology exceeded Wanfeng Auto's major business, and started to work as the upstream matching component supplier for the complex casting parts of the car, such as the cylinder head and the oil pump block of the engine. Later on, it exceeded its business in auto industry and started to develop the equipment for complicated casting parts used in the power industry.

Wanfeng Technology's active performance in the market had much to do with the operation model held inside Wanfeng Group. Since its initial participation in the market, Wanfeng Technology , sticking to the tradition of the entire group, attached much importance to the staff's initiative, and tried out the system in which project leader in each profession was in change of the project, making the high-tech company operated in the pattern that the project teams ,under the leadership of the experts, were responsible for the product research and development

Wanfeng Technology decomposed the complex foundry equipment into such modules as mechanical, electrical, hydraulic and pneumatic parts and the maintaining furnace, and allotted different projects to each of the project teams headed by a leading engineer according to their professions after organizing the value chain. In order to achieve higher working efficiency, technicians at expert level could choose the matching teammates freely. Through the connection of economic benefits, Wanfeng Technology linked the experts and its marketing together.

This strategy brought Wanfeng Technology two major advantages. For one thing, now that its strength in technology , research and development kept grwoing in the system, Wanfeng Technology thus had its talent advantage. For another, as the parent enterprise, Wanfeng Auto Group, during its extraordinary development, provided Wanfeng Technology endless markets and the most urgent need of a technology development company: demands.

The Next direction — Robots

Based on their understanding of the casting field, after 2006, Wanfeng Technology planed the next step for the company's development. It was to gradually have the hub manufacturing process fully automated by applying robotics in workshops of poor working conditions, and then to popularize robotics in the whole foundry industry.

It was obvious that the development in this direction would be supported by Chen Ailian. During each summer, because of the heat in the environment, there were always workers in the front line of production having sunstroke in Wanfeng Auto's casting workshops. Therefore, it was the yearly time when the executives at all levels in Wanfeng Auto visited the workshops to bring the workers there water in recognition of their hard work.

Although strong-willed in business, Chen Ailian is very tender in her heart. The deputy party secretary, Xu Zhiliang, of Wanfneg Auto had a deep impression about that. One year, as he recalled, Chen Ailian went to tell him seriously that the company's logistics service didn't keep pace the production, for the rest room arranged for the staff with sunstroke was too small. It was not until Xu Zhiliang changed a more spacious room near the staff canteen into an air-conditioned transfusion room and invited her to have a look at it herself did she feel relieved.

Such operating environment of high temperature was very common in domestic foundry industry. Besides the low pressure casting machines, there was also plenty of gravity casting equipment in the industry. Even if there were low pressure casting machines in the market, in many simple casting fields, being simple and convenient to operate and cheap in price, gravity casting equipment was still the main force of casting equipment .

Wanfeng Auto had tried a lot of measures to deal with the high temperature in the foundry workshop. The most interesting one was to install an air supply system in the workshop. At the end of air supply system where wind was sent out there was a stuff with water inside that decreased the temperature of the air passing through so that the workers on operation platform could be cooled down by the cool air directed to them.

This was indeed a way better than no way. Because on the casting field, aluminum needs high temperature to be melted into liquid, it is impossible to cool the field down with air-conditioners. Therefore, it had been the best choice to cool off the fixed operation platform with cool air.

The fundamental solution to the high temperature in the foundry field is to reduce the number of workers needed in the process as much as it is possible through automation, or just to have the entire process unmanned.

Since 2008, once entering Wanfeng Auto's foundry workshop, people can find , after several years' research and development, there have been great changes in the company's production field of gravity casting.

Now, between the aluminum melting furnace and the gravity casting machine, there is a huge semi-circular area segregating the two from each other. In the middle of the separation area stood steadily an agile industrial robot, who can continuously work 24 hours without tiredness or complaints, filling up the six gravity casting machines neatly arranged in front of the semi-circle with melted alloy aluminum liquid according to the procedures. The six gravity casting machines can be looked after by one employee. After the solidification casting process of the gravity casting machine, the operator pushes the operating button beside the casting machine, and the robot can quickly finish the following steps within seconds — taking the aluminum water out of the melting furnace, bringing the aluminum water to the sprue gate of the gravity casting machine, and injecting the aluminum liquid into the machine. If done by manual labor, the same work could be finished by 18 strong robust young laborers of three work shifts working for a day and a night. That's to say, an industrial robot can replace 15 workers during 24 hours' work. This is of great significance in Zhejiang Province where there is now an acute shortage of labor force.

When the robot is working with the procedures, the casting machine operator takes a small amount out of the aluminum water sent by the robot. After the robot finishes the injection, the operator adds the injection to the gravity casting machine with the aluminum water he has taken. This is because the aluminum water will shrink in volume during the process of solidification.

About a minute later, after the aluminum water inside the casting machine has solidified, the machine pushes out the aluminum body in desired shape, and the casting process of a semi-finished wheel hub is then completed.

The seemingly simple process is not only an indication that the domestic foundry industry has moved to the forefront of the international level, but also the fruit of the engineers' hard work during more than a year's time in Wanfeng Technology. Because all the robot's abilities to take and inject the aluminum water of determined amount and quickly react to the demands of several casting machines and its every movement during the operating process have contained complicated computing programs.

A robot in the operation can decrease the operator's close contact with the aluminum water, greatly improving the traditional situation that the casting field was always covered with high temperature.

And for the foundry enterprises, the benefits lie in two aspects. Firstly, the number of workers in the high temperature field can be of course reduced. Secondly, when the robot is used to cast the aluminum liquid in the molder, the stability and amount of the aluminum liquid become controllable, so it is greatly helpful to improve the quality of the casting process.

Wu Jun, the general manager of Wanfeng Technology, had a very deep impression about the development process of the pouring robot. For quite a long time , he and Wanfeng Technology's engineers were confused about the shrinkage of aluminum water after the liquid has solidified in the gravity casting machine. According the design requirements of automation, the shrinkage undoubtedly should be mended by the robot automatically with additional aluminum liquid, but the process could be hardly done in robot programs.

In the beginning, the pouring robots were not welcome by workers in the front line of production, when they were applied in the hub factories of Wanfeng Auto. Because in Wanfeng Auto's workshops, there was a quota assessment for each station. Workers with robots on their stations worried that they couldn't finish their quotas if the robots on trial failed to work as effectively as were wished, and their wages would be negatively influenced accordingly.

However, as time went on, the robot revealed its advantage. Everything carefully taken into consideration in design by Wanfeng Technology's technical personnel, the robots, once assembled and installed, enabled the workers on the station to finish their quotas with improved working conditions and productivity. As a result, they soon took to the robots and even began helping the engineers to solve the problem of solidification shrinkage.

The staff came up with a simple and effective solution. They advised the engineer to make the robot take more aluminum water each time so that the operator could directly take the aluminum water from the robot's crucible to mend the shrinkage while the robot was pouring the aluminum liquid. The tough problem that had long troubled the technical personnel now was easily solved with artificial feeding.

Entering into the Robot Industry

If it was by accident that the low pressure casting machine led Wanfeng Technology to the field of industrial intelligence , in the era of industrial robots, Wanfeng Technology began to enter into the industry in scale.

The industrial robot began developing as an industry in 1960s throughout the world. The popularization of intelligence control and the industrial computer made it technically feasible for man to produce robots. In the seventy and eighty's , since mass production had been very common in western industry, industrial robots began to be applied in some dangerous station, and the earliest application appeared in auto manufacturing. Stations involving repeated and labor-intensive work like welding in the assembly lines of auto production had early become the positions taken by welding robots. As a result, a batch of influential famous industrial robot companies appeared successively, including ABB in Sweden, FANUC and YASKAWA in Japan, KUKA in Germany, Adept Technology in America and COMAU in Italy , which had already become the pillar enterprises in their own countries.

Following the technological development in the world, China's robotics emerged in about the 1980s. During that time, the government launched the Program of High-Tech Research and Development (863 Program in short) to research and develop robotics. The local Ministry of Machinery Industry ,working as the head, organized the research and development in industrial robots of spot welding, arc welding, spray paint, handling and stacking , and other ministries also actively set up projects to support the development. Under this circumstance appeared the first upsurge of industrial robot development in China. By the 90s, China had successively developed 7 types of series industrial robot products and 102 kinds of special robots, and had implemented more than 100 robot application projects. By the end of the 90s, China had established 9 industrialization bases of robots and 7 scientific research bases, including Xisong Robot Company of Shenyang Research Institute of Automation, Boshi Automatic Equipment Co., Ltd of Harbin Institute of Technology, and Robot Development Center of Beijing Automation Research Institute of Industrial Machinery.

But technical development only provided the possibility of robot application. It is manufacturing enterprises with mass production like Wanfeng Auto that finally realized the application of robots. When automation had become a must to the production lines of gravity casting, more working positions brought by mass production made it possible for robots to be applied in industrial enterprises in that they can noticeably increase the industrial efficiency.

And what 's more important is the detail of robot application. Just as the problem in the process of re-pouring the aluminum liquid mentioned by Wujun, technical personnel are unable to take very detail into consideration so clearly inside the laboratory, if without sufficient practices in the enterprise.

After China has had the world largest development scale in industrialization and meanwhile the rise of labor price has opened up the market for the mass use of robots, the problems of robot industrialization can be solved with great ease.

To clearly understand Wanfeng Technology's operating space in the robot industry, we can first read a report on robot industrialization in enterprises in Chongqing.

March 20th, in a laboratory of about 40 square meters in Chongqing Institute of Chinese Academy of Science.

The room was fully filled with high-tech products — robots.

"We've already had 6 robot projects, and we 're still developing robots of many different types." Dr. Zhang Qi, who had studied in France, said excitedly.

Beside him, the deputy director of the robotics research center of the institute, Zheng Bin, was full of worries on the face. He said: " We do have produced the robots, but they can only be locked inside the laboratory, impossible to be purchased outside."

Research institutes could do nothing but worry, while there was no way for the robot to be industrialized.

A huge-shaped robot not only has good eyesight for high-speed and high-precision optical automatic location , but also has flexible hands and feet. With servo control system, it is able to deftly complete the movements such as LED polarity sorting, plugging in kits of three mixed colors, shearing and bending.

"This is called 'high-speed LED plug-in robot, still under improvement." Zhen Bin told the reporter that the kits used to be plugged in manually with low efficiency yet high error rate in the LED industry. With robots, these problems could be effectively handled. "The prototype can be produced in June.Though it can replace 8--10 workers, yet its costs were less than 1/3 of the foreign product's .

"This kind of LED plug-in robot has filled a gap in LED automatic equipment production in the south-west areas. Now we 're seeking for trial bases and cooperative partners in China. Yet it's a shame that till now no enterprise has contacted us." Zhen Bin sighed.

Actually, Zhen Bin was not the only that had been troubled by industrialization.

"We've researched and developed the robot for more than 20 years, yet for lack of market, the technology has developed very slowly." Shi Weiren , the professor in the school of Automation of Chongqing University, pointed it frankly that there was industrialization assessment of all the scientific research projects to be applied, not matter they were of state-level or city-level. However, with no corresponding responses from the local enterprises, the research institutes could do nothing but let it be.

Were the enterprise really not interested in the robot projects?

It was actually not.

On the afternoon of March 5th, the commission of economy and information technology of the city organized a forum on the development of the robot industry for the enterprises.

Initially, about 20 enterprises had been invited , but in fact more than 30 enterprises sent their representatives to the meeting. And many enterprise presidents attended the meeting together with their chief technical leaders. The meeting room was fully occupied with more seats being added to the room from time to time.

The entrepreneurs took the forum so seriously, because the enterprises, confronted with the bottleneck in key technology when developing their own robot systems, wanted to seek cooperative partners through the face-to-face communication.

In Zhen Bin's opinion, it was not so difficult or complicated to develop robot products as many enterprises had believed. "An enterprise in ShenZhen marketed the sweeping robot,and sold more than 600 thousand of it robot products within last year, 70%–80% of which were sold abroad , making an income of over 0.2 billion yuan. Actually the sweeping robot is not demanding in technology. But the company quickly realized its industrialization with the focus on the demands in market.

The report from Chongqing clearly stated the problems in robot industrialization. Scientific researchers in colleges can produce robots with technology but they knew little about the enterprises' demands, making the mass use of robots, or robot industrialization impossible. The difference between the reality and the ideal lies in the fact that enterprises work for profits. Only when robots applied in the enterprise could first solve the difficulties during its operation can the robot be produced in large scale.

In Wanfeng Technology, because the research and development team, composed of Chen Guodong, Zhang Shuiyong, Zhang Xuxia and some others, had taken the high temperature in the foundry field into consideration when producing their own robots, these robots won over the staff as soon as they were applied in the workshop. In the whole production chain of robots, the management of Wanfeng Technology were open-minded. They actively cooperated with Harbin Institute of Technology and ABB , the world famous company in robot application, in technology, and then produced the pouring robots that we now see.

Dream

"Intelligent network manufacturing, the future of Made-in-China, is the only path to Created-in-China." Lu Yongxiang, the vice chairman of the Standing Committee of NPC and former president of Chinese Academy of Sciences, said with enlightenment On 13th June 2014 on the 2014 Mobile Internet Summit of Zhejiang Entrepreneurs Convention on the theme of New imagination & New Start.

In Lu Yongxiang's opinion, intelligent network manufacture is the new form of manufacturing civilization, and is the key stage for us to realize China Creation. Faced with the external economic circumstances, such as the global financial crisis, the industrial transformation, the development of collaborative robots and unmanned plants in Japan, and the revival of high-end manufacturing in America,China carried out the development strategy of intelligence manufacture to revitalize China as a scientific power. This accelerated the transformation of manufacturing civilization in China and propelled manufacture technology and industries to transform into global intelligent network manufacturing. He especially reminded the entrepreneurs that Zhejiang Province with active private businesses should seize the opportunity to develop its intelligent network manufacturing. Zhejiang Province should develop with innovation by saving energy, lowering pollutant discharge and downsizing for efficiency. In this way the province could promote the status, value and competitiveness of its manufacture service in national and global industrial chains so as to upgrade its economy on the whole.

On the meeting, Wang Yongchang, the deputy leader of Standing Committee of Zhejiang Provincial People's Congress and president of the Department Research Institute of Zhejiang Entrepreneurs, said in his speech that China now needed new industry support and growth engine while striving toward a higher goal. Zhejiang, as the earliest birthplace of private economy and market economy, was now promoting its development with strategic measures known as "Branding with changes" (It referred to establish well-known enterprises, to create branded products and to cultivate famous entrepreneurs by means of replacing the incapable and unsuitable business leaders , substituting the robots for labor workers, opening up new markets outside of the province and encouraging the development of e-commerce.).And Zhejiang was hopeful to accelerate its transformation and development and go ahead of others as the first province with scientific coordinated development.

Wanfeng Technology did seize the development opportunity of the global intelligent manufacturing and entered the huge industry of automation. The company's team , composed of the current board chairman Ni Weiyong and the general manager Wu Jun , have put forward their enterprise demands. The global and domestic experts of the field will come out with solution plans for Wanfeng Technology and other research organizations to carry out cooperatively. The way to operate the technology industry in company form develops very well in Wanfeng Technology.

Now, Wanfeng Technology has its own independent factory located beside the industrial park of Wafeng Auto in Xinchang Industrial Zone. In the small factory yard stood four independent factory buildings. In terms of Wanfeng's great capacity, the technology company, though not large in size, has its own advantage in robot industry. It enjoys scale experiment conditions , which are unavailable in many scientific research institutes, together with the profound industry foundation of Wanfeng Auto, so many research institutes are willing to cooperate with it to develop new products.

Wanfeng Technology's idea is still highly relevant to the casting industry. After the successful application of pouring robots in Wanfeng's hub production, Wanfeng Technology has started to work hard to realize automation in the next field of casting. Now, Wanfeng's robot hasachieved a single manipulator controlling of six casting machines for pouring, breaking the international records ofa single manipulator controlling of four casting machines.

Of course, this is only a direction of machinery automation. The change in the foundry field of gravity casting with fewer labors is related to the current shortage of domestic workforce. The application of robots is to cope with the economic change of the country. As the country promotes the equipment revolution of substituting robots for labors with better command of the entire technology, Wanfeng Technologyhas been growing up rapidly, and now has become one of the country's ten largest robot manufacturers, especially one of the leading companies to develop national industry standards.

Clearly,Wanfeng Technology's goal is not limited to this. Just as general manager Wu Jun said, Wanfeng not only provides robot products, but alsoall services, including design, operation and maintenance of the whole production line.

"Other enterprise's robot can only replace2 workers, but in the production linewhichwe designed,a robot can replace 4 to 6 workers. In the order of China National Nuclear Corporationthat we have just completed, workers can'tmanipulate for a long time in the production linedue to radioactive contamination. We offered a complete unmanned production line, which are not subject to time constraints now."

Wanfeng Technologyhas entered into a high-speed development channel.

Wanfeng Auto's way: building the company's competitiveness with open mind

Wanfeng Auto more belonged to the traditional manufacturing when it initially started its business. Therefore, the company actually has shifted from a traditional manufacturing business to an advanced one since its development of low pressure casting machines and robots.

It is not a simple relationship of replacement between the traditional manufacturing and the advanced manufacturing, as is clearly demonstrated in the relation between Wanfeng Auto's intelligent industry and its component industry. Because of its advantageous role in the market of hub production, subjectively Wanfeng Auto has the demand for low pressure casting machines and robots. Such demand has opened up the basic market for Wanfeng Auto's intelligent department. Wanfeng Auto's liberal attitude to its hub business has enabled the intelligent department to get a foothold in the market and then expand later on. Meanwhile, well based on the company's own demand, the intelligent department of Wanfeng Auto gradually widens its market after its establishment.

In a company's operation, whether the technical section can seek its own market independently outside the company's main business is a major test for the management of the company. Usually, the key equipment independently developed by a company such as the low pressure casting machine is carefully saved as the company's core competitiveness without being marketed. What Wanfeng Auto has done may make its low pressure manufacture sector lose competitiveness in the market years later. Yet because of Chen Ailian's liberal attitude, Wanfeng Auto's intelligent department can gain a foothold in the market, which not only has trained the competitiveness of the company's hub production, but also enabled the intelligent department to build its own market strength under pressure.

第六章
镁业曲折路

863 计划的进与退

无论是在摩托车轮毂、汽车轮毂还是在低压铸造机产业领域，万丰奥特一经进入，都做得风生水起，体现了这家出身新昌的民营企业在生产和市场方面灵活的机制优势，也体现了陈爱莲带领的各级团队长袖善舞的经营才干。

但是时代还在进步，逐渐长大的万丰奥特，自然会接受更多的邀请，在更新的领域去接受新的挑战。

让万丰奥特管理层没有想到的是，2001 年，万丰奥特主动把握的镁合金制造的机会，会使万丰镁业踏上长达十年的曲折道路，最后意外地为集团迎来一个巨大的产业机会。

万丰奥特进入镁合金产业的机会，来得十分偶然。

2001 年，万丰奥特在完成对山东都瑞轮毂有限公司的收购之后，重组设立威海万丰。

重组成功，对于万丰奥特来说当然是件大事，因此在山东威海举行了一个隆重的开业仪式，邀请了政府、行业、客户单位相关领导前来见证。看到万丰奥特成功收购中外合资企业，当时来观礼的政府领导们都很吃惊。因为在 2001 年中国公司收购国外企业，还真是不多见。

机会总在不经意间光临。在前来观礼的领导中，有一位是威海市政府的科技顾问，国家科技部高新司巡视员（原副司长）陈贤杰。因为认可万丰奥特在产业上的成就和方向，他就把一个新的机会推荐给了陈爱莲。

这个信息的具体内涵，确实与万丰奥特高度相关。当时科技部高新司的863 计划正面向全国招标，其中一个重大专项就是"高强高韧镁合金材料研制及其在车轮上的应用"。此前，中国科学院金属研究所和上海交大两个团队已经摩拳擦掌准备投标，而吉林大学、沈阳工大、北京有色金属研究总院等高校、科研院所的一批专家虽然对镁合金材料及工艺有所研究，但在产业化方面缺乏一个有力的合作者，因此投标工作尚未最后落实。

而万丰奥特恰恰在汽车铝合金车轮制造领域是行家里手，与这批专家正好可以各尽所能，优势互补。因此，陈贤杰出于对中国镁合金产业化以使资源优势转化为产业优势的责任感，牵线搭桥，为这个专项的产学研合作尽一份心力。

科技部的这个专项，有着重大的产业背景。

我国是镁资源大国，总储量约占世界的 22.5%，位居第一；我国已探明菱镁矿 34 亿吨，同样居世界第一。镁及其合金是至今在工业中应用的最轻的金属结构材料，具有质量轻、密度小、强度高、刚性好、压铸性能好、降低噪声、电磁屏蔽性和减震性好、可循环利用等特性，被材料专家誉为 21 世纪最具有开发和应用潜力的绿色工程材料。近几年，镁及其合金开始替代铝材和钢材，广泛用于飞船、飞机、导弹、汽车、计算机、通信产品和消费类电子产品的制造等，生产和消耗呈快速上升趋势。

进入 21 世纪之后，由于全球对镁合金的需求量不断上升，但镁的加工技术的发展却极为落后，总体局面是出口原镁而进口镁合金。

也正是因此，科技部启动了 863 计划专项，引导着国内科研院所、高校和有实力的企业，通过产学研合作攻关，来改变这一局面。

而在车轮制造产业的发展方向上，鉴于中国汽车产业高速发展，能源需求带来巨大压力，科技部预期汽车的节能，呼唤部件的轻量化。而镁合金在汽车零部件上的应用，正好符合了轻量化的方向。

对于万丰奥特来说，进军镁合金行业，在一定意义上，是其在主业轮毂制造乃至汽车产业上又一个塑造竞争优势的重要行动。陈爱莲同样认识到，在国际汽车产业的前沿，节能是汽车和摩托车等交通工具竞争的方向。在强度不变的情况下，整车的部件越轻，汽车行驶的油耗就越低。因此，当汽车用户实现"有车"之后的下一步，节能就是影响用户选择汽车的重要因素之一。而镁合金材料在汽车和摩托车上的运用，可以在强度相同的情况下，比铝合金进一步减轻整车的质量，使得汽车和摩托车具备更为节能的功效。

在某种意义上，镁合金材料的开发，正是万丰奥特用铝合金轮毂取代早期市场上钢质轮毂的又一个重大进步。因为看中了这一点，经过讨论之后，董事会决定尝试性地进入这个领域，投资镁合金汽车部件的开发，并于2002年成立威海万丰镁业科技发展有限公司（以下简称万丰镁业）。

这种应用的第一步，就是开发镁合金轮毂。

万丰奥特承担的镁合金新材料研发，实际上是863计划科研项目的规模化生产阶段。一个科研项目，从最初的动议，经过论证，实验室试制之后认为可行，再到中试及大规模试验，常常要经过很长时间的试制。而863计划的镁合金项目，正是在已经完成了前期的工作之后，才进入万丰奥特进行大规模试验的。

陈爱莲派出了参与最初创业，后来又担任采购经理的盛晓方来带领团队执行这个项目。考虑到初期投资的风险控制，万丰镁业最初的创业地点就在威海万丰内，虽然没有独立的地点，但威海万丰拥有完整的生产设备，以及从生产到经营的完整团队。董事会的考虑是，要用万丰奥特集团汽轮的产业能力，来帮助万丰镁业解决从研发到规模生产可能遇到的障碍。

盛晓方经过充分了解，对镁工业的情况心里已经有谱：镁和铝相比优点是强度高，其密度要比铝小三分之一，而且熔铸之后的强度会更高，像F1方程式赛车用的都是镁合金车轮。虽然有这些优点，但要把镁铸造成镁合金部件，面临的主要难题是，镁的化学性能活泼，易燃易爆，给工艺流程带来许多难题。

波折

万丰奥特刚进入这个项目的时候，构想是相对简单的。

董事会决策的基础，在于科研的一般流程。按照最初的构想，既然确认院校的研究已经完成规模运营的生产准备，那么万丰奥特只需要投入资本，生产出来就可以了。也正是因此，万丰奥特在镁业项目上的投资，按正常情况，已经足够镁合金项目展开大规模生产。

但当双方的合作真正开始之后，盛晓方发现，院校的镁合金应用研究，基本还停留在理论研究阶段。

对于镁合金制造，院校在理论上研究得很透，但在工业企业中实现规模生产，其实还有很多障碍要跨越。

镁合金要熔铸，缺点在于它的流动性差，又容易氧化，而且在常温条件下液态镁合金凝固非常之快。它会迅速凝固，甚至不会像铝一样在液态时可以把铸造型腔填满。而原来研究计划当中提供的设备安排，只是在成熟的铝材熔炉基础上增加气体保护。它的设备改造基础来源就是万丰奥特在生产中常用的低压铸造机，而由于镁合金的特性，实际投入运用之后，包括万丰奥特在内的合作方很快发现，大规模生产当中这些设备在镁合金的熔融上存在问题。

万丰奥特的公司平台在产业化研究过程中，起到了预期的作用。威海万丰与汽车制造企业有着广泛的合作，经过联系，当时国内的一汽和奇瑞两家汽车公司都给出了试验样车，在万丰奥特的镁轮试制完毕之后，用以做各种试验。万丰奥特的镁轮在生产设备调整之后，一旦形成产品，可以迅速地在汽车厂的试车平台上试验轮毂的强度和耐久性。

　　然而产业化研究中的生产工艺问题，并不容易解决。威海万丰把铝合金生产的设备都按要求做了改进，而后按照镁合金的要求开始生产，在 2001 年万丰奥特与各方达成合作后的一年多时间，总共进行了 163 次试验，但最后的结果是，不管怎么改进设备，生产出来的镁合金轮毂在耐久性和疲劳强度上，很难达到汽车车轮的苛刻要求。

　　这种情况的出现，表明了万丰奥特已经开始进入技术前沿。在这方面，由于面对的都是没有人做过探索的领域，因此充满了不确定性。就镁合金而言，从技术研发到规模生产，就会存在各种各样的问题。碰到意外，其实是非常正常的，甚至整个项目失败，也不足为奇。而在这个过程中，企业与科研机构之间因为长期形成的价值取向不同，常常会产生矛盾。科研机构会视失败为兵家常事，而像万丰奥特这样的企业，因为有了投资，就一定要追求实现项目的结果。

　　万丰奥特开始寻求自我研发以外的道路来解决这个问题。时刻关注万丰镁业进展的陈爱莲引导专家们与国际镁合金研究机构和生产厂商对接，试图通过在生产设备上转让技术的方式，来解决镁合金生产规模化上的问题。

　　2003 年 10 月，在国家科技部国际合作司的支持和资助下，以万丰奥特为主、有三所高校的专家和三个省市科技厅高新处领导参加的中国首个镁业科技考察团前往欧洲进行考察。

　　考察团受到了欧洲镁业暨德国镁业秘书长、中国国家科技部外籍顾问克莱恩教授的热情接待，万丰奥特作为考察团领队，在欧洲镁业的贵宾留言簿上写下了对此行和未来合作的美好祝愿："要友谊更要合作"，得到了克莱恩教授的高度评价和欣然认同。

　　但是，友谊归友谊，"天下没有免费的午餐"，欧洲毕竟是高度发达、非常成熟的市场经济社会，为万丰奥特提供全套镁合金车轮的完整技术解决方案，克莱恩教授开价 2 500 万欧元（相当于 2.5 亿元人民币），这个数字远远超过了万丰奥特可以接受的底线。

中国有句俗话叫"外行看热闹，内行看门道"。镁业科技考察团的欧洲之行，绝非"游山玩水"，他们走一路、看一路、学一路，好比"捅破一层窗户纸"，考察团在欧洲之行中，悟出了不少道理。万丰奥特虽然没有与国外的科研机构达成技术转让协议，但在考察的过程中发现，这些规模生产镁合金的企业，都没有采用现成的生产设备，而是研发了新的专用设备。

这次考察之后，万丰奥特切入镁合金产业的思路发生了变化，认为万丰镁业不能只靠投入，在经过两年的探索之后，要靠自身的产出来平衡地推动企业向前走。

万丰镁业团队开始认为研发机构其实存在一个思维的误区。镁合金是一种新型材料，几家科研机构在前期研究的过程中，对它的生产设备都试图采用生产企业当下已经普遍采用的低压铸造机和重力铸造机设备，因为它们是比较先进的。但是这些设备都是基于铝合金的特性而设计的，对化学性能更为活泼的镁合金并不适用。

于是，万丰镁业开始尝试各种铸造方式，首先采用的就是万丰奥特最早进入轮毂产业时使用的压铸方式。令人意外的是，这种方法铸造出来的镁合金轮毂，虽然还是存在气泡，但却非常容易有效成型。

虽然找到了可能行得通的路径，不过，此时万丰镁业作为一家公司的经营情况却非常不容乐观。因为有了试验当中的这个波折，整个万丰镁业的投资已经消耗过半，股东们也开始信心不足了。

万丰镁业此时已经不能仅靠投资生存，必须要靠部分的生产来支持科研。这样才能使股东和员工对这家新生的公司产生信心。

这个市场策略，正是之后万丰镁业走上正途的关键所在。

谁会是创新的采用者？

从 2002 年开始试制的过程中，万丰镁业和科研机构解决了很多问题，在强度、耐冲击等方面，万丰镁业当时生产的镁轮（镁合金车轮），都已经通过了国家级的测试。尤其是在生产过程当中，万丰镁业的团队成员，已经得出了大量的生产试验数据。只是不能跨过抗疲劳这个门槛，公司的既定目标——在市场上大规模推广镁轮，很难实现。

无法大规模推广，万丰镁业是否可以采取小规模生产方式来进入市场呢？万丰镁业开始试图超越原来在镁合金领域承担的产业化推广者的角色定位。

这就是后来万丰镁业的镁轮主要的市场方向所在。

专业化公司对于市场的理解自然有所不同。到2004年，万丰奥特进入轮毂制造行业已经整整10年，而且已经拥有了全球化的营销网络。万丰镁业的市场人员知道，虽然都是轮毂，但不同的顾客对于轮毂有不同的要求。镁合金强度高，而且减重效果好，因此是否可以利用万丰奥特对整个产业熟知的优势，寻找相应的顾客群体呢？像欧美发达国家非常流行的卡丁车，是完全可以使用这种镁轮的。因为用于国际汽联F4系列赛的卡丁车的轮胎，几乎跑两三圈就要换，几乎不存在耐久性要求。但是卡丁车对于减重的要求极高，能减几十克，对卡丁车手也是一个巨大的进步，对于他们提高比赛成绩大有帮助。

在万丰镁业生死存亡的关键点上，它显示了一家专业化公司的价值。从2004年起，万丰镁业动作频频。先是拿下了自营进出口权，紧接着以压铸方式研制的镁合金车轮通过了多项检测，又被评为山东省重点扶持发展新材料产品领域的依托骨干企业。

这些动作背后的核心是，万丰镁业及时调整了市场方向。

一切准备就绪之后，万丰镁业联系了美国一家顶级卡丁车生产厂商——道格拉斯，来推广公司新试制的镁轮。

这个动作的本身，也包含着万丰镁业整个管理团队对市场的理解。这体现在对顾客的选择上，他们选择顶级企业。因为顶级企业提供的卡丁车，在

F4系列赛上，成绩傲然，在各方面都已经达到了最佳状态。而这同时意味着，顶级企业很清楚，要取得更大的突破越来越难了。除非在技术上取得更大的突破，而镁轮的减重，就是一个重大突破。

万丰镁业为道格拉斯卡丁车独家供货

果不其然，万丰镁业与道格拉斯建立了独家供货配套关系，道格拉斯不仅是一家卡丁车制造厂商，同时它还拥有一支在赛场上相当活跃的车队。万丰镁业提供的镁轮各项指标当中，减重指标是非常突出的，所以道格拉斯旗下的车队表现出极大的兴趣，很快派出专业人员来现场了解情况。

道格拉斯旗下的这支车队，是F4系列赛中的一支顶级车队。车队内部分工很细，每个方向上都有专业人员，而且很内行，动作更是十分迅速。他们来中国考察之后，拿样品回去试验，很快向万丰镁业提出要尝试性地采购一批，但要求以标价的一半来做试验。

这样的要求自然得到了万丰镁业迅速的回应，公司决定立即发货。虽然只以半价成交，但万丰镁业不管是管理层还是一线员工都觉得这一机会的出现，证明公司的生存和发展充满希望。

对于道格拉斯车队来说，镁轮并非全新产品，欧美市场当时已经出现了镁轮产品。但万丰镁业的镁轮还是很具创新性的，标准轮的重量比欧美的镁轮轻了十几克。就是这十几克的减重，使得这支著名的卡丁车国队决定要尝试一下万丰镁业的镁轮。

而第一批镁轮，就这样从威海驶向了美国——这就是万丰镁业在 2004 年要获得自营进出口权的原因。

万丰镁业的镁轮后来占到了卡丁车比赛用轮 30% 的市场份额，这很大程度上归功于万丰镁业当时选择了道格拉斯车队作为市场的切入口。可以说，万丰镁业选择道格拉斯这家厂商旗下的卡丁车车队的眼光为推广自己的镁轮起到了关键的作用。如果万丰选择的是一个普通车队，很可能镁轮作为车队胜绩的一个关键要素会被保密起来。而道格拉斯是一家包括卡丁车生产在内的汽车厂商，所以他们有动力去推广以镁轮为轻量化基因的卡丁车，而这引起了卡丁车比赛圈内的一个重大变化。只有装了万丰镁轮的卡丁车，才有可能在比赛中获胜。于是万丰镁业的镁轮，成了卡丁车生产厂商的标准配置。

万丰镁业在市场上站住了脚。

镁业拓新路

拿下了卡丁车的市场，万丰镁业站到了盈亏平衡线。不过，对于一家企业来说，达到盈亏平衡，还只是一个新项目的起点。仅仅拥有卡丁车的市场，根本不是万丰奥特进军镁业的目的。2008 年，万丰奥特一位"非常喜欢钻研"的创业元老朱训明被派遣到了万丰镁业，带领团队开始新一轮的创业。

要做大万丰镁业，关键还是要看市场的变化。此时，镁合金的应用市场，也开始向万丰镁业招手。2006 年之后，国内市场出现了两个非常有利于镁合金发展的趋势。

最有利的趋势当然还是来自汽车行业。在万丰奥特的这个主业领域，随着中国在 2000 年之后一步步地成为汽车大国，并走上全球汽车产销第一的位置之后，整个产业出现了更为积极的技术进步趋势。一方面，汽车的普及使得汽车的节能环保变得越来越重要，这就使汽车厂商对新材料的采用开始感兴趣；另一方面，国内大型汽车厂商的规模效应和赢利水平提高，也使得汽车厂商对采用新材料来保持自己的竞争优势有着强烈偏好。

另外一个有利趋势来自其他高科技产业，尤其是 IT 产业。

进入 21 世纪，由于 IT 和互联网技术的发展与行业竞争，计算机、手机等 IT 产品出现了轻量化趋势，激烈的竞争使得 IT 产品越做越精巧；同时，由 IT 技术衍生出来的工业控制技术，也使得像高铁、航空航天领域的产品小型化和轻量化变得可能。

这种变化，对于高强度、低比重的镁合金产品应用，是巨大利好。市场上开始大量出现使用镁合金材料的笔记本电脑、手机和一些高技术产品。

不过，市场的变化，仍然需要国内产业界的努力才能实现。而从 2004 年就开始进入镁合金铸造前沿的万丰镁业，在 2008 年确实也走到了可以进一步做大的门槛上。

朱训明到万丰镁业后，首先带领徐国松、杨亮等人的技术团队对镁合金的使用和开发方向做了研究。仅仅半年时间，万丰镁业就开始向政府申请多项专利——镁合金的重力铸造又重新进入万丰镁业的研究范围。不过这一次，有了卡丁车镁轮的基本业务做支撑，万丰镁业重新开始对镁合金的铸造方式进行研究就有了底气。

在对产业进行了研究，开始有信心重做镁合金的重力铸造的前提下，万丰镁业在威海开始了第二轮创业过程。在加大投资的基础上，建设了新厂房，脱离了初创时期借用威海万丰的厂房，完全进入了独立运营状态。

经过两年多时间的努力，万丰镁业的成绩开始显现。

2010 年，在中国国际汽车零部件博览会上，经过艰苦努力的万丰镁业开始亮相，展出了多样化的镁合金产品，其中包括了镁合金汽车零部件、高铁和航空航天领域的产品。

而在技术领域，这一年万丰镁业在科技部"十二五"国家科技支撑计划重点项目中，以镁合金在卡丁车上的集成应用得到了认可。

同时，万丰镁业还主导了关于镁合金生产的多项国家标准的起草制定。

万丰镁业成为国家标准起草单位之一

转型的先声

在万丰镁业向产业纵深前进的时候，负责万丰资本运作的陈伟军团队认为，从更为广泛的意义上来理解，镁的应用，是万丰奥特在产业发展上遇到的又一重大机遇。

万丰奥特在轮毂领域的成功，得益于国内交通运输领域的需求强劲增长，万丰奥特抓住了这个时代给予的机遇。同时，从公司以往的经历可以看出，万丰奥特的崛起，也伴随着铝合金材料取代钢材的过程。正是因为铝合金的强度大、密度小、造型容易，而广受下游主机厂商的欢迎。

随着产业的发展，材料的多样化将会有更大的空间。尤其中国又是一个镁原料大国，因此在国内发展镁合金产业，是有很大的发展空间的。这可以为万丰奥特从传统制造业向先进制造业的企业转型，提供一个平台。

万丰镁业董事会探索转型升级方向

企业转型升级是 2005 年之后陈爱莲与集团高管团队经常议起的话题。进入 21 世纪，国内民营企业已经占据了中国经济的半壁江山，而且我们也可以清晰地看到，像万丰奥特这样的民营企业，从一降生开始就是在全球经济的背景下运营的。不过，从经济全球化的格局当中看，万丰奥特也是国内民企的一个典型——顺从市场，以成本和规模为公司赢利的主导，比较缺乏的是在全球范围内的创新和引领地位。

这样的角色地位，虽然具有高度的活力，却也是一个时代的缩影。政府之所以引导民营企业向创新驱动转型，正是因为其缺乏创新，国内民企的赢利水平普遍较低，而且这样的赢利水平也还是基于劳动力价格低下的国家因素。

也正是因为这样，虽然万丰镁业此时的赢利水平不高，在万丰奥特以轮毂制造为主体的产业格局中只是一家小公司，但是它却代表着整个集团的一个方向——因为它已经触及真正创新的边缘。这是万丰奥特向新型材料科学产业化迈进的一步。万丰奥特团队关注的一个问题是：万丰镁业究竟是以材料供应企业的身份，去应对所有对镁合金材料的需求，还是预先把自己定位在某一领域，成为这个领域的领先供应商？

对于 2005 年前后的万丰奥特和万丰镁业来说，这已经是一个现实的问题了。

当时，对于高强轻质的镁合金，国内的产业界已经出现了需求。不过，最早的需求出现在 IT 和家电领域，而不是万丰奥特与科研机构早先预想的汽车配件。由于 IT 和家电领域变革迅速，而且需求旺盛，所以有较大的空间来采用镁合金这种新材料。

但万丰奥特的核心能力，是在汽车零部件的制造和营销上。一旦这个领域开始应用镁合金，它的需求量会更大，而且会与万丰奥特现有的市场结合得更为紧密。

所以是坚守汽车零部件这个领域，还是把万丰镁业的市场能力向其他领域转移？这不仅关系到万丰镁业这一家公司，更关系到整个万丰奥特未来的定位。同时，万丰镁业是要进一步做镁合金轮毂，还是可以扩散到整个汽车零部件，也是一个问题。在镁合金应用中，轮毂因为涉及整个汽车的安全性，因此是要求很高的一个细分市场。从万丰镁业的经历当中，我们可以看到，万丰镁业对镁合金制造的全套工艺技术，并没有彻底掌握。是继续投资研究，还是通过其他途径获得技术？

在这些问题上，万丰奥特决策层最终得出了结论，而它将导向万丰奥特作为企业的一个巨大变革。

万丰奥特之道：万丰镁业是万丰奥特作为企业转型的先声

就全球而言，国内企业尤其是民营企业都是后发的。我们可以从万丰奥特的公司历史中清晰地看到后发的优势：在万丰奥特的轮毂产业中，需求的瞬间爆发和国外现成的产业格局，使得万丰奥特能抓住轮毂产业向中国转移的机会实现迅速崛起。

而陈爱莲"长袖善舞"的运营能力，使企业很早就遇上了镁合金技术产业化的机会，接触到了科技前沿。

科技前沿的特点就是充满了想象，也充满了不确定性，有很高的失败概率。万丰镁业的公司经历，充分表明了这个特点。不过，万丰奥特整个集团不惧困难、灵活机动的特点，也在万丰镁业的经历当中表现了出来。坚信镁合金的中国优势，以及这种新型材料的广泛应用前景，使得企业坚持了下来。

实体企业向技术引领型企业转型，通常都要经历一个相当长的痛苦时期。因为企业是以市场和赢利为导向的，而先进技术背后的新事物，总是需要一个相当长的时间才能被市场接受，而后企业才能壮大。关键在于追求利润的实体企业，能否有足够的耐心等待，并且推进这一新事物的发展，直至其被市场接受。

而万丰奥特对镁业的坚守和投资，正是这家企业向技术前沿转型，从而努力争取在产业当中取得创新和主导地位的先声。

Chapter 6
Winding Road of Magnesium Industry

Plan 863

Wanfeng Auto excelled in whatever fields it had marched into: whether it was motorcycle hub, automobile wheel hub or low pressure casting. It showed the advantage of a flexible mechanism in both production and marketing, as wells as the management expertise and social activeness of Ailian's team.

However, with the time moving forward, Wanfeng Auto would naturally encounter more challenges in new fields.

In 2001, Wanfeng seized the opportunity of magnesium alloy manufacturing which unexpectedly took Wangfeng Magnesium onto a ten-year winding road and finally, the group experienced a nirvana like a phoenix.

It was very accidental for Wanfeng Auto to enter into the magnesium alloy industry.

In 2001, after its acquisition of Shandong Dooray Wheel Co. Ltd, Wanfeng Auto reshuffled and established Weihai Wanfeng.

The reshuffling was certainly a big event for Wanfeng Auto. On the grand opening ceremony held in Weihai, Shandong Province, government officials, experts and leaders of counterparts came to celebrate. Government officials were impressed by Wanfeng's successful acquisition of joint ventures since such acquisition in 2001 was rare in China.

Opportunities always come as surprise. Among the government visitors, there came a technical advisor to Weihai Municipal Government, Chen Xianjie, Patrol Officer from China's Ministry of Science and Technology (former Deputy Director of the High-Tech Department), who was impressed by the achievement and ambition of Wanfeng Auto and brought a message as a gift to Chen Ailian. This message was highly correlated with Wanfeng Auto. Right then, the High-tech Department of Ministry of Science and Technology was inviting bids for Plan 863 nationally, a major special project of which was the development of magnesium alloy material with high strength and high toughness and its application in wheels". Institute of Metal Research, Chinese Academy of Sciences and Shanghai Jiao Tong University had been gearing up for the bid, and Jilin University, Shenyang University of Technology. Meanwhile, Beijing Nonferrous Metal Research Institute and other universities and research institutes were still struggling for the bid with some experts who had researched on the magnesium alloy material and the technique, but desiring for a powerful partner.

Wanfeng Auto was just the powerful partner they wanted, the expert in the auto aluminum alloy wheel manufacturing field. Therefore, Chen Xianjie was determined to bridge the gap and transform China's resource advantage into industrial advantages.

The background for the plan was that China, as a country with abundant magnesite resources, accounting for 22.5% of the world's total reserve, ranking the first in the proven 34 million tons. Magnesium and its alloys are the lightest metal structure used in the modern industry, which feature light weight, low density, high strength, high ductility, good casting performance, low noise, good electromagnetic shielding, shock absorption and recyclability. In recent years, magnesium and its alloys began to replace aluminum and steel, widely used in the manufacturing of spacecrafts, aircrafts, missiles, automobiles, computers, communication products and consumer electronic products, with production and consumption rapidly increased.After entering the 21st Century, in contrast to the rising global demand for magnesium alloys, the development of magnesium processing technology lagged behind. Despite the large amount of raw magnesium export, China's demand for magnesium alloys still had to be met by imports.

Therefore the Ministry of S&T launched Plan 863 to stimulate domestic research institutes, universities and enterprises to change this situation through cooperative research.

The Ministry also anticipated a trend of energy-saving and light-weight components in view of the rapid development of China's automobile industry and the tremendous energy demand. The application of magnesium alloy in auto parts was just in line with the trend.To march into the magnesium alloy industry was to some extent an important action for Wanfeng to sharpen its competitive edge in the auto industry. Chen Ailian also recognized that in the forefront of the international auto industry, energy saving was the direction of competition for vehicles like motorcycles and automobiles. With the strength unchanged, the lighter the vehicle, the less fuel it will consume. Therefore, when car users have the ability to own a car, energy saving would be an important factor affecting their choice. The use of magnesium alloy in both automobiles and motorcycles can further reduce the weight of the vehicle while maintaining the strength so as to save more energy.

In a sense, the development of magnesium alloy material was another vital step further for Wanfeng to substitute aluminum alloy wheel hub for the earlier steel wheels. After discussion, the Board of Directors decided to enter the field and invest into the development of magnesium alloy car parts. Soon in 2002 Weihai Wanfeng Magnesium Science and Technology Development Co., Ltd. (hereinafter referred to as Wanfeng Magnesium for short) was founded.

The first step of the application was to develop magnesium alloy wheels.

The research and development of magnesium alloy, the new materials taken by Wanfeng Auto was actually the mass production phase of Plan 863. Normally, a scientific research project would take a rather long time of trials and tests from the proposal, demonstration, laboratory trial, and then to the pilot medium-scale and large-scale testing. Magnesium alloy project of Plan 863 was taken to Wanfeng Auto for large-scale trials after preliminary work had been done.

Chen Ailian assigned Sheng Xiaofang to lead the project, who had participated in the initial venturing and later acted as the Purchasing Manager. To control the early investment risk, the initial venturing place of Wanfeng Magnesium was located in Weihai Waifeng. Except for an independent site, Weihai Waifeng had complete production equipments, as well as a whole team of production and operation. The Board of Directors tried to borrow Wanfeng Auto's capacity to help Wanfeng Magnesium bridging the gap from R&D to mass production.

Sheng Xiaofang had a whole picture of the magnesium industry after a thorough research. He learned that, compared with aluminum, magnesium is of higher strength, with only two thirds of aluminum's density and will be even stronger after casting. That's why Formula Racing sports cars all adopt magnesium alloy wheels. Despite these advantages, it is more difficult to cast magnesium alloy parts, for that the chemical property of magnesium is unstable, flammable and explosive which brings many problems to its processing.

Twists and Turns

Wanfeng Auto didn't expect any twists and turns when first entering this project.

The Board of Directors made such a decision based on the normal process of a scientific research. They anticipated a smooth mass production as long as the investment was poured in, since the research institutes had already completed the research and preparation. It ought to be that case normally.

Unfortunately, however, it was not until the cooperation really started, did Sheng Xiaofang found the application research by those institutes still remained in theoretical stage, which means there were many obstacles to cross before they could achieve the real mass production.

Magnesium alloy has poor liquidity and is easy to be oxidized. It is solidified quickly especially under normal temperature, even not able to fill the cast cavity. The original research plan only added gas protection to the mature aluminum melting furnace. The basic equipment was Wanfeng Auto's low pressure casting machine, which soon proved to be incapable in the large-scale magnesium alloy melting.

Wanfeng Auto had played its expected role in the cooperative research. Weihai Wanfeng had a wide range of cooperation with automobile manufacturers, among which, FAW and Chery soon offered test vehicles. After an adjustment to the producing machines, the wheel hubs, once completed, could immediately be tested for strength and durability on the testing platform.

However, problems in producing technique were not easy to solve. Weihai Wanfeng made reforms to the aluminum alloy casting machine as required and tried to produce in accordance with the requirements of magnesium alloy. Unfortunately, in the year after, Wanfeng Auto had made all together163 tests only failed to meet the demanding requirements of durability and fatigue strength no matter how it improved the equipment.

Wanfeng Auto had entered the forefront of technology in an unexplored field, which was full of uncertainty. In the development and mass production of magnesium alloy, it would naturally come across a variety of problems and accidents, even failures. During this process, the value orientation of the enterprises and scientific research institutes encountered conflicts; with research institutes taking failures for granted while Wanfeng Auto being more eager to pursue successful result as a reward to its investment.

Wanfeng Auto began to seek other approaches than self research to solve the problem. Chen Ailian suggested that experts tried to contact international counterparts and transfer technology by purchasing production equipments.

In October 2003, funded by the International Cooperation Department of China's Ministry of Science and Technology, Wanfeng Auto sent a delegation to Europe to make research, accompanied by experts from three universities and some governmental officials.

The delegation received warm welcome from Prof. Kline, Secretary General of European and German Magnesium Industry, foreign advisor of China's S&T Ministry. Wanfeng Auto as the delegation leader also expressed its best wishes to the trip and their future cooperation: "To friendship and cooperation", which was highly acknowledged by Prof. Kline.

However, business is business. Prof. Kline form Europe, a highly developed and mature market economy society, offered a full set of magnesium alloy wheel technology solutions at the price of 25 million Euros (about 2.5 billion yuan), which far exceeded Wanfeng Auto bottom line.

As a Chinese proverbs goes "Experts grasp the essence, while the amateurs notice the surface". The delegation didn't make the trip for fun. Instead, they watched and learned, and grasped the essence by "piercing through" the technology. Although Wanfeng hadn't reached any agreement with European counterparts on technology transfer, it noticed that European manufacturers with mass production of magnesium alloy didn't use existing production equipments, but research and develop their special equipments.

After the trip, Wanfeng Auto changed its mind and decided to rely on its own research instead of investment only to promote a balanced development of the enterprise.

The research team of Wanfeng Magnesium began to consider the possibility that the R&D institutes had stuck in a myth by using low pressure casting machine and gravity casting machine simply because the two were most up-to-date equipments. But these machines are designed for the characteristics of aluminum alloy while magnesium alloy is a entirely new type of material, to which the machines may not be applicable.

So Wanfeng Magnesium began to try all kinds of casting techniques, starting with die-casting used by Wanfeng Auto at its early stage. Surprisingly, despite some bubbles, magnesium alloy wheel hubs cast this way were easier to take shape.

Although a feasible way dawned, the company was then faced with a not positive situation for the drawbacks in the previous tests: more than half of the investment had been run out and the shareholders began to doubt the project.

The young Wanfeng Magnesium could not continue to live on the investment only. It must rely on production to partially support its scientific research and to win the shareholders and employees back.

That market strategy was the key to Wanfeng Magnesium's path to success.

Who Will be the First User of Innovation?

Since 2002, Wanfeng Magnesium together with those scientific research institutes had solved many problems. Index like strength and impact resistance had passed the national test. A lot of test data had been achieved in the production process. However, without crossing the threshold of durability value, a large-scale promoting was almost impossible.

Then would it be possible to break the ice with small-scale production? Wanfeng Magnesium attempted to change its role as a mass production promoter of magnesium alloy.

And that became Wanfeng Magnesium's main marketing strategy in the field of magnesium wheels.

Professional companies understand the nature of the market in a different perspective. Wanfeng Auto had entered into the wheel manufacturing industry for 10 years by 2004 and had owned a global marketing network. The marketing staff of Wanfeng Magnesium had learned that different customers have different requirements for the wheel hubs. Magnesium alloy is of high strength and low weight. Then is there any possibility to use Wanfeng Auto's network to find a corresponding target market? Magnesium wheels are good enough for kart racing, a popular sport in developed countries like Europe and the United States. For instance, tyres used in FIA F4 series need to be changed every two or three laps and thus there is almost no durability requirement. Instead, the weight loss counts a lot and a cut of dozens of grams means huge to kart racers in improving their performance.

On the critical point for its survival, Wanfeng Magnesium showed its advantage as a professional company. From 2004 onwards, it took frequent actions in marketing: getting a license to self-running import and export, passing a number of tests for magnesium alloy wheel, winning the honor of key enterprise of new material products in Shandong Province.

The core of these actions was timely adjustment to its positioning in the market.

When everything was ready, Wanfeng Magnesium contacted a top go-kart manufacturer — Douglas, to promote its newly-developed magnesium wheels.

The choice conveyed Wanfeng's understanding of the market: the go-karts provided by top companies had already achieved stunning performance in F4 series in all aspects, which means every bit of progress would be increasingly difficult unless to achieve breakthroughs in technology — weight loss in magnesium wheels would be a major one.

Unexpectedly, Douglas soon promised to establish exclusive supply matching relationship with Wanfeng. Douglas is not only a go-kart manufacturer. It owns a quite active racing team, who showed great interest to Wanfeng's magnesium wheels with prominent weight-loss index and promptly sent professionals to make more research.

The racing team owned by Douglas is a top team in the F4 arena. The division of the team is very specific with professionals in each specification who acted efficiently. Soon after their visit to China and their study to the samples back home, they requested to book a batch of samples from Wanfeng Magnesium for tests, but only at half the price.

Wanfeng made a rapid response to the request: agreement arrived and shipment immediately dispatched. Although a sale at half the price, the booking was a sign to the company's survival and potential.

Magnesium wheel is not new to the Douglas team. Such products had already appeared in the European and American markets then. But Wanfeng's product was innovative in the weight ratio of standard wheels. It was the dozen-gram weight loss that persuaded the famous karting team to try Wanfeng's product.

The first batch of magnesium wheels soon left Weihai for the United States, thanks to the license of self-running import and export Wanfeng obtained in 2004.

Wanfeng Magnesium's production later accounted for 30% of the market share in kart racing vehicles. It should be attributed to a large extent to Wanfeng's cooperation with Douglas team as the entrance to the market. If Wanfeng had selected an average team, it is very likely that magnesium wheel as a key element of the team's victory would have remained a secret. Douglas as a go-kart manufacturer had high motivation to promote racing cars with magnesium wheels of low-weight genes, which brought about an earthquake in the field-- only cars equipped with Wanfeng's magnesium wheels had the chance to win in the competition. Thus, Wanfeng's magnesium wheels naturally became standard parts of go-kart manufacturers.

Wanfeng Magnesium finally laid a solid foundation for its role in the market.

Expansion in Magnesium Industry

Winning the go-kart market, Wanfeng Magnesium managed to make a profit-loss balance. That was just a starting point for this new project instead of the destination. Wanfeng Auto started a new round of venturing in 2008 led by Zhu Xunming, the senior researcher of the enterprise.

The key to expand in magnesium industry was to make use of the market changes. Since 2006, the domestic market showed tendency preferable to the development of magnesium alloy: the application market of magnesium alloy began to boom.

The most favorable trend came from the automotive industry. Since China became an auto giant and gradually took the first position in auto production and sales volume globally, more positive trends for technological reform have appeared in the industry. On the one hand, energy saving and environmental protection became increasingly important, which encouraged auto manufacturers to adopt new materials. On the other hand, mass production and increased profit of the domestic large auto manufacturers stirred even stronger preference for new materials in order to maintain their competitive edge.

Another positive trend came from other high-tech industries, especially the IT industry.

Since the 21st Century, due to the development and industry competition in IT and Internet technology, weight loss became a prevailing trend in computers, mobile phones and other IT products. IT products became more sophisticated; meanwhile industrial control technology derived from which, made miniaturization and low weight possible in fields such as express railway and air space.

Such change is good news to the application of magnesium alloy for it features high strength and low density. Laptops, mobile phones and some high-tech products made of magnesium alloy began to swarm into the market.

Despite the changes in the market, the domestic industry needs to make efforts to grasp the opportunity. Wanfeng, as a forerunner in magnesium alloy casting industry since 2004 was at the threshold to expand its market then in 2008.

As soon as Zhu Xunming came to Wanfeng Magnesium, he first led technicians including Xu Guosong, Yang Liang to make a research on the application and development trend of magnesium alloy. In only half a year, Wanfeng Magnesium had applied for a number of patents – Wanfeng resumed its research on gravity casting of magnesium alloy only to become more confident this time, with the support of the go-kart magnesium wheel order.

After a research to the industry, Wanfeng Magnesium confidently started the second round of the venturing with increased investment and the construction of new plants. It set off again by leaving the borrowed plants in Weihai Wanfeng and became fully independent in its operating.

With two years of endeavor, Wanfeng Magnesium came to the harvest season.

In 2010, at the China International Auto Parts Expo, Wanfeng Magnesium brought a variety of magnesium alloy products for display, including auto parts, products for express railway and aerospace.

In the same year, Wanfeng Magnesium gained recognition by China's S&T Ministry as one of the key projects during the "12th Five Year" with its integrated application of magnesium alloy in go-karts.

Meanwhile, a number of national standards for magnesium alloy production were drafted by Wanfeng Magnesium.

Preface to Transformation

When Wanfeng Magnesium tried to expanded, the team responsible for Wanfeng's capital operation, with Chen Weijun as the leader, pointed out that the application of magnesium might bring a great opportunity to Wanfeng Auto in a more extensive means

Wanfeng Auto's success in the field of wheel hub could be attributed to the booming domestic transportation demand. Reviewing its history, we found Wanfeng Auto's rise was accompanied with the process of aluminum alloy taking place steel. The new material was widely welcomed by the downstream host manufacturers because of its high strength, low density and high ductility.

With the development of the industry, the diversification of materials will create more space. China as a country rich of magnesium raw materials especially has great potential in magnesium alloy industry. This can provide a platform for Wanfeng Auto to transform from traditional manufacturing to advanced manufacturing.

Enterprise transformation and upgrading was a topic often discussed by Ailian and the group's executives since 2005. Entering the 21st century, the domestic private enterprises have dominated half of China's economy. Wanfeng Auto, although born under the background of globalization, was still a typical Chinese private enterprise, which was subjected to the market, conflicted by its scale and cost, lacking in innovation and leading position in the global scope.

Its role was just a typical microcosm of the time. Chinese government tried to guide private enterprises to be innovation-driven because they were generally in low level of profitability due to their lack of innovation and the low labor price.

Thus Wanfeng Magnesium, as a small company in Wanfeng Auto Group, represented the direction of the group's development for it first reached out to innovation and brought Wanfeng Auto a step further to the scientific industrialization of new material. Wanfeng Auto's management team was concerned about its positioning: should Wanfeng Magnesium be a material supplier or should it be a leading supplier of a particular field?

Such concern became fiercer for both Wanfeng Auto and Wanfeng Magnesium around 2005.

A demand for strong and light magnesium alloy had arisen in the domestic industry. However, the earliest demand appeared in the field of IT and home appliances rather than auto parts, much beyond the expectation of Wanfeng Auto and those research institutes. Because of the rapid changes and the demand in IT and home appliances, there was a large space for the application of magnesium alloy. Wanfeng Auto was more competitive in the manufacturing and marketing of auto parts. Once the application of magnesium alloy started to take off in this field, the demand would be astonishing and more closely related to Wanfeng Auto's existing markets. So it was a hard decision whether to stick to the market of auto parts, or to shift to other areas. This decision would not only impact the future of Wanfeng Magnesium, but also decide the positioning of the entire Wanfeng Auto Group. Another problem was whether to stick to the producing of magnesium alloy wheels, or should it expand to other auto parts. Since wheel hub is highly related to the safety of the vehicle, it is a highly demanding market segmentation. As long as Wanfeng Magnesium had not yet mastered the whole set of magnesium alloy processing technology, should it continue its investment in research, or should it obtain technology by other means?

Wanfeng Auto's management finally came to the conclusion as for all these problems, which would lead to a great reform.

The Way to Success: Wanfeng Magnesium as a Forerunner of Wanfeng Auto's Business Transformation

Chinese enterprises, especially the private enterprises, are mostly followers. Followers could take advantage of the explosive market demand and their foreign counterparts' ready-made industrial pattern, which created opportunity to their rapid rise.

While this time, Chen Ailian led Wanfeng to seize the cutting-edge technology and take the opportunity of the industrialization of magnesium alloy technology.

The frontier of technology is full of imagination and uncertainty, as well as high probability of failure. Wanfeng Magnesium's experience fully demonstrated this characteristic. However, Wanfeng Auto Group as a team fear of no difficulty, flexible in reforms also showed its features in the experience. Convinced of magnesium alloy's advantages in Chinese market, and the wide application prospect of this new material, the team decided to hold on.

To transform to a technology-based leading enterprise usually has to cost an arm and leg of an industrial enterprise. New technology always takes time to be accepted by the market, while the enterprises are market-and-profit-oriented. It is a problem whether the enterprise can be patient and strong enough to wait for the dawn of the new technology.

Wanfeng Auto's perseverance and investment in the magnesium industry was the preface to its transformation to the technology forefront and its leading role in the industry.

第七章

万丰汽车梦

艰难时刻的抉择

2006年3月12日，对时任万丰奥特副总裁的夏越璋来说，是一个难忘的日子。这天他在上海浦东张江高科东区上海万丰汽车制造有限公司（以下简称万丰汽车）厂房的会议室里，主持一次特殊的会议。参加会议的是万丰汽车的中层以上干部，不过他受命宣布的不是什么好消息，而是集团经营了6年的汽车项目（即万丰汽车），要暂时进入休眠期。

让夏越璋团队备感压力的是，陈爱莲召开三次公司会议后决定下达给他们工作小组的任务。他心里很清楚，要暂停万丰奥特的汽车项目，这个任务非常棘手。当时在国内，企业退出汽车市场的案例并不是没有。同处浙江的另一家民营企业（三星奥克斯）的"退市"，在整个国内汽车市场上引起了一场轩然大波。

汽车不是低值易耗品。企业退出市场后，已经购买了这家公司产品的消费者没有了售后服务的保证。大连、北京都曾发生车主将企业告上法庭，闹得不可开交，严重破坏了企业的信誉和市场形象。

三星奥克斯从2003年进军汽车业到宣布"退市"前后不到两年时间，业内人士估计这个品牌的汽车在全国销售量为 2 000 辆左右。而万丰汽车在国内外汽车市场的保有量近 30 000 辆，是前者的 15 倍。因此一旦公司暂停经营，面临的市场风险非常大。

除了消费者，企业中断某一领域的经营，意味着将给供应商、经销商、内部员工带来一定的风险。在某种意义上，市场经济就像一个彼此联系的有机体，企业与供应商、经销商和内部员工是利益攸关方彼此是血脉相连的纽带关系。一旦万丰奥特的汽车项目暂停经营，各方的矛盾可想而知。

当然，此前万丰奥特集团董事会已经就万丰汽车的休眠讨论了无数次，并且已经无数次地演练过休眠之后各种可能出现的场面以及万丰奥特的工作小组相应采取的应对措施。董事会派出的这个工作小组成员包括夏越璋、俞林、杨旭勇，以及主管万丰汽车生产的副总经理梁品松等高管。

工作小组此次的任务，就是要把万丰奥特在经营上的变更，所造成对供应商、经销商和消费者权益的损失，降到最低。他们召开此次会议，就是为万丰汽车的休眠做出内部的部署，对与会的中层以上干部"约法三章"。

第一，所有干部都要坚守岗位，恪尽职守，关键时刻要经受住考验。

第二，采购、营销、财务和售后服务人员要为合作伙伴、用户着想，绝不允许以权谋私，400 用户热线要保持 24 小时畅通响应，为客户排忧解难。

第三，富余人员按劳动法律法规妥善处理，绝不能给企业带来负面影响。

同时，董事会为清理万丰汽车休眠时的各方利益关系拿出了方案。

第一，加强售后服务，承诺按汽车三包规定 24 小时处理消费者投诉和售后服务事项。

第二，所有万丰汽车的债务，除了希望供应商帮助消化部分库存汽车外，万丰奥特将全额兑付；经销商与万丰汽车之间的债务关系与供应商一样处理，但经销商手中的万丰汽车应维持正常销售。

第三,万丰奥特成立善后小组和善后基金，通过采购配件，来帮助经销商、售后服务商维持万丰汽车的维修和配件服务。

使工作小组感到压力巨大的是清理万丰汽车相关的债权债务关系。

我们都知道，公司在运营的过程当中需要大量的社会资源，一旦退出，光债权债务的清算就是一项海量的工作，更何况公司退出某一市场，通常情况下是因为没有利润或者前景不被看好，这种时刻是极易爆发纠纷和冲突的。再加之汽车制造是大型项目，起码都要涉及数百家配件供应商。6 年的经营使得万丰汽车与每一家供应商之间都累积下错综复杂的债权债务关系。

万丰汽车的供应商和经销商，都与万丰奥特的轮毂制造主业处于同一市场当中。俗话说，"好事不出门，坏事传千里"。如果万丰奥特在暂停汽车项目时引起了很大的纠纷，那么多年以来在轮毂制造主业上形成的金字招牌，就可能会毁于一旦了。

因此万丰奥特暂停汽车项目的核心工作是，工作小组必须一家一家地与万丰汽车的供应商和经销商们商讨，针对他们与万丰汽车应收应付款，结合公司董事会提供的资源，基本按库存汽车加现金的比例，给他们提出兑现方案。

在善后的过程当中，万丰奥特最为关注的是买了万丰 SUV（运动型多用途汽车）的用户。从 2000 年进入整车制造领域，到 2006 年董事会下决心暂时退出这个市场，6 年当中，万丰汽车已经在市场上销售了近 10 万辆 SUV。这 10 万用户的权益，是万丰奥特最为关心的。就当时而言，以 2001 年批量销售汽车开始计算，就算是最早一批万丰汽车也才用了 5 年时间，还有 5 年的售后服务期限。

因此，万丰奥特暂停汽车项目时专门设立了一个小组，帮助万丰汽车的经销商采购配件，用以维修服务。这个小组一直到万丰奥特售出的汽车全部出保之后才撤销。

在对万丰汽车做善后处理的背后，是董事会的正确决策和工作小组强大的团队合力。

此时，陈爱莲已经提出了万丰百年经营的自我要求。而暂时退出汽车制造业，则是万丰奥特迈向目标所面临的第一道门槛。

万丰奥特团队此时已经非常清楚，公司的百年经营，是以社会的信任为核心的。进入汽车制造业，本身是万丰奥特作为一家企业对市场更为前端领域的一种追求。而一家企业因为各种原因，没有达到原来的经营目标，也是经营当中非常正常的情况。未来，万丰奥特肯定会不断面临这样的情况，为追求公司永续经营的目标，就一定要跨过类似汽车项目"休眠"这样的门槛。

万丰奥特的金字招牌，是用诚信构筑而成的。正是社会对万丰奥特的信任，才使得公司不断壮大，只有对企业生态链条各个环节中的商家和用户都负责，公司才能追求百年经营的目标。

因此，万丰奥特在善后汽车项目时，也必须维持社会对其的信任，这就形成了万丰奥特"商誉高过利益"的原则。在万丰奥特看来，只有对业务的增长和衰退都有正面的处理方法，才能在市场潮起潮落时与整个产业的各个方面保持良好的合作关系，这是成熟企业必须要面对的门槛。

就这个意义上说，万丰奥特在 2006 年经受了考验。万丰汽车虽然退出了市场，不过万丰奥特却还在汽配业内，因此万丰奥特的管理团队仍然与万丰汽车的供应商们发生各种各样的关系。而由此，他们可以听到万丰奥特在退出汽车制造业之后的各方面反馈，有很多原来万丰汽车的供应商都对万丰奥特的管理层表示，2000 年前后进入汽车制造业的企业不少，后来退出市场的也有一批，而万丰奥特在退出市场的企业当中，善后处理是最圆满的。

万丰奥特汽车项目善后处理的社会满意度，为 2006 年媒体对万丰奥特的一则报道证实。

2006 年下半年，万丰奥特旗下的汽轮业务成功上市，当时上海的一家媒体发表过一篇质疑万丰奥特的报道：为什么万丰汽车没有进入上市的资产？

我们来看看这份报道①。

---

① 卫金桥，《万丰奥威上市弃置整车资产》，《第一财经日报》，2006 年 11 月 29 日。

昨天（2006 年 11 月 28 日），国内最大汽车轮毂制造商之一浙江万丰奥特控股集团（以下简称万丰奥特）旗下浙江万丰奥威汽轮股份有限公司（以下简称万丰奥威）在深交所上市，其主营铝合金轮毂研发、制造、销售业务。

一年前尚且大红大紫的整车制造部分——上海万丰汽车制造有限公司此次被剔除在上市公司之外。万丰奥威目前在国内市场上稳居前三名。其网上定价公开发行 6 400 万股新股，上市表现不俗，发行价格为每股 5.66 元。昨天一上市便以每股 8.4 元的价格开盘，最后以每股 8.2 元报收，上涨幅度达 40%。

海通证券分析师胡松分析指出，汽车零部件行业的工业全球化趋势和零部件工业独立化为该公司产品提供了广阔前景。万丰奥威在产品定价上有主动权，获利能力有保障。

本报昨天致电万丰奥特时，该公司办公室工作人员表示，负责人都在深圳参加上市活动，对汽车资产为何不纳入上市公司一事避而不谈。

其实，此次万丰奥威的上市解开了一个最大的悬念。今年以来，全线停产的万丰汽车已经被万丰奥特剔除在主要资产之外，已有其他机构接洽万丰汽车制造基地事宜。

位于上海浦东新区合庆工业开发区的万丰汽车，由万丰奥特投资兴建，主要从事中高档多功能商务车生产经营。

这个记者的消息基本是正确的，报道中提到万丰奥特的轮毂制造受到市场的追捧，也注意到万丰奥特可能会退出汽车制造领域。不过，正是由于万丰奥特在退出汽车制造业时正确处理了善后事宜，没有引起纷争，因此涉及面非常广的万丰汽车供应商和经销商，没有一个向媒体投诉，使得上海这家素以消息灵通著称的媒体只是提出了疑问而已。

不过，成功的退出，并不能掩盖陈爱莲在万丰奥特进入汽车制造领域之后又调整休眠的遗憾。万丰奥特进入汽车制造领域，是集团产业的升级，更是她的一个梦。

造车的决策

如果说1998年万丰奥特进入汽车轮毂领域时，国内人均GDP达750美元已经使得中国出现了汽车需求萌芽的话，那么中国真正进入汽车时代的年份是在2004年。这一年，中国人均GDP达到了3 000美元，相应地，汽车开始正式走入国内家庭，中国的汽车时代到来了。

汽车进入中国家庭是一个巨大的变革，形成了一个新的巨大市场。1998年亚洲金融危机爆发之后，国内的居民储蓄开始大幅上升，为了把这种储蓄转化为消费，政府开始提倡公众以"新三样"来取代原有消费当中的彩电、冰箱和洗衣机为主的"老三样"。所谓的"新三样"，指的就是住房、汽车和消费类电子产品。

住房和汽车，都属于十万甚至几十万的产品，以国内消费者的习惯来看，要跨越这样的台阶很难，不过，因为当时国内的改革开放已经接近20年，人们的收入差异已经较大，在相当一部分先富阶层当中，住房和汽车消费，已经开始形成风气。

这种市场的变化，迅速演变成了企业的转变。与我们之前描述的摩托车市场增长一样，国内汽车市场同样是由年产销几百万辆，骤然上升到2013年国内汽车产销量达1 800万辆。正是这样的变化，使得在1998年到2004年之间，国内相当一批改革开放之后起步的民营企业嗅到了这个市场散发出来的商机。从各个领域起家的企业，纷纷进入汽车制造领域。

在这其中，我们可以清晰地看到内行与外行的差别。最早一批进入汽车制造领域里的企业，有生产摩托车的浙江吉利控股集团和重庆力帆实业（集团）股份有限公司；接下来是从家电业起家的宁波奥克斯集团和广东的美的集团；再接下来像比亚迪这样的公司，也在 2003 年进入了汽车制造领域。

　　像吉利和力帆这样的公司，因为身处业内，所以了解市场的这种变化，从而提前进入。而万丰奥特当然也不会在这股浪潮面前无动于衷。陈爱莲有浓厚的汽车情节，早年就有过去北大荒当一名女拖拉机手的梦想，后来成为全县第一位女驾驶员，接着带领十几个人的团队上马铝轮毂制造创办万丰奥特——最终领导万丰奥特造车，是她梦想的升级。

　　尽管看到了市场可能形成的消费热潮，万丰奥特董事会对于进入这个市场，还是相当谨慎的。因为与万丰奥特传统的经营不同，汽车是直接面向消费者的产品，本身就有相当高的门槛，包括资本、技术、人才和销售四个方面。对于民营资本来说，这些门槛每个都不好跨越。

　　此时已经形成自己鲜明管理风格的陈爱莲，在董事会决策之后，把前期的市场调查和初步形成生产能力的任务，交给了万丰奥特创始人之一的杨旭勇。

　　杨旭勇首先要做的市场调查是，汽车市场是否会迎来热潮？而更为重要的是，适合万丰奥特的，是什么车型？对于前者，经过一段时间的熟悉之后，杨旭勇领导的调查小组很快得出了肯定的结论。而对于后面一个问题，万丰奥特的董事会成员与调查小组都觉得，万丰奥特适合避开与国家资本投资的国有大型车厂正面竞争，进入以高端的 SUV 为核心的市场。

　　这条路径的选择，是董事会对公司综合实力评估后的谨慎决策。万丰奥特身处汽车业，因此组织汽车生产相对于其他民营企业较为容易。不过当时整个万丰奥特处于大发展时期，各板块都需要大量投资。因此选择 SUV，使得万丰奥特避开了当时竞争更为激烈、投入更大的家用轿车市场，处于一个更为细分的市场当中。

　　在起步之初，万丰奥特采取了非常小心翼翼的姿态，为了保证投资的平稳，在大规模投产汽车之前，2000 年，首先采取了小规模试生产的方式，与一家国企的轻型客车部门，在新昌本地尝试合作生产。同时，项目小组还努力开辟人才来源，当时东北的重工业处于衰落的过程当中，由于万丰奥特在汽车业内已经形成了相当的品牌效应，项目小组从东北几家轻型客车厂的研究所，招聘了相当一批研发和生产管理人才。

因为在市场调研的过程当中熟悉了整个产业的状态，所以杨旭勇在接下来的试生产过程中对汽车项目实行了总体领导，通过试生产的过程，逐步实现外来人才与万丰奥特企业文化的融合。

根据当时的市场情况，决策层给首批万丰SUV定价在8万元左右。

万丰汽车SUV成功上市

这个定价是足以引爆市场的。就万丰汽车最早销售的2001年而言，当时市场上主流普及型轿车桑塔纳、富康和夏利等都在10多万到20万元的水平上。2000年左右，民营的吉利汽车推出早期款的豪情汽车，价格在3万多元，不过豪情汽车早期并不是流水线生产产品，而是手工制作产品，因此其在整车的舒适度水平上，与引进流水线生产的万丰SUV，在用户体验上相差甚多。

当然，更为重要的是，当时国内汽车市场处于"从无到有"的阶段，消费者在意的是"有没有车"。此时，价格因素对市场来说，极为重要。

在试生产期间，万丰SUV迅速地在本地市场受到了欢迎。由于万丰奥特在长三角地区的良好声誉，公司生产的头几批SUV很快销售一空。这使得万丰奥特对进入汽车制造业有了信心。管理层认为，公司可以进一步把汽车这个领域做大。

减速的汽车

要做大，万丰汽车当然不可能还像在试生产期间那样，只做现有国企的合作生产方。万丰汽车做大的第一步，就是启动并购方式获得正规的入市许可。

并购的机会来自"国退民进"。此时万丰奥特已经在上海设立了自己的子公司，当时在上海主持工作，后来成为集团副总裁的陈伟军发现，上海有一家名叫长丰客车的轻型客车制造厂，因为产品不对路，当时已经处于全面停产状态，其上属的国有资产管理部门正在考虑盘活它的资产。早就对此非常留意的陈伟军把这个动向汇报给了陈爱莲。董事会当即决定，收购长丰客车，让万丰奥特通过"正门"进入造车市场。

拿到了造车的牌照，万丰奥特的汽车项目搬迁上海就成了必然之举，这是由当时国内汽车业的状态决定的。从政府的角度来看，汽车是一个对质量要求很高的产业，关系到用户的生命财产安全，需要政府部门深入管理，因此有很强的属地管理要求，所以政府在很长时间内不允许汽车异地生产。

另外，一直以来，汽车生产牌照是各个地方的重要资源，汽车业是个大投资的产业，对地方经济有很大的拉动作用，所以各地方政府对于本地的汽车业资源都非常重视，万丰奥特要并购上海的汽车厂，在上海投资建厂就是顺理成章的事。

上海长期以来都是汽车工业的重镇，拥有大量的产业资源；同时上海的工业产品，一直以来也在市场上享有盛誉，有很强的号召力。

所以并购完成之后，万丰奥特决定与已经合作多年的上海浦东新区合庆镇再次合作拿到了土地使用权，进行大规模投资，而且投资建设一条完整的汽车生产线。

不仅如此，对于汽车项目进军上海，万丰奥特还做了人事上更进一步的安排。除招聘各类专业人才外，还抽调相当一批万丰奥特的优秀管理者如梁品松等进入上海的汽车项目。万丰奥特的汽车梦，就这样开始了。

就进入汽车制造业的时间点来说，万丰奥特选择的市场时机相当正确。国内汽车市场的爆发点就在 2003 年，而且在政府频频出台的产业扶持政策的扶持下，整个市场的汽车供应和需求都进入了蓬勃发展的阶段。万丰奥特早在 2002 年决定大规模投资汽车制造，给自己留了相对宽裕的时间去迎接这个市场高潮。

不过，市场的高潮，并不意味着每家企业都能扩张。相反，它常常意味着更为残酷的竞争，"蜂拥而入"与"洗牌退市"并存。市场通过竞争，出现领先者，进而形成领导者。

中国汽车工业协会会长胡茂元（左二）、时任中国机械工业联合会副会长张小虞
（左一）参观万丰汽车展台

此时的万丰汽车，赢下了两个关键点，除了在时机把握上十分准确之外，初期的投资也比很多民营汽车制造企业要宽裕，由此衍生出万丰汽车的另外一个优势——相对而言，它已经拥有了一批汽车技术人员。比起早期通常只有两三个核心技术人员的其他民营企业，万丰汽车的起点不低。

不过，当时的万丰汽车在运作一年之后，尚有两大门槛需要跨越。

其一，汽车制造是个大投资、综合性的领域，需要有相当数量精通技术同时又熟悉行业状态的技术和管理人员进入，因为只有这样的人才来领导企业，才能协调供应商、经销商和整个公司向统一的目标前进。

其二，汽车是个大市场，消费者对于汽车种类和车型的选择具有高度的多样化，所以对一个汽车制造企业来说，能制造出一辆车，并不意味着它就能在市场上生存。只有纯熟地掌握汽车设计和制造的各个环节，进而不断推陈出新的企业，才能确保持续生存。

这都要求万丰汽车在运营的过程当中，有一个坚强的领导权威，快速地对日常事务进行决策和处理。只有这样，才能使企业中来自五湖四海的技术和管理人才比较快地融合成一个团队，去实现目标。

搬迁上海之初，万丰汽车主要由三类人员构成：一类是对外招聘的各大汽车厂熟练的技术和管理人员；一类是由万丰奥特派出的自行培养的优秀工艺和技术骨干；第三类是对外招聘的作为后续储备的大学生和基层员工。

而由于万丰汽车搬迁到上海的速度过快，使得这支基础本来不错的团队，融合的速度大大降低了。

派遣到上海万丰汽车的梁品松、章益丹和袁林刚，见证了万丰汽车与市场之间的矛盾。

负责生产管理的梁品松很快发现，来自东北和武汉的外聘人员、来自万丰奥特内部的员工，以及万丰汽车招聘来的大学生之间，很明显有三种作风。来自国企的汽车技术人员掌握着技术，希望公司的决策更为重视技术层面，但国企的作风使得他们的效率较低，跟不上市场的节奏；而来自万丰奥特内部的员工，大多在市场一线，受市场的压力较大，而且对汽车的主机产业有一个适应过程，所以特别希望技术人员给他们以强有力的支持，也因此对技术线上的低效率非常不理解；同时，上述情况使得万丰汽车招聘来的新人有点无所适从。

这一切随着外在市场压力的加大，这种矛盾逐渐浮出水面。

由袁林刚负责的市场销售网络组建，在刚刚开始的时候，进展还是相当不错的。因为万丰奥特的品牌在经销商当中有一定的影响力，所以组网比较顺利。但他很快发现，SUV的经销商不好找，因为汽车经销商都在城市，他们销售的重点都在家用轿车上。一开始SUV作为一个新品种，经销商很愿意增加，不过几次下来，由于销售量不大，经销商们就会提出自己的看法，希望万丰汽车进行改进。

转到售后服务的章益丹的经历，则更具代表性，他差不多在半年之后才真正入行。他觉得自己一开始去做售后，是完全没有系统意识的：今天哪个经销商来电话说有辆车回来修了，是某个部件出了问题，他就马上让相应区域的备件仓库出货，把相应的配件给送过去；明天另一个经销商反映同样的问题，他还是做同样的处理。而没有去想这个问题背后说明了什么。

碰壁之后，他开始意识到了汽车专业人员所说的"系统"的重要性：要及时响应顾客的要求，不在于一个人忙得要死，而是要建立一个体系，让一批人来响应顾客的反馈，并把信息回传到生产，以便做出改进。

再接下来，他也逐步地意识到所谓"中国国情"是怎么回事。在逐步建立了汽车售后服务体系之后，章益丹带领团队开始对消费者做分析，他们意识到万丰汽车的产品，确实有可以改进的方向。

所谓"系统性思维"，就是要求处于管理者位置上的人对问题进行深入思考。章益丹曾发现市场上有一款产品销售得比较好，不过一直没有找到它旺销的理由。后来反复琢磨，终于发现是它的底盘载荷系数比万丰汽车的产品要大。

　　但这些来自外部市场的压力，并没能使万丰汽车内部的技术人员做出迅速的反应。一直到停产，万丰汽车的款型都停留于起步时的设计。在销售一线到处跑的袁林刚发现，时间长了之后，由于用户的"喜新厌旧"，万丰汽车的销售开始停滞了。各销售网点也从一开始很热心地卖万丰汽车，到销售遇阻后，销售人员都开始重点销售其他公司的汽车了。

　　万丰汽车销售的低迷，更主要的是遇上了 2004 年中国车市的分水岭。在经历了 2003 年市场的高歌猛进后，中国车市在 2004 年忽然打了个"结"，自4 月份开始，一下子跌入冰点，整个汽车市场的增长不足 10%，这与 2003 年汽车行业总体超过 35% 的增长判若云泥。不期而遇的车市调整、宏观政策的调控、消费者的持币待购、国际性能源危机和国内油价连续三次上涨等因素相互作用，传统的"油老虎"SUV 的销售日渐陷入低迷，中国车市在 2004 年给汽车生产商们上演了一部堪称《十面埋伏》的大片。

　　这就是万丰汽车决定休眠时，仍然保有相当数量库存的根源。由于外部整车市场的严峻环境，加上内部没有跟上市场的节奏，很快万丰汽车的决策变得非常艰难。一生产就是库存，停产更无法销售。

　　2004 年之后，陈爱莲感到压力倍增：因为几乎不存在销售回款，所以集团每月必须向汽车项目投入数百万元给予支撑，汽车项目成了一个很标准的"吸金"战役，必须不断向项目"加油"，一停止投入，各项支出就成问题。

　　为了改变万丰汽车的经营现状，董事会多次调整经营层班子，但无论外聘的顾彪、史践还是内部培养的张静，都没能扭转效益不断下行的局面。

休眠

　　提出让万丰汽车这个项目休眠的，是陈爱莲自己。核心原因是她发现，万丰汽车当中已经有"害群之马"——贪腐现象出现了。

　　这也是汽车项目内部矛盾进一步发展的表现。销售市场没有进展，再加上一系列的挫折，万丰汽车的人心开始变得散漫，在这种散漫的企业文化环境之下，就有人开始运用权力来谋私利了。

发现这种情况，陈爱莲开始考虑是否要暂停这个项目。她很清楚，企业要做起来，靠的就是创业精神。公司是为顾客服务的，需要的是管理者和员工都不畏艰难、不惧辛苦地工作。

创建一个优秀的企业文化，是企业管理当中最为重要也最需要保持的要素。陈爱莲的想法是，如果一家公司出现了贪腐，说明这个组织当中的文化已经出现了不小的问题。

这样的组织，要尽快从集团里切除掉。陈爱莲在这一点上的原则是非常坚定的——此时如果因为已经投入了多少资本，或者这个项目已经有一些进展而不敢或者是不忍下手裁撤的话，常常会把小问题拖成大问题。

身处售后服务线的章益丹，对陈爱莲观察到的现象，有着切身的感受。

以万丰奥特在业内的声望，再加上最初几款SUV车型，当时想成为万丰汽车经销商的人，数量相当不少。21世纪初，家用汽车在市场上供不应求，很多人认为汽车经销商这个领域有盈利，而万丰汽车的网点开设是有限度的，僧多而粥少，因此谁能成为经销商，就存在一个标准问题。

万丰奥特把选择经销商的权力下放到了基层，规定的要求是简单的：当然，汽车的销售是个大宗型业务，以万丰奥特的作风，要求经销商货款两清是肯定的，所以经销商需要有相当的经济实力。很快章益丹发现，在接纳新的销售商时，万丰汽车的经理人员中已经开始有向对方"伸手"的现象出现。

到2006年之后，万丰汽车内部有一批人已经对这个项目失去了信心，认为企业这样下去，很难在真正的市场上取得进展。因此动脑筋为自己谋私利的人开始增多，而万丰汽车管理层的手段又不够强硬，内部矛盾也不少，所以留下了很多漏洞。

最后，整个公司的阵脚开始乱了，甚至出现有人利用权力，把公司的产品拿出来倒卖的现象。

而且陈爱莲发现更多问题出现在生产领域,供应商结算被卡、采购价格虚高等,这些现象的出现,都在提醒陈爱莲,汽车项目面临关键时点。

这使得陈爱莲的内心十分痛苦。她明白,这是她作为一个决策者要痛下决心的时候了。

万丰奥特决定暂停汽车项目,背后有着更为全面的考虑。

久经商海的陈爱莲本能地觉得,从 2006 年到 2007 年,国内经济的繁荣度太高了。浙江有句老话,叫"晴天带伞,肚饱带饭",说的是人要居安思危。当时她看国内的经济繁花似锦,人人都在考虑投资,心里就有点警惕:这种繁荣能不能持久呢?

而回顾万丰奥特自 1994 年创业之后的经历,她更是心生警惕。1994 年,万丰奥特以摩托车轮毂制造为基础,一举进入国内产业界之后,以摩托车和汽车为主体的交通工具市场始终处于高速增长状态。在这个背景之下,董事会不断投资一个又一个领域,取得了比产业领域更高的增长速度。

这样的增长,是以整个市场快速增长的需求为背景的。可即便这样,万丰奥特也要控制好自己的扩张幅度。当时陈爱莲自我检视,万丰奥特所涉及的行业,是不是每个都有这种快速增长的可能? 万丰奥特所建立的企业,是不是每个都非常健康、充满活力呢?

反复思考之下,陈爱莲把自己的想法提交到董事会上讨论。董事会的结论是,万丰奥特的汽车产业,必须要暂停。因为集团为这个产业每月投入数百万元,而且短期内,没有很明显的指标可以说明它会有向好的迹象。

这个决定,在汽车界和她的朋友圈内引起了巨大反响。2007 年年底,万丰奥特的汽车项目成功整合,不仅保留了宝贵的汽车资质资源,而且弥补了项目投资的亏损,以富余的资金,为 2008 年全球金融危机的到来,备好了充足的现金流,被国内熟悉汽车工业和万丰奥特内情的政府领导认可为"进也正确,退也漂亮"。

陈爱莲被誉为中国女性企业家造车第一人

万丰奥特之道：低谷是考验企业的关键时刻

市场是波动的，一家企业进入一个市场，市场与企业的匹配度如何？能不能获得消费者的认可？同行的竞争是否激烈？这些都是企业要面对的风险。

万丰奥特进入汽车主机制造领域，从进入时间、细分市场的选择和进入路径上，都具有合理性。但是汽车市场本身竞争的激烈程度，尤其是万丰奥特对整车制造的把握程度，让这一决策存在风险。在实践过程当中，正是因为管理层对整车制造的把握存在不确定性，对外部引进的技术团队有比较大的依赖性，所以导致整车的制造规模不能起步，公司的文化不能覆盖新的产业，因此风险因素变大了。

万丰奥特在把握整车制造的进退时，整体上从集团的财务安全性出发，又考虑了万丰汽车的团队文化，非常周全。在企业文化上出现较大偏差，就意味着企业团队执行力下降，因此比较难以在市场上有所作为。而 2004 年之后，国内汽车业陷入低迷且竞争激烈，整车制造没有快速上升的市场，就不能启动规模，因此就很难在短期内达到盈亏平衡。此时如果万丰奥特的财务不能提供较高的保障，整个集团都有可能被整车制造拖入泥潭。

同时，由于整车制造与万丰奥特主业的轮毂制造存在相关性，使得万丰汽车退出市场非常受人关注。能否良性退出，一方面考验着企业管理层的能力，另一方面还关乎整个集团的业界信誉。

而万丰汽车进入休眠状态，只是暂停的，未来还有进入汽车产业的资质和空间；另外，陈爱莲视"诚信"为万丰奥特的生命，因此在处理债权债务关系上，集团负起了高度的责任。这也同陈爱莲以把万丰奥特"做成一个百年老店"作为经营目标有关。2008 年，她在接受《时代汽车》杂志采访时就曾说过："我觉得人生的价值在于创造财富，财富的价值在于奉献社会。"因此，长期以来，她在企业经营、为人处世上，倡导互利共赢。

在这种指导思想之下，以夏越璋、俞林、梁品松、杨旭勇为主力的执行层在处理善后时，有了比较大的空间，并非常圆满地完成了任务。

Chapter 7
Wanfeng's Automobile Dream

Choice in Hard Times

March 12th, 2006 was an unforgettable day for Xia Yuezhang, the vice CEO of Wanfeng Auto then. He was conducting a meeting in the conference room of Wanfeng Automobile Manufacturing Co., Ltd. (hereinafter referred to as Wanfeng Auto) in Zhangjiang Hi-tech District of Pudong Shanghai. Those attending the meeting are cadres above middle level. However, he was ordered to announce the bad news that the auto project, which had been operated for six years by the group was to go into the dormancy stage.

What makes Yuezhang's team pressured was the task assigned to their team after three meetings of Wanfeng Auto held by Chen Ailian. He was well aware that it was a tough task to pause the auto project. At that time, there were also cases to retreat from the auto market. It was sensational in the national auto market for a private enterprise (Samsung Aux), also in Zhejiang province, to retreat from the market.

Automobiles are not consumable consumer goods holding little value. After the retreat of the enterprise, the consumers of the products from the enterprise will lose the guarantee of after sales service. Car owners in Dalian and Beijing have ever brought the enterprise to court. The intense conflict severely damaged the credibility and market image of the enterprise.

It only took Samsung AUX less than two years from its entry into the automotive industry to its retreat. Insiders estimated the national sales volume of this brand to be about 2000 cars, while the international and domestic market volume of Wangfeng Auto was 30,000, 15 times of the former. Therefore, once the company suspended operations, the market risk was great.

Besides consumers, the business suspension of a sector of business will bring a certain risk to the supplier, dealers and internal staff. Market economy is like an organism, in which enterprises and suppliers, distributors and internal staff are linked to each other with shared interests. Once Wanfeng Auto suspended the project, the conflicts can be imagined.

Of course, previously board of Wanfeng Auto group has Wanfeng Auto discussed dormancy of Wanfeng Auto numerous times, and has rehearsed response measures to all kinds of possible situations after the dormancy for countless times. The board has assigned a work group from some of the senior management including Xia Yuezhang, Yu Lin, Yang Xuyong, and Deputy General Production Manager Liang Pinsong etc.

The task for the work group at that time was to reduce the loss of suppliers, dealers and consumers' rights and interests to a minimum because of the management change in Wanfeng Auto. They held the meeting to have an internal deployment of the dormancy plan in Wanfeng. The cadres above middle management who attended the meeting agreed on three pledges.

Firstly, all cadres should stick to their posts, fulfill their duties, and withstand the test at the critical moment.

Second, Procurement, marketing, finance and after-sales service personnel should have partners and customers in their mind. They are not allowed to abuse power for personal gains.   The users' hotline must be open 24 hours a day, to solve problems for customers.

Thirdly, the surplus personnel must be handled properly according to the labor laws and regulations, without giving a negative impact on the enterprise.

At the same time, the board of directors brought out measures to the various interests of the different parties when cleaning up Wanfeng Auto during the dormancy.

First, to strengthen after-sales service: committing to deal with consumer complaints and after sale service 24 hours a day according to three guarantees.

Second, all Wanfeng Auto debt, in addition to the hope that the suppliers helped deal with some of cars in stock, Wanfeng Auto would pay in full. Debt relations between Wanfeng and dealers and suppliers would be dealt the same. However, the dealers should maintain the normal sales of stock cars.

Third, Wanfeng Auto established rehabilitation group and fund to help distributors and service providers maintain Wanfeng Auto repair and spare parts service through the procurement of parts.

What made the working group feel the great pressure was to clean up the car related debtor creditor relationship related to Wanfeng Auto.

We all know that the company needs a lot of social resources in the course of operations. Once out, the liquidation of the debt is a massive amount of work. Not to mention the company to withdraw from a market. Usually because there is no profit or optimistic prospect, disputes and conflicts may break out easily. Furthermore car manufacturing is a large project, involving at least hundreds of spare parts suppliers. Six years of operation has formed a complex debtor creditor relationship between Wanfeng Auto and each supplier.

Wanfeng Auto's suppliers and distributors, and Wanfeng Auto wheel manufacturing industry are in the same market. As the saying goes, 'bad news has wings'. If Wanfeng Auto's suspension of a car project aroused great disputes, then the good brand reputation formed after many years in wheel manufacturing industry might collapse overnight.

Therefore the main task in Wanfeng Auto suspension of the car project was that the working group must discuss with Wanfeng suppliers and distributors one by one to give proposals on redemption, according to their receivables and payables with Wanfeng, together with resources provided by the board of directors and the proportion of stock cars and cash.

In the process aftermath, Wanfeng Auto was most concerned about the users who had bought Wanfeng SUV (sports utility vehicle). Since the entry into the vehicle manufacturing field in 2000, and until 2006 the board of directors decided to temporarily withdraw from this market. During the 6 years, nearly 100,000 SUV have been sold in the market Wanfeng was most concerned about the 100000 users' rights and interests. From 2001, when Wanfeng Auto began fleet sale of the cars, even the first batch of Wanfeng cars have been used for 5 years, and there are 5 years of after sale service period.

Therefore, Wanfeng Auto set up a team especially when the car project was suspended, to help Wanfeng Auto dealers buy accessories, and for maintenance services. After the team would continue until Wanfeng cars' insurance expired.

The dealing with the aftermath of the Wanfeng cars was the correct decision of the board and strong team spirit of the working team.

At this time, Chen Ailian proposed a self requirement for a century-old business.

And the temporary withdrawal from the automobile manufacturing industry was the first threshold Wanfeng Auto confronted towards the target.

Wanfeng Auto team was aware that the company's 100-year business should rely on the trust of the society. To enter the automobile manufacturing industry itself was Wanfeng's pursuit for a more frontier field of the market as an enterprise. It is very common in business that for various reasons, a business did not achieve the original business In the future, Wanfeng will certainly face such a situation continually. For the pursuit of sustainable management of the company goal, it must be cross such a threshold similar to car project dormancy.

Wanfeng Auto's reputation has been constructed with integrity. It is social the social trust in Wanfeng that makes the company continue to grow. Only when the enterprise takes responsibility for each link of the business and the users in ecological chain can the company pursue the goal of 100- year operation.

Therefore, aftermath of the car project for Wanfeng Auto must also maintain the social trust, which formed the Wanfeng Auto's principle "good business reputation outweighs high interest". In Wanfeng's view, only with a positive approach to the business growth and recession, can the enterprise maintain good relations of cooperation with all aspects of the industry in rise and fall of the market. This is the threshold every mature enterprise must face.

In this sense, Wanfeng Auto has withstood the test in 2006. Although Wanfeng cars have retreated from the market, but Wanfeng Auto remained in auto parts industry, and therefore Wanfeng Auto management team still maintained various relations with Wanfeng Auto suppliers. And thus, they can hear feedback from all aspects of car manufacturing industry. Many from the management of original Wanfeng Auto suppliers said, around the year 2000, many enterprises entered automobile manufacturing. Later a number of them withdrew from the market.

However Wanfeng's dealing with the aftermath is the most sound among the enterprises withdrawing from the market,

The social satisfaction in dealing with the aftermath of Wanfeng Auto's car project of has been confirmed by a media report on Wanfeng Auto in 2006.

In the second half of 2006, Wanfeng Auto's Automobile wheels business was successfully listed. A media in Shanghai published an article questioning Wanfeng Auto reported: why hasn't Wanfeng car been listed?

Let's take a look at the report.

Yesterday (28 November 2006), one of the largest automobile wheel manufacturer in Zhejiang Wanfeng Auto Holding Group (hereinafter referred to as Wanfeng Auto) whose subsidiary Zhejiang Wanfeng Aowei Automobile Wheels Co., Ltd. (hereinafter referred to as Wanfeng Aowei) has been listed on the Shenzhen Stock Exchange. Its main business is research and development, manufacturing and sales of aluminum alloy wheel hub.

Vehicle manufacturing section which was in the limelight a year ago--Shanghai Wanfeng Auto Manufacturing Co., Ltd. was excluded in the listed companies this time. Wanfeng Aowei is currently ranked top three in the domestic market. Its online public pricing of offered 64000000 new shares. The performance is good, with the issue price of 5.66 yuan per share. Yesterday, shortly after being listed, its opening price was 8.4 yuan per share price and closed at 8.2 yuan per share, with a 40% rate of increase.

Haitong Securities analyst Hu Song has pointed out that the trend of the industrial globalization of the auto parts industry, and the independence of the parts industry provide a broad prospect for the company's products. Wanfeng Aowei has initiative on product pricing, and security of profitability

When our staff reporter called Wanfeng Auto yesterday, calling Wanfeng Auto, the company's office staff said the person in charge was in Shenzhen to attend public activities, avoiding the issue why Wanfeng Auto assets were not included in the listed company.

In fact, the listing of Wanfeng Aowei unlocked a biggest suspense. Since the beginning of this year, Wanfeng Automobile which has stopped production has been excluded from the main assets and other institutions are already approached matters of Wanfeng vehicle manufacturing base.

Located in Shanghai Pudong Heqing Industrial Development Zone, Wanfeng Automobile, invested by Wanfeng Auto, mainly engaged in middle and high-grade multi-functional commercial vehicle production.

The reporter's message was basically correct. It was mentioned in the report that Wanfeng Auto Wheel Hub Manufacturing was sought after by the market, and it also noted that Wanfeng Auto might retreat from the automobile manufacturing field. However, it is due to the correct handling of the aftermath when Wanfeng Auto withdrew from automobile manufacturing industry that it did not cause disputes, and therefore none of the many Wanfeng Automobile suppliers and distributors involved complained to the media, making the well-informed media in Shanghai only raised some questions.

However, successful exit cannot conceal Chen Ailian's regret on Wanfeng Auto's entering the field of automobile manufacturing and dormancy adjustment. Wanfeng's entering the field of automobile manufacturing field, is the upgrading of the industry, and also one of her dreams.

The Decision of Automobile Manufacturing

In 1998 when Wanfeng Auto to enter the field of automotive wheel hub, the per capita GDP of $750 has made China auto demand bud. Then China really entered the era of automobile year in 2004 when China's per capita GDP reached $3000. Accordingly, the car began to formally enter the domestic family. The Chinese car era has arrived.

Entry of cars into the Chinese family is a huge reform, forming a new huge market. After the outbreak of the Asian financial crisis in 1998, the domestic household savings began to rise sharply. In order to transform savings into consumption, the government began to encourage the public to use the "new three" to replace the previous consumption of color TV sets, refrigerators and washing machines based "old three". The so-called "new three", refers to housing, automobile and consumer electronics products.

Housing and cars all belong to the products worth hundreds of thousand or even hundreds of thousand yuan. In view of the domestic consumer habits, it is very difficult to climb such a step. However, it has been nearly 20 years since the domestic reform and open policy. People's income gap is large. It has become fashionable for a considerable part of the rich class to have housing and car consumption.

The change of the market evolved into the enterprise change very soon. Similar to motorcycle market growth as mentioned before, the domestic car market the year of sales of cars also soared from several million to 18 million in 2013. It was such a change that made quite a number of domestic private enterprises founded after reform and opening up policy sense the business opportunities from the market between 1998 and 2004. Enterprises started from various fields have entered the field of auto manufacturing.

In this process, we can clearly see the differences between the experts and the lay. The earliest batch of enterprises entering the field of automobile manufacturing included Zhejiang Geely Holding Group that manufactured motorcycles and Chongqing Lifan Industry (Group) Co., Ltd. Next came Ningbo Aux group which started from the household appliance industry and Guangdong Midea Group, followed by companies such as BYD, which also entered the car manufacturing field in 2003.

Company such as Geely and Lifan, were in the auto industry, so they understood the changes of the market and entered it in advance. Wanfeng Auto certainly wouldn't be completely indifferent in the face of this wave. Chen Ailian has strong auto complex. She has been a woman tractor driver in Beidahuang in the past and became the first female driver in the whole country. Then she led a team of about ten members to launch aluminum wheel manufacturing company - Wanfeng Auto and finally led Wanfeng to manufacture cars, which was the upgrade of her dream.

Despite the consumption boom arising in the market, Wanfeng Auto's board of directors was still quite cautious when deciding to enter the market. Different from Wanfeng Auto's traditional operation, the cars are direct consumer-oriented products which have a very high threshold, including four aspects, namely capital, technology, talent and sales. For private capital, it is not easy even to conquer one of them.

At this time Chen Ailian who has formed her own distinctive management style, after board's decision assigned the task of the early market research and forming the production capacity to Yang Xuyong, one of the founders of Wanfeng Auto.

The market survey Yang Xuyong should conduct first of all was that whether the car market would embrace a boom? And more importantly, what type of car was most suitable for Wanfeng Auto? For the former, after a period of time research, investigation team led by Yang Xuyong quickly got the conclusion, but for the latter question, both Wanfeng board members and the investigation team felt that

Wanfeng Auto should avoid the direct competition with state-owned large car factories. Wanfeng should enter the market that based on high-end SUV.

This choice was the prudent decision after board's the evaluation of the company's comprehensive strength. Wanfeng Auto was in the automotive industry, so compared with other private enterprises it was easier for Wanfeng to start automobile production. But at that time the entire Wanfeng was in a major period of development, with every section needing a lot of investment. Therefore, choosing SUV, the Wanfeng Auto avoided the family car market which had more intense competition and needed more investment, in a more market segments among.

In the beginning, Wanfeng Auto was very prudent. To guarantee the security of investment, Wanfeng tried small scale production, attempting to cooperate with some sections of light bus manufacture in a state-owned enterprise and produce locally in Xinchang before mass production. At the same time, the project team also strived to open up talent sources. At that time heavy industry is in the process of decline in the northeast. Because Wanfeng has formed a considerable brand effect in the automotive industry, the project team has recruited a considerable number of management personnel in research and development and production from several Northeast institutes of light bus factories.

Because they know the state of the whole industry in the process of market research, so Yang Xuyong was the general leader in the following trial production process of the automobile project. Through trial production process, the newly recruited talents assimilated Wanfeng enterprise culture gradually.

According to the prevailing market conditions then, the decision layer priced the first batch of Wangfeng SUV at 80000 yuan.

This pricing is enough to set off the market. As early as the first sale of

Wangfeng vehicles in 2001, the most popular cars were Santana, Fukang and Xiali which were above the level from 10,000 to 20,000. Around 2000, the private Geely Automobile launched early models of Haoqin, at the price of over 30000 yuan. However, early Haoqin cars were not products on the production line instead they were handmade products. Therefore, compared with Wanfeng SUV produced on the introduced assembly line, Haoqin's comfort level of user experience was quite different.

Of course, the more important was that the domestic auto market went through the stage from nothing to ownership. What consumers cared was whether they have the cars. In is sense, the price factor was very important for the market then.

During the trial production, Wanfeng SUV was quickly welcomed in the local market. Because of Wanfeng's good reputation in the Yangtze River Delta region, the first batches of Wanfeng SUV quickly sold out, which made Wanfeng have confidence to enter the automotive industry. The management believed that the company could further expand the field of the car production.

Slowing Cars

To become larger, of course Wanfeng's automobiles couldn't stay in the level of trial production, by only cooperating with the existing state-owned enterprises in production. The first step to become larger was to start the ways of merger and acquisition to obtain the formal entry into the market.

The opportunity came from "the retreat of state-owned enterprises and entry of private ones". At this time Wanfeng Auto has set up its own subsidiary in Shanghai then. Chen Weijun who has been in charge in Shanghai then, and later becoming group vice president, found at that time, a light bus manufacturing factory in

Shanghai named Changfeng bus was in the state of production halts because the product is not right. The management department of its state-owned assets was considering revitalizing its assets. Chen Weijun who has keeping a close eye on it reported this to Chen Ailian. The board of directors decided to purchase, Changfeng bus to let Wanfeng Auto enter the automobile manufacturing market through the "front entrance".

After getting the license to manufacture cars, it was necessary for Wanfeng Auto car project to move to Shanghai, which was determined by the state of domestic auto industry. From the government point of view, the auto industry has a very high quality requirement, which is related to the user's life and property security, needing government's intensive management. Therefore there is a very strong territorial management requirement. Consequently, for a long time the government does not allow cars to produce in remote places.

In addition, vehicle production license has been an important resource for each region. The auto industry is a big investment industry, having a significant role in boosting the local economy, so the local government has attached great importance to local resources of the automobile industry. It was reasonable for Wanfeng Auto to merge and purchase Shanghai car factory, and invest and build factory in Shanghai.

Shanghai has long been an important city of the automobile industry, with a large number of industrial resources. Shanghai's industrial products have a good reputation in the market all the time, having a strong appeal.

So after the completion of the acquisition, Wanfeng Auto decided to cooperate with Shanghai Heqing town (which has been working together for many years) in the Pudong New District again to get the right to use the land and of, and make large investments, investing in the construction of a complete auto production line.

Besides, Wanfeng Auto also made further arrangements for personnel as for the entry of the car project into Shanghai. In addition to recruiting all kinds of professional talents, a number of outstanding persons of management such as Liang Pinsong in Wanfeng Auto are deployed to the car project in Shanghai. Wanfeng's dream for car manufacture began in this way.

The timing for Wanfeng Auto to enter the automobile manufacturing is fairly correct. The outbreak of the domestic automobile market was in 2003. With the government's frequent introduction of industrial support policies, the entire market's auto supply and demand have entered a stage of rapid development. Wanfeng Auto decided to make large-scale investment in the automobile manufacturing early in 2002, leaving itself a relatively ample time to meet the climax of the market.

However, the climax of the market does not mean that every enterprise can expand. On the contrary, it often means more cruel competition. "Flocking into the market" and "delisting" coexist. Through competition in the market, front runners appear and then become the leaders.

Hu Maoyuan (second from left); president of China Automobile Industrial Association, and Zhang Xiaoyu who was vice president of the China Machinery Industry Federation Zhang Xiaoyu (first from left) visited the Wanfeng car booth.

At this time, Wanfeng has won the two key points: in addition to the timing is very accurate, the initial investment is also more than a lot of private car manufacturing enterprises, resulting in another advantage of Wanfeng. Relatively speaking, it has already had a number of automotive technical personnel. Compared with other private enterprises which only had two or three core technical personnel at early time, Wanfeng's starting point is not low.

However, after Wanfeng Car has been in operation for a year, there are two major barriers to cross.

First, car manufacturing comprehensive field needs huge investments and a considerable number of management personnel who master technology and are familiar with the industry status. Only such talents, who are in charge of the enterprise, can coordinate suppliers, distributors and entire firm to move forward the common target.

Second, the car market is a big one. Consumers' choices for car types and models are of high diversification. Therefore for a car manufacturing enterprise, ability of producing a car does not mean that it will be able to survive in the market. Only the enterprises which skillfully master all aspects of the automotive design and manufacturing, and carry out continuous innovation, can they ensure the continued survival.

This required that in the course of operations of Wanfeng cars, there was a strong leadership authority that could quickly make decisions and deal with the daily affairs. Only in this way can technical and management personnel from all over the country in the enterprise blend into a team more quickly to achieve their goals.

When it moved to Shanghai, Wanfeng Automobile consisted of three types of personnel: the first type of personnel were skilled technical personnel recruited from different car factories and management personnel; the second type of personnel were excellent craft and technical backbone cultivated by Wanfeng itself; the third type were reserve university graduates and junior staff recruited outside Wanfeng.

Wanfeng Automobile moved to Shanghai too quickly, which greatly slowed down the speed of convergence of the team that was originally a good one.

Liang Pinsong, Zhang Yidan, and Yuan Lingang who were sent to Shanghai, witnessed the contradiction between Wanfeng car and the market.

Liang Pinsong who was responsible for production management soon found, there were obviously three kinds of styles in staff from the northeast and Wuhan, from Wanfeng Auto itself, as well as college students recruited outside. Automobile technical Staff from state-owned enterprises who mastered technique hoped that company's decision would pay more attention to the technical level. However, the style of state-owned enterprises made them inefficient, which was not in rhythm of the market. Most of the staff from internal Wanfeng Auto were in the forefront of the market and under great market pressure Besides, It took time for them to adjust to the automobile industry. Therefore, they particularly hoped technology personnel could give them a strong support, so they didn't quite understand the low efficiency of technical staff. Meanwhile, the above situation makes newly recruited staff of Wanfeng a little bit at a loss.

With the increasing pressure of the external market, this contradiction has gradually emerged.

The market sales network set up by Yuan Lingang went fairly smoothly at the beginning. Because Wangfen Auto brand had a certain influence among the dealer, so it was smooth to establish the network of sales, whereas he soon found it hard to find SUV dealers, because dealers are in the city. The focus of their sales was on the family car. SUV was a new product. The dealers were willing increase sales. After several times, due to low sales, dealers would put forward their own views, hoping that the car could be improved.

The experience of Zhang Yidan, who was transferred to after sale service, was more representative. He hasn't mastered the industry until half a year later. He thought that he had not system awareness when he began after-sale service. He will immediately sent the spare parts from warehouse from corresponding section. When tomorrow another dealer reflected the same problem, he still did the same without thinking the problem behind it. After hitting against the wall, he began to be aware of the importance of "system" mentioned by automotive professionals. To timely response to customer requirements did not rely on a person, but set up a system and let a group of people be in response customers' feedback, and the information is transmitted to the production in order to make improvements.

The so-called "systematic thinking" requires the management personnel to think over the problem. Zhang Yidan has found that a product sold well in the market, but he has not found the reason for its popularity. Later after repeated pondering, he finally found that its chassis load coefficient was greater than the product of Wanfeng.

However, the pressure these from the external market did not make the internal technical personnel in Wanfeng car to make rapid response. Until the suspense of production, Wanfeng car models remained the design at the beginning. Always in the frontline sales, Yuan Lingang found that Wanfeng Auto sales began to stagnate as time went by, due to the fact that the users love the new and loathe the old. In every sales outlet, the salesmen who were very enthusiastic about selling Wanfeng cars, began to sell cars of other companies after meeting obstacles in sales.

Wanfeng' sales downturn was mainly due to a divide in China automobile market in 2004. After the triumph of the market in 2003, Chinese car market suddenly hit a deadlock since April 2004, suddenly falling to the bottom with a growth of less than 10% in the entire car market, in sharp contrast with 35% in 2003. Unexpected adjustment of the auto market, macroeconomic policy regulation, consumers' keeping cash in hand, international energy crisis and domestic rising oil prices continuously for three times all caused the sales of the traditional SUV, the "gas guzzler" to gradually have a downturn. Chinese auto market was like a Chinese movie "house of Flying Daggers", which means ambush on all sides.

That was why there was a considerable amount of inventory, when Wanfeng decided to begin dormancy plan. Due to the severe environment of the external vehicle market, coupled with the internal Wanfeng did not keep up with the rhythm of the market, it was very difficult for Wanfeng Automobile to make decisions. Once it produced, there would be stock, but if it stopped production, it is harder to sell.

Since 2004, Chen Ailian has felt even greater pressure: because there are virtually no sales and accounts receivable, so the group must allocate several million yuan to car project monthly. The car project continuously consumed money. Once without input of money, there would be trouble in spending.

To change Wanfeng Automobile's operating status, the board of directors repeatedly adjusted the management team. Regardless of Gu Bia recruited outside Wanfeng, Shi Jian or Zhang Jing cultivated by Wanfeng group itself, they failed to reverse benefits the situation of downturn profits.

Dormancy

It was Chen Ailian herself who put forward the plan of dormancy to the Wanfeng Automobile project. The core reason was that she found, Wanfeng Auto had "black sheep" — the phenomenon of corruption.

This is also the performance of further internal contradictions of the automotive project. Sales in the market had no progress, coupled with a series of setbacks. In Wanfeng Automobile, people began to become loose. Under such a lax corporate culture environment, people began to use power to seek personal gains.

Facing this situation, Chen Ailian began to consider whether to suspend the project. She was very clear that the success of the enterprise was based on the entrepreneurial spirit. The company was for the customer service, needing the hard work of the management and staff who were not afraid of difficulties and hard work.

To create a good corporate culture is the most important element for the management of the enterprise. Chen Ailian's idea was that if a company has been corrupt, and then the culture of the organization had a big problem.

Such an organization should be removed as soon as possible from the group. Chen Ailian was very firm in this principle. If the group was unwilling to remove the project, because much capital was invested, or there was some progress in the project, and then the small problems might become big ones.

Zhang Yidan who was in the after-sales service had a personal experience towards the phenomenon observed by Ailian.

Owing to Wanfeng Auto's popularity in the industry, coupled with the several initial SUV models, there were quite a few people who want to be Wanfeng Automobile dealers. In early twenty-first Century, the domestic automobile market was in short supply. Many people thought that the field of car dealers was profitable. The limited number of Wanfeng Automobile sales network couldn't meet the demand of dealers, so who could become dealers was a common problem.

Wanfeng Auto gave the power of choosing dealers to the grassroots. The regulations were very simple: as car sale was large business, according to Wanfeng Auto style, dealers were certainly required be collected and delivered. Therefore, dealers needed to have considerable economic strength. Soon Zhang Yidan found that in the admission of new dealer, the manager of Wanfeng Automobile began to ask for bribes from the dealers.

By 2006, a number of people inside Wanfeng car have lost confidence in the project, thinking that if the enterprise continued in this way, it was difficult to make progress in the real market. Therefore, increasing number of people thought of their personal gains. Besides, the car management was not tough enough, coupled with many internal contradictions, leaving a lot of loopholes.

Finally, the company was in a chaos. Some even abused their power to sell the company's product for their own profits. Furthermore, Chen Ailian found more problems in the field of production,

And Chen Ailian found more problems in the production field: the supplier settlement was stuck; the purchasing price was illusively high. The emergence of all these phenomena reminded Chen Ailian that automotive project was facing a critical point.

This made Chen Ailian very painful. She understood that this was the time for her to make a decision as a decision maker.

Chen Ailian, as an experience businesswoman, felt instinctively that, the degree of economic prosperity is too high from 2006 to 2007. There is an old saying in Zhejiang, saying "bring umbrella on a sunny day; bring food when full", which tells people to be vigilant. When she saw the domestic economy flourishing and everyone considering the investment, she was cautious and doubt whether this prosperity could be sustained.

Looking back on the experience of the founding of Wanfeng Auto since 1994, she was more wary. In 1994, Wanfeng Auto entered the domestic industry based on motorcycle wheel hub manufacturing. The transportation market with motorcycles and automobiles as the main traffic tools was always in the state of rapid growth. In this context, the board of directors continued to invest in one area after another, achieving a higher growth rate than the field of industry.

Such an increase was based on the rapid growth of the entire market demand, but even so Wanfeng Auto should control its rate of expansion. At that time

Chen Ailian had a self-examination about whether every Wanfeng Auto industry involved had the possibility of rapid growth and whether every enterprise established by Wanfeng Auto was very healthy and vibrant?

After repeated reflection, Chen Ailian put forward her ideas to the board of directors for discussion. The board concluded that Wanfeng Automobile industry must be suspended, for the group has invested millions of yuan every month in the industry, but in the short term, there was no obvious indication that it would be better.

This decision caused a huge storm in the automotive industry and her circle of friends. By the end of 2007, Wanfeng Automobile project had had successful integration, not only retaining the valuable resource of automobile quality, but also making up for the loss of investment in the project. With surplus funds and cash, Wanfeng was well prepared for the arrival of the global financial crisis of 2008.The government leaders who were familiar with Wanfeng's internal situation thought Wanfeng had both a good beginning and a good ending in automotive industry.

Chen Ailian: known as the first Chinese female entrepreneurs of vehicle production

Wanfeng Auto style: trough is the critical moment to test enterprises

Market is volatile. After an enterprise enters a market, what is the level of matching between the market and the enterprise? Can it get the recognition of consumers? Is the competition among the peers fierce? These are the risks that enterprises should face.

It was reasonable in timing, market choice, and way for Wanfeng Auto to enter automobile engine manufacturing field. However, the decision was risky depending on the extent of fierce competition and mastery of vehicle manufacturing. In practice, it is because the management had uncertainty toward the vehicle manufacturing and depended largely on the introduction of the external technical team, which led to the stagnant scale of vehicle manufacturing. Besides, the corporate culture could not cover the new industry, so the risk factors became big.

When Wanfeng Auto decided to enter or retreat from vehicle manufacturing, they considered both the group's financial security and Wanfeng Automobile team culture, which was very comprehensive. A large deviation from corporate culture meant that the company's team executive power had declined. In this case, it was difficult to make achievements in the market. Besides, since 2004, the domestic auto industry had downturn and competition was fierce. Vehicle manufacturing couldn't start large-scale production without a rapid rise in the market. Therefore, it was difficult to strike a balance between profits and loss. If the Wanfeng Auto finance could not provide high security, the whole group was likely to be trapped in vehicle manufacturing.

At the same time, due to a correlation between the vehicle manufacturing and Wanfeng's main business of hub manufacturing, whether Wanfeng Automobiles could withdraw from the market well is a great concern among people. On the one hand, it tested the ability of the enterprise management on the other hand, it was also related to the entire group's industry reputation.

However, Wanfeng Auto's state of dormancy was just a pause. In the future, Wanfeng Automobile had qualifications and room to enter automobile industry. In addition, Chen Ailian considered integrity as Wanfeng Auto's life, so in dealing with the relationship between claims and liabilities, the group was highly responsible. This was also the same with the Chen Ailian's target of making Wanfeng Auto a century-old business. In 2008, when she was interviewed by Auto Age magazine, she said, "I think the value of life lies in the creation of wealth, while the value of wealth lies in dedication to the community." So, for a long time, she has been advocating mutual benefit in the business, in both enterprise operation and getting on with people.

Under such guideline, Xia Yuezhang, Yu Lin, Liang Pinsong, and Yang Xuyong as the main force of the executive layer in the treatment of the aftermath had greater room and completed the task successfully.

第八章

大公司格局

曲折上市路

2006 年 11 日 28 日是万丰奥特发展历程中一个重要的日子。这一天，深圳证券交易所（以下简称深交所）的开市宝钟被陈爱莲和中国机械工业联合会执行副会长张小虞共同敲响。它标志着万丰奥威正式翻开了作为上市公司的新篇章。

万丰奥特的陈列室内至今仍保存着敲响开市钟的木槌。

这是万丰奥特创业的第 12 个年头。万丰奥威是当时中小企业板上市公司开盘时，人来得最多的一家企业，这体现了已经形成大公司格局的万丰奥特整个集团高管层"共创共享"的风格。

从 1999 年收购上海二守合金开始，万丰奥特逐步进入了大公司格局，发展的机会纷至沓来。

2000 年，通过联合重组设立上海万丰汽车制造有限公司，选择 SUV 作为主打产品，实现从汽车零部件向整车的跨越；

2001 年，北上收购山东都瑞轮毂有限公司，将万丰奥特大旗插上齐鲁大地；

2002 年，建立重庆生产基地，将触角直接渗透到中国摩托车工业的发祥地，实现本土化生产、敏捷化供应；

2003 年，承担国家 863 计划项目，设立威海万丰镁业科技发展有限公司；

2004 年，在长三角地区的另一个经济重镇宁波，播下了中外合资企业的种子；

2005 年，迎来万丰奥威汽轮股份有限公司的大发展。

2000 年之后，万丰奥特的发展愿景已经越来越清晰，在基于自身积累的人才和技术基础上，这家浙江本土的民营企业试图成为汽车和机械领域里具有领先技术和规模制造的大型企业集团。

从最初创业团队的亲力亲为，到后来董事会的各司其职，万丰奥特作为一家民营企业，已经逐步地从轮毂制造一个产业迈向了多个领域，企业产值开始从几亿迈向了百亿的门槛。

万丰奥特能迈过这个门槛，与陈爱莲的个性高度相关。这位好学的女性，是个孔雀型的管理者：她乐意分享，知人善任，喜欢把事情分解之后由团队成员一起来承担，而在业绩分配上又从不吝啬。因此万丰奥特运营数年之后，越来越多有才干的人聚集到了这个平台上。万丰奥特在摩托车轮毂制造领域起步之后，机会和人才的快速积聚，使得这家企业实现了超常规跨越式发展。

而这也形成了万丰奥特的企业管理风格——这是一家长袖善舞的企业，在企业运作的各个方面，都建立了良好的关系。

也正是因此，万丰奥威上市成为整个集团相关方的一个节日，万丰奥威也成为当时深交所上市公司当中到现场祝贺嘉宾最多的一家企业。

2006 年 11 月 28 日 9 点 28 分，陈爱莲敲下万丰奥威的开市钟，代码为002085 的股票瞬间开盘。股价从发行时的每股 5.66 元，到以每股 8.20 元结束上市当天的交易，价格上涨 45%。

此时的万丰奥特已经从 1994 年创业时从银行贷款 50 万元的资本、15 个人的创业团队，以及新昌县城江南路 50 号中宝实业厂区两条夹道里的 4 台机

器，发展成为一家资产超过 50 亿元、员工超过 6 000 人的大型民营集团。在
国内的汽车零部件领域里，它已经成为一个重要的领跑者，在浙商群体当中，
也是少见的先进制造业企业。

万丰奥威成为国内行业第一股

　　之后，万丰奥特举行了答谢宴会，真诚感谢来自中国机械工业联合会、
浙江省、绍兴市新昌县及深交所的众多合作伙伴们。

　　万丰奥特的成长，确实与它所处的环境密切相关。

　　如果说在万丰奥特起步之初，这家小企业对环境并无选择的话，那么这
家企业的幸运之处，就是它降生在万商云集的浙江省，另外新昌的小环境，
又使它生长速度更得到加速。

　　浙江是中国民营企业的大本营。在改革开放的早期，由于浙江"七山
二水一分田"的现实，务农意味着贫困，这使得本地民众有转向工业的巨
大动力。

创业初期的浙商身上就具备了"历经千辛万苦、说尽千言万语、走遍千山万水、想尽千方百计"的"四千精神",使他们在各个领域达到了无坚不摧、攻无不克、战无不胜的境界。早期,在本地社会迈过了由农业转向工业的门槛之后,工业的发展得到了各级政府的支持。作为全国民营经济的发祥地,浙江历届省委省政府营造了非常好的环境和土壤,在市场上采取"无为"态度,按市场经济规律办事,在行政上采取"有为"手段,服务意识非常强,使浙商具备了"一有雨露就发芽,一有阳光就灿烂"的强大活力!

30 年积累下来,浙江出现了商业领域群星闪烁的局面。在浙商群体当中,2006 年已经迈过了 50 亿元资产的万丰奥特,虽然光芒闪耀,但还不是最亮的那颗巨星。而对于万丰奥特来说,生存于这样一个社会环境当中,无疑是一种激励。

万丰奥特的幸运之处,还在于其立身之地在新昌。新昌作为浙江不多的山区县,由于发展农业的要素缺乏,所以县委县政府和社会各界对于工业的支持力度很大。正是这种支持,造就了新昌这个山区县从农业时代的贫困地区发展成为改革开放之后的工业重镇。改革开放之前,新昌几乎没有工业,而改革开放 30 年之后,在这个人口不到 50 万的资源小县里,涌现出了 3 家上市公司。

在万丰奥特不长的历史当中,我们可以在它发展的每一个阶段看到包括政府在内的社会各界的支持身影。无论是陈爱莲带领团队独立创业获得银行贷款、征地建设工业园,还是奔赴上海、山东、重庆、广东等地建立生产基地,都得到了各级政府的高效服务。

作为新昌的一家标杆性企业,万丰奥特从 21 世纪开始就率先一步形成了多元化的经营结构。而在此之后,它将向哪里发展?从 2001 年开始,陈爱莲就考虑到了万丰奥特上市的需求。

这是水到渠成的一步,万丰奥特的轮毂主业已经获得了社会美誉度,而这使得社会将给它进一步的信任和机会,尤其是在万丰奥特依托的国内汽车业大发展背景之下，企业就有机会获得更大的空间来为社会服务。而此时，万丰奥特自身发展资本金的不足，一直是企业走向国际化大公司的一个重要障碍。

这个矛盾正是万丰奥特高度重视资产负债率的原因。实际上，万丰奥特整个发展过程当中始终面临矛盾：一方面，中国汽车和摩托车业高速成长，抓住了机会的万丰奥特要做大，始终面临资金上的压力；另一方面，高速成长的万丰奥特也难免出现像万丰汽车这样需调整的项目，因此企业又不能不为未来可能的问题保留充足的现金流。

办法当然是现成的，那就是上市。

不过，万丰奥特上市的这个想法，实现起来并不容易。

进入21世纪，上市成为国内公司的普遍追求。因为通过上市，公司可以获得一大笔募集资本。同时，掌握在创业团队手中的股份，也获得了一个变现的通道。因此大批国内公司试图通过上市来套现，而不是像陈爱莲领导下的万丰奥特一样，是为企业的未来发展来募集资金。

由此，国内A股市场上市公司的怪相频生。大批上市公司上市后从不分红，而只是一轮又一轮地稀释股份套现。A股市场上的中小投资者资本大量被套取之后失去了对A股的信任，市场普遍对上市公司的诚信产生了怀疑。而掌管着公司上市通道的政府机构也开始对企业上市加强了控制，像万丰奥特这样的民营企业上市的难度就大大提高了。

所以，国内民营企业在2003年前后，兴起了一股海外上市热潮。国内A股失去了融资功能，而大批民营企业急需筹资发展，海外的交易所纷纷向国内民营公司敞开大门，在2003年前后，新加坡、伦敦和纽约等地的交易所管理者纷纷到国内做推广，希望民营公司到这些交易场所上市。

万丰奥特的上市，集中体现了陈爱莲团队的价值观。在2003年启动上市进程之时，公司董事会本来是打算在国内上市的，成立了以夏越璋为首的上市工作小组，专门引进了吴延坤等专业证券人员，同时还邀请国内一家著名的投资银行来帮助企业做上市辅导。

上市工作小组提出的构想是清晰的。他们计划把万丰奥特的资产分为准备上市部分和非上市部分。企业内部已经有稳定产出的业务，主要是汽车轮毂制造，放入上市公司的资产包内，上市之后，企业可以通过这部分资产的收入，来回报外部投资者。

而其他的资产，比如当时万丰奥特已经进入汽车制造的部分资产，由于已经发现了它当时的风险，就由集团来集中投资和把握，决定其进入和退出；又比如说万丰镁业，当时还处于研发期，有相当的不确定性，也由集团来投资。

这样，万丰奥特的这两部分资产就可以在集团与投资者之间不断交易。万丰奥特作为一个投资主体，用融资部分不断投资新的业务，等新业务稳定之后，再由上市公司对集团投资的新业务进行收购。这样，集团就可以在上市公司之外不断投资新业务，并让它慢慢稳定发展起来。而上市公司的股东就可以通过上市公司向集团收购新业务，不断获得稳定回报；同时集团可以通过上市公司收购新业务得到风险回报，从而可以不断地向新业务进行投资。这就形成了一个良好的业务循环，让上市公司和万丰奥特之间形成双赢互动。

但是，因为2003年前后，国内的融资形势不容乐观，万丰奥特一再向政府部门提出上市申请，但却一直没有办法得到落实。

21世纪初，万丰奥特在轮毂主业上的市场地位稳固之后，因为汽车业大发展，所以机会之门频频向万丰奥特打开。如果有了集团公司与上市公司之间的互动，那么万丰奥特只要有优秀的管理团队、良好的运营机制，集团的事业就可以做到更大更强。而此时，万丰奥特急需的就是投资。

鉴于万丰奥特的业绩和成长性非常突出，被誉为财富园丁、在投资银行界赫赫有名的法国巴黎百富勤投资银行董事总经理蔡洪平看中，他多次上门建议万丰奥特可以到中国香港联合交易所有限公司（以下简称联交所）上市。

在这种情况之下，董事会指导着万丰奥特的上市转向香港联交所。

但从内心深处来说，陈爱莲并不希望万丰奥特在香港上市。因为她对于万丰奥特的定位，是一家中国内地企业。陈爱莲的这个信念，来自对汽车业的观察。她认为，汽车业在几十年内，都是中国发展非常快的行业，是国内市场上的消费者用货币选票让万丰奥特发展壮大。所以她更希望回馈的，是内地的投资者。

因此，到 2005 年政府开设中小企业板，市场的融资功能又重新启动之时，陈爱莲毅然将已经进展大半的在香港联交所上市的进程中止，重新启动在深交所中小企业板上市的进程。

万丰奥特上市工作小组成员吴延坤本是一名大学教师，之后去了一家投资银行工作。一个偶然的机会，他被万丰奥特的企业文化所吸引，到万丰担任董秘，经历了整个上市过程的酸甜苦辣。

2006 年 9 月 11 日，是他非常难忘的一天。这一天，他们在位于北京的中国证监会等待万丰奥威能否通过发审委审查的消息。当工作人员出来宣布万丰奥威通过发审委审查的时候，他们都高兴得跳了起来。陈爱莲也一样，她在打电话，显然是在给公司里的团队报告这个好消息。看起来一切都很正常，只是吴延坤看到她拿着手机的手在轻轻地颤抖，拨号码时拨错了好几次。

所有人都非常理解她，这么多年企业的经营通过上市这个环节，就都得到了认同。

不过，如果从更大的视角来看，万丰奥威上市，有着更为深远的背景。

2005 年到 2008 年，中国国内经济进入了又一个过热期。一方面，21 世纪以来政府主导的出口战略，此时已经达到了顶峰。在全面的外贸出口政策扶持之下，物美价廉的中国产品席卷全世界，下游膨胀的能源原材料需求给上游供应带来了巨大压力，另一方面，中国又进入了 2008 年北京奥运会的准备期，日渐庞大的基建规模，对原材料提出了数量巨大的要求。

这种外界的景象，落实在万丰奥特的轮毂制造主业里所带来的变化就是原材料的涨价。在 2006 年，铝锭价格上涨是万丰奥特人频频提起的一个关键词。

不仅如此，万丰奥特下游的摩托车和汽车市场同时进入了普及期。2006年，国内已经普遍出现摩托车最低售价触及 3 000 元；而同时，大批售价低于 10 万元的汽车开始进入市场。

下游产品的价格普遍下降，给万丰奥特带来的难题是，摩托车和汽车的主机制造公司出于自身市场竞争的需要，不接受配件企业上游原材料价格上涨所带来的价格上涨。这一现实的困难考验着万丰奥特：是迎接挑战，为未来的市场份额做准备，还是放弃部分份额，要利润？

万丰奥特用事实做出了选择：企业要走向汽车业的大公司梦想可以一步步来，但在核心业务的轮毂市场上，不但不能放弃市场，而且要进一步扩张。2006 年，正是万丰奥特的两个主要业务部门——摩轮提升印度业务、汽轮提升全球跨国汽车公司业务的关键年度。

正是因为市场的开拓不断要求万丰奥特扩张核心主业的产能，而同时原材料的价格上涨吞噬着万丰奥特的净利率，所以 2006 年年初，陈爱莲在万丰奥特内部发表了《全员参与降低成本提高核心竞争力》的讲话，要求全员努力通过控制成本来渡过原材料涨价的难关，同时通过打造成本的竞争力，来更好地适应市场的要求。

管理练内功

从某种意义上说，像所有民营企业一样，万丰奥特是由市场催生而成的。在这家企业前 10 年的发展历程中，万丰奥特伴随着中国市场对于交通工具的巨大需求而成立，由于创业团队抓住了市场的需求，万丰奥特得以白手起家，完成了从项目到企业的发展；又抓住了市场竞争对已有产能的淘汰机会，通过并购而形成了大型企业的初步架构。

在规模扩张的同时，我们看到，由于万丰奥特包容开放的信任文化，使得企业始终处于"各司其职"的分权状态。因此在万丰奥特的轮毂产品初步跨越了品质关之后,陆续又跨越了成本控制、关键设备和原材料内部化等关口,使得万丰奥特轮毂制造的核心能力进一步得到加强,把轮毂大规模制造的优势扩展到最初那 100 多家竞争对手无法追赶的地步。

可以想见的是,如果一家刚刚入行或者是入行之后没有扩张的同行,显然很难像万丰奥特一样,因轮毂的大规模制造在原材料采购、低压机制造这样的产业深处形成自己的能力。这种能力一方面降低了万丰奥特在轮毂制造上的成本,另一方面也使万丰奥特的客户因其在专业方向上的深入产生更大的信任。

但是到 2007 年,万丰奥特这棵大树虽然硕果累累,但也有部分业务不尽如人意。比如,万丰汽车的投资始终产生不了盈利,万丰镁业虽然达到了盈亏平衡,但还需要更进一步的投资。

因此万丰奥特在上市前后,对每一部分业务的运营进行反复讨论,最终把万丰汽车以及其他一些试探性业务,都进行了调整。如果我们把万丰奥特看成一棵参天大树的话,万丰汽车的休眠不过是集团主动削减这棵大树上的旁枝,其主干仍然是花繁叶茂、硕果累累。而且因为越来越多的高端主机厂与万丰奥特成为战略合作伙伴,所以万丰奥特的轮毂制造主业还在不断壮大。

2007 年万丰奥特的这一次"瘦身",在对整车制造等新公司忍痛割爱的同时,也有另一份收获:正是对于多元化战线的适当收缩,以退为进,才使得企业在 2008 年面对全球性的经济萧条,备上了一件厚厚的"棉袄"。全球金融危机中万丰奥特因为有足够的现金流,因此还可以考虑扩张。

当然,财务上的这种安排,是为万丰奥特向百年企业的迈进而做的物质准备。而对万丰奥特成为基业长青的企业起到实质性作用的,则是它向精益化和国际化方向的发展。

客观上,万丰奥特向生产精益化方向发展,也是公司开始与跨国汽车公司合作的结果。2005 年之后,万丰奥特的轮毂事业进入一个又一个大型跨国汽车公司的供应商行列,除了万丰奥特各级团队通过学习具有了国际化视野之外,与一系列国际企业的合作,主机厂开始以国际化企业的要求来衡量万丰奥特。

国际化的标志之一,就是主机厂开始要求万丰奥特具有自主的研发体系。主机厂每年会推出新的车型,零部件企业要根据主机厂的要求来自主完成设计,满足主机厂的要求。

此外,主机厂还会提出各种各样的精益生产要求。比如说,全面实施产品的可追溯管理,就是汽车产业开始实施召回制度之后的一个产物。进入 21 世纪,汽车产业的激烈竞争要求整车厂在发现投放市场的汽车由于设计或生产方面的原因存在缺陷,必须对该产品进行召回。在这样一种市场竞争态势之下,可追溯管理是相当有效的。整车厂发生系统性问题需要召回时,可追溯管理使得汽车厂在确定需要召回的产品数量上,可以很容易地针对同一批产品进行召回,把需要召回的产品控制在出现质量事故的最小数量。

更为重要的是,汽车是大宗的耐用消费品,有很长的使用过程。汽车制造厂采取了可追溯管理之后,如果整车出现故障,就可以非常方便地判定是生产企业在生产过程当中发生的问题,还是用户在使用过程出现了不当使用。

显然,这一管理方式,对于零部件企业来说,所构成的管理工作量不小。它要求万丰奥特对一个轮毂所涉及的每道工序都要有相关的生产数据记录。

但也正是这一系列高标准要求成就了万丰奥特。长期对于品质和工艺的不懈追求,使得万丰奥特在轮毂制造领域里成为一家高度专业化的企业。

万丰全景图

德国留学生杨华声是在万丰汽轮业务加快国际化进程中加盟企业的。2008 年之后,万丰已经与德国大众、奥迪等高端品牌建立了深入的合作关系,迫切需要一批既有专业基础又能非常熟练使用德语的营销骨干,所以他借此机会进入了万丰。

据杨华声回忆，那一次公司在德国宝马公司总部举办宣讲会，是他万万没想到的，而且对于万丰来说也纯属偶然。本来万丰营销团队去德国出差，主要目的是去德国大众谈一个项目。大众公司的总部在德国的沃尔夫斯堡，是德国南方的一个小镇。当时就有人提议说，干脆尝试去拜访一下宝马公司，看能不能与宝马公司形成供应关系。于是行前，万丰的营销人员就把自己的意向以邮件方式发给了宝马公司的供应商管理部门。

万丰这次偶然的提议，很快得到了宝马公司的回应：欢迎万丰的市场团队到慕尼黑宝马公司总部去做一次宣讲会。

不过还让杨华声没有想到的是，这次万丰的宣讲会，在宝马公司受到如此高程度的重视。

宝马公司总部所在的慕尼黑是德国第三大城市，慕尼黑奥林匹克公园附近的一幢 22 层高楼，是宝马公司的"心脏"。万丰团队到了宝马公司为他们安排的会议室才发现，宝马公司涉及供应商管理的技术、采购、商务和决策层人员，几乎全部都到会议现场来听万丰的宣讲。很显然，万丰在国内汽配业内的地位，已经使这家其实只有十多岁的年轻公司，早早就进入了宝马公司的视野之中。而德国人刻板外表下的严谨和高效，使得万丰一次就能接触到供应商管理的所有人员。

万丰的宣讲会由杨华声主持，这显然是因为他的德语最为流利。把万丰的汽车轮毂业务讲清楚，他花了一个多小时。再接下来一个多小时里，是整个万丰市场团队回答宝马公司供应商管理成员们提出的各种各样的问题。

万丰团队接下来体验到的是宝马公司的高效，仅仅两个多月之后，万丰迎来了宝马公司的现场工程师。宝马公司决定先让万丰试着与自己公司的技术人员合作，在一款年度车型上合作开发新型轮毂。在对万丰的现场进行查验之后，宝马公司的工程师提出了需要改进的报告，但宝马公司与万丰合作的意向并没有动摇。很显然，宝马公司的决策层已经明白，这是一家非常善于学习和改进的中国企业，而自己则非常需要在中国有一家优秀的零部件合作伙伴。

万丰与宝马公司之间的合作迅速展开。宝马公司高度认同万丰的价值观，所以双方在合作当中建立了战略伙伴关系，甚至超越了这种关系。比如说宝马公司甚至向万丰派出了驻厂工程师，帮助万丰提高精细设计能力，以满足设计宝马公司特有的复杂轮毂的要求。

除了宝马公司之外，万丰汽轮业务进一步提升与更多全球顶级整车厂的合作。这个市场策略不仅加大了万丰在国外市场的影响力，提高了企业的自身能力，也间接地使得国有汽车主机厂对出生草根的万丰奥特刮目相看。

而同时，上市之后，万丰奥威作为中小企业板当时一只表现非常活跃的股票，使得万丰奥特大大提高了知名度，摆脱了轮毂制造细分行业，进入了大众的视野。

万丰奥特之道：大公司的结构怎么形成

　　由于社会需求的变化，号称"百年老店"的大公司，通常都经过了多个业务的变迁。因此大型企业同时存在多个内在具有相关性的业务，对其业务结构的稳定是极其有利的。

　　同时，公司的经营，实际上就是不断获得社会认可和信任的过程。企业在一个领域的经营获得市场认可的过程，就是获得消费者和合作伙伴信任的过程。在这个过程当中，企业就有可能获得外界认可，经营多个业务。

　　万丰奥特搭建大公司结构的过程，就是陈爱莲领导下的万丰奥特在摩托车和汽车轮毂制造领域里有了卓越表现，获得外部资源来多元化经营的过程。而在万丰奥特形成多元化业务的过程当中，开放和自主经营，显然是万丰奥特把握多元化业务"进退"的原则，无论是万丰科技，还是万丰镁业，集团一经投资完毕，就要求子公司在市场上自己"找饭吃"，在市场的考验下快速成长。相形之下，万丰奥特对于整车制造的投入期，反而是众多新业务投资当中最长的一个。

　　我们在后面可以看到，陈爱莲的这种投资哲学，使得万丰奥特在上市之后，有了更大的发展空间。

Chapter 8
Pattern of a large company

Winding Road to Listing

November, 28, 2006 was an important day in Wanfeng Auto's development. On this day, the listing bell of Shenzhen Stock Exchange (hereinafter referred to as Shenzhen Exchange) was sounded by Chen Ailian and China Machinery Industry Federation executive vice president Zhang Xiaoyu. It marked the opening of Wanfeng Auto as a listed Corporation.

Wanfeng display room still has the opening bell mallet.

This was the twelfth year for Wanfeng Auto business. Among the small and medium board listed companies, Wangeng had the most people on the day of listing, which reflects the pattern of Wanfeng Auto as a big company – the whole group executive layer has formed the style of "co-creating and sharing".

Since the acquisition of Shanghai Ershou Alloy in 1999, Wanfeng Auto has gradually formed the big company pattern. Opportunities of development came in a throng.

In 2000, after uniting and recombining, Shanghai Wanfeng Automobile

Manufacturing Co., Ltd. was established, choosing SUV as the main product, advancing from the vehicle parts production to the vehicle manufacturing.

In 2001, the acquisition of Shandong Durui Wheel Co. Ltd. in the North, Wanfeng Auto spread into Shangdong province.

In 2002, with the establishment of Chongqing production base, Wanfeng Auto penetrated directly into the birthplace of the Chinese motorcycle industry, achieving localization of production and agile supply.

In 2003, Wanfeng Auto maintained the National 863 plan and established Weihai Wanfeng Magnesium Industrial Technology Development Co., ltd.;

In 2004, Wanfeng Auto sparked the Sino foreign joint ventures in another economic center in the Yangtze River Delta region of Ningbo.

In 2005, Wanfeng embraced the big development of Wanfeng Aowei Wheel Limited Company.

Since 2000, Wanfeng Auto developing prospect has become increasingly clear, which is based on their own accumulation of talents and technology. The Zhejiang native private enterprise tried to become a large enterprise group with leading technology and mass production in automobile and mechanical fields.

From doing everything in person at initial start-up of the team to the board fulfilling their respective duty later, Wanfeng Auto as a private enterprise, has been gradually transformed from a hub manufacturing industry into various fields, with the output value of enterprises starting from a few hundred million to the threshold of 10 billion.

Wanfeng Auto's achievements were highly correlated with Chen Ailian's personality. The hardworking woman is a peacock type manager: she is willing to share and good at use of personnel. She likes to delegate the things to team members and she is never stingy on the distribution of achievements. Therefore, after Wanfeng Auto has been in operation for a few years, more and more talented people gathered on this platform. Auto Starting up in motorcycle wheel hub manufacturing field, Wanfeng soon accumulated of opportunities and talents, making the company have supernormal and leaping development.

This also formed the Wanfeng Auto's enterprise management style - this is an enterprise good at management. Wanfeng has established good relationship in every aspect of the enterprise operation.

Therefore, Wanfeng Aowei listing has become a festival of the whole group. On that day Wanfeng Aowei also had the most guests on the scene of Shenzhen stock exchange to congratulate when it was listed.

At 9:28 on November 28, 2006, Chen Ailian sounded the opening bell for listing of Wanfeng Aowei. The stock whose code was 002085, opened instantly. With an issue price started at 5.66 yuan and closed at 8.20 yuan at the end of the day of listing, with an increase of 45%.

At this time of Wanfeng Auto has developed from a 15- people entrepreneurial team with half a million bank loaned capital, 4 sets of machines in a narrow lane of No. 50 Jiangnan Road of Xinchang County South, to a large private with assets of over 5 billion yuan and over 6000 employees. In the field of domestic automobile parts, it has become an important leader In the Zhejiang business groups, it is also a rare advanced manufacturing enterprises.

Wanfeng Auto become the first stock of domestic industry

Later, Wanfeng Auto held reciprocal banquet to sincerely thank many partners from China Machinery Industry Federation, Zhejiang Province, Xinchang County, Shaoxing City, and the Shenzhen stock exchange

Wanfeng Auto's growth is closely related with its environment.

When Wanfeng Auto started up, the small enterprise didn't choose the environment. But it was lucky for the enterprise to be born in Zhejiang province where thousands of businessmen gathered. Besides, Xinchang local environment accelerated its growth.

Zhejiang is the headquarters of Chinese private enterprises. Early in Chinese reform and opening, due to the reality that the largest proportion of the land is covered by mountains and waters and there is not much farming land, farming means poverty, which greatly motivates the local people turn to industry.

At early entrepreneurial stage, Zhejiang businessmen have the spirit of "tolerance of hardship, utterance of every word, traveling thousands of miles, trying to do everything possible", so that they reached the invincible and invulnerable state. At an early stage, after the local agriculture was successfully transformed into industry, industrial development has got support government at all levels. As the birthplace of the private economy, every previous Zhejiang provincial government has created a good environment for development. They handle everything according to the law of market economy, without much interruption. In the administration, they are very effective, with strong sense of service, making Zhejiang business have strong vitality.

After 30 years of accumulation, Zhejiang commercial sphere has been glittered with shining stars, of which Wanfeng Auto is not the most shinning one, though its assets have exceeded 2 billion yuan in 2006. As for Wanfeng Auto, living in such a social environment is a kind of drive.

Wanfeng is lucky, for it is located in Xinchang, which was one of the few mountainous counties in Zhejiang. Due to the lack of element for the development of agriculture, the county government and all sectors of society give great support towards the industry. It is because of this support that has transformed Xinchang, the mountainous from a poor agricultural county into an important industrial town after reform and opening. Before the reform and opening, there was virtually no industry in Xinchang. While 30 years after the reform and opening-up policy, three listed companies have appeared this small county with a population of less than half a million.

In the short history of Wanfeng Auto, we can see support from all walks of life including the government and the society in every stage of its development. Whether when Chen Ailian led the team to get bank loans, land acquisition and construction of Industrial Park, or when she went to Shanghai, Shandong, Chongqing, Guangdong and other places to establish a production base, Wanfeng got efficient service from all levels of government.

As a benchmark for companies in Xinchang, Wanfeng Auto has taken the lead to form a diversified business structure since the beginning of twenty-first Century. And after that, where should it develop? From the beginning of 2001, Chen Ailian has considered Wanfeng Auto market's demand for listing.

This was a natural step of ripe conditions. Wanfeng Auto's main wheel hub industry has gained good social reputation, which has made the society give it further trust and opportunity. Especially under domestic auto industry development background, Wanfeng Auto has the opportunity to obtain greater space to serve the society. However at the same time, Wanfeng Auto's lack of capital for development was always a huge obstacle to large globalized large companies.

This contradiction was the reason why Wanfeng Auto attached great importance to the rate of assets and liabilities. Actually, throughout Wangfeng development process, it has always been confronted with the contradictions: on the one hand, China's automobile and motorcycle industry had the rapid growth, Wanfeng wanted to seize the opportunity to become bigger but it has been facing financial pressure; on the other hand, fast-growing Wanfeng may have projects like Wanfeng

Automobile that needed adjustment . Therefore, the enterprise has to retain sufficient cash flow for future possibilities.

The existing way was of course listing.

However, this idea for Wanfeng Auto listing was not easy to achieve.

In the twenty-first Century, listing has become a universal pursuit of Domestic Company, because the company can raise a large amount of capital through the listing. At the same time, the shares in the hands of the entrepreneurial team obtain a channel to cash. Therefore a large number of domestic companies try to cash through the listing, different from Wanfeng Auto under the leadership of Chen Ailian, Wanfeng raise funds for the future development of enterprise.

Thus, strange phenomena of listed companies frequently appear in A share market. Many companies after listed have never distributed dividend; instead they dilute stocks successively to cash. Medium and small investors' stocks have been cashed and then they lost trust in A-share market. The integrity of listed companies has generally been doubted in the market. At the same time government agencies in charge of the channel for listed companies, strengthen the control over companies to be listed. It has become increasingly difficult for private enterprises like Wanfeng Auto to be listed.

Therefore, in 2003 there was an overseas listing boom for the domestic private enterprises. Domestic A share market has lost financing function, while a large number of private enterprises were in urgent need of financing for development. Foreign exchanges opened the door to domestic private companies in 2003, management in exchanges from Singapore, London and New York etc. came to promote in China, wishing those enterprises to get listed in their exchanges.

Listing for Wanfeng Auto embodies the values of the Chen Ailian team. In 2003, when starting the listing process, the company's board of directors had intended to be listed in the domestic market, and set up a working team led by Xia Yuezhang. Professional securities personnel Wu Yankun and others were recruited, and they also invited a well-known domestic investment bank to help the enterprise with listing counseling.

The idea that the listing working group proposed was clear. They plan to divide Wanfeng Auto's of assets into listed and unlisted parts. Enterprises have already had a stable output of business, mainly in the production of car wheels. This section would be included into the assets of the listed corporation. After the listing, the enterprise could return the external investors through revenue of the assets.

As for other assets, such as parts of the assets of Wanfeng Auto in the automobile manufacturing, have been found risky at that time, these parts of the assets would be invested and controlled   by the group, which determine its entry and exit. Another example is Wanfeng magnesium, which was at the stage of research and was of great uncertainty and should be invested by the group.

In this case, the two parts of the assets of Wanfeng Auto can be traded between groups and investors continuously. Wanfeng Auto, as a principal investor, uses a portion of the financing to continue to invest in new business. After the new business gets stable, it will be acquired by the listed company. In this way, the group can continue to invest in new business besides the listing Corporation, and let it grow slowly and steadily. And the shareholders of the listed Corporation can acquire new businesses through the listed Company, getting a stable return. At the same time, the group can get a risk return through the acquisition of new business, so that it can continue to invest in new business. This is a good business cycle, forming a win-win interaction between listed Corporation and Wanfeng Auto.

However, around 2003, domestic financing situation was not optimistic; Wanfeng Auto's repeated listing application to government departments was not approved.

At the beginning of the 21st century, Wanfeng Auto's main business of wheel hub had a firm position in the market. Because of the great development of automobile industry, the doors of opportunity were frequently open to Wanfeng Auto. With the interaction between the group company and listed company, Wanfeng's excellent management team and good management mechanism, cause for the group can become bigger and stronger. At the same time, what Wanfeng was in urgent need of was investment.

In view of Wanfeng Auto's outstanding performance and growth, the well-known managing director of BNP Paribas peregrine investment bank, Cai Hongping who is famous in the field of investment banking and hailed as the gardener of wealth, has fanced Wanfeng. He has repeatedly visited Wanfeng and advised Wanfeng Auto to get listed in the China stock exchange of Hong Kong Limited company (hereinafter referred to as the Hong Kong Stock Exchange)

In this case, the board of directors guided Wanfeng Auto's listing to the Hong Kong Stock Exchange.

But deep down, Chen Ailian didn't want Wanfeng Auto to get listed in Hong Kong, because her orientation for Wanfeng was a China mainland enterprise. Chen Ailian's faith came from the observation of the automotive industry. She believed that the automobile industry would be the fastest developing industry in China. It was consumer support by money that made Wanfeng grow stranger and bigger, so she preferred to return to the mainland investors.

Therefore, when government established of the SME board in 2005 and restarted the financing function of the market, Ailian resolutely stopped the listing process which has progressed more than half on the Hong Kong stock exchange and restarted the listing process of SME board in Shenzhen exchange.

One of Wanfeng Auto listing working group members, Wu Yankun was formerly a university teacher, and then he went to work for an investment bank. By chance, he was attracted by Wanfeng Auto's corporate culture to attract. He came to Wanfeng to serve as the board secretary. He experienced the ups and downs of the listing process.

September 11, 2006 was a very memorable day for him. On this day, they were in the Beijing China Securities Regulatory commission, awaiting the news whether Wanfeng Auto could pass the examination by Issuance Examination Committee. When the staff came out to announce that Wanfeng Auto has passed the examination of the Issuance Examination Committee, they all jumped with joy. Chen Ailian was also the same. She was on the phone to report the good news to the company's team. Everything seemed normal, but Wu Yankun noticed that her hands holding the phone trembling gently, and that she dialed the wrong number several times.

All the people understood her well. Many years of business has been recognized through the listing.

However, from a larger perspective, Wanfeng Auto's listing has a more profound background.

From 2005 to 2008, China's domestic economy entered another period of overheating. On the one hand, the government's leading export strategy has reached its peak since the twenty-first Century. With the support of comprehensive foreign trade exporting policy, inexpensive and high quality Chinese products wiped across the world. The downstream expansion of supply of the energy raw materials posed great pressure to the upstream supply. On the other hand, China had begun to prepare for 2008 Beijing Olympic Games. The growing scale of the construction demanded a huge number of raw materials.

The outside influence on Wanfeng Auto's main industry of wheel hub manufacturing was the increasing price of raw materials. In 2006, increasing aluminum price is a keyword Wanfeng people frequently mentioned.

In addition to that, Wanfeng Auto's downstream motorcycle and car market has also entered the period of popularization. In 2006, the lowest price of a motorcycle hit 3000 yuan, while at the same time, a large number of cars priced at less than 100000 yuan entered the market.

A general decline in the prices of downstream products is a difficult problem to Wanfeng Auto: motorcycle and automobile engine manufacturing companies did not accept upstream accessory enterprises' rising price brought by increasing raw material price for the needs of market competition. The practical difficulty was a test of Wanfeng Auto: to meet the challenge and prepare for the future market share, or to give up part of the share for profits?

Wanfeng Auto made a choice with facts: the enterprise's dream of becoming large companies in the automotive industry could be realized gradually, but the core business of hub market could not be given up; instead it should be further expanded. 2006 was a critical year for Wanfeng Auto's two major divisions - increasing India business in motorcycle wheels, and enhancing auto wheels business in the global multinational auto companies.

Because markets exploration continued to require Wanfeng Auto to expand capacity of its core business, while at the same time the rising price of raw materials devoured Wanfeng Auto Net profit rate, so in early 2006, Chen Ailian's speech in published in Wanfeng Auto: "All participation to reduce costs and to enhance the core competitive force". The speech called on all the staff to conquer the difficulty of increasing price of raw materials by controlling the cost and at the same time by building cost competitiveness to better adapt to market requirements.

Management Skills

In a sense, like all private enterprises, Wanfeng Auto is bred by the market. In former ten years, Wanfeng was set up along with huge demand for transportation tools in the Chinese market. The entrepreneurial team met the market demand to make Wanfeng Auto start from scratch, and develop from the project to the enterprise. In addition Wanfeng seize the opportunity of the market competition and selection of existing production capacity, forming the primary structure of large enterprises through mergers and acquisitions.

At the time of expansion, we could see that Wanfeng's trust culture of openness and inclusiveness auto inclusive open trust culture has made the enterprise always in a decentralized state with their duties. After Wanfeng Auto's wheel products preliminary met the standard of quality, Wanfeng has conquered one obstacle after another: cost control, internalization of key equipments and raw materials, etc., making Wanfeng Auto wheel hub manufacturing's core competence further strengthened. The advantages of large-scale hub manufacturing have expanded to the point where over 100 initial competitors cannot catch up with.

One can imagine that it is unimaginable for a new peer business or a new business without expansion to be like Wanfeng Auto. Wanfeng has formed its competence in purchase of raw materials and in industry like low compressor manufacturing because of large-scale wheel hub manufacturing. The competence on the one hand reduced the Wanfeng Auto wheel manufacturing cost, on the other hand also enabled Wanfeng Auto customers to have greater trust due to its professional depth.

But by 2007, though Wanfeng Auto was generally fruitful, there were also parts of the business not satisfactory. For example, the investment in Wanfeng car has not been profitable. Though Wanfeng Magnesium managed to achieve a balance between profits and losses, it also needed further investment.

Therefore before Wanfeng Auto's listing, the operation of each part of the business went through repeated discussions. At last, the Wanfeng Automobile and other some tentative business have been adjusted. If we regard Wanfeng Auto as a towering tree, Wanfeng Automobile dormancy plan was that the group has taken the initiative to cut the branches of tree and the trunk is still flourishing and fruitful. Furthermore, because more and more high-end motor plants become Wanfeng Auto's strategic partners, Wanfeng Auto wheel manufacturing industry is continuously growing.

In 2007 Wanfeng Auto endured the pain of loss for suspending vehicle manufacturing company but this "downsizing reap another benefit: proper contraction of diversification production line – retreat for the sake of advancing, which makes the enterprise well prepared for the global economic depression in 2008. During the period of the global financial crisis, Wanfeng Auto could also consider expansion because there was enough cash flow.

Of course, the financial arrangements were making material preparation for Wanfeng Auto's development toward a century-old enterprise. It was the orientation towards simplification and globalization that made Wanfeng Auto become an everlasting enterprise.

Objectively, Wanfeng Auto's development direction to lean production is as a result of cooperation with multinational automobile company. After 2005, Wanfeng Auto wheel hub business ranked suppliers for large multinational automotive companies one after another. Through study and cooperation with a series of international enterprises, Wanfeng Auto Team at all levels obtained global vision. Motor plants began measuring Wanfeng Auto by the requirements of international enterprise.

One of the symbols for globalization is that the motor plant began to require Wanfeng Auto to have independent research and development system. The motor plant will launch a new model every year, requiring part manufacturing enterprise to design according to the requirements of the motor plant and to meet the requirements of the motor plant.

In addition, the motor plant would also put forward a variety of requirements for lean production, for example, the full implementation of management on the product traceability, the outcome of the implementation of the recall system of the products in automotive industry. In the twenty-first Century, the automotive industry's fierce competition requires that the vehicle factory should recall their products when discovering defects in the design or production of their vehicles in the market.

In such a competitive market situation, management on the product traceability is quite effective. When the vehicle factory has a systematic problem and needs recalling, management on the product traceability can determine the number of cars to be traced back and can also make it easy to recall the same batch of products, controlling number of vehicles that have quality accidents to the minimum.

Even more important is that the cars are large consumer goods, lasting a long period of use. The traceability management of vehicle manufacturing plant may easily determine whether the problem existed in the production process of the manufacturing enterprises or improper use of the users, if the vehicles fail.

Obviously, this management approach has brought much more work to the management of part production enterprises, for the management of the composition is not small. It requires production data be recorded for each procedure of a wheel hub production.

However, it is the series of high standards of achievements that make Wanfeng Auto successful. Long-term relentless pursuit for quality and process has made Wanfeng Auto become a highly specialized enterprise in wheel manufacturing field

Wanfeng's panorama

Yang Huasheng who has studied in Germany joined Wanfeng, when the globalization of auto wheel business accelerated. After 2008, Wanfeng have established in-depth cooperation with Volkswagen, Audi and other high-end brands, having urgent need of a group of marketing backbone of both professional foundation and very skilled in the use of German, so he would like to take this opportunity to entered the Wanfeng.

According to the memories of the Yang Huasheng, Wanfeng was given a chance to give a speech of publicity in Germany's BMW headquarters. The chance was quite out of his expectation and it was purely accidental for Wanfeng is. Originally, Wanfeng marketing team had planned to go on a business trip to Germany, with the main purpose to discuss a project in German Volkswagen. Volkswagen's headquarters are in Wolfsburg, Germany, which is a small town in the south of Germany. At that time, some suggested paying a visit to the BMW Company, to see whether it was possible to form a supply relationship with BMW. Therefore, before leaving for Germany, Wanfeng's marketing personnel sent an e-mail of their intention to supplier management department of the BMW Company.

Wanfeng's accidental proposal, quickly got BMW's response: Wanfeng marketing team was welcome to BMW headquarters in Munich to give a speech of publicity.

However what was out of Yang Huasheng's expectation was the speech of publicity of Wanfeng received great attention by BMW.

BMW's headquarters are located in Munich, Germany's third largest city. Near Munich Olympic Park there is a 22-story building, which is BMW's "heart". When Wanfeng team arrived at their conference room arranged by the BMW Company, he found that the personnel concerning technology, purchasing, business and decision-making all come to the meeting room to hear Wangfeng's speech of publicity. Obviously, Wanfeng, a young company with 10-years-old position in the domestic auto industry, has actually entered the BMW's vision very early. And German people's strictness and efficiency under their rigid appearance make Wanfeng contact all the personnel of supplier management.

Wanfeng's speech was presided over by Yang Huasheng, apparently because of his most fluent German. He spent more than an hour on the clear explanation of the Wanfeng Automobile hub business auto. In the following hour, the Wanfeng market team to answer a wide variety of problems proposed by members of the BMW company supplier management.

Next Wanfeng team experienced BMW's efficiency. Just over two months later, Wanfeng ushered in the BMW's site engineers. BMW has decided to let Wanfeng try to cooperate with the technical staff in his company. They would cooperate to develop a new type of hub for the car of that year. After the field inspection of Wanfeng, BMW engineers proposed report for places needing to be improved. However, BMW did not waver in its intention to cooperate with Wanfeng. Obviously, the decision-making level of the BMW has understood that Wanfeng is a very good Chinese enterprise good at learning and improvement, and BMW are in urgent need to have an excellent partner of spare part plant in China.

Cooperation between Wanfeng and BMW was launched rapidly. BMW is highly identified with Wanfeng's values, so the two sides established strategic partnership in the process of cooperation. For example, BMW even sent engineers to Wanfeng factory, to help Wanfeng improve the ability of delicate design, in order to meet the requirements of BMW's own complex hub design.

In addition to BMW, Wanfeng wheel further enhance cooperation with many more top global vehicle plants. The marketing strategy not only increased the Wanfeng's influence in foreign markets, improving the enterprise's own ability, but also indirectly makes state-owned automotive factories to look at Wanfeng born grassroots with new eyes

While at the same time, after the listing, Wanfeng's stock as SME board was a very active, making the Wanfeng Auto's popularity greatly enhanced, getting rid of the wheel manufacturing industry segments and getting into the public view.

Wanfeng Auto way: how to form the structure of large companies

Due to the change of the social demand, the so-called century-old large companies usually experienced the change of multiple businesses. Therefore, that there are many related businesses in a large-scale enterprise at the same time is very favorable to the stability of the business structure.

At the same time, the company's management is actually the process of gaining social acceptance and trust. The process for enterprises to gain market recognition in a field of business is the process to get trust from consumers and partners. In this process, the enterprise has the potential to obtain external recognition and have quite a few business operations.

The process for Wanfeng Auto to build corporate structure is the outstanding performance in the field of motorcycle and automotive wheel hubs of Wanfeng under the leadership of the Chen Ailian and the process of getting access to external resources for diversified operation. On the way to diversified operation, open and independent operation is apparently principle for Wanfeng Auto's "advance and retreat". Whether Wanfeng technology, or Wanfeng magnesium industry, after group investment, should depend on themselves in the market and have a rapid growth by the test of the market. In contrast, Wanfeng's investment period on vehicle manufacturing is the longest among the many new business investments.

We can see in the following that Chen Ailian's investment philosophy brings Wanfeng Auto greater space for development after the listing.

第九章

万丰文化和公司治理

社区支柱背后的团队精神

新昌天姥山区的地点多以"岙"命名，赵婆岙就是天姥山在新昌县城的一支余脉，这个山村没有什么特别，只是因为有一座铁佛寺，平时有一些本地游客来游玩。

2013 年夏天，新昌在中央电视台新闻联播里露了一次面：当地的气温创下了全国纪录，达到了 44℃。而就在气温最高的 8 月，赵婆岙的山林发生了一次长达两天的火灾。

起火原因很简单，本地的一户村民去铁佛寺烧香，拜佛结束，在寺外燃放了两只爆竹。当这两只爆竹带着火星落在寺周围的无人山林中，因为天干物燥，迅速引发了山林大火。等 8 月 12 日晚人们发现山林出现明火时，大火已经扩散到周围几百亩山林了。

当时，陈爱莲正在外地参加一场论坛，刚演讲完，她就接到县领导打来的电话："赵婆岙大火难以控制，需要万丰奥特派出 200 名民兵参与救援！"

县领导打电话给陈爱莲，除了万丰奥特是本地大企业之外，更是因为万丰奥特内部有着严密的民兵组织。这支民兵队伍在县人武部的统一指挥下，近年来先后出动民兵 1 800 多人,参与抗击"桑美"台风新昌江堤坝险情、"莫拉克"台风新林乡抗洪、破冰除雪和森林灭火等抢险救灾任务,万丰奥特的民兵听令守规、敢打硬仗的战斗意志赢得了社会的高度赞誉。

陈爱莲在电话里想都没想,就立即答应县领导把万丰奥特的民兵营派到赵婆呑参与灭火。浙江各大媒体在报道新昌大火时,都提到当地组织了几百人的灭火队伍,而其中万丰奥特民兵组成的灭火队,就达到了 200 多人。

民兵汇报表演

接到命令后,负责这次灭火行动的万丰奥特人武部部长丁金潮马上组织了杨利平、王宇浩、俞光耀、张惠成、梁晓明等骨干民兵带头人,分组迅速召集力量。他们知道,除消防队、政府干部之外,万丰奥特的民兵队伍是参与灭火的人群中最大而且最有纪律的一支队伍了,所以他们必然会面对艰巨的任务。不过他们并不紧张,因为这支队伍的参与人员,曾多次参与县级应急抢险救灾任务,平时还有像拉练这样的活动,因此彼此都认识,合作起来非常熟练。

消防部门制定的灭火方案,由两部分组成。一方面要在着火林区周围开辟一条防火隔离通道，使明火不至于无限扩大；另一方面由消防部门从山下的水库抽水，对着火林区进行灭火。

任务果然艰巨，消防部门安排给万丰奥特民兵队伍的任务，一是把不能用车带上去的设备搬到山上。因为火情在山上，道路崎岖，很多地方汽车无法上去，像灭火袋、消防水龙带都需要人力搬运上山。二是要开辟一条宽20米左右的防火隔离通道，分配到万丰奥特民兵队伍的，总共有近千米长。最后算下来，万丰奥特的民兵们共开辟了6 000多平方米的防火隔离带。

这两个任务都不好完成。

搬东西这项工作，看似不起眼，但其实非常辛苦。因为着火点是在山上。提着大量物品山下山上来回几十趟，不是年轻员工，很难完成。不过万丰奥特200多人的队伍很快完成了这项工作。

万丰奥特民兵勇救火山，被当地人武部授予锦旗

但接下来的开辟防火隔离带工作量更大，这项工作要求要把隔离带内的树木全部砍掉移开，使火势不至于进一步扩散。因为是夜晚，所以根本看不清楚，且新昌的山上多是荆棘，万丰奥特的民兵几乎全部被荆棘刺出了血口

子，很多人砍树时还拉伤了自己。不过，让他们感到自豪的是，因为有了他们的共同努力，大火在两天之内被扑灭了。救火虽然是项公益工作，不过它集中反映了万丰奥特的民兵招之即来、来之能战、战之能胜的群体文化，尤其展现了万丰奥特在长期良性企业文化引导下形成的团结、上进、纪律严明的作风。

万丰奥特企业文化的形成

万丰奥特的团队在救灾等公益事件上表现出来的企业文化，并不是一朝一夕形成的，是陈爱莲和万丰奥特的管理团队多年来有意塑造的，与整个企业的创业历史同步。

不过，真正把企业文化作为一个单独的概念加以培养，在万丰奥特始于1998 年。那几年，陈爱莲和万丰奥特的管理层连续对国外同行进行考察，从各国的同行当中吸收了很多企业管理要素。

陈爱莲一行东渡日本，对 12 家百年以上著名企业进行考察

　　1998 年，陈爱莲一行 8 人东渡日本，对 12 家百年以上的著名企业进行考察。在考察的过程当中，陈爱莲觉得这些企业的经营者的水平也不怎么样，有几个总经理甚至没有万丰奥特的车间主任水平高，那为什么这些百年企业还能很好地发展呢？

　　在当时，这支还非常年轻的团队就已经养成了遇事讨论的习惯。考察期间，他们在宾馆里展开激烈讨论，得出的结论是文化在起作用。

　　这一讨论成为万丰奥特自身企业文化的起源。当时考察团的成员发现日本最长寿的企业经营的历史可以达到 300 多年，是典型的百年老店。而万丰奥特团队去考察学习的企业，最少的也有五六十年，100 多年的企业也很多。而这其中，既有股份制的大企业，也有完全属于个人的家族企业。

　　万丰奥特的这支管理团队发现，这些长寿的企业往往经历过很多起伏，传承过几代人。以家族企业论，常常是创业的曾祖父的时代是非常辉煌的，祖父的时代一般，到了父辈的时代再现辉煌到了当下又表现平平。不过，起起伏伏，公司总是能生存下来。

　　万丰奥特团队仔细讨论他们走访过的这些企业，发现它们之所以能持续经营，其实与经营者个人能力的关系已经不大，关键在于它们都把产业布局在社会需要的领域，所以社会总是需要它们。另外，公司用制度来保障基础的经营管理，这使得企业的产品有稳定的品质。

　　当然，更为重要的是，这些长期经营的公司，虽然管理层和员工不断变迁，但整体上都有一种上进、相互信任、遵守既有纪律和规章、懂得分工和协作的良好氛围。有了这种氛围，一方面，新的管理者和员工会不断融入这种氛围；另一方面，它保障了企业的基础制度能得到执行，这就使得这些长寿企业的产品非常稳定，能够得到消费者的认可。

　　陈爱莲和万丰奥特的团队，就这样触及了国外公司的企业文化。当时考察团队感到豁然开朗：有了这些，一家企业的业绩虽然会随着经营者的个人能力而有所起伏，但却不会有根本性的生存问题。

认识到了这一点的考察团队一致认为，企业文化建设非常重要。

进修 EMBA（高级管理人员工商管理硕士）课程之后，陈爱莲开始用长期规划来运营万丰奥特，提出了"营造国际品牌、构建百年企业"的目标。而在万丰奥特随后的五年规划当中，企业文化建设成为陈爱莲打造万丰奥特"百年企业"目标的核心手段。为此，陈爱莲从党校引进了从事十几年政治教育工作、具有深厚马克思主义理论基础的吴艺担任专职党委副书记，走出了一条独具特色的文化经营之路。

本来，党校教师这一工作使吴艺很有机会进入政府部门工作，但他说喜欢做点实事。在某种程度上，可以说是吴艺带领团队推动了万丰奥特企业文化的发展。

在作为决策者的陈爱莲和管理团队的高度重视下，万丰奥特通过吸收广大员工的集体智慧，以领导团队的精神为主导而提炼形成了成体系、可表述的万丰奥特企业文化。它的核心层是精神，教导员工如何做人；第二层是理念，教导员工如何做事；第三层是制度，是员工的行为准则。这些，对经营活动和经营结果都会产生直接的影响。

万丰奥特企业文化分为公司使命、愿景、价值观、目标、方针、作风和万丰奥特的五种精神，一共七个部分，这七个部分构成了一个比较完整的体系。

由陈爱莲主导的万丰奥特管理层提出：

万丰奥特的使命是为客户提供满意的优质产品。

为客户提供满意的优质产品是作为企业存在的最基本也是最核心的价值。一家企业，如果忽视了提供优质产品的使命，不管它曾经多么强大、多么辉煌、多么有竞争力，都是一家没有生命力的企业！

通过公司的使命，我们可以清晰地看到，在产品的质量方面，陈爱莲希望万丰奥特达到国际优秀水平。她曾经用一个案例来做警示：

万丰奥特有客户发现某轮毂产品一直到最后一道检验程序时，才发现最初加工的过程当中有一个小瑕疵，因此就向万丰奥特的检验员提出非议。而该检验员为了不使客户挑刺，就轻描淡写地说："回去补补就可以了。"

那位客户把这件事情告诉了陈爱莲，而它也成为陈爱莲用来警醒全体员工的案例。她想以此告诉员工的是，所谓的优质产品，是靠一丝不苟的态度执行出来的。这个案例当中，万丰奥特的检验员讲的是事实，但如果像这个案例当中的生产检验过程还存在，就说明万丰奥特的生产过程还没有达到品质上的国际化，万丰奥特就不能算是达成了公司存在的使命。

万丰奥特的公司愿景是营造国际品牌、构筑百年企业。

万丰奥特主要有两个商标。

一是"ZCW"商标：这是集团第一个自创商标，Z代表浙江（Zhejiang），C代表中国（China），W代表车轮（Wheel）和世界（World）；寓意万丰奥特品牌要立足全球平台，通过跨越式发展，为从地方级的品牌上升为行业级的品牌、从民族级的品牌上升为世界级的品牌打好基础。

二是"萬豐"商标：外围是两束环绕的麦穗，意为丰收，内部则是希腊字母"W"的变体，是万丰奥特的首个拼音字母，这样的设计体现了集团成立时中西合璧、接轨国际、适应开放、迈向21世纪新时代的产业特征。

万丰奥特创立十周年高管团队

万丰奥特希望自己成为一家国际级的企业，而且融入整个社会，从而基业长青。当前，万丰奥特已获得了中国名牌、中国出口名牌、中国驰名商标和全国质量奖等诸多荣誉，但要从中国名牌上升为国际名牌，还得进一步提升：以产品质量为核心、知识产权为内涵、企业形象为引力、用户亲和力为源泉，通过广告宣传等手段，最后达到市场占有率目标。

万丰奥特的价值观是，永恒提升价值，不断奉献社会。

在万丰奥特的企业文化当中，其价值观是有非常具体的要求的。

"永恒提升价值"包括了三个层面：首先是提升企业价值，要求管理层引领企业不断创造效益，创造就业，持续发展；其次是要求员工在具体执行的过程中，不断提升用户价值，包括创新产品、保证品质、全面服务；最后还要求公司内部管理层和员工要努力提升自我价值，要求管理层与员工相互之间要引领成长、用人之长。

"不断奉献社会"包括四个方面：提高股东回报，使资源达到最优化配置；提高员工生活水平，引导员工奔向小康生活；通过参与竞争，推动行业进步；通过承担社会责任，推动社会发展。

为达到万丰奥特的愿景，陈爱莲提出了具体的目标体系，包括"百强万丰"、"百誉万丰"和"百年万丰"三个阶段。

第一步要实现"百强万丰"，也就是要进入世界行业百强（包括研发、工艺、规模、市场占有率、品牌影响力、赢利能力、资本运作等达到行业细分市场的领跑地位）；第二步则要实现"百誉万丰"，达到客户满意度高、合作伙伴评价好，行业竞争力强、品牌知名度高，社会美誉度好、责任贡献度大；而后第三步则要通过几代人的努力，将万丰奥特打造成为一个可持续发展的企业，实现"百年万丰"的目标。

当我们具体了解万丰奥特整个公司的历史之后就会发现，陈爱莲和管理层为万丰奥特制定的目标体系非常具体，给员工们以强大的激励，从而使得这个公司有可能开始形成一个事业共同体，去追求"百强"、"百誉"、"百年"目标。

　　除了目标之外，陈爱莲和万丰奥特的管理层也总结了万丰奥特创业以来养成的工作习惯，这是企业实现未来目标的保障。

　　万丰奥特企业文化当中的方针，强调的是：万里之行，始于轮下；丰功伟业，基在创新。

　　"万里之行，始于轮下"：激励全体万丰奥特人要大处着眼，小处着手，不断进取，同时也揭示了以轮代步的时代特征和企业所处的行业特征。

　　"丰功伟业，基在创新"：创新是企业发展的永恒主题，包括体制机制创新、科技创新、经营模式创新、管理体系创新等，要有否定自我、超越自我的信心和勇气。

　　两句话的句首结合起来，为"万丰"二字，解释了公司名称的独特文化内涵。

　　万丰奥特企业文化当中的作风，强调的是：实事求是，艰苦奋斗，雷厉风行，一抓到底。

　　万丰奥特管理层强调的作风，实质上就是万丰奥特的执行文化。"实事求是"强调的是客观规律性，要求在执行的过程中要从市场和企业的实际出发，讲究工作方法，遵循市场规律；"艰苦奋斗"强调的是曲折性，要求员工坚信前途是光明的、道路是曲折的，要有希望，更要有顽强的斗志和勤俭节约的品质；"雷厉风行"强调迅速性，要求员工在充分领会、服从上级指令的同时，行事要果断有力，专业迅速；而"一抓到底"则强调彻底性，要求公司上下，"事事有人做，人人有事做，人人负责任"。

　　万丰奥特企业文化当中的五种精神，分别是敬业精神、竞争精神、实干精神、学习精神和团队精神。

　　管理层认为，这五种精神，是万丰奥特创业和壮大的保障，也只有这样的精神，才能在万丰奥特成为百年企业的过程中，起到关键作用。

　　万丰奥特作为一个中国本土公司所形成的企业文化，也具有鲜明的时代特征。由于中国市场经济还远未达到成熟状态，很多领域的市场竞争并没有充分开放，所以像万丰奥特这样高度市场化的企业，公司的构想和使命常常没有十分具体化，因为市场开放给市场化企业带来的，往往是蓝海式发展。

红色风景线

红色，在万丰奥特是一道亮丽的风景。很多初次走进万丰奥特的人会惊讶，一个地道的民企怎么会有类似国企的各种组织：党、工、青、妇、兵，一应俱全，民营企业不是以人员精炼、机构精简而著称吗？

"浙江省是民营经济大省，民营企业党建作用发挥越来越重要。党组织可以说是企业发展的导航器，发挥党组织的政治引导作用，能够使企业准确把握党和国家的方针政策，把握产业发展趋势；同时，党组织还是企业发展的助推器，通过发挥党员先锋模范作用和党组织战斗堡垒作用，能够进一步构建和谐劳动关系。"在陈爱莲心中，听党话、跟党走，是天经地义的事，企业能有今天，前提就是党的改革开放政策，党组织治理国家的力量强大而有效，党应该成为民营企业的政治核心。

万丰面向全国"外聘直选"党委副书记，为民企党建探索新路子

为此，万丰奥特像设计产品规格标准一样，从制度上设计"万丰奥特的党建制度"，制定了全省第一个非公企业党建工作标准，通过了ISO 9001体系认证。

更具特色的是，党委书记陈爱莲响应浙江省委建设"发展强、党建强"企业的号召，面向全国"外聘直选"党委副书记。而负责这次"外聘直选"的，就是万丰奥特原党委副书记吴艺。

经过了解，吴艺发现浙江省在进入21世纪之后，有一批党政干部先后下海到民企工作。他认为，这些干部既有政府工作经验，对政府的部门结构和工作流程有深入的了解，又在民企长期工作，熟知民企的运营，所以是万丰奥特选拔党委副书记的最佳选择。

恰巧在2010年，浙江温州25家民企公开招聘"红色CEO"，吴艺两次赴温州市委组织部，在1 200多位报名者中筛选适合人选，而后逐个以电话和面谈的方式，把万丰奥特招聘党委副书记的动机以及万丰奥特要加强党建工作的构想清晰地表达给他们，邀请他们来参加应聘。

吴艺的诚挚，感动了这批干部当中的相当一部分人。有了他们的积极参与，万丰奥特的"外聘直选"党委副书记的举措，就有了成功的基础。为了既让社会认可，又让企业党员拥护，万丰奥特在当地组织部门指导下，设计了"外聘直选"党委副书记的流程。在经过信息发布、初审筛选、面试答辩、竞职演说四个阶段的筛选之后，万丰奥特全体党员以无记名投票的方式，选举产生了专职党委副书记——徐志良，一位来自绍兴本地组织部门的专业人才。

徐志良在竞职演说中这样讲道："我在不惑之年从体制内转到体制外，这将是我人生中的一个转折点。来之前朋友为我算了'三本账'：经济账、政治账、家庭账，劝我留在政府组织部门，但我还是坚定地怀着'三颗心'、'三个梦想'来了，对万丰奥特、对陈爱莲董事长的敬畏之心、敬重之心、敬佩之心，将激励我不断地探索万丰奥特党建模式，不断地实现自己的人生价值。"

"外聘直选"为万丰党建注入了新的活力。为进一步充实党建力量，

2015 年 12 月，万丰再次面向全国"外聘直选"党委副书记，在绍兴组织部门工作过的金亦伟成功当选，万丰党建工作实现了传承与弘扬。

三任集团党委副书记的交接与传承

万丰奥特的党建，除了党组织日常工作以外，主要职能在两个层面体现出鲜明的特色：一是抓实基础。参照"把支部建在连队"的方式，在各车间、工段建有党、工、青、妇、兵 5 个小组，协助车间主任、工段领班做好凝聚力工作，分别负责先进人员培养、帮助解决员工实际困难、丰富员工业余生活、关心员工家庭建设、加强现场安全生产管理。二是抓住核心。集团层面，党委通过参与战略建议、制度建设，起到引导物质文明、政治文明建设的作用；通过主抓企业文化、社会责任，起到领导精神文明、社会文明建设的作用。

万丰奥特党建工作中最具人文情怀的，是集团工会与当地医院和省级重点医院沟通协商设立了"万丰奥特医院绿色通道"，为员工及家属们提供及时的医疗服务。

2014 年 3 月，一位员工的父亲突发脑出血，这位员工第一时间想到了打工会主席杨旭勇的电话。当时已经是中午 12 点半，万丰奥特在当地医院的联络医生已经下班，杨旭勇马上打电话请他赶回医院，把最好的脑科专家找来，做好动手术的准备。紧接着，他和工会副主席陈宝根立即赶往医院，等那位员工父亲的救护车一到，他们就已经在门口迎接了，帮助将他立刻送往手术室。手术非常成功，一个星期之后这位员工的父亲就康复出院了。这位员工回到公司上班后，逢人就感激地说，是万丰奥特和工会救了她父亲。

这样的例子还有很多，万丰奥特各级工会组织真正成为员工的当家人，切切实实地为员工解决好衣、食、住、行问题，还成为员工的贴心人，无论是员工结婚、生育，还是生病住院、家属离世，工会组织都会赶在第一时间、按照公司制度规定进行慰问，尽心尽力地帮助员工解决实际困难，让员工感受到万丰奥特大家庭的温暖。

万丰奥特工会委员会成员

所以，在万丰奥特已经达成了这样一种共识，那就是有困难就找工会组织。陈爱莲也常常说，只要有工会组织在，她晚上就能睡个安稳觉了！

速写野马特训

每年，在新昌天姥山区，都有一次或者几次，上百名年轻的小伙子和姑娘们，皮肤晒得黝黑，打着野马旗，穿着统一的迷彩服，背着整齐划一的行李包，穿越过这些古老的村落。在旁观的村民看来，这些人多少有些奇怪，因为跟随着整个队伍的，有大小好几辆车，但这些年轻人当中，即使有几个人脚肿得一瘸一拐地被人扶着艰难地跟在队伍后面，却一个也不愿意坐上车。

万丰奥特的员工都知道，这就是"野马特训"当中最考验人的野外拉练训练。这支队伍在一天内，要徒步行军 50 多公里，而目的只有一个，那就是考验这些未来万丰奥特管理者的意志。而紧跟在队伍后面的那几辆车，是万丰奥特为野马特训这一项目准备的后勤车辆。上面的装备从饮用水、食物到救急药品，应有尽有——在新昌天姥山区进行拉练训练，由于山势陡峭，落差很大，受训人员常有疲劳、脱水、划伤的现象，而万丰奥特为训练做的准备是非常完善的。

万丰奥特的"野马特训"，对全体学员提出了 6 个方面的基本要求：强大的活力、不驯服精神、良好的环境适应性、群体协同性、强健的体魄和吃苦耐劳特性。

万丰奥特野马特训营

为了磨炼员工的精神，万丰奥特每年通过层层选拔优秀员工和后备干部，送往山区军校进行为期一个月的全封闭式特训，内容主要包括三个方面：企业文化、管理技能和体能训练。因此，无论是骄阳似火，还是风雨交加，学员们都要与自己的意志进行较量：5 公里的负重越野跑、50 公里的徒步拉练、高难度的铁人三项、野外生存拓展训练……

每一期特训，陈爱莲无论在哪里出差，都会赶回去看望学员，给学员上企业文化课，和学员面对面交流，谈创业经历，谈人生感悟。每当看到学员在操场上一站就是几小时，说趴下不管是水是泥都得趴下……虽然明知铁不炼不成钢，而且这种特训方式也是自己所倡导的，但她又会忍不住要掉眼泪，会向教官求情，能不能减少一点这种高强度的训练。因此，她每次去特训营看望学员，总会带一副茶色眼镜，因为她不想让大家看到她心疼落泪的样子。

在万丰奥特成为多元化的大型企业集团之后，"野马特训"对于万丰奥特整个企业集团的作用非常明显。通过这项培训，万丰奥特的基层骨干人员能够全面深入地了解整个集团的过去、现在和未来，增加对公司的感情；另外，通过训练这些基层骨干成员之间凝聚了特殊的感情，增加了跨部门相互之间的了解和各个公司之间的协同，良好的人际关系有了保障；而同时，万丰奥特的核心管理团队成员，尤其是陈爱莲，通过深入培训现场，亲身接触基层的公司骨干，有机会关注这些年轻人的成长，并提拔人才。

事实也正是如此，只要经历过特训的学员，都会感到获益匪浅。虽然训练是异乎寻常的艰苦，皮肤黑了，嘴唇裂了，但学员们收获的是坚毅和勇敢、自信和力量。参训归来的学员都会说，三十天虽短，但一辈子够用，什么是服从，什么是纪律，什么是意志与毅力，什么是团队意识和团队精神全都知道了，只要能挺过来，今后就再也没有什么事能难倒自己。即便后来离职的员工，也对这段经历念念不忘，无不感叹："受训一月，受益一生。"

"野马特训"使来自五湖四海不同专业、不同文化、不同年龄的各种人才，形成了一种声音、一个方向、一股合力，具备了强大的团队作战能力。

因此野马特训营也成为万丰奥特培养精英骨干的大熔炉，被称为万丰奥特的"黄埔军校"。

2004年，王兴东、高松年、乔迈等100多位著名作家相约万丰奥特，对万丰奥特企业文化做了高度评价。他们说，作为一家民营企业，用"野马精神"来诠释恰到好处。它有强大的活力、良好的环境适应性，更有优秀的群体精神，"希望以'野马精神'为主的企业文化能够发扬光大"。

对于万丰奥特整个公司来说，重要的是，这些都已经在初步形成大公司格局的企业当中，以文字的形式固定下来，成为可传承的精神财富。

"四会式"治理结构

万丰奥特之所以能形成大公司格局，核心因素是因为万丰奥特在轮毂制造领域的卓越业绩，使得它的市场触角所及，社会各方都对企业产生了信任。正是因为有了这种信任，万丰奥特得以从摩轮业务顺利扩张到汽轮业务，并衍生出装备智能机器人、镁合金等一系列业务。

在形成大公司格局的过程中，万丰奥特的经验是，社会给予企业的信任和资源，要小心使用。现在看来，跨半步，是万丰奥特做产业能成功的前提。

所谓的半步，就是从万丰奥特经营的产品发展过程中看，必须要有不变的部分。从摩轮车铝轮毂到汽车铝轮毂，是原料不变产品变；从铝轮毂到镁轮毂，是产品不变原料变；从轮毂制造，到万丰科技的低压铸造机和智能机器人，虽然原料与产品都发生了巨大的变化，但万丰科技的客户是万丰奥特和它的同行，客户群还是万丰奥特非常熟悉的群体，因此也获得了成功。

而在这种多元化格局形成的背后，万丰奥特面对着不同的行业、市场、技术以及人才的要求，如何实行管理？

这是陈爱莲在万丰奥特做强做大之后遇到的又一个挑战。

万丰奥特在长期摸索之后，形成了独具特色的"四会"（党委会、董事会、监事会和经营管理会）体制治理结构。

党委会的主要职能是对接政府部门，准确传达、落实国家的方针、政策；同时主抓企业党、工、青、妇、兵精神文明体系建设，服务于生产经营。

董事会的主要职能是科学决策，定战略、把方向、用高管，批制度、批计划、批投资。

经营办公会的主要职能是，贯彻实施董事会的战略决策以及所审批的计划、制度、投资，通过各级团队的经营管理，把董事会给予的综合资源价值最大化。

而监事会的主要职能是，监督公司对战略规划、经营计划、制度和投资的实施过程和实施结果，确保队伍健康成长、确保企业稳健发展。

万丰奥特制定"四会"制度的目的，是使体制更加畅达、机制更加灵活、运行模式更加高效，能更好地设置职权关系、依法治企、统一思想，既分工负责又集体领导，提升执行能力，真正体现民营企业的灵活机制和国有企业的规范程序以及上市公司的科学治理。

万丰奥特的这个"四会"制度，实际上是党的宏观治国思想在企业中的微观实践。而在这个做法的背后，陈爱莲和万丰奥特的管理层，是有着深刻的构思的。

万丰奥特之所以采取这种"红色"的治理结构，是因为陈爱莲和现有万丰奥特管理层的成员，都认为治企与治国虽然不同，但都是组织管理，有相通之处，企业管理的原理、思维方式、工作方法都可以借鉴，直接而效益明显，并容易获得认可。

万丰奥特虽为民企，但在企业实践当中把党的治国思想转化为公司的管理标杆方面，已经有了很深的实践心得体会。

万丰奥特的"四会"制度其实是一个表象，内在的原则是通过会议把尽可能多的管理层的智慧，纳入到公司决策的过程当中；同时，党组织在每个领导层上多元结构，体现了权力的制衡因素；把决策制定和执行过程分开，也保证了董事会的权威性。

当然，更为重要的是要让万丰奥特在成为大公司之后，依旧保有小公司的灵活性。这一点，陈爱莲在"四会"制度的结构当中，特意形成了一个临时决策机构，就是在日常事务的处理当中，一旦形成紧急而重要的事务时，陈爱莲可以召集"四会"相关成员，扩大到具体事务的相关人员，临时形成组织，对待决策事项临时听取汇报，当即做出决策，并由相应管理者执行，确保了民企的活力。

在成功交接党委副书记一职后，吴艺的工作重点就是带领吕雪莲、曾昭岭团队建立完善的监事会管理体系。经过几年的探索，万丰奥特的监督体系原则开始显山露水。根据万丰奥特的发展目标，通过树立风险管理理念和廉洁自律理念建立起完整的内控体系，它以企业文化为灵魂，以法人治理架构为基础，以内控制度为保障，以风险管理为重点，并以各级行政自我监控为主线，以党、工、青、妇、兵为辅线，以事前法律、事中财务、事后审计、事发监察调查为防线。

这是一个多层次、立交式、全方位的"三线防范体制"，它意味着万丰奥特把每一个决策的执行流程都视为一个过程。在长期规划和董事会决策决定了一项工作得到开展之后，万丰奥特集团所有的业务都自动进入这个有监督的执行过程。

公司的审计体系会对每宗流程的整个展开过程进行监督，审计的依据主要是三个规章制度：《年度计划》、《管理制度》、《VI》（ Visual Identity，视觉识别系统 ）。审计的内容主要包括四个方面：一是"责"，以经营管理数据说话，经营指标是否完成、项目投资是否有漏洞、各级干部是否运行好职权范围内的资源配置；二是"权"，人、财、物的运用过程中，是否有越权、贪私、受贿现象；三是"利"，考核指标设置是否科学、考核业绩数据是否真实；四是对各级公司的经营班子成员的调整、离任，进行实事求是的审计，把握原则、尽心尽责、正确评价。

针对审计出来的问题，有三个方面的处理结果：一是与各级经营管理团队进行面对面交流，提出解决方案，限期整改，直至跟踪整改完毕，有违反公司制度的，按制度处罚；二是对于审计出来的不完善的制度和流程，提出方案，提交法律部门改进；三是违反国家法律、公司制度、公民道德底线的，任何一项违规（越权、受贿、私欲膨胀等）的查处，提交董事会（或"四会"会议）讨论决定，根据情节轻重，按照制度规定，或是"治病救人"，或是提交当地公安机关。万丰奥特内部审计的目的，是弘扬"君子爱财，取之有道"的文化理念，让各级干部健康成长、家庭幸福、事业有成，使公司稳步、健康、可持续发展。

在这样的一个体系结构上，万丰奥特的大公司结构是非常具有特色的。既有大公司的严谨，又有小公司的灵活。当然，它还要有对员工的提升和关爱。

发挥团队威力

在万丰奥特的大小会议上，陈爱莲常常倡导：一个人的力量是有限的，团队的威力是无穷的。这句理念作为万丰奥特企业文化的核心之一，已深入人心。

陈爱莲在为人处世时讲究平等、乐于分享。前者使得万丰奥特有一个相当大范围的可以平等议事的高级管理层，在平等的讨论当中，公司的大事可以从众多方法当中讨论出一个最优的来执行；而她的乐于分享表现在，她不仅分享决策，她还愿意与成员分享公司经营的成果，保证了万丰奥特管理层和员工有创新的构想时，不仅能得到公司的支持予以实行，而且在为公司创造效益之后，自己也能得到精神和物质上的激励。

陈爱莲送给每位总经理一块匾，上面书写着她的题词"敬天爱才，共创辉煌"。"敬天"就是要遵循自然规律、遵循市场规律、合乎党和国家的方针政策；"爱才"就是要尊重知识、尊重人才，实现共话、共创、共享。她认

为，一个领导者持续优秀，一是看他能否源源不断地打胜仗，打到哪里成功
到哪里，优秀队伍也集聚到哪里；二是看他胜利后是否能把成果与大家分享，
包括精神激励和物质激励。而要想实现这一目标，领导者的胸怀至关重要。

"万丰功臣"评选表彰

　　每逢中秋佳节大团圆之日，万丰奥特都要隆重表彰"感动人物"、"建设
功臣"、"好母亲、好父亲、好妻子、好丈夫、优秀小万丰奥特人"，使企业
文化深入到每一个家庭。万丰奥特还把员工的住房安置率指标纳入战略规划，
通过团购商品房等方式，以最优惠的价格为优秀员工解决住房问题。

为优秀骨干奖配奔驰、宝马等高级轿车

在吸引人才、激励人才、留住人才方面，陈爱莲往往都是大手笔。从1999 年开始，当人们把拥有一辆轿车当作家庭梦想的时候，万丰奥特就在年度总结表彰大会上奖励汽车。近年来，还开始给一批优秀骨干和员工奖配奔驰、宝马等高级轿车，使其在万丰奥特舞台上更加努力地施展才华、体现价值。

除此之外，陈爱莲认为，对员工最好的福利是培训。

万丰奥特每年投入上千万元通过"送出去、请进来"的形式，安排一批批优秀骨干到著名高校研修，派遣一批批技术人员赴国外深造；同时，还邀请专家学者到企业授课。

在这方面，陈爱莲为员工做出了很好的表率。从1995 年开始，她每年都要到高等院校进修，从杭州商学院到浙江大学，从香港公开大学的MPA（公共管理硕士）到复旦大学的EMBA，从清华大学到北京大学，完成这些进修课程都是靠其锲而不舍的学习精神实现的。在进修学习时，为了上第二天的课，她常常是连夜赶路。

有趣的是，当陈爱莲在读复旦大学MBA的时候，老师们看她学得很认真，就对她说："你可以再去报名，尝试读个EMBA。"她就问："EMBA在哪里报名？"老师指了指楼上，陈爱莲下了课就跑上去了。当时就读复旦大学EMBA需要考试，陈爱莲英语不好，考试时就在试卷上面这样写道："尊敬的老师，我英语不好，但是我很想读EMBA，我现在已经读了好几个MBA了，希望老师能够允许我一边读，一边学。"

当时的复旦大学管理学院陆雄文院长觉得一位女性有这么强烈的学习欲望，很不容易，所以他非常诚恳地在面试中和陈爱莲进行了深入的交流。

陈爱莲是一个擅长学习、学以致用的人。在复旦大学学习内部控制的课程时，老师布置作业后，她以公司的实际情况为例第一个上交了作业。老师拿着她的作业在课堂上展开讨论，提出整改意见，她就把这份成果带回企业实施。每次出差或学习回来，陈爱莲也总是召集相关人员，讲述她听到的新观念和感悟，从而带动了整个团队的学习氛围。

"学习是员工进步的起点，培训是企业发展的基础。"万丰奥特还筹建了"万丰商学院"，使每一名员工、每一级干部，都能接受分层级、系统化、专业化的培训。

在一年一度的"泰山企业文化论坛"上，陈爱莲与300多名万丰奥特精英分享自己的人生体会。她说，每个人的价值体现无外乎"物质与精神"两个方面。在物质价值体现上，包括报酬、待遇、更好的生活品质。人对物质的追求是很正常的，但应该循序渐进、量力而行，要对自己有个正确的评价。任何一个人，只要能沉下心来、立足岗位、踏踏实实工作、兢兢业业付出，随着经验的积累、阅历的沉淀、能力的提升、岗位的升迁、业绩的创造，物质利益自然会有，而且贡献越大、报酬越高。

复旦大学EMBA同学会与陆雄文院长（第二排中）合影

而在精神价值体现方面，则包括更好的工作岗位、学习培训机会和各种荣誉，被上级赏识、被同事学习、被部下信任、被家庭尊重、被社会认可。只要努力，人人都能做到，如果做到了这些，都应该是具备了高贵品格的人，也不枉来到世上走一遭！

万丰奥特企业文化，为其进一步架构大公司的格局铺平了道路。

这家公司还有更大的未来吗？

万丰奥特之道：大公司运营靠文化

本章揭示的主要是，万丰奥特在集团化格局初步形成之后，开始形成万丰奥特企业文化的过程。陈爱莲在万丰奥特多元化业务形成之后，及时地认识到，大公司的经营靠的是文化，只有良好的企业文化才是万丰奥特的规模进一步扩展的保障。

一个集团的企业文化形成过程，包括两个来源。一个是公司在长期的实践过程中体现在公司人群当中的文化习惯；另一个是企业经营者和管理层希望自己经营的公司所要达到的文化要求。

陈爱莲认为，世界上凡是基业长青的企业都是有灵魂的企业。万丰奥特的企业文化是从企业发展过程当中提炼出来的，以领导团队的精神为主导，并吸收了广大员工的集体智慧。虽然它看不见、摸不着，但无形地印在全体员工的头脑里，发挥着无比强大的动力和战斗力，成为企业的灵魂。万丰奥特的企业文化就是全体万丰奥特人的灵魂。

Chapter 9
Wanfeng's Culture and Administration

The Team Spirit of the Community Pillar

In the district of Tianmu Mountains in Xinchang, many places are named with Ao. Zhaopo'ao is part of the mountain range of Tianmu Mountains. There is nothing special in the mountain village except that some local visitors usually visit the Iron Buddha Temple located here.

During the summer of 2013, Xinchang was first reported in CCTV news, because the local temperate of 44 degrees centigrade set a new national record. In August, the hottest period of the summer, a forest fire broke out in Zhaopo'ao and lasted for two days.

The bush fire was simply caused by a local villager who went to burn incense in Iron Buddha Temple. After the villager finish praying, he set off two firecrackers outside the temple. The firecracker fell with flame in the undeveloped forest around the temple and quickly caused the forest fire in the dry season. When the flames in the forest were noticed on the night of 12th August, forest of several hundred mu were all covered in flames.

Chen Ailian was then attending a forum outside Xinchang. Just after her speech, she received a call from the county leader who said to her:" The forest fire in Zhaopo'ao is hard to put out, and we need 200 militiamen from Wanfeng Auto to take part in the rescue."

As a large enterprise in Xinchang, Wanfeng Auto has its own well-organized militia, and that was why the county leader called Chen Ailian for help. The company militia, under the leadership of the people's armed forces department in the county, had joined many emergency and disaster rescues with more than 1800 people, such as protecting the river dam and river banks of Xinchang against the typhoon Sangmei, fighting against the flood brought by the typhoon Moraque in Xinlin Xiang, removing ice and snow and fighting fires. Wanfeng Auto's militia are well-disciplined and strong-willed and have won high praise from the public.

Without hesitation, Chen Ailian promised the county leader at once on the phone that Wanfeng Auto would soon send its militia to fight the forest fire in Zhaopo'ao. When reporting the bush fire in Xinchang, the media throughout Zhejiang Province all mentioned the local fire-fighter team of several hundred members, 200 of whom were from Wanfeng Auto's militia.

On receiving the order, the secretary of Wanfeng's people's armed forces department Ding Jinchao, leader of the fire-fighting action, immediately appointed the backbones of the militia, Yang Liping, Wang Yuhao, Yu Guangyao, Zhang Huicheng and Liang Xiaoming, to gather their group members as the leaders. They knew that besides the fire bridade and the local government leaders, Wanfeng' militia was the largest and most-disciplined team of all the groups that joined the fire fighting, so they were responsible to handle the tough task. They were not nervous, for all the team members here had participated in emergency and disaster rescues for many times in the county. Besides, they usually had had such camp and field training activities, so they can work together very skillfully as close acquaintances. The plan made by fire fighting department consisted of two parts. Firstly, they should dug a firebreak to prevent the expansion of flames; secondly, the fire fighters should fight the fire with water drained from the reservoir at the foot of the mountain.

This indeed was a tough task. One of the tasks assigned to Wanfeng Auto's militia was to take the device that couldn't be transported by vehicles up to the mountain. Because of the forest fire on the mountain and the rugged roads, many of the devices such as the fire-extinguishing bags and fire hosepipes had to be handled onto the mountain . Another task for them was to dug a nearly 1000-meter-long part of the 20-meter-wide firebreak to be opened up. Finally, the fire isolation belt to be dug by Wanfeng Auto's militia totally would cover more than 6000 square meters.

Neither of the tasks was easy to handle.

Though seemingly simple, handling the devices onto the mountain in flames was really a hard job. But for the young militiaman, one could hardly go up and down the mountain with large amount of goods for tens of times. Yet the team ,composed of more than 200 militiamen, from Wanfeng Auto quickly finished the tiring task.

But next, it was a great workload to open up a fire isolation belt inside which all the woods and bushes should be cut down and removed so as to prevent the forest fire from further spread. It being the night, almost all the militia from Wanfeng Auto had their bodies cut in darkness by the thorns that were everywhere on the mountain, and many of them pulled their muscles while cutting down the woods. However, it brought them much self-pride that the bush fire was put out within two days because of their joint efforts. Though Wanfeng Auto only performed a public service by sending its militia to fight the fire, it demonstrated the team culture of the militia who could be easily organized to work jointly till the task was fulfilled. In particular, it revealed the militia's united, ambitious and disciplined work style nurtured by the good enterprise culture in Wanfeng Auto.

The Formation of Wanfeng Auto's Enterprise Culture

The enterprise culture demonstrated by Wanfeng Auto's team while performing the public service as fire fighters was not shaped suddenly. The enterprise culture has been purposely cultivated for years by Chen Ailian and Wanfeng Auto's management team and it grows in pace with the company since the start-up.

In fact, it was in 1998 that Wanfeng Auto started to cultivate its enterprise culture as an independent concept. During those years, Chen Ailian and the company's management went abroad to visit and investigate the foreign counterparts successively, and learned a lot about management from the foreign enterprises of the same trade.

In 1998, Chen Ailian, together with another 7 team members, went to Japan to visit 12 famous enterprises all with a history of more than 100 years. During her visit, Chen Ailian didn't think these enterprise operators were not outstanding in management, and even none of their general managers was superior to Wanfeng Auto's workshop director. But why could these enterprises of long history still develop so well? She wondered.

At that time, the newly-established team had already had the habit of discussing any issue they met among team members. During their visits, after heated discussions in hotel rooms, the team came to an conclusion that the company culture was playing an important role in each of these famous enterprises' successful development.

The discussion has become the origin of Wanfeng Auto's enterprise culture later on. The team members found that the oldest enterprise in Japan had a long history of more than 300 years, a typical century-old company. Of all the enterprises that Wanfeng Auto's investigating visited ,many were more than a hundred years old, and even the youngest one had a history of at least 5-60 years. There were both big stock corporations and completely private family businesses among these enterprises.

Wanfeng Auto's management team found that these long history enterprises usually had been passed down for several generations with lots of ups and downs . Take the family business as an example, usually it was at prosperously brilliant during the great-grand father's time when the business was founded, ordinary in grand-father's time, yet greatly successful again in father's time, and flatly plain in current time. In spite of the good and bad times, the enterprise could always survive.

Wanfeng Auto's investigating team carefully discussed these enterprises they had visited and found that the long-lasting operation of these enterprises had little to do with the operators' capability but was vitally attached to the necessary industrial field they were in. In the fields of social needs, these enterprises were always needed. In addition, with their operation guaranteed by the company regulations, the products of these enterprises had been enjoying steady quality.

Of course more importantly, these enterprises of longevity generally were filled with a kind of nice atmosphere of ambition and mutual trust, in which the staff, disciplined and regulation-abiding, knew how to work independently and how to cooperate with each other, despite the changes of the management and the staff. Because of the atmosphere,for one thing, the new administrators and employees could integrate with the enterprise gradually. For another, the atmosphere guaranteed the implementation of the long-lived company's basic rules, which ensured the company's steady product quality and the consumers' recognition of their products.

Chen Ailian and her team thus touched the corporate cultures of the foreign companies. Suddenly enlightened, the investigating team started to understand that because of the corporate culture, the business performance of a company may fluctuate with the operator's capability, but the company wouldn't be troubled by the fundamental problem of its survival.

With this idea, the team members reached the consensus that the construction of corporate culture was of vital significance.

Having finished her EMBA (Executive Master of Business Administration) courses, Chen Ailian started to operate Wanfeng Auto with long-term plans and set the goal "to transform Wanfeng into an international brand and to develop Wanfeng into a century enterprise". In the following five-year plan of the company , the company culture construction became the key measure to realize Chen Ailian's goal to make the Wanfeng Auto as a century enterprise. As a result, Chen Ailian invited the Party School teacher Wu Yi, who,with a good command of Marxist theories, had been working for more than ten years in the field of political education, from the Party School to work as the full-time vice party secretary in Wanfeng Auto. The company was thus led to a unique path of cultural management.

Actually, as a Party school teacher, Wu Yi had great chance to work in the government bureaus. But he likes to do practical jobs. To a degree, it is the team led by Wu Yi that has promoted the development of Wanfeng Auto's enterprise culture.

With great concerns from the decision-maker Chen Ailian and her management team, Wanfeng Auto's company culture was formed with the staff's wisdom and the leadership's leading spirit as a system expressive of the company's operation concept. The core of the enterprise culture is attached to the employee's spirit of how to be a true man. The second layer of the culture is linked to the staff's concepts of how to deal with their jobs. And the third layer is the company's rule system serving as the code of conduct of the staff. All the three aspects of the company culture would have direct influence on Wanfeng Auto's business and operation.

Wanfeng Auto's company culture consists of seven parts — the company's mission, anticipation, values, goals, policies, working style and its five principles — which has formed a complete system.

Under Chen Ailian's leadership, Wanfeng Auto's management put forward:

Wanfeng Auto's mission is to provide the customers with products of satisfyingly high quality.

It is the most fundamental core value of an enterprise' existence to provide the customers with satisfyingly high quality products. No matter how strong, how successful and how competitive an enterprise once was, it will be of no vitality if neglecting its mission to provide customers with high quality products. .

Through the company's mission, we can clearly see that in terms of the product quality, Chen Ailian wished Wanfeng Auto to achieve an internationally high level. She once cited a case warn her employees.

Once a customer of Wanfeng Auto noticed in the final round of test that there was a small defect in a certain hub product caused by the initial processing. So the customer pointed it out to Wanfeng's quality inspector. To avoid the customer's criticism, the quality inspector said airily: "It will be OK only with a little repair."

The customer told Chen Ailian the case, and it later became the typical example Chen used to caution her staff that products of high quality were produced with scrupulousness. In the case mentioned above, what Wanfeng Auto's quality inspector said was the true fact. But if there were such cases in its inspection process, it would indicate that Wanfeng Auto's production didn't achieve the international level in quality, and the company in no sense fulfilled its mission.

Wanfeng Auto's prospect is to develop into a century enterprise of an international brand image.

Wanfeng Auto has two major trademarks.

One is ZCW , the first trademark created by Wanfeng Group itself, of which Z stands for Zhejiang Province, C for China and W for Wheel and World. The trademark indicates that Wanfeng Auto's brand based on the global platform will promote itself from a local brand into a famous one in the industry and develop from a national brand into a world-class one by making brave leaps in its development.

萬豐(Wanfeng) is the second trademark. The logo is composed of two beans of wheat, meaning harvest, outside and a variant of the Greek letter W , also the first initial of Wanfeng Auto, inside. Such design is a good combination of Chinese and western elements, and it demonstrates the industry characters of the group's establishment time when China adapted to opening-up began to integrate with the world and advance to the new era 21st century.

The CEO team of Wanfeng Auto

Wanfeng Auto wishes to become a world-class enterprise that is integrated with the whole society with a solid growing base in business. Currently, Wanfeng Auto has been honored as the recognized China's famous brand and China's famous export brand, and has won prizes such as China's well-known trademark and the national quality award. But it still needs to improve itself from a national well-known brand into a world-class brand. To take bigger market share , besides advance publicity for itself, Wanfeng Auto still should be centered on its product quality, be driven with its good enterprise image as the exterior motive and the intellectual property rights as the interior one, and meanwhile base its development on the friendly relationship with the customer.

Wanfeng Auto's values: eternal enhancement in value and constant dedication to society

In Wanfeng Auto's company culture, the values are something with specific requirements.

It includes three aspects in the requirement for eternal enhancement in value. Firstly, it is to enhance the enterprise value, which requires the management to lead the enterprise to sustainable development while making profits and creating more jobs. Secondly, the staff are required to keep increasing the value of consumers by innovating new products, ensuring product quality and providing comprehensive service when they are implementing their own specific jobs. Lastly, both the company's management and the staff should try to improve their own self-values so that both parties can develop with their own strong points as well as the mutual influence between them .

There are four specific requirements in the principle of constant dedication to society. The first is to improve shareholders' returns so that the resources can be optimized. Another one is to improve the staff's living standards by leading them to a well-off life. The third one is to advance the industry by participating in the competition. And to promote the social development by shouldering corresponding social responsibilities is the last requirement.

To achieve Wanfeng Auto's goal, Chen Ailian has proposed specific steps, including making Wanfeng one of the top one hundred business successes, gaining Wanfeng honorable reputations in business, and developing Wanfeng into a century enterprise.

To make Wanfeng Auto one of the top one hundred business successes is to make the company one of the world's top successful enterprises in the industry (i.e. it should take the lead in each field of the industry market segmentation, including in the fields of development, technology, scale, market share, brand influence, ability to make profits ,capital operation and so forth.). The second step — gaining Wanfeng honorable reputations — is to gain good evaluation from cooperative partners and satisfied customers, to enjoy strong competitiveness and high brand popularity, to win good social fame, to shoulder more responsibilities and dedicate more to the society. Well, the third step can only be realized through ceaseless efforts from several generations who will finally transform Wanfeng Auto into a century enterprise of sustainable development.

After we thoroughly understand Wanfeng Auto's history, we may find Chen Ailian and the management have set a very specific and systemic goal for the company. Inspired by the goal, the whole company, both the employers and the employees, are thus likely to work together as a united team for the same cause — to make the company one of the top one hundred business successes, to gain it honorable reputations and to develop it into a century enterprise.

In addition to the target, Chen Ailian and her management team have also summarized the working habit cultivated since the company's establishment, for this working habit is the guarantee of the achievement of the enterprise's goal in future.

Wanfeng Auto's enterprise culture stresses that the company's long journey starts from the wheel and its splendid achievement is based on innovation. The sentence that the company's long journey starts from the wheel reveals the characters of the auto age and those of the industry that Wanfeng is in. Also it inspires all Wanfeng Auto's staff to be ambitious in life, to be far-sighted to future and to be cautious in daily work.

Wanfeng Auto's splendid achievement is based on innovation: innovation, the eternal theme of a company's development, involves innovation in system and mechanism, technology, business model and management. It is a kind of self-faith and courage in surpassing the company's former image.

The two sentences perfectly interpret the unique cultural implications of the company's title by delicately inlaying the two Chinese characters , i.e. the company's name — (万) Wan and (丰) Feng — in the slogan.

The working style emphasized in Wanfeng Auto's enterprise culture requires down-to-earth attitude, trying efforts, prompt actions and consistently clear responsibility. Wanfeng Auto's working style in management actually is reflected in its staff's execution of tasks. The down-to-earth attitude requests the staff to observe the market laws with proper working approaches according to the market and company situations while carrying out tasks in work. Trying efforts are demanded because no job can be successfully finished without setbacks or difficulties. And therefore, they are expected to have faith in the promising future with high spirits and diligence in spite of the hardships. Prompt actions require the employee to take immediate actions after thoroughly understanding orders he has received. With consistently clear responsibility, each of the staff in the company, from the management to the common workers, are responsible for what is in his charge. So everyone is respectively in charge of something, and everything is properly in the change of somebody.

Wanfeng Auto's enterprise culture embodies commitment spirit, competing spirit, hard-working spirit, study spirit and teamwork spirit.

The company's executives believe the five kinds of spirit mentioned above ensure Wanfeng Auto's growth and development. It is such spirit that will play a vital role in Wanfeng Auto's gradual development into a century enterprise.

Wanfeng Auto is a native Chinese enterprise, so its corporate culture is definitely marked with distinctive characters of the time. Since China's market economy was then still far from mature, with many fields not fully opened to market competition, in a highly market-driven enterprise like Wanfeng Auto, the company's development plan and mission were usually not clearly specified. After all, the open market tends to lead the market-driven enterprise to develop in the Blue Ocean.

Red Landscape

There is a kind of unique landscaped of Wanfeng Auto formed by different social and political organizations in the company. To those who first visit the company, it seems amazing that like in the state-owned enterprise, there are different kinds of social and political organizations in the private enterprise Wanfeng Auto, such as the Party organization, labor union, the Communist Youth League, women's federation and the militia. Shouldn't it be typical to for a private enterprise to operate with streamlined administrative structures and downsized personnel?

"Zhejiang Province has the largest private economy, so the Party building plays an increasingly important role in the private enterprises. The Party organization can guide the enterprise to understand the policies of the Party and the state and grasp the development trend in the industry as the enterprise's political compass in its development. Meanwhile, the Party organization can advance the enterprise's development and further establish a harmonious labor relations with the Party members' good examples and the teamwork of the Party organization in Wanfeng Auto." In Chen Ailian's opinion, it is only right and proper for her and her enterprise to follow the Party, since it was due to the Party's reform and opening-up policy that Wanfeng Auto has welcome its success in business. As an effective and powerful political force that is administrating the country, the Party organization should also be the political core in the private enterprises.

Therefore, like it did in the design of its own product quality standards , Wanfeng Auto has designed its own Party building system, and laid down the first work criteria for Party construction in private enterprises. The criteria later passed the ISO 9001 system certification.

Moreover, in response to the call for enterprises to develop with Party construction from Zhejiang provincial Party committee, Chen Ailian, the Party Secretary of Wanfeng Aut , directly recruited the company's vice Party Secretary from throughout the country. Wu Yi, the former vice Party Secretary of Wanfeng Auto, took charge of the direct recruit. After his study, Wu Yi found that a batch of Party administrators in Zhejiang Province resigned and went to work in private enterprises as the 21st century started. He held that these former government administrators could be the ideal candidates for Wanfeng Auto's vice Party Secretary, for they not only thoroughly understood the structures in government departments and the related working processes due to their early working experiences in the government bureaus, but also were familiar with the operation of private enterprises after working there for a long time.

Right in 2010, 25 private enterprises in Wenzhou, Zhejiang Province publicly recruited suitable Party members as their CEOs. Wu Yi visited the Organization Department of WenZhou Municipal Council twice and figured out suitable ones from 1200 applicants.After that, he called each of the chosen candidates telling them about Wanfeng Auto's motive for recruiting the vice Party Secretary and its plan to strengthen Party construction, and invited them to participate in the coming interview.

Wu Yi moved a considerable number of the candidates from the government departments with his sincerity. With their active participation, Wanfeng Auto's recruitment for the vice Party Secretary was successful in the first step. To win recognition from society and the support from party members inside the company, Wanfeng Auto designed its work process for the recruitment under the guidance of the local Organization Department. After the four rounds of selection, from the initial advertising to the first round selection, and from the interview to the final competition speech, Xu Zhiliang, a professional from the local Organization Department of Shaoxing , was voted as the full-time vice Party Secretary of Wanfeng Auto by secret ballot by all the Party members in the enterprise with

In his competition speech, Xu Zhiliang said: "It will be a turning point of my life that I transfer myself from the government department to the enterprise this year when I am 40 years old. Before I resigned from the government department, my friends tried to persuade me to stay where I was in the government organization department by listing my possible losses in economy, politics and family. Yet inspired by my dreams, I have resolved to join Wanfeng Auto with awe, respect and admiration to the company and its board director Chen Ailian. Here I will go on working hard to explore suitable mode of Party construction in Wanfeng Auto so as to realize my own value of life."

The direct recruitment injected new vitality into Party construction in Wanfeng. In December 2015, Wanfeng restarted direct recruitment for Deputy Party Secretary from all over the country to further strengthen Party construction. Jin

Yiwei, once worked in Shaoxing Organization Department, was successfully elected. Wanfeng's Party construction work had realized inheritance and development.

Besides the routine work in the Party organization, Wanfeng Auto's Party organization has two major characteristic duties, one of which is to strengthen the foundation of the Party in the enterprise. With the reference way from the army to build the Party branch on each company , Wanfeng Auto has the Party organization, labor union, the Communist Youth League, women's federation and the militia in each of its workshops and work sections. These organizations assist the workshop directors and work section chiefs to cultivate staff with excellent performances, to solve the staff's practical problems, to enrich the staff's life in spare time, to care the staff's family life, and to strengthen the on-site safety management in production. Another job of Wanfeng Auto's Party organization is to lead the enterprise's development as core spiritual guide . In the group level, Wanfeng's Party committee guide the construction of material and political civilization in the company by offering it strategic proposals and participating in its system construction. Also the Party organization lead the company's development of spiritual and social civilization by attaching great importance to its corporate culture and social responsibilities.

The effort of great humanity made by Wanfeng Auto's Party organization is that they've opened up the green medical channel for Wanfeng Auto to provide timely medical services for its employees and their families, after the group's labor union exchanged and negotiated with the local hospital and the key hospital of the province.

In March 2014, when an employee's father suddenly had cerebral hemorrhage, she immediately called the union chairman Yang Xuyong for help . It was half past 12 at noon time, and the doctor who was responsible especially for Wanfeng Auto's medical service in the local hospital was then off duty. So Yang Xuyong called the doctor right away and asked him to return to the hospital to invite the best brain medical specialist and prepare for the surgery. And then, he and the vice chairman of the labor union immediately went to receive the employee's father at the hospital gate. When the ambulance arrived, they , already waiting there, helped to send the patient to the operation room at once. The surgery was very successful and the employee's father was discharged from hospital a week later. After returning to work in the company, the employee said gratefully to her co-workers she met that it was the company and its labor union that had saved her father .

There are a lot of such examples. Wanfeng Auto's labor union at all levels , working as the real housekeepers of the staff, do help to solve the basically practical problems in the staff's life. Furthermore, the union is considerate to all the staff. No matter it is when an employee gets married, gives birth to a baby, gets ill or hospitalized , or when his family member passes away, the union leaders will arrive immediately to send regards or show sympathy to him/ her according to the company's rules. All the staff feel the warmth here in the big family of Wanfeng Auto because of the union's great efforts to help them with practical problems in life.

Members of the Labor Union Committee in Wanfeng Auto

Therefore, in Wanfeng Auto, the staff have reached the consensus that they should turn to the labor union whenever they have any trouble. Chen Ailian always says she can sleep peacefully as long as the labor union is there in Wanfeng Auto.

The "Wild Horse" Camp Training

Every year in Tianmushan District of Xinchang County, there is more than one occasion when a line of about a hundred sunburned young people, men and women, all dressed in uniform camouflage, walk through the old villages , flag with wild horse logo in hand and uniform backpack on back. To the villagers, these people, to a degree, look a little weird. Usually the team is followed by several vehicles, big or small, yet all of the young people would rather walk on foot than take the car. And even those with swollen feet struggle to follow the team with limp under others' help rather than having a rest in the car.

As is known to all Wanfeng Auto's staff, the forced march is the most trying part of the "Wild Horse" field training. The team should march on foot for more than 50 kilometers within one day, which is aimed to train the wills of Wanfeng Auto's future administrators. The cars following the team are the logistic vehicles prepared in particular for the "Wild Horse" Camp Training by Wanfeng Auto. Having field training in Tianmushan District where the mountains are steep, the trainees are likely to become fatigued, dehydrated and cut. So the company has made full preparations for the training by loading the the logistic vehicles behind the team with all the necessary items, like water, food, first-aid medicines and so on so forth.

Generally All the trainees from Wanfeng Auto are expected to become vigorous, undefeated, hardy, cooperative, muscular and hard-working through the "Wild Horse" camp training.

In order to steel the staff's willpower, every year after rounds of selection, Wanfeng Auto sends its outstanding employees and reserve administrators to the Military Academy located in the local mountains to have a one-month fully closed camp training. It involves special training in corporate culture, management skills and physical training. Therefore, to fight against their ow willpower, the trainees should take tough activities despite the nasty weather. They take the five-kilometer cross-country running with heavy backpacks, participate in the 50-kilometer march, have the highly demanding triathlon and join the field survival training.

Each time, Chen Ailian will make the camp training to visit the trainees, no matter where she is on business. Once there, she will give lectures to the staff about Wanfeng Auto's company culture and talk with them face to face about her own business experience and her thought about life. In there training, the trainees are always asked to stand still for hours on the playground or quickly lie prone on the ground be it in water or mud. Though aware of the training aim and supportive of the training, Chen Ailian still hate to see her staff suffering and feel sorry for them. Sometimes, eyes filled with tears, she even pleads with the instructor not to push her employees so hard in the training. Unwilling to let others see her tears, Chen Ailian always wears a pair of brownish tinted glasses each time when she goes to the training camp to visit her staff.

After Wanfeng Auto has become a large enterprise groups with diversified businesses, Wild Horse Camp Training has obvious influence on the entire group's development. Through the training, the backbones at grass-roots level can strengthen their feelings towards the enterprise with a thorough understanding of the group's history and development in the future. Moreover, the training increases the bonds between the basic-level cadre, improves the cooperation between different departments and companies, and guarantees good personal relations inside the group. Meanwhile, by visit the training field personally, Wanfeng Auto's core administrators, especially Chen Ailian, have opportunity to contact the basic-level backbones , pay attention to their development and even promote talents from them.

It is virtually true that all the trainees have reaped a lot through the training. Though they become sunburned with dried and cracked lips, the trainees have built up their perseverance, courage, confidence and strength. After returning from the training, the trainees all hold that what they've learned during the 30 days can be beneficial to them for the rest of their lives, since they have known what are obedience, discipline, willpower, perseverance, teamwork and team spirit. Once they have pushed through all the sufferings in the training, they'll be set back or defeated by nothing. Deeply impressed by the experiences in the camp training , even those who have later left the Wanfeng Auto say: "Though only a one-month training, it is a lifetime benefit."

Through Wild Horse Camp Training, the talents of different walks and ages from different places have formed into a strong team working for the same goal with competitiveness.Therefore, Wild Horse Camp Training , the melting pot to cultivate Wanfeng Auto's elites, has been regarded as the company's Huangpu Military Academy

In 2004, about 100 famous writers, such as Wang Xingdong, Gao Songnian and Qiao Mai, met at Wanfeng Auto and spoke highly of its enterprise culture. They said the private enterprise Wanfeng Auto's corporate culture can be perfectly illustrated by the wild horse's characters. Due to its better environmental adaptability and team spirit, the vigorous wild horse resembles Wanfeng Auto in character. The writers wished Wanfeng Auto's corporate culture featured as the wild horse spirit, to prevail.

To the entire corporate of Wanfeng Auto, it is more important to make its corporate culture, which has been primarily formed in the company, fixed in written form so as to turn it into the heritable spiritual wealth.

Four-Committee Governance

The core factor that Wanfeng Auto can develop into a large enterprise lies in the its outstanding performance in wheel hub production , which has gained it wide social trust in the market it touches. Because of the trust, Wanfeng has expanded its business from motorcycle wheel hubs to auto wheel hubs, and even opened up a series of other businesses, such as its production of industrial intelligent robots and magnesium alloy. During its growing process, Wanfeng Auto has gained the experience that it should take the social trust and resources seriously. It seems that making a half step each time is the premise of its success in business.

A half step means the production part that can't be changed in Wanfeng's development. From motorcycle aluminum hubs to auto aluminum hubs, the raw material hasn't been changed together with the new products, while from aluminum hubs to magnesium hubs, except the raw material, the product hasn't been changed in other aspects. Furthermore, from wheel hub production to Wanfeng Technology's production of low pressure casting machine and intelligent robots, though both the raw material and the product have been greatly changed, the customers have been no other than the familiar partners, i.e., Wanfeng Auto and other enterprises of the same trade. And the new change is therefore another success of Wanfeng Auto Group.

Faced with such diversified business, how can Wanfeng Auto be managed according to different industrial, market, technological and personnel demands?

This is another challenge that Chen Ailian has encountered after the enterprise has developed into a powerful large group.

The board of directors and board of supervisors in Wanfeng Auto Holding Group

By trial and error for a long time, Wanfeng Auto has formed a unique four-committee governing system ------ the Party organization committee, the board of directors, the board of supervisors and the management committee.

The Party organization committee is responsible for contact with the government departments so as to accurately transmit and implement the country's policies; and meanwhile it takes charge of the construction of the Party organization, labor union, Communist Youth League, women's federation and the militia in the enterprise so that they can better serve the Wanfeng Auto's production and business operation.

The board of directors shoulder responsibility of making scientific and strategic decisions about regulations, plans and investments, steering the enterprise's development and selecting CEOs.

And the management committee is to carry out all the strategic decisions and plans made by the board of directors and take full advantage of the comprehensive resources provided by the board through the management team of all levels throughout the enterprise.

As for the board of supervisors, its mission is to supervise the implementation of the company's strategic and business plans, system and investment so as to guarantee the healthy development of the business team and steady growth of the enterprise.

Wanfeng's Auto's four-committee system is aimed to run the enterprise with smoother and more efficient operation in a more flexible system. In this way, with the authority power set better , the enterprise can be operated according to the law and its administrators can improve their management ability with respective duties under collective leadership. And the flexible system of the private enterprise, the standardized procedures of the state-owned corporate, and the scientific management of the listed company are thus demonstrated properly in Wanfeng Auto.

Wanfeng Auto's four-committee system is actually the practice of the Party's state governance in microcosm in the enterprise. Behind the practice, it is the profound insight from Chen Ailian and Wanfeng Auto's management

It is simply because of Chen Ailian and the administrators in the current management of Wanfeng Auto that the enterprise has adopted the governance method mentioned above. They all hold that an enterprise resembles a state in administration and operation, though the two are actually different. Therefore, the enterprise can learn from the government and even adopt its the administration principles and working methods so as to achieve obvious benefits and approval more quickly and easily.

A private enterprise as it is, Wanfeng Auto has taken advantage of the Party's concepts of state governance in its company administration and has gained great experience in practice.

The four-committee system is the external appearance of Wanfeng Auto's administration. The interior principle of its governance is to collect and adopt as much management wisdom as possible in the company's decision-making process through meetings. Meanwhile, the multi-structure of the Party organization at all levels demonstrates a balanced relation of power. And the division of decision-making and implementation process ensures the authority of the board of directors.

Of course, what's more important to Wanfeng Auto is to remain as flexible as a small business after it has developed into a large enterprise. As a result, Chen Ailian has particularly set an organization to make temporary decisions in the four-committee governance system. If there is any urgent or important affairs in daily routine, Chen Ailian can gather the related members from the four committees and those in charge of the specific affair to form a temporary organization. Thus they can make decisions right after listening to related reports about the issue and then assign responsible administrators to carry out the decision, which ensures the vitality of the private enterprise.

After handing over his jobs to the new vice Party secretary, Wu Yi starts to focus on promoting the administrative system of the board of supervisors with his team members Lv Xulian and Zeng Zhaoling. By trail and error for years, Wanfeng Auto's supervision principles begin to take shape. According to Wanfeng Auto's development objective, the enterprise's comprehensive inner supervision system, established with concepts of risk management, incorruptibility and self-discipline, treats the corporate culture as its soul on the basis of corporate governance, focuses on risk management guaranteed by the inner control rules. In addition, the supervision system mainly demands the self-supervision of the administrative departments at all levels, with all the Party organization, labor union, Communist Youth League branch, women's federation and militia working as supervisors. And it requires the enterprise to be law-abiding in operation with finance, audit and investigation supervising steps.

This is a multi-leveled, interchange-typed and comprehensive prevention system. It means there is a process to carry out each decision in Wanfeng Auto. Once a long-term plan or a decision of the board is implemented, all the following businesses in Wanfeng Auto Group will naturally be supervised during the processes when they are implemented.

Wanfeng's audit system can supervise the whole implementation process of each business operation mainly on the basis of three rules and regulations — the annual plan; the administrative rules and the VI system. The company's audit mainly involves four parts of jobs. The first is to examine the duty performance of each sector, according to related operation and management data. Specifically it is to check whether the business objective is fulfilled, whether there is loophole in investment and whether the leaders at all levels have operated the allocation of resources within their province. The second task is to supervise the power, i.e., to check whether there phenomena of power abuse, corruption and bribery. The third task is to assess the profit — to examine whether the assessment target is scientific and whether the performance assessment data are genuine. The last task of the audit is to examine the administrator's performance and financial records when he is transferred to a new post or has left office in order to make a correct and responsible evaluation of him.

There are three ways to deal with the problems discovered in the company's audit. Firstly, the board of supervisors will exchange with the management team of all levels face to face, put forward solutions for them , set time limits for their reform and consolidation and have follow-up supervision until the reform job is done. Anyone who violates the company's system will be punished according to the rules and regulations. Secondly, to the incomplete rule or process, the board of supervisors will come up with revising plan or bring it to the company's rule-making department for improvement. Thirdly, once any illegal conduct — power abuse, corruption or bribery — is discovered, it will be reported to the board of directors (or the four committees) for the final settlement. Usually according to the serious degree of the illegal conduct, the board of directors will either punish the person involved according to the company's own regulations or just bring the man to the local police. Wanfeng Auto's inner audit is aimed to ensure the healthy development and promotion of its administrative leaders at all levels, as well as the steady and sustainable growth of the company.

As a large company, Wanfeng Auto is very distinctive in its corporate structure system, for such a structure has both the rigorous character of a large company and the flexibility of a small one. Moreover, it also cares for the staff and their promotion.

The Power of A Team

In all the meetings in Wanfeng Auto, Chen Ailian often advocates that one person has only limited strength, while a team enjoys endless force. As a core part of Wanfeng's corporate culture, the concept has been deeply rooted in the staff's minds.

Chen Ailian always treats others as her equals and is used to sharing. Her principle of equality leads to a wide range of equality in Wanfeng Auto's senior management which can finally reach a better agreement on the company's big issue after equal discussion among themselves. She is willing not only to share with her management in decision-making, but also to share business fruits with her staff. As a result, not only will the management or the staff be supported for their innovative ideas by the company, but they also can enjoy spiritual and material rewards after the company has made profits with their innovation.

Chen Ailian have sent each general manager in Wanfeng a plaque, on which is written her inscription — With awe to nature and respect for talents, we're working together for splendid achievements. Awe to nature here actually means they should not only follow the laws of nature and those of the market, but also comply with the state laws and the Party's policies. Respect for talents actually is to respect knowledge and intellectuals so as to achieve and share profits together with the talents in an equal environment. She believes there are two ways to judge whether a leader is indeed excellent. Firstly, whether can he keep achieving success and gather an outstanding team along with his success? Secondly, whether can he share with others in rewards, including spiritual and material incentives? The leader's mind counts much in whether he can achieve the goal to be an excellent leader.

Each year on the Mid-Autumn Festival, Wanfeng Auto will hold grand award ceremony to honor the inspirational role model, the construction hero, the good mother, the good father, the good wife, the good husband or the nice kid in Wanfeng Auto among the employees and their families. Such an activity enables the enterprise culture to enter into each family throughout the company. Besides, in Wanfeng Auto, the staff's housing placement rate has been taken in its strategic plans, and the outstanding employees can buy their own houses with favorable prices by group purchase.

To invite, motivate and retain talents, Chen Ailian is always very generous. Since 1999 when it was a dream for a household to own a car, Wanfeng Auto has begun to award cars to its outstanding staff in its annual summary commendation meeting. In recent years, the company starts to award luxury cars like Mercedes Benz and BMW to a batch of backbones and staff so that they can work even harder with their talents to achieve greater values on the stage provided by Wanfeng Auto.

In addition, Chen Ailian holds that training is the best welfare for the staff.

Therefore, Wanfeng Auto invest tens of million yuan each year to send its outstanding backbones to study in famous universities and its technicians to further their studies abroad, and meanwhile to invite experts and scholars to give lectures in the enterprise.

Chen Ailian has set a good example for her staff in this way. Since 1995, she goes to study in higher educational institutions each year. From Hanzhou University of Commerce to Zhejiang University, and then from the MPA (Master of Public Administration) in the Open University of Hong Kong to the EMBA in Fudan University, and later from Tsinghua University to Peking University, she has completed all the courses with her perseverance in learning. During the studies, she usually made trips to the university during nights just to make for the classes on the next morning.

Interestingly, when Chen Ailian was studying the MBA course in Fudan University, seeing that she was working so hard, the teachers said to her: " You can enroll for the EMBA course." She asked: " Where can I get registered?" The teacher told her it was just upstairs. So she went there and got registered right after the class. At that time, the students should pass examinations before they were admitted to the EMBA course in Fudan University. Being poor in English, Che Ailian wrote on her paper during the exam " Honorable teachers, poor in English as I am, I am long to studying EMBA. I've learned several MBA courses, and I do wish you to accept me in the course so that I can study for EMBA course while learning English.

At that time, Lu Xiongwen, the dean in the School of Management of Fudan University, thought it was not easy for a woman to have such a strong desire to study, so he communicated sincerely with Chen Ailian in depth in the interview.

Chen Ailian is not only good at learning but also adept in applying what she has learned to practice. When learning the lessons of inner control, she became the first to hand in the homework with her company as a case in point in it, after the teacher assigned the assignment. The teacher held a discussion on her homework in class and put forward rectification suggestions, and she carried out the suggestions in the company on her return. Whenever she returns from business or study, Chen Ailian will gather related staff and share with them her inspiration and the new ideas she has known, greatly promoting the studying atmosphere in the whole team.

Believing that learning is the starting point for the staff's improvement, and training is the basis of the enterprise's development, Wanfeng Auto has built Wanfeng Business School, so that all its employees and cadres at all levels can receive hierarchically different, systematic and professional training.

In the annual Taishan Corporate Culture Forum, Chen Ailian shares her life experiences with more than 300 elite of her staff. She says the value of each person is reflected in material and spiritual aspects. The material value includes material rewards, like the higher salary and the better life quality. It is normal for one to have material pursuit, but one should gradually achieve material satisfaction with a correct self-evaluation according to his own ability. Whoever can focus on his job with endless hard work and trying efforts will be rewarded with material satisfaction as he accumulates his experiences, improves his abilities, promotes his position and betters his work performance. And the greater contribution he has made, the more rewards he will be granted.

And the spiritual value embodies in a better job, learning and training opportunities, kinds of honors, the superior's appreciation, the co-worker's admiration, the inferior's trust, the families' respect and the social recognition. Everyone can achieve them as long as he works hard. He who has achieved all of these is a noble man with a worthy life.

Wanfeng Auto's corporate culture has paved a way to a big company for its development.

Will the company have a much better future?

Wanfeng Auto's way of development: the operation of a big company relies on culture.

In this chapter, it has mainly elaborated the formation process of Wanfeng Auto's corporate culture. After the company diversified its businesses, Chen Ailian realized in time that the operation of a big company depends on culture. Only with the good corporate culture could Wanfeng Auto be ensured to further expand its scale.

There are two sources of a group's enterprise culture. One is the staff's habit formed during the company's long-term business operation, and the other is the cultural demand that the operator and the management wish to achieve in the enterprise.

Chen Ailian believes that all the long-lived enterprises in the world are ones with souls. Evolving from the enterprise's development , Wanfeng Auto's corporate culture is led by the concept of the leadership and meanwhile has absorbed the staff's collective wisdom. Though invisible and untouchable, it is marked in every employee's mind as a powerful motivator and is playing an important role in the enterprise's competitiveness as its soul. In fact, Wanfeng Auto's corporate culture is just the soul of all those working in the enterprise.

第十章

正在展开的未来

加拿大小镇的中国客

2013 年 10 月 8 日，加拿大一家叫做镁瑞丁公司的会议室。

因为行业细分的缘故，镁瑞丁公司（MLTH Holding Inc.）在公众当中并不是一家著名公司。不过，在整个西方，如果用"汽车配件"和"镁合金"两个关键词细分一下，人们就会发现，镁瑞丁其实是一家处于领导者地位上的隐型冠军公司。这家公司不仅占有了整个北美地区镁合金汽车配件 65% 以上的市场份额，而且在全球的镁合金汽配市场上也有占三成以上的份额。它的公司总部在加拿大一个小镇上，有着顶级的技术研发力量，而且在美国、英国、墨西哥、中国等设有生产基地，是一个标准的全球化企业。

这一天会议的主题，是镁瑞丁公司股权收购。坐在会议桌一边的，是以总裁艾瑞克·R·修瓦尔特为首的镁瑞丁公司管理层团队，而在另一边的，则是一群中国人。

被人们通常叫做艾瑞克的镁瑞丁总裁，一开始主要的谈话对象是对面一位叫做齐向民的中国人。他并没有注意齐向民边上坐着一位年纪刚刚三十出头、戴眼镜的年轻人。虽然他已经发现齐向民总是在与这个年轻人说话，不过，艾瑞克对此不奇怪，他觉得他已经摸到了中方收购者的底牌。

万丰奥特高管团队与镁瑞丁团队合影（前排左四陈滨、左六陈爱莲）

那个年轻人就是万丰的总裁陈滨。

陈滨与父母在一起

20世纪80年代出生的陈滨对实业经营有着强烈的兴趣，北京大学法律系毕业后赴英国深造工商管理硕士，2008年学成归来相继担任万丰车业公司总经理、万丰奥威上市公司副总经理、总经理职务，经过 3 年培养和历练，2011 年擢升为万丰奥特控股集团总裁。

此时的陈滨肩负着万丰集团董事会赋予的重任，在董事局主席陈爱莲对并购项目进行三次谈判并战略决策之后，由总裁陈滨进行战术上的实施，带领团队奔赴加拿大开展为期一个月的紧张尽调。到一个月后，当陈滨已经完成对镁瑞丁公司的尽职调查，收购接近尾声的时候，艾瑞克把项目并购当中的一些过程全都告诉了陈滨。

其实在 10 月份，镁瑞丁公司的管理层已经对中方此次的收购预期已经很小。不过当时他们并不担心，因为此前中方已经对收购付出了 800 万加元的预付金。镁瑞丁管理层已经做好了收购不成之后，没收中方定金的准备。

但镁瑞丁公司的管理层没有想到，以齐向民为核心的中国收购方找到了万丰，就在陈滨出现在镁瑞丁公司的会议室时，万丰已经做好了收购这家公司各方面的准备。虽然陈滨是第一次出现在尽调现场，不过通过各种各样的材料，陈滨带领的收购团队，已经对这个公司熟得不能再熟了。

这是一宗极其复杂的并购交易。要看明白这宗交易的来龙去脉，我们必须从万丰在 2010 年制定集团十二五战略规划时的企业定位开始回溯。

2010 年 10 月，万丰集团 300 多位精英骨干汇聚黄山，召开集团十二五发展战略研讨会。研讨会的由来，是因为陈爱莲一直以来都非常重视企业战略规划的制订，她认为战略是对企业未来发展全局性、长期性、基本性的谋略和对策，是纲，纲举则目张，没有战略就没方向。所以，万丰始终与国家保持同步，五年制订一个战略。在制订战略的过程中，陈爱莲总会认真汲取行业专家的集体智慧，中国机械行业的一批领导，何光远、陆燕荪、蔡惟慈、张小虞、朱森第、李新亚、宋天虎、孙伯淮、陈蕴博、屈贤明、张书林、闫建来、金艳丽等专家和好友，总是非常热忱地给予万丰奥特以悉心指导。时至当年，万丰已经走过了三个五年、三个阶段，制定了九五、十五、十一五三个五年规划作为指导，从而保持了健稳、可持续发展。

　　正是通过此次"黄山论道",陈爱莲提出了"实现百年企业目标"应该定位于做"国际化企业",实现资本、管理、人才、科技、品牌五个方面的国际化,成为一家跨国集团公司。这一讨论,也成为万丰新一轮产业布局的根本。在讨论中,陈爱莲提出,万丰的集团产业布局,应该基于"大交通"概念,也就是在航天、航空、海洋、陆地等交通领域里快速进行国际化并购的动作。

　　对于万丰集团来说,这是一个思维上的突破,也是一个纲领性的提出。事实上,做"大交通",已经使得万丰转向了顾客需求定位的企业。

　　我们从万丰的经历当中可以看得非常清楚,万丰创业时所从事的摩托车轮毂,从属于摩托车产业,这个市场是有起伏的。从长期来看,摩托车作为一个交通工具,可能有高潮,也可能不被市场所需要;而后来万丰进入的汽车轮毂领域也是一样。

　　不过,在所有这些市场变化的背后,有一点是不变的:那就是作为消费者对于交通运输的需求。随着经济的发展,消费者们总的活动范围是越来越大,频率也越来越高,虽然交通工具从早期的摩托发展到汽车,后来又发展到多样化的如轮船、飞机这样的交通工具,但如果总的来看,交通工具的使用越来越频繁的趋势不变。

　　而把万丰定位于一个做"大交通"领域的公司,因为顺应了这种趋势,首先就奠定了万丰进一步做强做大的可能性。而其次,也定义了万丰可以努力的方向,因为像摩托车、汽车、轮船和飞机,其实都是交通工具,但背后它所涉及到的学科领域又是具有统一性的——大致在能源应用、机械设计及制造、材料、智能控制领域及管理领域。

　　在确定了这样的方向之后,万丰整个集团,就有了一个努力的方向。

　　在对万丰有了这样一个定位的前提下,我们就很容易看清楚为什么会收购镁瑞丁公司了。

万丰奥特精英"黄山论道"，探讨"十二五"发展战略

　　因为材料本身是大交通战略当中的一个布局，又加上因为万丰之前运营过威海镁业，所以对镁合金材料方面的应用就非常关注，万丰非常清楚的是，镁合金材料的应用与交通业当中的轻量化方向高度相关，因此有着广泛的应用。

　　而在镁合金领域，镁瑞丁是一家领导型企业，不仅在材料研究和制造方面处于产业的前沿，而且他们也把应用的方向主要集中于大交通配件上。与众多跨国级的汽车企业建立了长期的战略合作伙伴关系。

　　所以在整个万丰董事会的版图当中，镁瑞丁如果能被纳入，将会是整个企业一个强有力的业务。收购这家企业，绝不仅是它的盈利被纳入到了万丰，更重要的是，镁瑞丁的镁合金技术与万丰的市场能力，以及中国的资源，将带来深层的整合作用。

　　那么，镁瑞丁作为一家在业内处于领导者地位上的企业，怎么会处于股权出售的状态呢？这里有两个原因。

　　其一是镁合金的生产原料是镁，而我们已经知道，镁在全球的主要分布带，处于中国，当然在北美地区也有一些分布。在2008年前后，中国政府开始控制单纯的产业原料出口，造成全球镁矿石原料价格大涨。

　　这个变动，使得镁瑞丁公司与各大汽车企业的合作关系出现了较大问题。

一方面，由于镁原料的价格上涨，使得镁瑞丁与汽车公司已经订立的合同出现了部分的亏损，另一方面，镁瑞丁要求对镁合金部件涨价的要求，使得汽车制造企业对更大范围应用镁合金部件心存疑虑，使得镁瑞丁公司的市场前景发生了动摇。

这样的状态，使得镁瑞丁原来的股东们也开始对公司的盈利产生信心缺失。加上 2008 年的全球性金融危机，镁瑞丁的股东们把股权低价转让给了包括 GE 金融和冰岛银行在内的金融机构持股。

我们知道，金融机构虽然可以持有股份，但却是标准的财务投资人。对他们来说，只有流转的资本才能不断产生效益，因此他们对镁瑞丁的要求是，尽快找到产业投资者，把自己手里的股份变现，出于信任，这些金融机构把股权变现的机会寻求委托给了镁瑞丁的管理层。

这个机会被一群精于金融运作的中国人得到了，这就是万丰并购镁瑞丁的"过桥方"，也就是在会议桌上出现的谈判者——山西天硕投资公司。

天硕公司收购镁瑞丁，虽然实力上存在很大的差距，不过在金融上却有着深厚的基础。作为一家投资公司，天硕精明地看到，由于国内的产业发展，有相当一批企业具备了全球收购的能力，也有了相应的需要；而 2008 年金融危机之后，由于西方有相当一批实业型企业在资本层面出现了断裂，因此存在一种可能：即这些公司成为稀缺资源，成为国内产业资本追逐的对象，所以发现了镁瑞丁有出售股权的可能性之后，天硕抢先与镁瑞丁达成了收购意向。而后，天硕公司再试图以其名下另一家名叫"山西联合镁业"的实体企业为平台，聚集资本试图来完成这项收购。

山西联合镁业公司一出现，我们就大致明白镁瑞丁公司的管理层为什么愿意与天硕达成收购意向了。在国内，山西是镁资源集中的一个省份，山西联合镁业作为一家实体企业，是拥有镁业资源的。因此对于镁瑞丁公司来说，天硕如果作为拥有镁业资源的企业完成收购，就解决了镁瑞丁在运营过程中"镁原料供应不稳定"的困局，可谓是一举两得。

不过，镁瑞丁的管理者们没有搞明白的是，天硕投资与山西联合镁业虽然有同一个管理者，不过股份的组成却不太一样。天硕投资是独资公司，而山西镁业却是由多家股东组成的股份公司。因此，天硕其实并不能完成镁瑞丁的收购。

在万丰集团确定了自己的战略定位之后，在上海区域总部成立了以陈伟军、任心刚为主要成员的资本运作小组，并在 2013 年初得到了镁瑞丁寻求股权转让的消息。陈伟军团队在第一时间向董事局主席陈爱莲作了汇报，并转达了天硕公司一定要求见她一面的想法。

当收购小组把镁瑞丁公司的材料拿到陈爱莲面前之后，陈爱莲很快答应与天硕公司面谈。通过参观和交流，天硕公司马上看到了万丰的优势：这是一家先进制造业企业，有着行业首位的制造业资源，同时是一个大公司结构，可以容纳作为单一产业隐型冠军企业的镁瑞丁；另外万丰的一个重要优势在于，它已经拥有了万丰奥威的上市平台，可以通过直接融资完成收购；

而天硕的管理者们也明白的是，对于镁瑞丁来说，万丰也是具有吸引力的企业。一方面，万丰旗下有镁业公司，已经对镁合金材料的研发和市场有了相当的认识，因此与镁瑞丁的管理层有着相当的共识；而同时，两家公司有着重要的共同点——同处汽配产业，尤其是万丰服务于全球顶级的汽车制造企业，因此并购之后有着巨大的协同效应。

由此，本来就定位为中介方的天硕，认定万丰是镁瑞丁公司在中国国内最合适的买方。如果有万丰成为收购方，天硕的收购中介功能是能圆满完成的。

除了大交通领域的定位使得万丰从大的战略方向上可以达成收购之外，具体促成万丰董事会明确对镁瑞丁收购意向的，是万丰在威海镁业创业道路上的十年摸索。

因为有了威海镁业的十年起伏，万丰对于镁合金技术在汽车及多个市场前沿的应用，有着清晰的了解，也知道镁瑞丁公司在镁合金技术上的优势。

在接下来的两个月里，陈爱莲与天硕公司进行三次谈判后，就召开了董事会迅速作出决策：收购镁瑞丁符合万丰国际并购优质项目的五条要求，第一，产业是行业细分市场的全球领跑者；第二，具有国际化的地域布局；第三，拥有行业核心技术、掌握着市场的话语权；第四，收购价格便宜；第五，发展提升有盈利空间。大家一致认为这一宗并购对万丰有着重大的战略意义，将有利于进一步提升万丰在未来产业界的先导地位。但并购劣势是时间短、有风险。

作出收购决定以后，万丰马上"兵分三路"：一是以陈滨为首的陈荣等海外尽调团队，二是以陈伟军、陈黎军、杨铭兴、曾昭岭为主的国内资源整合和法律团队，三是以赵亚红、丁锋云、陈韩霞为主的资金运作团队。三支团队都由陈爱莲为总指挥，把握收购大局和时间进度，把控上下、左右、内外等一切风险，真正体现了"个人力量有限，团队威力无穷"的万丰理念。

从 2013 年 8 月谈判开始，到 10 月份，万丰首先完成了对天硕投资公司 100% 的股权收购。而后，陈滨总裁带领的四支海外尽调团队与天硕公司一起赴加拿大，开始了对镁瑞丁的尽调过程。

对于万丰来说，虽然镁瑞丁有着非常大的重要性，不过要在半年内完成总金额 15 亿元人民币的大宗收购，确实不易。

不过，陈滨第一次出现在镁瑞丁公司的尽调桌上时，总裁艾瑞克并没有太在意他，其实也是正常的。这是因为天硕既然完成了对镁瑞丁的收购意向确认，同时自己实力又有距离，就必然会选择其他投资人来继续对镁瑞丁的收购。艾瑞克对陈滨说，在万丰之前，已经有好几拨中国投资人已经在镁瑞丁的会议桌上出现过，而他们的共同特点是来过一次就再也不出现了。

这种现象，与国内对海外企业的并购热潮特点有关。国内产业投资人的海外并购，要么追求大规模、要么追求有名声。而镁瑞丁是一家处于细分行业的技术引领型企业，所以规模名声都不大，并不符合中国买家的兴趣点。只有像万丰这样与它同处一个领域的同行，才会有格外的兴趣。

接管

董事会决定由陈滨总裁去尽调和接管镁瑞丁，主要是因为陈滨有海外留学的经历，走遍了世界各个国家；不仅了解欧美企业的背景，而且他毕业后在上市公司积累了经营管理的实践经验，专业、勤奋、认真，是他的个性特点。

陈滨在第一次尽调会议中就意识到，必须把镁瑞丁管理层的注意力转过来。

因此开谈之后，他很快就告诉对方，现在万丰已经全资收购了天硕，所以镁瑞丁股权出售的交易对象已经转向万丰集团。而坐在艾瑞克对面的就是万丰集团的代表，所以交接过程当中的所有事项，都由万丰的代表负责。

陈滨这种直接的态度，固然有他一直留学于英国，了解英美文化有关，同时也是被收购过程后半段紧张的时间逼急了。天硕与镁瑞丁达成的收购意向计划中，9 月份已经付清了收购的定金，双方规定，到 2013 年 12 月，中方必须完成整个收购的付款和交割过程，否则镁瑞丁是有权没收定金，取消交易的。陈滨深谙这个时间表，而同时 10 月才开始介入这宗交易的万丰，还需要时间来重做尽职调查和法律框架。短短两个月时间内要完成这一切，不由得陈滨在虚礼上客套，他必须直接了当。再加上他英语纯熟，不需要翻译，所以一开腔就与镁瑞丁的管理层形成了直接沟通。

不过，就算是这样，要在两个月内完成对镁瑞丁的收购，对万丰来说，还是一个非常大的挑战。那一段时间，万丰收购小组和管理层都处于高速运转状态。

在陈爱莲的有力战略决策和万丰管理层的全力配合之下，陈滨在第二次赴镁瑞丁之时，就已经可以带领着顶级的财务顾问公司和法律顾问公司的代表一起开始与镁瑞丁的管理层进入了为期一个月的实质性尽调阶段。

但尽调一开始，镁瑞丁公司管理层并不太乐意再一次把所有的公司财务数据开放。这其实是可以理解的，因为天硕在达成收购意向之时，已经进行过一次调查，数月之内，连续两次把财务数据开放，镁瑞丁的管理层需要确认万丰是不是有明确意向收购他们。

因此在第二次尽调之初，万丰就拿出了详尽的并购计划表，把时间安排和需要了解的技术细节都陈列在内。从这张安排表上，可以一眼看出万丰不仅有收购的诚意，而且对镁合金和汽车零部件市场两个方向都非常内行。

双方的合作开始变得顺利起来了。

很快，陈滨团队迅速开始了解镁瑞丁公司的情况：迈瑞丁公司创立于1981年，至今已有33年发展历史。由于加拿大本地的矿产资源丰富，有着很长时间的开采和冶炼历史，所以镁瑞丁是一家拥有行业尖端核心技术的镁合金行业的全球领导者，与特斯拉、保时捷、奥迪、奔驰、宝马、沃尔沃、路虎、丰田、本田、福特、通用、菲亚特、克莱斯勒等世界高端品牌作为长期战略伙伴，在加拿大本地的州和镇上，是一家支柱型企业，员工有着非常强的自豪感。

因此，在2008年之后，镁瑞丁公司股权发生变更，进入财务投资人之手后，公司的员工对于"为谁工作"这件事上，失落颇大。因为象征着公司归属权的股权不断交易，就意味着公司的所有者不停地发生着变化，所以同样作为员工的管理层，也希望尽快能找到一个真正的产业投资来接手这个公司，让企业尽快能做较为长期的打算。

而在产业上，镁瑞丁由于技术先进，生产稳定，所以在北美地区的汽车生产厂商当中有着稳定的形象，因此占领着汽车制造多种镁合金配件65%以上的市场。不过，因为镁价在2008年之后的波动，北美汽车厂商对于是否进一步扩大采用镁合金配件保持了一种怀疑的态度，所以镁瑞丁公司才会希望能有一个有实力的中国企业来对它控股，使汽车厂商们重新对镁瑞丁产生信任。

欧洲是镁瑞丁需要大力开拓的市场——北美的汽车厂商之所以愿意采用镁合金，是因为加拿大有一部分镁矿，所以汽车厂商有理由认为镁瑞丁可以生产品质优秀的镁合金产品，而在欧洲，因为基本没有镁矿资源，所以欧洲厂商并没有采用镁合金配件的强烈动机，只是因为近年来汽车环保的要求越来越高，所以镁合金才开始进入市场。因此同样，有了来自镁矿大国中国的企业控股，是非常有助于镁瑞丁在欧洲打开市场的。

而镁合金配件在中国市场上的应用，则是镁瑞丁和万丰可以高度共赢的领域：中国是汽车的后发市场，同时也是全球范围内产销量最大、增长最快的市场。但是在国内，能使汽车通过轻量减重而达到节油降污的镁合金应用，现在还近乎于零。这主要是因为国内汽车业当下大干快上，约束因素还较少，同时也是由于国内镁合金技术并不成熟的状态。所以万丰一旦控股镁瑞丁，既为国内带来了成熟的镁合金生产技术，又可以更大规模和范围地投入资源，帮助镁瑞丁打开中国市场，强化万丰旗下镁瑞丁在全球镁合金领域的优势地位。

陈滨荣获浙江年度经济人物奖（中间为陈滨）

在巨大的共赢点推动下，万丰与镁瑞丁的并购进行得非常顺利，12 月份，双方顺利地完成了尽职调查、签约和股权交割的工作。而陈滨团队尽调时间之短、效率之高、速度之快，真正发扬了万丰人"变不可能为可能、变不成功为成功"的万丰传统精神。

从并购产能到并购影响力

收购镁瑞丁的工作完成之后，陈爱莲发现，这宗收购，看起来是收购了一家企业，实际上是给万丰一个机会在全球范围内做一个细分的行业。

此话看起来很大。不过只要通过一个数据，我们就可以了解，其实还是非常切实的：当下，全球每年原镁的产能约在七十万吨，大部分产于中国。而镁瑞丁全球工厂的用镁量，就达到 7 万吨的水平，而一旦镁瑞丁在万丰控股之后，在中国诸多市场上有所开拓，这个比例还会进一步提高。

在这种需求的情况下，最初万丰承接国家 863 计划当中的政府意图，现在就可以有所实现了：其实在镁瑞丁头疼于镁价不稳定的同时，作为镁资源大国，中国政府也在为镁资源得不到广泛应用，而苦恼于镁应用的范围不够大。中国的镁储量占世界第一位，但相对于资源优势来说，中国在镁合金深加工及应用领域仍然非常落后。因此，国家工信部发布了《新材料产业十二五发展规划》，大力发展高性能的镁合金产品，重点满足汽车、大飞机、高铁等装备需求。而万丰通过并购引进世界最先进的镁合金工艺技术，就可以使中国从镁资源大国，迅速走向镁产业强国。

所以万丰认为，在下游有了广泛应用之后，万丰未来数年内，在镁产业内首先要做的事情，很可能是与地方政府合作，以开发镁矿资源为轴心，把万丰旗下的镁产业原料稳定住。必要的话，也可以投资开采镁矿。另外，出于扩大国内镁产业应用范围的目的，也可通过与各方资源合作，开设镁的交易市场。

关于这一点，陈滨有着深入的考虑：正如镁瑞丁在欧洲推广镁资源所遇到的阻力显示的那样，要扩大某种资源的应用范围，必须给应用者，也就是镁瑞丁的下游汽车厂商顾客以稳定的预期。那么在镁资源的应用上，要给下游的汽车制造企业、IT和家电制造企业以一个稳定预期，最为稳定的办法，无疑是建立一个公开、透明的交易机制，因为中国是一个镁资源大国，这个责任无疑是需要中国企业来承担的。

有了这种宏观的考虑，再加上万丰与镁瑞丁共处于汽车配件领域，有着共同的客户，所以万丰希望达到的结果是，通过资源和市场两端，引领镁瑞丁共同创造新的价值。

当然，同时镁瑞丁可以贡献给万丰的价值在于，万丰正在从传统制造业向先进制造业转型，镁瑞丁则是一个技术引领型的企业。他们在科研和技术成果产业化的具体环节当中，可以与万丰转型过程分享的要点很多，可以加速万丰的转型升级，同时实现细分行业市场的全球领跑。

这个进程，则是万丰董事会更为关注的。

细心的读者自可以发现，从收购镁瑞丁，以及我们马上将要看到的收购上海达克罗工业公司过程中，万丰的收购策略发生了很大的变化。早期万丰在收购上海二守合金和韩国都瑞集团威海工厂之时，都采用的是低价收购，尽可能地让收购价格接近净资产。而到2013年之后，陈爱莲引领下的收购却转向了另一个方向，万丰此时的收购对象都转向了业内首屈一指的企业，具有较强的国际竞争力，随之而来的是，收购过程当中也给出了较高的溢价。

在企业已经定下了真正要做国际化企业的目标，同时定下了在"大交通"的领域里做强做久企业的自我定位之后，万丰的收购，当然与之前发生了根本性的变化。在新世纪之初，万丰的收购过程目标非常明确，就是在下游市场需求快速上升的时候，通过收购来尽快扩张自己的产能。这样的收购从根本上是进入了万丰制造的成本，而且万丰也有能力来领导这种扩张。而到了现在，事情反了过来，在定位于大交通领域之后，万丰发现自己的可扩张空间非常大，同时，进入新的领域要遇上的挑战也会非常多。

　　然而，跨国收购并不是交易双方达成了意向上的一致就可以完成的。在陈滨带领的海外尽调团队完成了与镁瑞丁的交易之后，陈伟军团队才开始紧张地进入下一步工作，也就是收购交易在国内各级政府部门的审批工作。

　　因为根据万丰与山西天硕达成的协议，收购审批本应由天硕方完成，而且应于陈滨团队在收购前方的工作同步进行。但当海外尽调团队在前方与镁瑞丁的股东方、管理层达成一致之后，天硕方面的审批工作却出现了问题。

　　陈爱莲和收购小组迅速接手这个工作。因为时间确实是太紧张了，陈滨团队在前方完成工作已经是 2013 年的 10 月初，万丰要想收购成功，必须在 2013 年底之前完成政府审批。而跨国收购的审批要获得多个中央政府部委的同意，而且必须是一环扣一环地去完成。通常情况下，审批时间最起码半年以上。

镁瑞丁公司与特斯拉汽车成为战略合作伙伴

陈爱莲与特斯拉副总裁*Diarmuid O'Connell*合影

在这个紧要关头，万丰可谓是尝到了新一届政府简政放权的甜头。项目上报国家发改委短短 5 个工作日就顺利批出、商务部短短 1 天时间就完成审批。各部委审批速度之快、效率之高，令镁瑞丁管理层刮目相看。他们认为在这么短的时间内完全不可能办成的事，通过中国的深化改革，万丰顺利地完成了！

所以在参加 2014 年全国两会时，作为一名全国人大代表，陈爱莲在浙江代表团审议李克强总理所作的政府工作报告时，发自内心地表示，作为来自经济界的代表，切实享受到了国家深化改革的成果，全国上下政令畅通，浙江省在全国率先响应打造"办事最快的政府"，要求各级干部当好企业的后勤部长，倡导"店小二"文化，为浙商加快国际并购步伐提供了快速高效的服务。

2014 年的 4 月，当陈爱莲率领万丰高管团队出现在镁瑞丁加拿大公司、美国公司、墨西哥公司门口时，镁瑞丁的外籍高管们早已站在门口列队迎接，并以热烈的掌声欢迎他们来自中国的新董事长。面对一家有着 1680 名外籍员工的公司，收购之后如何在企业文化之上进行融合，在很多人看来都是很大的挑战，然而，陈爱莲却信心满满，她认为最关键的在于双方价值观能否实现高度一体，要以莫大的胸怀、信任和尊重容纳天下有识之士。

陈爱莲在全国"两会"上发言

为此，陈爱莲团队每到一个工厂，就召开交流座谈会，倾听镁瑞丁管理层的想法，并明确地告诉他们，收购以后，一不裁员、不换人，二要提高工资福利待遇，三要帮助他们切实解决经营当中存在的问题，包括加大投资、优化市场、制定战略。通过现场办公、现场解决问题，万丰高管团队使镁瑞丁管理者迅速统一了思想、产生了共识，使他们更加明确了万丰收购的目的不是为了转手投资，而是真正要把企业不断地做强做久。并购整合之后，镁瑞丁的市场空间之大、产业生命力之强，使他们有充分体现价值的舞台和家的归属感，双方价值取向和经营理念迅速融为一体。

收购完成之后，原本只有 70% 开工率的镁瑞丁工厂很快就恢复了满负荷生产，而外籍员工也从前期对于中国新股东的怀疑，慢慢转向了充分的信任，并对完成年度经营计划充满了信心。

进军达克罗

陈爱莲定位的"优势收购"，当然不止收购镁瑞丁这一家公司。

达克罗本是一种涂料的名称，最早诞生于二十世纪五十年代末。在北美、北欧寒冷的冬天，道路上厚实的冰层严重阻碍机动车的行驶，人们用盐撒在地上的方法来降低凝固点的温度以缓解道路畅通问题。但是紧接而来问题是，氯化钠中的氯离子侵蚀了钢铁基体，交通工具严重受损，严峻的课题出现了。

美国科学家迈克·马丁研制了以金属锌片为主、同时加入铝片、铬酸、去离子水做溶剂的高分散水溶性涂料，涂料沾在金属基体上，经过全闭路循环涂覆烘烤，形成薄薄的涂层，达克罗涂层成功地抵抗氯离子的侵蚀，防腐技术进入了新的台阶，革新了传统工艺防腐寿命短的缺陷。到八十年代之后，达克罗工艺得到进一步改良，配方当中对环境有污染的铬成份被去除。

万丰奥威收购上海达克罗签约仪式

作为设备涂覆的一种手段，达克罗工艺是电镀工艺的一种替代。由于这种工艺当中不含有对环境的污染成份，所以随着中国国内对于环保要求越来越高，它有着广泛的应用空间。

上海达克罗涂覆工业公司在上海北部的宝山区，无论从规模、知名度和工艺的复杂度来说，它都不是一家惹眼的企业，在宝山区僻静的市一东路，有一座进深几十米、宽度几百米的厂区，这就是上海达克罗工业公司的地址。

上海达克罗涂覆工业公司的创始人是一位留学德国并从事贸易的企业家，在国内汽车工业起步的时候，因为深入了解了达克罗工艺的未来，所以就回到国内，开始从国外引进达克罗工艺对汽车企业的零部件进行服务，后来这项服务还延伸到高铁、重要的机械部件等多个领域。

这种经历而成的优势，使得上海达克罗在这个细分领域里形成了自己独有的竞争规模优势。由于这家企业在达克罗涂覆这个工艺上起步早，运营精细，而且管理优秀，所以它的业务范围覆盖了国内大多数高端的制造业企业，成为它们可靠的合作伙伴。而由此，上海达克罗虽然规模不大，但效益却不错，不仅加工数量饱和，而且利润率也不低。

上海达克罗之所以愿意出售股权，主要是因为创始人的主观意愿。这家民营企业的第一代创始人已经到了退休的年龄，而家族成员当中又没有人愿意接手这家公司，因此拥有全部股权的创始人就希望把这家公司转手给一家进取心强烈，而且正在蒸蒸日上的国内公司。

这位老先生其实是个性含蓄而理性的人，在整个谈判的过程当中都非常冷静。但是在与万丰达成合同之后，在签约的仪式上，老先生终于感慨地说，今天他来签这个合同，心里的感受，与当年嫁女儿差不多。恳请万丰接手之后，能善待这个公司，把既有的优势进一步放大。而他自己，也答应再工作三年，到七十岁再退休，以便万丰能顺利地接手企业。

万丰与达克罗形成的这一次企业并购，除了上海达克罗自身意愿之外，更多的还在于国内产业变化的形势。

　　从具体的产业形态来看，由于国内当下各方面对于环保的意识和要求正在不断提高，所以从整个市场份额上看，作为涂覆手段的达克罗工艺未来将取代传统的电镀工艺的可能性也在变得越来越大。

　　这对已经从事这一工艺多年的上海达克罗公司来说，优势在于市场总份额的扩大，可以进一步扩展它的优势；但同时，未来的市场风险在于一旦达克罗工艺成为涂覆工艺的主流手段之后，也可能有更为大型的竞争对手进入这一市场，与上海达克罗公司形成激烈竞争。

　　上海达克罗公司的规模不大，是有它工艺上的道理的，因为与电镀一样，作为一种涂覆手段，达克罗工艺的竞争力在于它的涂覆料配方和溶液。就形态上看，它的门槛并不是很高，是个轻资产企业。

　　因此在大规模竞争当中，陈爱莲认为，万丰并购达克罗，还有一个可以共赢的市场之道在于双方合作顺畅的情况下，万丰可以利用遍布全球的生产基地，快速地把这个工艺复制到全球去，为所有需要达克罗工艺服务的汽车、高铁生产商提供同样是门对门的服务。我们知道，正是因为上海达克罗本身已经走出了一条轻资产、重服务的经营道路，这样的运营模式，是可行的。

　　经过几个月的谈判，万丰最后与上海达克罗达成收购达克罗所有股权的协议。到11月份，万丰奥威首先就收购上海达克罗的全部股份发布了公告。

　　不过，万丰关于大交通的战略定位，以及万丰在一系列运营上的变化，此时还并不为市场所知。市场能认同这一相当大的变革吗？

　　在对达克罗和镁瑞丁发起收购之前，由于万丰已经确定了一系列正确的经营方针，而且国内资本市场一直看好汽车产业，所以在A股市场并不景气的情况下，万丰奥威的股价却一直在上行。

　　达克罗的收购行动因为先行完成，所以万丰率先公告达克罗项目。11月13日，万丰首份公告发出之后，市场的第一反应是在公告前后，万丰奥威的股价从每股16元一直跌到最低每股13元。

　　对此，并购小组的理解是，资本市场认为万丰奥威收购上海达克罗所给出的溢价太高，从而不看好万丰一系列的收购行动。但他们相信一旦机构和投资者真正看明白上海达克罗的价值，同时理解了万丰与达克罗之间形成合作共赢前景，万丰奥威的股价就一定会重拾上升通道。

为加强与资本市场的有效沟通，并购小组在公告次日就安排了相当一批机构投资者去现场考察。

那一天，上海是个下着小雨的天气。不过，随着二十多位基金经理和投资研究部门的研究员们从走访现场，到听取上海达克罗公司高管的介绍，投资机构的运作者们脸色也是由多云转向了晴天。很明显的是，国内涉及到复杂机械制造的行业对于涂覆的市场需求巨大，相对应的数据是中国国内共有一万余家电镀厂，这些工厂在实现涂覆要求之余，它们所排出的废水对环境造成了很大的危害。因此未来，达克罗工艺对电镀有巨大的替代空间。

在这个条件下，万丰并购达克罗，是在大交通领域布下了一枚重要的棋子，而对于上海达克罗来说，有了上市公司的融资平台和万丰的大公司格局平台，就是进一步重新构成未来竞争当中核心的优势因素，有可能保持其产业领导者地位。

真正深入的了解之后，万丰奥威的股价，就像上海接下来的天气一样，开始由阴转晴了。不仅从那个'V'字形每股13元的底部走出来，而且最高攀上了每股24元的高位，为未来万丰进一步使用资本平台布局大公司产业，打下了基础。

资本市场对于万丰奥威并购达克罗的肯定，更多来自于万丰从传统的轮毂制造领域向整个大交通领域转型升级成为先进制造业的努力。陈爱莲团队所做的转变，不仅是并购几家企业，获得更高的利润，关键在于要实现万丰向真正的国际化企业迈进。

收购宁波达克罗，提升行业细分市场的龙头地位

　　为巩固万丰达克罗的龙头地位，收购上海达克罗后，2014 年 11 月，万丰收购宁波达克罗的股权转让协议在新昌签订，宁波达克罗创始人蒋佳宏因二代无意接班，出让公司全部股权。由此，万丰在达克罗涂覆行业的龙头优势地位得到进一步的巩固和加强。

新能源卡达克

　　2013 年 11 月 12 日，十八届三中全会通过《中共中央关于全面深化改革若干重大问题的决定》，《决定》提出，要完善产权保护制度，积极发展混合所有制经济，推动国有企业完善现代企业制度，支持非公有制经济健康发展。

　　在中央首次明确提出积极发展混合所有制经济之前，浙江省作为全国民营经济的发祥地，早在 2011 年 12 月，时任浙江省委副书记夏宝龙全力促进国务院国资委与浙江人民政府签署了战略合作备忘录，107 家央企负责人与 2000 多家浙江民营企业代表参加洽谈活动，当场签署了 2721 亿元的合作项目。

在浙江省委省政府的号召下，2012 年 8 月 9 日，陈爱莲与中国汽车技术研究中心主任赵航在上海举行了"新能源混合动力"项目的签约仪式，标志着万丰成功牵手央企，拉开战略合作序幕，共同开启新能源混合动力时代。

陈爱莲在致辞中说，从 2000 年以来的 12 年当中，万丰与中汽中心的合作非常愉快，彼此之间结下了非常深厚的情谊，也结出了灿烂的信任之花，双方的价值观达到了高度一体。她相信，央企的实力加上民企的活力，一定能创造出强大的国际竞争力，为使中国从汽车大国走向汽车强国贡献更大的力量。

而赵航主任也满怀深情地说，中汽中心在投资领域的第一桶金就是在万丰，此次携手是双方发挥各自优势的双赢。新能源混合动力项目是中汽中心专家团队研究八年的成果，在技术、性能指标等方面到达了国内领先，中汽中心将积极发挥技术后盾作用，调动各院所的技术力量来为项目提供技术支撑，并致力于不断革新、升级，使开发的产品能够在市场竞争中始终处于领先地位。

中国汽车技术研究中心是国内权威的汽车老牌研发机构转型而成的科技型企业。在中国汽车工业发轫的八十年代，中央政府成立了中国汽车工业总公司（简称中汽总）统一管理国内的汽车工业，中国汽车技术研究中心（简称中汽中心）就是中汽总下属的汽车研究专业机构，它于 1985 年成立，汇聚了当时中国汽车工业当中的一大批人才。

万丰奥特成功牵手央企，拉开战略合作序幕

九十年代，政府对汽车工业实行放权管理，中汽总公司撤消。中国汽车技术研究中心几经转折，归属国资委管理，成为科技型企业。一方面它原有的试验设备承担了国内第三方的汽车检验工作，而另一方面，它运作自身的技术优势，内引外联不断推进国内汽车新技术。

这样的一个科研机构，自然会针对全球范围内汽车工业的前沿变化做出一些部署。新世纪之后，汽车业面临的一个巨大问题是，现在，能源真的成为了一个汽车业发展的大瓶颈。从2000年开始，石油的价格从每桶十到二十美元开始，一直涨到了一百多美元，价格远远高过了七十年代两次石油危机时的水平。因此节能和开辟新能源汽车，真实地成为汽车业所面临的新挑战。

在长期的汽车工业实践当中，万丰和中汽中心两家企业之间结下了很深的合作基础。同时因为理念相同，又有很深的产业互补优势，所以在新能源汽车浪潮到来的时候，这两家企业，在多个领域开始了合作。

新能源汽车的技术路线，在国内主要有两种实践：

比较激进的整车厂商推进的是纯电动汽车，这种汽车以电池提供动力，由电机驱动。采取更换电池或者给电池充电的方式提供外在能源，与汽油汽车类似的是，纯电动汽车一旦被普及使用之后，厂商会大量建设充电站以方便消费者使用。

在纯电动汽车的研发方面，比较领先的车型是美国的特斯拉汽车，这款纯电动汽车在 2013 年一经上市，就引起了全球汽车爱好者的轰动。据媒体实测，它的续航里程达到了 420 公里，达到了纯电动汽车的实用标准。但它的缺点在于因为没有量产，所以价格较贵；

而相对稳健的整车厂商则倾向于采用混合动力汽车。所谓混合动力，就是以汽油为主要动力，同时辅之以电机驱动。并在常规动力使用时，对辅助动力的电池进行充电，以达到降低能耗的目的。

混合动力汽车的优势在于它涉及到的厂商变化比较小，也无需在现有的加油站进行大规模的更替。这个方向上，丰田的普锐斯是领先车型，相对于特斯拉，丰田普锐斯的价格就要便宜得多。

2011 年 5 月，万丰奥威宣布，公司以 3600 万元入股上海卡耐新能源公司，与中汽中心及韩国一家电池研究机构合作开发电动汽车的电池技术，万丰取得 15% 的股份；

一年之后的 2012 年 8 月，万丰与中汽中心联合宣布，总投资 20 亿元，通过分步实施、滚动发展，开始研制被称为"卡达克"的汽车混合动力总成项目。

这意味着万丰与中汽中心在新能源的两个项目当中都布下了棋局。

不过，相较于电池技术，万丰与中汽中心在混合动力汽车上的布局更大。在新能源汽车的两个主要方向上，未来很可能发生的是，由于混合动力汽车对于汽车业格局引发的变动较小，企业较为乐意向市场率先推广混合动力汽车，因此混合动力汽车率先在市场上成为新能源汽车的主流；而后，当消费者习惯于较低的能源之后，电动汽车也达到了一定的普及程度，作为一种更新能源、更低能耗的汽车，开始占据市场的主导地位。

而在中国国内，由于政府开始率先引导新能源汽车的使用，因此新能源汽车首先萌芽的市场，存在于大巴车上。政府投资的各地公交汽车开始引进新型的混合动力大巴，它的使用，开始为普及度更高的乘用轿车先扫清技术障碍。

所以在实践的层面，在万丰开始大规模生产新能源汽车混合动力总成——卡达克之前，实际上卡达克作为中汽中心的研究项目，已经在天津进行了早期的小规模生产。经过两年的正常经营生产和销售，万丰混合动力建立了"十大城市、六大客户"的市场布局定位，品牌影响力已阶段性地成功打响，在第一轮的行业洗牌中站稳了脚跟，正在不断地迈入行业细分市场的领先地位。

航空梦

2015 年 8 月，一架加拿大庞巴迪型公务机徐徐降落在杭州萧山机场。到这一年的 11 月，这架公务机从杭州顺利实现首飞济南。

改革开放之后，国内的先富阶层购买私人飞机的已经不少。因此这两条消息虽然对万丰集团来说是大事，但它出现在浙江、绍兴和新昌的媒体上时，却是相当平静的。

但如果有心人把这两条消息与万丰集团的一系列动作，还有政府政策层面的变动联系起来看的时候，它就显得有些不寻常了。

2015 年，万丰专门成立了万丰航空工业有限公司，该公司旗下还相继组建了万丰通用航空有限公司、新昌万丰机场建设管理有限公司、万丰（捷克）飞机工业有限公司等公司，并着手并购海外知名飞机制造企业。2015 年 12 月，万丰收购了加拿大 DFC 航空培训学校——这是加拿大最具实力的航空飞行员培训学校之一。

万丰收购加拿大DFCtsDC航校

　　这一系列的动作，让人一望而知，万丰集团在航空领域不是简单为之，而是有不小抱负的。

　　万丰的这一番抱负，背景首先是国内政府开始逐步开放低空领域的航空。自2009年开始，政府逐步开放了低于1000米以下的空域，特别是2016年5月，国务院办公厅正式发布《关于促进通用航空业发展的指导意见》，中国通航产业迎来了春天。

　　政策的开放，使得通用航空领域里的企业不断涌现。这一时期，国内航空领域的企业从百余家上升到了千余家。而万丰所在的浙江，低空航权的开放是全国率先的试点省，浙江省在全国率先提出建设"大航空、大交通、大平台"战略，打造全省"空中1小时交通圈"，制定了《浙江省通用机场发展规划》，大力发展通航产业，为投资通航产业创造了良好的政策环境，万丰占有着地利。

通过战略规划，将公司发展定位于大交通领域的万丰集团，自然也会把航空纳入自己的视野。

万丰通航首飞仪式

如果说当年陈爱莲带领着万丰的创业者们进入轮毂制造领域带有一定的偶然性，缘于陈爱莲个人对交通工具的喜好和坚持的话，那么 2015 年进入航空领域时的万丰集团，则早已是有战略，规模化进军航空领域。在陈爱莲看来，航空产业是大国崛起和综合国力的象征，飞机就好比 20 年前我们想都不敢想的汽车，再过 20 年，万丰完全有能力给优秀员工奖配飞机，让来自全球各地的万丰精英们能够畅游蓝天！而随着政府对低空航行权的放开，先富阶层一定会喜欢上代表着自由和梦想的航空，因此航空的产品和服务市场在未来会有相当时间的供求不平衡，足够使进入这个市场的万丰获得利润并建立自己的竞争力。

到 2014 年 6 月，万丰集团成立了航空项目组，正式启动航空产业的相关调研。

市场调查的结果决定了万丰在航空领域的出击，是全方位的。万丰看中了航空领域的五项产业：通用飞机的制造、机场服务、通航经营、飞行培训和飞行服务站。经过市场调查，万丰发现，这些领域是低空航权开放之后供需最为不平衡的领域。

仅仅三个月之后，万丰董事局审议决定进入航空产业，浙江省有关领导听取了万丰的汇报，新昌县委县政府为此召开了两次项目论证会议，并专门成立以县委书记、县长为组长的领导小组和工作推进组。

新昌县委县政府专题召开万丰通用航空项目现场论证会

之后，万丰集团的项目组在欧美多地对国外的航空产业进行了考察，落实了两家可收购的对象。这样，万丰在进入航空领域时就有了强大的技术基础保障，并为企业未来在这个领域的创新提供了一个重要基础。

与意大利阿古斯塔开展战略合作　　　与捷克布尔诺科技大学签署战略合作协议

2015 年，万丰制订了"十三五"发展规划，确定了将通航产业作为未来 20 年的"蓝海"产业，并提出了"万里之航、丰行天下"的经营理念，按照成为全国发展通航产业的领导者的目标，借鉴美国、英国航空小镇成功开发运营经验，结合"智慧航空小镇"、"工业 4.0"、"中国制造 2025"、"O2O"等先进理念，在转型升级过程中全面进军航空全产业链，努力打造一家集整机制造、机场建设管理、通航运营、航校培训、飞行服务等为一体的通航产业龙头企业，建设国际布局的固定翼飞机和直升机制造工厂、世界级的通用飞机设计和研发中心、世界级通用机场设计和建设公司、覆盖全省的通用机场网络和航空小镇体系、覆盖全省的飞行服务站系统、国际布局的飞行学院和航空工业技术学院，集政府紧急救援、空中 Tax、VIP 飞行、公共运输等项目的航空公司。

此后，万丰十分注重发挥国外知名航空企业品牌优势，在国外收购夏威夷航校、国内组建万丰航校的同时，在意大利、加拿大、捷克建立飞机设计研发平台，与意大利莱昂纳多公司合资合作生产系列高端直升机；收购加拿大钻石飞机，生产钻石系列固定翼飞机；收购捷克 DF 项目，生产拥有万丰自主知识产权的系列轻型运动飞机，在国内打造飞机生产销售基地，形成国际研发、万丰制造、全球销售的航空产业格局。

考察奥地利钻石飞机总部

万丰收购捷克DF项目

于此同时，万丰积极响应浙江省委、省政府提出的在全省打造100个特色小镇的号召，决定在绍兴市新昌工业园核心区内建设万丰航空小镇。小镇总规划面积5.5平方公里，总投资100亿元，第一期就投入30亿元。按照"3年成园，5年成镇，8年达产"的建设计划，以飞机研发制造为核心，结合当地旅游、文化、环境等资源基础，以通航运营、观光旅游、航空运动、飞行体验、驾照培训为亮点，带动服务业、建筑业、文化创意产业等关联产业发展，形成产业、文化、旅游三位一体，生产、生活、生态融合发展，工业化、信息化、城镇化联动发展，宜业、宜居、宜游的美丽生态小镇，目标是打造成为全国城镇化建设和产业转型升级的新样板、中国通用航空特色小镇的典范、国家级通航产业综合示范区、国家级工程中心。

与其他航空小镇相比，万丰航空特色小镇呈现出四大亮点：一是突出飞机制造业，万丰把飞机整机制造作为整个航空小镇的核心产业，将建成固定翼飞机制造厂和直升机制造厂，以生产国际先进水平的轻型运动飞机、公务机、直升机为主，同时带动一批飞机核心零部件的生产制造。二是打造民族自主品牌，万丰在海外收购、兼并的同时，注重知识产权的所有权，注重飞机设计研发平台、工程中心的建设，生产拥有万丰自主知识产权的飞机与核心零部件。三是全产业链建设，对整机制造、机场建设管理、通航运营、航校培训、飞行服务等方面进行统筹规划，整体协调推进。四是国际化视野，非常注重全球优质航空资源的整合配置，实现产业布局国际化、团队国际化、经营管理国际化、资本国际化。目前，该小镇已列入第一批国家"十三五"100 家先进制造基地、浙江省 100 家特色小镇之中。

万丰航空特色小镇奠基仪式

万丰团队在航空特色小镇合影

2016 年 6 月，国家发改委领导在实地调研万丰航空特色小镇时如此评价，这是他迄今为止听到的方案中最系统完整、计划最详细、起点最高、贯穿全产业链、具有国际视野的航空产业发展方案，而且是实实在在推动项目落地，万丰对通航行业把握非常准确，发展通航产业非常契合国家战略，是经过精心调研、精心论证、深入评估的，万丰将对中国通航产业发展作出重大贡献。

万丰航空特色小镇总体规划图

这是一个徐徐展开的未来，它具有高度的不确定性。不过未来就是这样，正是因为不确定性才迷人。

并购派斯林

在万丰集团先进制造业板块取得行业细分市场全球领跑的基础上，金融投资板块在担保、基金、租赁、银行等业务领域也做得风生水起。

万丰金融投资产业诞生于 2008 年全球金融危机时期。在经济寒冬里，有现金就是王。而陈爱莲早在 2007 年底就看到国内经济过热的繁荣度，心生警惕，判断出"冬天"要来的信号，因此果断"瘦身"整合汽车项目，确保了资金流的健康，同时以退为进，进入金融投资领域。因为这一年，按照国务院的战略部署，上海将建设成国际金融中心。陈爱莲敏锐地发现，相比较于国外成熟的金融市场，中国金融市场还刚刚处于成长阶段，拥有非常好的发展前景。中国的资本市场正在向多层次体系迈进，PE 投资也如雨后春笋般地迎来了"基金潮"。

经过八年发展，到 2015 年万丰金融投资遵循"万源融汇，丰泽天下"的经营理念，担保业务已跃居"浙江省十佳融资性担保机构"前三强，租赁业务实现了上海地区行业细分市场领先，基金业务通过与优秀基金战略合作，每年有多个项目成功上市，锦源投资品牌已成功打响。

但集团董事会在决策十三五战略规划时，一致认为，万丰金融投资产业要实现华东地区领先的战略目标，必须要以先进制造业为依托，以上市平台为支撑，通过海外并购，把万丰科技的工业机器人产业不断做精做专、做强做久，金融资本与产业资本相结合，实现行业领跑目标。

正在这时，2015 年 6 月，陈爱莲 27 岁的儿子吴锦华加盟万丰。吴锦华，一个风华正茂的年轻人，从中国人民大学金融系毕业后，就读英国诺丁汉大学投资学士专业获硕士学位，具有金融投资的专业背景和国际化视野，2015 年 6 月刚从政府部门副处长职位上"下海"，出任万丰科技董事长。"初生牛犊不怕虎"，吴锦华挑战的是他人生中的首次海外收购。

吴锦华带领江玉华等并购团队，肩负使命，踏上了跨国并购之旅，前往美国、欧洲、日本等地积极寻找项目资源并不断筛选，最后把目标锁定在美国 Paslin（以下简称"派斯林"）机器人公司身上。

吴锦华与父母在一起

　　该公司成立于 1937 年，总部位于美国密歇根州沃伦市，是国际领先的焊接机器人应用系统服务商，以其领先的自动化系统概念、工业设计、施工和生产装配经验，为美国汽车产业和重工业提供自动化系统解决方案。同时，该公司具有强劲的研发能力，在全体 805 名员工中有 400 个技术工种，一半以上是工程师及编程人员，拥有了全美铸造机器人市场 70% 的份额。这是个优质标的，在市场结构上缺乏欧亚大客户，刚好也在积极寻求中国合作伙伴，对万丰机器人具有很强的互补性。

　　这些都令吴锦华团队兴奋不已，充满激情。大家全力以赴、忘我工作，克服时间紧、任务重、对手强等困难，国内外密切配合、日夜奋战，经过 3 个月艰苦卓绝的实地考察、周密尽调和机智谈判，不辱使命，在众多收购竞争对象中脱颖而出，全资收购派斯林公司，成为迄今为止国内机器人企业规模最大的一起跨国并购案。

　　同时，这次并购，缘于万丰对产业战略的准确把握和收购的莫大气魄，也吸引众多产业基金的垂睐，最终万丰选择了国字号的先进制造业产业基金作为合作伙伴，极大的提升了这次收购的影响力。

　　三个月时间就拿下拥有近百年历史的美国机器人巨头，这样的结果也同样震惊了全球机器人制造行业。要知道，当初有 21 家企业与万丰同台竞争并购派斯林，其中有来自国际一流的企业，也有来自中国机器人行业其他知名企业。全程参与并购的美国智鼎金融顾问公司总裁范钦华和美国明康律师事务所合作人王树盛却认为，这完全是意料之中的事。因为万丰的并购团队年轻化、专业化、国际化，在当时激烈的竞争中，从尽职调查、谈判签约到政府审批和交割，万丰团队展示了务实高效的作风，才会在众多国际买家中后来居上。

　　2016 年美国当地时间 3 月 23 日下午 16:30，在百年企业美国通用汽车公司总部大楼举行了万丰科技收购派斯林的交割仪式，意味着万丰锦源集团正式迈向国际化，而此时，距吴锦华出任锦源集团总裁刚满 3 个月。

万丰并购美国 *Pasling* 公司签约仪式

　　在陈爱莲看来，成功并购派斯林无疑可利用其 80 年来积累的业务渠道，通过通用、福特、本田等老客户在中国的主机厂进行业务拓展，快速扩大市场份额，并产生较大品牌溢价，这样一来，万丰机器人至少提前 10 年登上了国际竞技舞台，今后的视野变得更为宽广，制造水平与世界领先技术的差距就会不断缩小。

　　初战告捷的吴锦华认为，派斯林在焊接自动化领域积累了顶级的技术和客户群，万丰科技公司并购派斯林后，将在工业自动化领域，为客户提供从毛坯获得到机械加工与部件连接一体化的自动化解决方案，打破国内焊接机器人技术的局限，摆脱国内机器人产业受制于人的局面。

　　当然，完成跨国并购后，管理才是真正的考验。尽管前期曾有过数次深入的沟通，但被收购方仍充满疑惑，这家来自中国一个山区县城的民营企业，究竟会把有着悠久历史的派斯林公司带向何方？

　　2016 年 8 月，陈爱莲带领高管团队专程前往美国派斯林公司实地考察，通过召开交流座谈会，使派斯林管理者迅速统一思想、达成共识。

万丰美国 PASLIN

　　"什么是真正的重组？是要形成合并后大家都认同的一种文化，对合并后的企业的自我认同。"陈爱莲认为最关键的在于双方价值观能否高度一体，万丰要以宽大的胸怀、信任和尊重容纳天下有识之士。

　　派斯林公司高管团队都这样认为："我们很高兴能够加入万丰集团，并相信此次整合将有利于我们的客户、员工和业务合作伙伴，帮助我们快速实现显著增长和扩大。万丰的资金实力和运作能力，其卓越的研发精神，将推动派斯林继续成长。"

　　为进一步释放并购协同效应，实现公司产品竞争力和产能的进一步提升，撬动中国工业机器人行业的崛起。万丰集团在成功收购美国派斯林后，通过"送出去、请进来"的方式，马上着手同步布局设立中国派斯林公司。2016年5月18日，总投资15亿元的万丰锦源高端装备园奠基动工。

　　"心有多大，舞台就有多大"。引进国投战略投资、实施海外收购兼并、建设中国生产基地、借用上市公司平台、购置上海大楼，这五大战略布局，使万丰锦源集团真正实现了腾飞与转型升级。

上海市浙江商会响誉海内外，大佬云集、资源共享、携手共进

　　追根溯源，万丰一系列成功的海外并购，更为直接的影响是，作为上海市浙江商会轮值会长的陈爱莲，总能从郭广昌、马云、周成健、郑永刚等会长身上，感受到资本的魅力。郭广昌执掌复星集团，通过"中国资源嫁接全球动力"模式，一举成为全球最具影响力的投资控股集团之一，成为万丰进军金融投资产业的标竿。

万丰：基石与新梦

　　在万丰科技园办公楼的二楼，穿过记载着万丰历史照片的长廊，就到了陈爱莲的办公室。在偌大的欧式办公室里，总会被她座位后面的大幅牡丹图所吸引。不过，在这间商务活动非常频繁的办公室会客区外，有一个小门。

万丰奥特控股集团董监高团队合照

万丰锦源控股集团董监高团队合照

万丰奥特与全球最高端品牌成为长期战略合作伙伴

一推开这个小门，出现在访客面前的是别有洞天的风景。这是一片绿茵茵的芳草地衬托下的屋顶花园，大约有三百平米左右。在大片的草地中间，有一条交叉成"人"字形的鹅卵石小路穿过，而"人"字形小路的交叉点上，种了一棵郁郁葱葱的桂花树，它如伞状般打开，黄灿灿的桂花，满枝头，一簇簇，一团团，香气浓郁，沁人心田，树下摆放着一套欧式的白色桌椅。

2016 年的秋天，已是硕果累累的季节，在这个地方为万丰梦奋斗了二十二年的陈爱莲，忙中偷闲地在这个花园里的桂花树下总结着过去，展望着未来。

回顾过去，万丰是灿烂的。万丰人喜欢梦想，陈爱莲作为创始人，带领各级团队把一个个美好的梦想变成了灿烂的现实。"如果说我们有一点成绩的话，要感谢天时、地利、人和。从天时来看，中国改革开放三十年，万丰正好在这样一个时代诞生、切入市场。那么地利呢，浙江省是中国民营经济的发祥地和民营经济大省，各级政府为民营企业提供了非常好的环境和土壤。人和就是尊贵客户的厚爱、万丰各级优秀团队的努力。如果没有客户的信任，万丰发展就是无源之水。特别是各级万丰团队，从创业时的十个人到一万多人，从全球各地汇聚万丰大舞台，尽情地施展才华、体现价值，共同建设万丰大家庭更加美好的未来。"

正视现在，万丰是稳健的。十三五开局之年，万丰控股已经做好了五个科学布局：一是在体制上，形成了万丰奥特与万丰锦源两大集团，齐头并进、协调发展；二是在机制上，两大集团均形成了完善的"四会"治理体系、信息化管控体系、万丰文化体系，"法治万丰"理念形成共识；三是在产业上，万丰奥特集团以先进制造业为核心，以汽车部件、通用航空等"大交通"领域为产业定位，而万丰锦源集团则以金融产业为核心，以智能装备（工业机器人集成系统产业）先进制造业为支撑；四是在资本上，两大集团都致力于"营造国际品牌，构筑百年企业"的愿景，通过产业资本与金融资本相结合，实现科技、人才、资本、管理、品牌五个全球化；五是在团队上，培育了各级优秀的接班团队，实现了年轻化、知识化、专业化、全球化，正如长江后浪推前浪，一代更比一代强！

展望未来，万丰是辉煌的。万丰十三五宏伟蓝图已经描绘，万丰奥特集团和万丰锦源集团将依托各自上市平台，通过不断地并购整合，分别实现双千亿市值的战略目标，进一步提升行业全球领跑地位。

可以说，万丰22年的创业历程，其实就是中国改革开放伟大历史变革的缩影。在万丰20周年典礼上，陈爱莲不禁心潮澎湃、感慨万分："我们有幸赶上了改革开放大浪潮，贡献了我们的智慧和汗水。伟大的时代造就了千千万万中国企业的精彩，也造就了我们每一个人今天的幸福生活！"

当你真正走近陈爱莲时你会发觉，"听党话，跟党走"的思想从小就在她的心灵深处扎下了根。出生于红色家庭的陈爱莲，父母都是革命年代的老党员。她出生时，光明磊落的父亲陈忠炎借鉴《爱莲说》，为她取名为"爱莲"，希望女儿将来在做人的品质方面如莲花一般。所以，陈爱莲常常在公司大小会议上倡导全体万丰人要"常存敬畏之心"，敬畏国家的法律、敬畏公司的制度、敬畏组织的原则；同时，还要"常怀感恩之情"，感恩国家的强大、感恩组织的培养、感恩团队的付出，每一个万丰人只有真正懂得知恩、感恩、报恩，才会更好地珍惜政府给予的环境、珍惜社会给予的资源、珍惜客户给予的市场，才能以美丽的眼睛看世界、以快乐的心态做工作。

所以，陈爱莲认为，作为企业家的职责和使命，就是要通过创新创造，把社会资源实现价值最大化。她要求各级总经理经营团队，要遵循"永恒提升价值，不断奉献社会"的价值观，肩负起历史赋予的五个方面的责任：实现企业可持续发展、为客户提供优质产品、为国家创造税收、为员工提高生活质量、为股东提高投资回报、支持社会公益事业。

为了回报社会，万丰在支持教育、体育、文化和新农村建设上累计投入3亿多元：建立希望小学、设立慈善基金、主动带头捐资1000万元用于当地农村的"五水共治"等，陈爱莲还个人出资设立了浙江省首个美丽乡村建设基金，凡是年满 60 岁以上的老人、升读幼儿园的儿童、考入大学的学子以及喜结良缘的夫妻，每年都能享受到"长寿金、优学金、幸福金"。基金会理事长徐高松最能感受到陈爱莲的那份爱心，每年重阳节"三金"发放，看到村民们一张张幸福灿烂的笑容，那是他一年当中最开心的事。

而让陈爱莲最开心的时候，则是与她的强鹰学子们在一起，帮助他们在兴业强国奋斗中实现人生梦想。求是强鹰俱乐部是浙大阮俊华老师创立的全国"导师带徒"新模式，目的是推动青年创新创业，引领青年正能量。在"陈家军"中，才俊辈出，有多人成功走上创业之路。王孟秋创立零零科技，研发出全球首部真正意义上的便捷式自拍无人机；王旭龙琦创立利珀科技，通过万丰的融资及平台支持，成功打响品牌；徐属斌在父辈的基础上二次创业，陈爱莲亲自到学生的工厂，在战略、研发、市场、资金上给予全方面的指导和支持……浓浓师生情，让创业精神不断地传承与弘扬。

陈爱莲的强鹰学子们才俊辈出，多人成功走上创业之路

陈爱莲的强鹰学子们才俊辈出，多人成功走上创业之路

　　且歌且行，在创业的道路上，陈爱莲忙碌着、快乐着、幸福着，"我对万丰的未来充满了信心！"

　　而跟随陈爱莲多年的秘书大团队，每年在她生日的时候，总会送上一份特殊的礼物：一朵玫瑰花、一个红苹果、一根棒棒糖、一张音乐碟、一本休闲书，祝福被她们尊称为"慈母和导师"的董事长永葆健康、美丽、快乐、优雅……

万丰奥特之道：坚守先进制造业的专业化道路

先进制造业水平是国力的象征，是衡量国与国之间、区域与区域之间、企业与企业之间生产力综合水平的核心体现。作为中国工业化进程中的中坚力量，中国制造业要追赶上国际水平，靠的就是有一大批实业家对自身使命的追求。

作为民营企业，万丰奥特成长于改革开放之后的市场化进程，它创造了被媒体誉为"万丰奥特现象"的关键有三个：一是坚定不移地走先进制造业道路，坚持有所为、有所不为，做自己最擅长的"大交通"领域，从汽车零部件及整车制造，到飞机及零部件制造，以"一览众山小、再览众山无"的高端产业和高端市场战略定位，形成了超百亿先进制造业规模；二是胸怀全球走国际化道路，充分利用资本市场平台，主动整合全球资源，从经营国际化，走向资本、管理、人才、科技、品牌的国际化，使企业既有民营企业体制机制的灵活高效，又有国际企业百年沉淀的科学管理系统，成为有中国特色的国际化企业集团；三是走法治化道路，引进大批法律人才，培养员工的法律意识，严格遵守国家的法律法规，严格执行企业的规章制度，外部审计与内部审计相结合，确保企业健康发展、确保干部健康成长。

变革给民营经济带来的是活力和机会，同时也使得它们有动力和需求来接纳科学技术发展的成果，推动自身及所在行业和整个国家的进步。陈爱莲和她的各级万丰奥特团队在一轮轮的行业洗牌和变革中激流勇进，把企业成长过程当中的经验总结毫无保留地奉献出来，成为国内企业界的典型案例之一。无论对企业的经营管理者，还是对正在梦想路上奋勇前行的创业者们，无疑都是一种贡献。而同时，我们可以清晰地看到，陈爱莲带领团队为实现全体万丰人"快乐工作、幸福生活"的"万丰梦"，仍然保持着感恩的心态和奋斗的激情，他们以强烈的愿望、坚定的信仰和锲而不舍的努力，用"万丰梦"的力量共同推动中华民族早日实现伟大复兴的"中国梦"。

这是一个仍在征途中昂首前行的灿烂之梦！

Chapter 10
Brilliant Future

Chinese Visitors in a Small Canadian Town

It was in the meeting room of a Canadian company named MLTH Holding Inc. on October 8, 2013.

MLTH Holding Inc. was unknown to most people due to market segmentation. But if searching with the two key words "auto parts"and "magnesium alloy", you will find MLTH a hidden champion which sustained world market leadership. It captured over 65% market share in North American magnesium alloy auto parts business and meanwhile held more than 30% share of the global market. Headquartered in a small town in Canada though, MLTH was truly an international enterprise, having top R&D staff and production bases in U.S., U.K., Mexico and China.

The topic for the meeting was share acquisition of MLTH. President of MLTH, Eric R. Showalter, and his management team were sitting on one side of the conference table and on the other side were some Chinese businessmen.

At the start, Showalter spoke directly to the Chinese called Qi Xiangmin most of the time, who was sitting opposite to him. Sitting next to Qi Xiangmin was a young man wearing glasses in his early 30s. Showalter noticed that Qi Xiangmin had frequent discussion with the young man but he paid little attention to him and felt no surprise as he believed he had known everything about the Chinese acquirer.

The young man was the president of Wanfeng Auto--Chen Bin.

Born in 1980s, Chen Bin who graduated from law department of Peking University and then went to England to study MBA, has strong interest in industrial management. In 2008, after Chen Bin returned from England, he served as general manager of Wanfeng Automobile Company, deputy general manager and general manager of the listed company. In 2011, he was promoted to President of Wanfeng Auto Holding Group after training and experience for 3 years.

After three rounds of discussion about the takeover proposal, Chen Ailian, chairman of the board of directors, made strategic decisions. Entrusted by the board of Wanfeng Auto Group, Chen Bin was now shouldering the responsibility of implementing those decisions by launching a one-month due diligence investigation in Canada as the head of the team. One month later, when Chen Bin completed the due diligence investigation and the takeover was drawing to an end, Showalter disclosed some details about the takeover deal to Chen Bin.

In October, the management of MLTH was not quite optimistic about the takeover, but they didn't concerned much about the deal because the Chinese acquirer had left an advance payment guarantee of 8 million Canadian dollars. Actually they were ready to receive the deposit once the buyer called the whole deal off.

However, they did not quite expect that Qi Xiangmin, the central character of the Chinese acquisition team, had found Wanfeng Auto and when Chen Bin appeared in the meeting room, Wanfeng Auto was well prepared for the acquisition. Though it was the first time for Chen Bin to come to a due diligence investigation, but with the help of comprehensive materials relating to MLTH, he and his acquisition team knew ins and outs of the targeting company.

This was an extremely complex merger deal. To understand the whole story, we have to begin with the strategic positioning of Wanfeng Auto dating back to 2010 when the Group introduced its 12th Five-Year Strategic Plan.

In October 2010, on Mountain Huang more than 300 elite staff of Wanfeng Auto gathered together to hold the development strategy seminar of the 12th Five-Year Strategic Plan. Chen Ailian had always attached great importance to the development of corporate strategic planning, so here was the seminar. Chen Ailian believed development strategies were the overall, long-term and essential tactics and reflections on the future of an enterprise. The strategies were guidelines, and specific moves always came after guidelines. No strategies, no directions. Therefore, Wanfeng Auto kept pace with China's economic growth all the time, developing a strategic plan every five years. In the process of strategy development, Chen Ailian would draw on the collective wisdom of experts, while a number of the former leaders of the Chinese machinery industry, such as He Guangyuan, Lu Yansun, Cai Weici, Zhang Xiaoyu, Zhu Sendi, Li Xinya, Song Tianhu, Sun BoHuai, Chen Yunbo, Qu Xianming, Zhang Shulin, Yan Jianlai, Jin Yanli etc., would always do their utmost to offer suggestions with enthusiasm. By 2010, Wanfeng Auto had gone through three Five-Year periods. Guided by the 9th, 10th and 11th Five-Year Strategic Plan, Wanfeng Auto maintained a stable and sustainable development.

It was on the seminar that Chen Ailian brought up "the objective of building a long-standing business" and positioned Wanfeng Auto as "a multinational corporation". A multinational enterprise meant the globalization of five aspects: capital, management, personnel, technology and brand. The discussions in the seminar gave rise to the new business planning of Wanfeng Auto. During the discussions, Chen Ailian put forward the concept of "multi-modal transportation" on which the strategic planning of Wanfeng Auto Group was based. That is to say, globalization must be accelerated via merger and acquisitions in various transport sectors such as, aerospace, sea and land.

To Wanfeng Auto, this was a breakthrough in thinking, marking the birth of guiding principles. In fact, the entry into "multi-modal transportation" sector transformed Wanfeng Auto into an enterprise offering product customization.

Wanfeng's history has shown that motor-hub as an industry relying on motorcycles will fluctuate as motorcycles may not be highly demanded by the market any more as a transport means. So is the case in auto-hub industry.

However, shifts in the market demands cannot deny consumers' needs to transport in general. Although means of transport have experienced a long evolution with various changes, ranging from motorcycles and cars to ships, and airplanes, the overall trend of more frequent use of vehicles would not change.

By following this trend, Wanfeng Auto positioned itself as an enterprise providing "multi-modal transportation" products, which made growing bigger and stronger possible. Meanwhile, this indicated the desired direction of development, because motorcycles, cars, ships and airplanes are a variety of vehicles. They may belong to different scopes, but these scopes share a lot in common — energy applications, mechanical design and manufacture, materials science, intelligent control and management.

Elite staff of Wanfeng Auto participating in the seminar on Mountain Huang, discussing the twelfth Five-Year Strategic Plan

After establishing the strategy, the whole Group knew what they were striving for.

With the positioning decision mentioned above, now it is very clear to see why Wanfeng Auto had to buy MLTH.

One key component of the "multi-modal transportation" strategy was materials, and since Wanfeng Auto had operated Weihai Wanfeng Magnesium S&T Development Ltd., the Group was attentive to magnesium alloys and their application. It was fully aware of the wide application of magnesium alloys because it was highly related to the lightweight trend of automotive industry.

MLTH was a leader in magnesium alloy industry, and a world top-level enterprise on the aspects of material research and production technology. What's more, it focused on the production of "multi-modal transportation" parts and was a strategic partner of many transnational auto-makers.

Therefore, in the blueprint of the board of directors of Wanfeng Auto, MLTH would be an essential part of the picture for the entire group if the acquisition turned successful. The takeover of MLTH was not simply because it was a huge profit-making enterprise; more importantly, the deep integration of MLTH's cutting-edge technology, Wanfeng Auto's huge market power and together with China's resources, would generate remarkable impact.

But how could a world leading company like MLTH end up selling stakes?

The raw material for magnesium alloy production is magnesium, and China is a top magnesium reserve holder in the world. North America, of course, has the resources. Around 2008, the Chinese government began to implement export restrictions on raw industrial materials, causing prices skyrocketing in global magnesium alloy market.

This led to troubles to the cooperation between MLTH and major auto companies. One reason was that the increasing price caused MLTH to suffer loss according to the original contracts with its business partners, the other was MLTH stated that price rise of its products was required. The auto producers started to doubt about the wider application of magnesium alloy auto parts, and predicted a bleak outlook for MLTH.

The gloomy prospect also shook the confidence of the shareholders in MLTH and the situation was worsened by the global economy crisis happened in 2008. As a result, financial institutions like GM Financial and National Bank of Iceland received shares at low equity transfer prices from shareholders of MLTH.

Financial institutions can be shareholder but they are, in essence, investors. They know only the flow of capital can produce benefits. For this reason, they required MLTH to locate industry investors as soon as possible so they could sell the equity stakes and out of trust, they commissioned the investor-seeking mission to MLTH management.

The opportunity was caught by a group of Chinese businessmen who were masters of financial operations and played"matchmaker"for the acquisition. They were also those who were Chinese negotiators sitting in the MLTH conference room -- Shanxi Tianshuo Investment Co, Ltd. (hereinafter referred to as Tianshuo).

As an investment company, Tianshuo was shrewd enough to see the emerging possibility as well as demand for a considerable number of Chinese enterprises to make global acquisitions due to the development of domestic industry. A number of the Western industrial enterprises were facing a shortage of liquid capital because of the 2008 global financial crisis, so it was a possible that these companies became a scarce resource. Namely, they became the magnet of industrial capital of China. Hence, when Tianshuo discovered MLTH was willing to sell shares, it managed to sign the letter of intent to purchase share with MLTH.

Afterwards, Tianshuo tried to use Shanxi United Magnesium Industry Co. Ltd., an industrial company owned by itself, as a platform to attract massive capital for the acquisition.

The appearance of Shanxi United Magnesium Industry Co. Ltd. may help to understand why MLTH management was willing to accept the acquisition proposal. Shanxi province was abundant in magnesium resources in China; as a corporate entity, Shanxi United Magnesium Industry Co. Ltd. was bound to be a holder of magnesium reserves. To MLTH, if Tianshuo, a holder of magnesium resources, completed the acquisition, the difficulty of "unstable supply of magnesium material"in its operations could be solved, which was absolutely killing two birds with one stone.

One thing that confused MLTH management was Tianshuo and Shanxi United Magnesium Industry Co. Ltd. had the same manager, but differed in equity structure. Tianshuo was a wholly owned company, but Shanxi United Magnesium Industry Co. Ltd. was composed of a number of shareholders. That is to say, Tianshuo couldn't afford the takeover on its own.

Now that Wanfeng Auto determined the strategic positioning, a capital operation team was founded in the regional headquarters in Shanghai with Cheng Weijun, and Ren Xingang as the key members. In early 2013, the team learnt the news that MLTH was seeking equity transfer and immediately reported to Chen Ailian, chairman of the board of directors, and also passed on Tianshuo's requirement to meet her in person.

Shortly after the team presented MLTH's material to Chen Ailian, she agreed to meet with Tianshuo. Through visiting and view exchanging, Tianshuo instantly saw the strengths of Wanfeng Auto: It was an advanced manufacturing enterprises, with top level manufacturing resources; at the same time it had a big corporate structure that can accommodate take the hidden champion enterprise with single products. Another advantage of Wanfeng Auto was Wanfeng Aowei which was a listed company could be used as platform for direct financing for the acquisition.

The management of Tianshuo also understood that for MLTH, Wanfeng Auto was an attractive buyer. On the one hand, it could be easy for Wanfeng Auto and MLTH to reach consensus, considering a fairly comprehensive knowledge Wanfeng Auto had about research and development of magnesium alloy materials and the industry market because it was the owner of Wanfeng Magnesium S&T Development Co., Ltd. On the other hand, the two enterprises had one important thing in common -- both were involved in auto parts industry, especially Wanfeng Auto, which offered service for the world's top automobile manufacturers. There would be a lot of synergy between the two companies after the merger.

Thus, Tianshuo which had positioned itself as the go-between concluded that Wanfeng Auto was the most suitable buyer in China. With Wanfeng Auto as the suitor, Tianshuo could complete the acquisition with success.

Because of the "multi-modal transportation" positioning, Wanfeng Auto would like to make the acquisition based on its strategic direction. What contributed to the decision of Wanfeng Auto board on the takeover was the lessons it had learnt from 10 years' exploration of running Wanfeng Magnesium S&T Development Co., Ltd.

The ten-year operation gave Wanfeng Auto a clear picture of the latest applications of magnesium alloy in automotive industry and other markets, and it also helped Wanfeng Auto understand the technology advantage MLTH possessed.

In the next two months, after three talk between Chen Ailian and Tianshuo, a quick resolution was passed at the Board meeting: the acquisition of MLTH should be undertaken, because it met the five requirements of quality projects concerning international acquisitions: first, target company was the world leader in market segmentation; second, target company had an international geographical layout; third, possessing the key technology, target company holds the pricing power in international market; fourth, the takeover price was reasonable; finally, further development of the acquired firm could produce greater profit. It was agreed that the acquisition was of great strategic significance for Wanfeng Auto, for it would further strengthen Wanfeng Auto's leading position in the future. Difficulties also existed. The acquisition was a risky project and there was not enough time for preparation.

Once the decision was made, three teams were immediately set up to work on the acquisition: the first team was the due diligence investigation team heading overseas led by Chen Bin; the second team responsible for integration of domestic resources and legal, had key members like Chen Weijun, Chen Lijun, Yang Mingxing and Zeng Zhaoling; the third team was the capital operation team including Zhao Yahong, Ding Fengyun and Chen Hanxia. Chen Ailian was the commander of all three teams, taking charge of overall situation, acquisition schedule, and risk control of all aspects. This truly embodies the phisosophy of Wanfeng -- a person's strength is limited, the team's power is infinite.

The negotiations between Wanfeng and Tianshuo started from August 2013, and on October, Wanfeng completed the purchase of 100% stake of Tianshuo. After that, Tianshuo and President Chen Bin together with his four overseas due diligence investigation teams went to Canada.

For Wanfeng Auto, the acquisition of MLTH was critical, but to complete the huge acquisition with the total amount of 1.5 billion RMB within six months was not easy at all.

It was normal for Showalter, president of MLTH, not to take much notice of

Chen Bin in his first presence at the due diligence investigation conference. MLTH had other candidates for the acquisition visited before. Showalter told Chen Bin that before Wanfeng Auto, several groups of Chinese investors had come into the meeting room, though never came back.

Such craze was caused by the overseas mergers and acquisitions boom in China. Domestic industrial investors were in the pursuit of either large-scale or fame of the target company in the overseas mergers and acquisitions. MLTH was a technology-oriented business in a sub-sector industry, failing to attract most Chinese investors with scale or reputation. However, Wanfeng Auto had great interest in MLTH because the two enterprises were counterparts in the same specified field.

Taking over

The board of Wanfeng Auto assigned Chen Bin, president of Wanfeng Auto, to carry out due diligence and to take over MLTH, mainly because Chen Bin traveled around various countries while studying abroad. Apart from understanding the background of European and American enterprises, he had earned practical management experience in listed companies after graduation. In addition, he is a professional, diligent and conscientious person.

Chen Bin realized he had to strike the attention of MLTH's management at the first due diligence investigation meeting.

So right after the meeting begun, he stated that Wanfeng Auto had wholly acquired Tianshuo; thus became the trading negotiation partners of MLTH. Those who were sitting opposite to Showalter were representatives of Wanfeng Auto, from now on Wanfeng Auto would take charge of everything about the equity transfer process.

The straightforwardness was partly due to Chen Bin's knowledge of Anglo-salson culture based on his education in the UK, and of course also because of the shortage of time in the second half of the acquisition. According to the acquisition intention agreement between MLTH and Tianshuo signed in September, a deposit was paid by Tianshuo, and both sides agreed that the deposit would be confiscated by MLTH and the transaction would be canceled if Wanfeng Auto failed to complete the acquisition and transaction by December, 2013. Chen Bin had a clear understanding of the consequences, however, Wanfeng Auto was not involved in this transaction until October, and it took time for Wanfeng Auto to do the due diligence investigation again and reestablish the legal structures of the transaction. If all these had to be done in just two months, there would be no time for courtesy and directness was the only option. As Chen Bin had a good command of English, he could communicate effectively and directly with senior executives of MLTH without a translator.

Even so, it remained a huge challenge for Wanfeng Auto to complete the acquisition within two months. In those days, the acquisition teams as well as all senior executives were in high tension.

With Ailian's efficient decisions and the support from the management, the second time when Chen Bin took his team of superior financial law consultant to MLTH, they could carry on substantive investigation right as they arrived.

At first, MLTH's management was not willing to provide the financial data once again, because a survey had been conducted when acquisition intention was reached. MLTH would reveal the finical data to Wanfeng Auto several months later only if the MLTH executives could make sure they were really serious about the purchase.

Therefore, at the beginning of the due diligence investigation, Wanfeng Auto offered a detailed merger plan, with the timetable and all the necessary technical details on display. From this timetable, it was easy to tell Wanfeng Auto's earnest and sincerity about the acquisition, and it was a professional enterprise in both magnesium alloy market and auto parts market.

Everything then went smoothly.

Soon, Chen Bin's team quickly began to understand the company's situation: MLTH was founded in 1981 and walked through a 33-year developing course. Due to the abundant mineral resources and a long history of mining and smelting, MLTH was a company with cutting-edge core technology and a world leader in magnesium alloy industry. It had long-term strategic partnership with high-end brands in the world, such as Tesla, Porsche, Audi, Mercedes-Benz, BMW, Volvo, Land Rover, Toyota, Honda, Ford, General Motors, Fiat, Chrysler etc. Its employees were proud of the company, because for the town and state where in MLTH was located, MLTH was a pillar enterprise.

Because of the change in stockholding MLTH was controlled by financial investors after 2008. The staff felt frustrated as they were not sure about "for whom they work". The constant trade of shares represented the continuous change of ownership. Thus, the executives, also the staff of MLTH hoped to find a real industry investor for this company who could made a long-term development plan for the enterprise.

From the perspective of the industry, the advanced technology and production stability enabled MLTH to enjoy a good reputation among the North American auto manufacturers as well as secure over 65% of magnesium alloy automobile parts market. However, around 2008, magnesium prices fluctuated; the North American auto makers became doubtful about whether to further expand the use of magnesium alloy parts. Hence, MLTH hoped to invite a powerful Chinese enterprise to be the controlling shareholder so as to reestablish car makers' trust.

Europe was the market worth vigorous expansion — North American car makers were willing to use magnesium alloy, because Canada has some magnesium resources. It is reasonable for them to believe that MLTH could produce magnesium alloy auto parts with excellent quality. On the contrary, European manufacturers had little interests in magnesium alloy parts for the lack of magnesium resources in Europe. But in recent years, European makers were forced to use magnesium alloy auto parts by the higher requirement for environment production. For this reason, a Chinese controlling shareholder coming from a country enjoying abundant magnesium resources would be very helpful for MLTH to explore European market.

In addition, the Chinese market of magnesium alloy car parts was where MLTH and Wanfeng Auto could achieve win-win situation: China was a latecomer of car market, but it was the largest and fastest growing market in car production and sales. But in China, magnesium alloy was seldom applied to reduce the car weight for fuel-efficiency and less pollution. The current domestic auto industry developed rapidly and there were few compulsory regulations on environment protection. Moreover, domestic magnesium alloy technology was not mature. As a result, once Wanfeng Auto became the controlling shareholder, Wanfeng could introduce the mature and sophisticated magnesium alloy technology into China, help MLTH enter Chinese market with investment on larger scale, and reinforce the dominant position of MLTH as the subsidiary of Wanfeng Auto in the field of magnesium alloy.

Chen Bin (5th from right), the winner of Zhejiang Economic Figure of the Year.

Based on the mutual interest of two parties, the merger went very smoothly. In

December, the two sides successfully completed the due diligence investigation, agreement signing and equity transaction. That the due diligence investigation completed with efficiency and speed on such a short notice by Chen Bin's team demonstrated the long-held spirit Wanfeng Auto -- "making the impossible possible."

From Production Merger to Influence Merger

After it had been completed, Chen Ailian found out that this acquisition of MLTH was more than a simple acquisition of an enterprise, it actually offered an opportunity for industry segmentation in global market.

This may sound irrational. But we can understand it was quite reasonable after checking the following data. The world annual total production of magnesium was about 700,000 tons, most of which was produced in China. And the magnesium demand of MLTH factories all over the world was about 70,000 tons. Once Wanfeng Auto became the controlling share holder of MLTH and expanded in Chinese market, the ratio would be further raised.

With this huge magnesium demand, the government's purpose that Wanfeng undertook the project of National High Technology Research and Development Program (i.e. Plan 863) could be finally realized: When the fluctuation of magnesium price became the headache of MLTH, China, a country with abundant magnesium resources, was worrying about the limited application of the resources. China's magnesium reserve ranks the first place in the world. Despite China enjoys advantage in resources, the magnesium alloy deep processing technology and its applications lagged far behind. Therefore, the Ministry of Industry and Information Technology issued The *12th Five Year Plan for New Material Industry* to develop high quality magnesium products, which could satisfy the need of automobiles, "Large Aircraft Project" and high speed rails. Now, Wanfeng Auto's got access to the cutting-edge magnesium alloy technology through the acquisition, helping China quickly become a nation with strong magnesium industry.

Thus, Wanfeng Auto believed that with wide application in the downstream industry, the top priority in the following years was to stabilize the magnesium raw material source and price by means of cooperating with local government and developing magnesium mining resources. Besides, Wanfeng Auto should build magnesium trade market through collaboration with all parties to expand the domestic application.

Chen Bin had a deep insight about this. Just like the barriers MLTH encountered in Europe, the prerequisite of widening the application of a certain resource was offering a stable expectation for users, namely, MLTH's downstream auto manufacturers. To provide a stable expectation for the downstream automobile businesses, IT and household appliance companies, the most effective method was to establish an open and transparent trade mechanism. Undoubtedly, a Chinese enterprise shall take the responsibility of this, as China is abundant with magnesium ores.

With this macro consideration, coupled with the mutual auto parts clients Wanfeng Auto and MLTH had, Wanfeng Auto hoped to lead MLTH to create new value through the two channels of resource and market.

Certainly, there was a lot more that MLTH could contribute to Wanfeng Auto. Wanfeng Auto was transforming from traditional manufacturing to advanced manufacturing, so it could learnt a lot in all aspects of the industrialization of scientific research and technological achievement from MLTH which was a technology leading enterprise, and speed up the transformation then achieve the global leader of industry market segments at the same time.

This was what the Wanfeng Auto board cared more.

From the acquisition of MLTH to the acquisition of Shanghai Dacromet Surface Treatment Co., Ltd. which we'd like to talk about later, it can be seen that the acquisition strategy of Wanfeng Auto changed greatly. In the early stage, Wanfeng Auto purchased Shanghai Ershou and Shangdong Dooray at relatively low prices which were close to the net asset. However, after 2013, under the leadership of Chen Ailian, Wanfeng Auto changed manners of acquisition by targeting at top enterprises in the industry with strong international competitiveness, and usually provided a high premium.

Firmly aiming to become a globalized enterprise and achieve sustainable development in the field of "multi-modal transportation", Wanfeng Auto made fundamental changes in acquisition strategies accordingly. At the beginning of the 21st century, the specific acquisition target of Wanfeng Auto was to expand production capacity through acquisition when the downstream market demand increased rapidly. This kind of acquisitions was counted into the production cost and Wanfeng Auto was competent to play a leading in the acquisitions. But the situation was quite different after of Wanfeng Auto targeted at the "multi-modal transportation" field, Wanfeng Auto found great potentials for expansion, but in this new field, more challenges would arise.

However, transnational acquisition cannot simply be accomplished when transaction parties reached an agreement. After the due diligence investigation team led by Chen Bin finished the transaction with MLTH, the team of Chen Weijun proceeded to gain the administrative approvals of this acquisition from different levels of governments.

According to the earlier agreement, Tianshuo was responsible for going through the administrative approval procedures while Chen Bin's team conducted investigations in Canada. But when the due diligence investigation team reached a consensus with the shareholders and management team of MLTH, Tianshuo was trapped in gaining permission for the acquisition from the government.

Chen Ailian and the acquisition teams took over this job immediately after learning that. They were running out of time. It was in the beginning of October, 2013 that Chen Bin's ream finished the transaction. If Wanfeng Auto wanted to take over MLTH successfully, administrative approvals must be obtained before the end of 2013. A transnational acquisition requires approvals from different central ministries and commissions, and they must be done one after another. Usually, the whole process would take half a year.

At the critical moment, Wanfeng Auto greatly benefited from the new session of government's policy: streamlining administration and delegating power to lower-level governments. The acquisition was approved by National Development and Reforms Commission within five workdays and then approved by Ministry of Commerce within one day. The management team of MLTH was amazed at the high administrative efficiency of Chinese ministries and commissions. Owing to comprehensively deepening reforms in China, Wanfeng Auto accomplished the "mission impossible"!

Thus, during the session of NPC &CPPCC in 2014, Chen Ailian, a member of NPC, said sincerely as a deputy from business of the delegation of Zhenjiang province, she and her enterprise did gain benefits from the reform results of the government when she reviewed the Report on the Work of the Government done by Premier Li Keqiang. The resolutions and decisions were carried out effectively in the whole country. Zhejiang province advocated to build "the most efficient government", and required officials of all levels to wholeheartedly provide full support and prompt service for Zhejiang businessmen to speed up international mergers.

In April, 2014, when she visited the MLTH branches in Canada, US and Mexico, together with senior executives of Wanfeng Auto, Chen Ailian, the new president of the board from China, was warmly welcomed with applause given by those foreign senior executives lining up at the gate. MLTH had 1680 foreign staff, so integration of two different cooperate cultures was a huge challenge. Nevertheless, Ailian had great confidence and believed that the key was if the staff of both parties shared a highly universal values and Wanfeng Auto welcomed every talent with great generosity, trust and respect.

For this reason, in every MLTH's factory Chen Ailian's team visited, symposiums were held to listen to the advice of the management team and the following specific promises were made: after the acquisition, first of all, no layoff and staff substitution would occur. In addition, the salary and well-being would be raised and finally, problems existing in the company operation, concerning investment increasing, market optimizing and strategy making, would be solved. With solving problems on-site, the executives of MLTH reached consensus and understood that the purpose of the acquisition was to build MLTH into a top enduring enterprise rather than selling it again. With greater market potential and more vitality brought by the acquisition, the staff of MLTH regained their sense of belonging and found a platform to fully demonstrate their talent. The values and business philosophy successfully blended in a short time.

Prior to the acquisition the factories of MLTHs had an operation rate of 70% only. After completing the acquisition, all factories operated at full capacity. The foreign staff who had doubted about the Chinese owner now had full confidence in fulfilling the yearly operation plan.

The acquisition of Shanghai Dacromet

The MLTH was just one of Chen Ailian's targets of "advantage acquisition".

Dacromet used to be name of coating which was invented in the late 1950s. The thick ice was a severe impediment for vehicles in the severer winter in North America and North Europe. To solve this problem, salt was spread on the ground to lower the freezing point of ice. Nevertheless, because the chloride ions in salt eroded the steel substrate, the vehicle would be seriously damaged, a sticky problem arose.

American scientist Mike Martin invented a type of aqueous dispersion paint with de-ionized water as solvents, mainly contained zinc and aluminum flakes in a chromium binder. When the aqueous dispersion is applied to steel substrate by repeated immersion and stoving, a thin-film coating shall be produced. The coating has a good performance against corrosion caused by chloride ions. The metal anticorrosion had entered a new era, for the correction protection provided by previous technology never lasted long. In the 1980s, Dacromet technology was improved to be chromium free, eliminating chromium, a pollutant for the environment, from the formula.

Dacromet coating is an alternative to electroplating and it is environmental-friendly. With an increasing demand for environmental protection in China, Dacromet has versatile application in the future.

Shanghai Dacromet Surface Treatment Co., Ltd.located in Baoshan District, North of Shanghai,was not big in neither its scale and reputation, nor the complexity of its technique. It was somewhat hidden in a quiet place covering several thousand square meters in East Shiyi Road in Baoshan District.

The founder of Shanghai Dacromet is an entrepreneur who had studied in

Germany and engaged in trading. When domestic auto industry started to develop, being optimistic about the future of Dacromet technology, he returned to China, introducing Dacromet technology to China and offered service to automobile manufacturers for parts processing. Later, his business extended to various fields like high speed railway, important mechanical components etc.

The accumulated experience through years gave Shanghai Dacromet a unique competitive edge in this specialized field. It had head start in development, refined operation, and excellent management. Its business covered most major domestic high-end manufacturing cooperates, and was their reliable cooperative partner. For this reason, despite its relatively small scale, Shanghai Dacroment could operate at its full capacity and enjoy high profit margin.

Selling its share equity was the decision of the founder himself. At that time, the entrepreneur was about to retire and no one in his family had the willing to take over his business. Therefore, the founder who possessed all share equity of the company intended to sell his company to a thriving domestic enterprise with great ambition.

This founder was a reserved and rational old gentleman, who was calm during the whole process of negotiation. At the signing ceremony after the contract was concluded, however, he emotionally said that this reminded him of his daughter's wedding ceremony. He pleaded Wanfeng Auto to take good care of his company and magnify its existing strengths. He promised to work three more years and retire at the age of 70 for sake of Wanfeng's smooth takeover.

Besides the initiation of Shanghai Dacromet, the changeable situation in domestic industry also promoted this merger between Wanfeng Auto and Shanghai Dacromet.

From the perspective of industry development, with the continuously increasing awareness and requirements of environment protection in China, it was getting highly likely that Dacromet coating would finally replace the traditional electroplating.

For Shanghai Dacromet which has engaged in this coating technology for years, it can give full play of its advantage in the expanding market. But meanwhile, once Dacromet coating becomes the mainstream technology, more powerful companies possibly will enter this market and compete fiercely with Shanghai Dacromet.

The small scale of Shanghai Dacroment resulted from the coating technology. Just like electroplating technology, as an approach of coating, the key to Dacroment lies in the coating formula and the solvent. Therefore, the threshold of coating technology is not high, and in turn, Shanghai Dacromet is asset-light enterprise.

Therefore, in the large scale competition, Chen Ailian believed among other good sides brought by the acquisition, a win-win situation could be achieved in marketing. As long as two parties cooperates well, Wanfeng Aowei will be able to spread the technology worldwide and offer B2B Dacromet coating service for automobile manufacturers and high speed train producers. Shanghai Dacroment created an "asset-light and service-oriented" business mode which has been proved practical.

Several months later, Wanfeng finally reached an agreement with Shanghai Dacromet that Wanfeng purchased all the equity of Shanghai Dacromet. In November Wanfeng Aowei issued the announcement about the acquisition.

However, the strategic positioning of "multi-modal transportation" and a series adjustments on operation remained unknown to the market at this time. Would the investors accept the rather bold reform?

Before launching the acquisition bid for MLTH, Wanfeng had made a series of correct operation policies. Moreover, domestic capital market had been optimistic about the automotive industry. The stock price of Wanfeng Aowei kept climbing despite the fact that A share stock market was gloomy.

The acquisition of Shanghai Dacromet was completed earlier than other projects, so Wanfeng Aowei made announcement on 13, November. The stock market didn't respond well to the news. The stock price of Wanfeng Aowei decreased from 16 RMB per share to 13 RMB per share.

The acquisition team believed this negative reaction was resulted from the high premium Wanfeng Aowei paid for acquiring Shanghai Dacromet and investors' pessimistic attitude toward all the mergers conducted by Wanfeng Aowei. But the team also believed once institutional investors and individual investors got to understood the real value of Shanghai Dacromet and foresaw the win-win future, the stock price of Wanfeng Aowei would go up again.

In order to communicate with the capital market effectively, the acquisition team arranged a field trip to Shanghai Dacromet for a group of institutional investors.

On that day, in the drizzling rain, more than 20 fund managers and researchers from Investment Research Department paid a visit to Shanghai Dacromet and listened to the introduction delivered by the senior executives, and then the investors came to know the strong demand from domestic industries involving complicated mechanic manufacturing. There were more than ten thousand electroplating factories in China, producing waste water in coating process which had done great harm to the environment. Dacromet coating had great market potential in China. Therefore, investors dispelled the misgivings concerning the acquisition and felt optimistic about the future of Wanfeng Aowei.

Under this context, the acquisition of Shanghai Dacromet was an important step toward the "multi-modal transportation". And with the financing platform of a listed corporate and support from Wanfeng Auto, a powerful and ambitious enterprise, Shanghai Dacromet could rebuild the core advantage in future competition and maintain its leading position in the industry.

Afterwards, like the cleared-up days in Shanghai, the stock price later climbed up to 24 RMB from the bottom of 13 RMB per share and finished a V type inversion, which laid the foundation for further use of capital platform to build a big company.

The positive reaction from the capital market was more of result of the efforts of Wanfeng Auto to update and transform the corporate from traditional wheel manufacturing to advanced manufacturing in "multi-modal transportation". The significance of the changes made by the team led by Chen Ailian was far more than acquiring some enterprises for higher profits. It was the changes that helped to make Wanfeng Auto a true international enterprise.

On November 2014 after acquisition of Shanghai Dacromet, Wanfeng acquired Ningbo Dacromet to strengthen the leading position of Wanfeng Dacromet, and signed the equity transfer agreement in Xinchang. Jiang Jiahong, the founder of Ningbo Dacromet sell the entire stake for his child had no intention to take over. As a result, the leading role of Wanfeng in Dacromet coating industry was further consolidated and strengthened.

New energy vehicles of CATARC

On 12 November, 2013, the Third Plenary Session of the 18th Central Committee of the Communist Party passed the "Decision of the Central Committee of the Communist Party of China on Some Major Issues Concerning Comprehensively Deepening the Reform." (hereinafter referred to as the "Decision"). The "Decision" proposed guiding thoughts on deepening the reform comprehensively, including improving the property rights protection system; developing a mixed economy vigorously, promoting a modern corporate system for SOEs and supporting the healthy development of the non-public sector.

Before the idea of vigorously developing a mixed economy was clearly put forward, Zhejiang province, the birthplace of the private economy, had attempted to advocate cooperation among central government-owned enterprises and private enterprises. As early as in December 2011, Xia Baolong, deputy secretary of the Zhejiang provincial Party committee, promoted the SASAC and the Zhejiang Provincial People's Government to sign a strategic cooperation memorandum. Heads from 107 central government-led enterprises negotiated with entrepreneurs from more than 2000 private enterprises and finally signed projects of cooperation worth 27.21 billion RMB.

In response to the appeal of Zhejiang provincial Party committee and provincial people's government, Chen Ailian and Zhao Hang, the director of China Automotive Technology & Research Center (hereinafter referred to as CATARC) appeared at the signing ceremony for the project of "new energy hybrid vehicles"in Shanghai, a symbol of Wanfeng Auto's strategic cooperation with central government-led enterprises to jointly open an era of hybrid cars.

In the speech, Ailian said Wanfeng Auto had been maintaining a cordial cooperation relationship with CATARC since 2000. The partnership and mutual trust had been forged between the two parties. And the values of the two sides had reached a high degree of consistency. She believed that the strength of the central government-led enterprise, coupled with the dynamic of the private enterprise, was bound to create a strong international competitiveness and contributed more to make China a nation with strong auto industry.

At the ceremony, Zhao Hang, the director of CATARC also addressed with great emotion. He claimed that CATARC made its first pot of gold in the field of investment by investing in Wanfeng Auto, and this cooperation would be a win-win situation where both sides could give play to respective advantages. The new energy hybrid vehicle was the 8-year research result of the expert team in CATARC. In terms of technology and performance indicators, products reached the advanced level in China. By providing technical support in the project and devoting to technical innovation and products update CATARC's products could maintain its leading position in fierce competition.

CATARC is a high-tech enterprise originated from an authoritative automobile R&D institution. In the 1980s, when Chinese automobile industry started budding, the China National Automotive Industry Corporation (hereinafter referred to as CNAIC) was founded by central government in 1985, where a lot of talented people in automotive industry converged.

CNAIC was dissolved because the central government adopted decentralized management in automotive industry in the 1990s. CATARC is now affiliated to SASAC and has transformed into a tech-based enterprise. On the one hand, with advanced equipment it has already possessed, CATARC engages in third-party vehicle testing operations. On the other hand, exploiting its own technology advantages, CATARC promotes the domestic automotive technical innovation in China by means of attracting talents and cooperating with other companies.

Naturally, a scientific research institution like CATARC has made some planning in reaction to the latest changes in the global automotive industry. In the 21century, automotive industry is facing the bottleneck of energy shortage in the development. Since 2000, the price of oil rose from 10 to 20 US dollars a barrel to more than 100 US dollars per barrel, which is far higher than that of the two oil crises in the 1970s. Therefore, energy conservation and the development of new energy vehicles are new challenges to the automotive industry.

In the long term practice in the auto industry a solid foundation has been laid for the cooperation between Wanfeng Auto and CATARC. Meanwhile, the two share the same philosophy and have mutual complementary advantages, so it's natural to start their cooperation in other fields at the advent of new energy car era.

There are two major innovation directions in producing new energy vehicles. The relatively radical way is the pure electric car promoted by automobile manufacturers. This sort of vehicle is battery-powered and driven by an electric motor. The external energy is provided through replacing or recharging the battery. Like petrol-driven vehicles, once electric cars are widely used, the manufacturers will build plenty of charging stations.

As for pure electric vehicles, Tesla is the most advanced products. This electric vehicle triggered the pursuit of global automotive enthusiasts the moment it was launched into market. According to the performance testing done by media, it can cruise 420 kilometers on a single charge, which proves that pure electric vehicle is practical. However, Tesla is relatively expensive because it hasn't been massively produced.

The relatively rational vehicle manufacturers tend to produce hybrid vehicles. A hybrid vehicle normally includes a conventional internal combustion engine and also a high voltage electric motor. When the vehicle is driven by conventional energy, the batteries which serve as the auxiliary power are recharged. Thus, energy consumption can be reduced.

Hybrid vehicles production doesn't require much alternation for manufacturers, and also no massive changes to gas stations. That's why Toyota Prius is a leading model among all hybrid vehicles, and is much cheaper than Tesla.

Wanfeng Aowei announced in May, 2011 that it had bought 15% stock share of Shanghai CENAT New Energy Co. Ltd at the price of 36,000,000 yuan, and started to develop a battery technology of electric vehicles with CATARC and a Korean battery research institution.

A year later, Wanfeng Auto and CATARC jointly announced in August 2012 that a total 2 billion RMB would be poured into a CATARC hybrid vehicle powertrain project which was going to be completed in several stages.

This means Wanfeng Auto and CATARC have made strategic planning in both directions of new energy vehicles.

However, in contrast with battery technology, Wanfeng Auto and CATARC put more resources on hybrid vehicles. The enterprises are more willing to promote hybrid vehicles now because the change required in the automotive industry for hybrid vehicles is relatively small. Therefore, hybrid vehicles are more likely to become the mainstream of new energy vehicle market first. After the new energy vehicles become generally accepted, electric vehicles will be dominant in the market as an alternative with lower energy consumption.

In China, the government is the first advocate of the application of new energy vehicles. Therefore, the new energy technology has been first applied to public transport buses. The state-owned public transport bus service companies all over China introduced buses with hybrid power, which eliminates the technical barrier of wider application to more commonly used household vehicles.

Before Wanfeng Auto massively produced CATARC — a type of hybrid vehicle powertrain, the small-scale pilot production had been conducted in Tianjin as a research project of CARTAC research center. After 2 years of production and marketing, the target in market positioning of"ten major cities and six major clients"has been reached, and the brand influence has basically come into being.

Wanfeng Auto has survived in the first round of industry competition and held the leading position in the market segmentation.

The dream of making aeroplanes

In August 2015, a Bombardier commercial aircraft landed on Xiaoshan Airport, Hanzhou and made its first flight to Jinan in November that year.

After the reform and opening up, it is not unusual for China 's rich class to buy a private jet. Therefore the news didn't arouse big fuss in the media of Zhejiang , Shaoxing and Xinchang althrough they were major events to Wanfeng Group.

It these two messages were related to a series of actions by Wanfeng, as well as changes in government policy, they would seem a little unusual.

In 2015, Wanfeng set up Wanfeng Aviation Industry Co., Ltd. which established Wanfeng General Aviation Co., Ltd., Xinchang Wanfeng Airport Construction Management Co., Ltd., and Wanfeng (Czech) Aircraft Industry Co., Ltd., and started to acquire well-known overseas aircraft manufacturing enterprises. In December 2015, Wanfeng merged Durham Flight Centre, one of Canada's most powerful aviation pilot training schools.

These actions revealed its ambition in aviation field.

Wanfeng's ambition was based on the background of China's gradual relaxation of the aviation market in lower altitude space, Since 2009, the government gradually opened up the airspace under level of 1000 meters. Particularly in May 2016, the State Council officially released "The guidance on promotion of general aviation industry development", then China's aviation industry ushered in the development of the spring.

The relaxation of policy has led to a springing up of enterprises in aviation, with a sharp increase of the enterprise number from a hundred to a thousand. Wanfeng occupied a geographical advantage for Zhejiang is the pilot province of opening up low level space, who first proposed the construction of "multi-modal aviation, multi-modal transportation, and multi-modal platform" strategy and to build the "one hour transport circle in the space" in the province. It also formulated "Zhejiang General Airport Development Plan" to develop the aviation industry and create good policy environment for investment.

Wanfeng Group, which has positioned itself in multi-modal transport will naturally include aviation into its field of vision.

If there was certain chance of Ailian's personal preferences and adherence for vehicle in Wanfeng's early entrepreneurship, in 2015, its entering into the field of aviation was already strategic with scale. In Ailian's opinion, the aviation industry is a symbol of the rise of a country's comprehensive national strength. Aircrafts are much alike automobiles 20 years ago. In another 20 years, Wanfeng will be fully capable to award outstanding employees with the planes to enable Wanfeng elites to travel around the world. With the government's relaxation to low-altitude navigation, elite class will take to airplane flying which represents freedom and dream. Therefore, aerospace products and services will face an unbalance of supply and demand in the future for a considerable period of time, enough for Wanfeng to make profits and create its own competitiveness.

By June 2014, Wanfeng formed its aviation developing team to make research on the industry.

Research showed that Wanfeng should make an all-round investment in aviation industry including manufacturing of general airplanes, airport service, navigation operations, flight training and flight service stations. Wanfeng found greatest unbalance of supply and demand in these areas after the relaxation of low-altitude aviation.

After just three months, Wanfeng's Board of Directors decided to enter the aviation industry and briefed to the provincial governors of Zhejiang.

Wanfeng's project developing team then made an and more investigation in European and American aviation industry and targeted at two goals for acquisition. Thus, Wanfeng found a strong technology guarantee when entering the aviation sector and paved an important basis for future innovation in this field.

In 2015, Wanfeng developed "the 13th Five-Year Plan" for developing aviation industry, decided aviation as the "Blue Ocean" industry in the next 20 years, and put forward the business philosophy – ensure miles flying to all over the world. A goal of becoming national leader of navigation was made by borrowing experiences from the United States and British Airway towns. Concepts including "wisdom aviation town", "industry 4.0", "Made in China 2025", "O2O" were proposed. In the process of transformation and upgrading into the whole aviation industry chain, Wanfeng is striving to become a leading enterprise devoted to plane manufacturing, airport construction management, navigation operations, aviation training, and flight services. Wanfeng is going to build manufacturing plant with international layout for fixed-wing aircraft and Helicopter, world-class general aircraft design and development center, world-class general airport design and construction company, general airport network covering the whole province and aviation town system, flight service station system covering the whole province, flight schools and institute of aviation technology with international layout, as well as projects such as government emergency rescue system, air Tax, VIP flight and public transport.

Since then, Wanfeng attaches great importance to play a well-known brand of foreign aviation enterprises. Wanfeng acquired Hawaii aviation school abroad, and set up Wanfeng aviation school in the domestic. At the same time, Wanfeng established aircraft design research and development platform in Italy, Canada, Czech Republic; joint venture with Italy Leonardo to manufacture high-end helicopters; acquired Canada Diamond Aircraft to produce diamond-series fixed-wing aircraft; acquired Czech Republic DF project to make light-sport series aircraft with Wanfeng's independent intellectual property rights; established aircraft manufacturing and sales base in domestic to form an aviation industry pattern including international R & D, Wanfeng manufacturing, and global sales.

In accordance with the construction call of "three years to become industrial park, five years to become industrial town, and eight years to achieve production", Wanfeng actively responded to the call of building 100 characteristic towns in the whole province proposed by Zhejiang Provincial Party Committee and Zhejiang provincial government. Wanfeng was determined to establish an aviation town in the core area of Xinchang Industrial Park in Shaoxing. The total planned area of the Wanfeng aviation town was 5.5 km2, with the total investment of 10 billion RMB and 3 billion RMB for the first phase. Wanfeng aviation town will take airplane R&D as the core, combining with local tourism, culture, environment and other resources, taking navigation operations, sightseeing, aviation sports, flight experience, driver's license training as the bright spot, promoting the development of related industries such as service industry, construction industry, cultural and creative industries. Thus, the town will become a beautiful ecological town that appropriate for industry, living and tourism with trinity of industry, culture and tourism, with integrated development of production, life and ecological, and with linkage development of industrialization, information and urbanization. The goal is to build a new model of national urbanization construction, industrial transformation and upgrading, a characteristic town model of China's general aviation, a comprehensive demonstration zone of state-level navigation industry, and the national engineering center.

Compared with other aviation towns, Wanfeng's characteristic aviation town presents four highlights. Firstly, highlighting the aircraft manufacturing industry. Wanfeng takes aircraft manufacturing as the core industry of entire aviation town, and will build a fixed-wing aircraft and helicopter manufacturing plant to produce light sports aircraft, business jet and helicopter with international advanced level, and drives a number of manufacturing industry for aircraft core parts. Secondly, building national brands. When acquires and mergers overseas, Wanfeng focuses on the ownership of intellectual property rights, construction of aircraft design and development platform, and engineering center, producing aircraft and core components with Wanfeng's independent intellectual property rights. Thirdly, construction of the whole industrial chain. Wanfeng overall plan the whole plane manufacturing, airport construction management, navigation operations, aviation school training, flight services and other aspects to promote overall coordination. Fourthly, international vision. Wanfeng attaches great importance to the integration of the world's high-quality aviation resources to realize the internationalization of industrial layout, work team, management and capital. At present, the town has been included in the first batch of national "the 13th Five-Year Plan" 100 advanced manufacturing base, and 100 characteristic town of Zhejiang Province.

In June 2016, a leader of National Development and Reform Commission evaluated Wanfeng's aviation town that, the town was an aviation industry development program with the most complete system plan, the most detailed plan, the highest starting point, throughout the whole industry chain, international perspective, actually implementation that he heard so far. Wanfeng had a very accurate grasp of navigation industry which is corresponding with national strategy, and had carefully researched, demonstrated and assessed in depth. Wanfeng would make a significant contribution to the development of China's aviation industry.

The future is reviled before us, though with great uncertainty; while no one could deny that uncertainty is just what composes the mystery and charm of future.

Acquisition of Paslin

When the advanced manufacturing sector of Wanfeng Group obtains the leader position in global segment industry market, the financial investment sector also has done very well in guarantee, funds, leasing, banking and other business areas.

Wanfeng financial investment industry was born in the global financial crisis in 2008. In the harsh economic winter, those who have sufficient cash are the king. As early as in 2007, Chen Ailian sensed it as a signal of the coming of "winter", and decisively "downsized" the integration of automobile project, ensuring the health of capital flows. Meanwhile, she decided to enter into the financial and investment fields. Because in this year, Shanghai was planning to be built as an international financial center in accordance with strategic plan of the State Council. Chen Ailian was keen to locate development prospect of China's financial market in the growth stage, compared with mature foreign financial markets. China's capital market was moving towards a multi-level system, and PE investment also sprung up with a "fund tide".

By the year of 2015 after eight years of development, Wanfeng financial investment industry, following the philosophy of "Integrating resources, benefiting the world", had achieved great development. The guarantee business had ranked third in "Top Ten Financing Guarantee Institutions in Zhejiang". In Shanghai, the leasing business had also achieved a leading position in the segment market. While in fund business, it was able to ensure at least one project listed with brand of Wanfeng Jinyuan every year through strategic cooperation with excellent Funds.

However, when making the 13th five-year strategic plan, the Group Board of Directors all agreed that, Wanfeng financial investment industry must rely on advanced manufacturing industry, listing platform and overseas mergers and acquisitions in order to achieve the leading strategic objectives in East China. Wanfeng Technology must continue to do industrial robot more fine, more specific, stronger and longer. Financial capital and industrial capital should be combined to achieve the target of industry leader.

At this time, in June 2015, Wu Jinhua of 27 years old, son of Chen Ailian, joined Wanfeng. Wu Jinhua, a young man graduated from the Department of Finance, Renmin University of China, and then studied at University of Nottingham, UK with a master's degree, has professional background of financial investment and international perspective. In June 2015, he served as chairman of Wanfeng Technology after resigned from government department as deputy Director. "Newborn calves are not afraid of tigers". Wu Jinhua challenged the first overseas acquisition in his life.

Wu Jinhua shouldered the mission, led Jiang Yuhua and other M & A team, embarked on a cross-border M & A trip to U.S., Europe and Japan to actively search for project resource. Finally, the target was locked in U.S. Paslin robot company.

Paslin, founded in 1937 and headquartered in Warren, Michigan, was a top worldwide provider of welding robot application service for automotive industry and heavy industry production, with its international advanced automation system concept, industrial design, construction and production, as well as assembly experience. Meanwhile, Paslin had strong R & D capability. Among all 805 employees, there were 400 technical jobs, and more than half of them were engineers and programmers. Paslin held 70% share of the whole U.S. casting robot market. This was a high-quality subject. In the market structure, due to lack of large customers from Europe and Asia, Paslin was actively seeking Chinese partners, and indeed had strong complementary with Wanfeng robot.

All these made Wu Jinhua team excited and full of passion. They worked hard both at home and abroad, day and night to overcome tough issues, such as tight schedule, heavy task, strong competitors and other difficulties. After investigation, careful due diligence and tactical negotiation for 3 months, they stood out from many competitors, and succeeded in carrying out wholly-owned acquisition of Paslin. Then, this became the largest cross-border mergers and acquisitions initiated by domestic robot enterprise so far.

At the same time, the merger also attracted a large number of industry funds due to Wanfeng's accurately grasp of industrial strategy and their courage of the acquisition. Finally, Wanfeng chose an advanced manufacturing industry fund as a partner, which greatly enhanced the influence of the acquisition.

Wanfeng took only three months to merge a giant U.S. robot company with nearly a hundred years of history, which shocked the global robot manufacturing industry. It should be noted that, Wanfeng was competing with 21 enterprises including world-class enterprises and other well-known robot enterprises from China. Fan Qinhua, the president of U.S. Zhiding financial adviser, and Wang Shusheng, the partner of U.S. Mingkang law firm, were both involved in the acquisition. They believed that this is completely expected. Because the merger team of Wanfeng was younger, professional and international. In the fierce competition from due diligence, negotiating to government approval, they demonstrated pragmatic and efficient work style, and would catch up from behind among these international buyers.

At 16:30 on March 23, 2016 U.S. local time, Wanfeng took over Paslin at U.S. General Motors Corporation headquarters, which means Wanfeng Jiyuan Group formally stepped onto the international stage. At this time, Wu Jinhua was just appointed as president of Wanfeng Jinyuan Group three months ago.

In the view of Chen Ailian, the successful acquisition of Paslim no doubt can help Wanfeng to use the former's business channels accumulated for 80 years. By aid of OEM factory of GM, Ford, Honda and other old customers, Wanfeng could expand business, market share, and generate a greater brand premium. As a result, Wanfeng robot will board the international stage at least 10 years in advance with more extensive vision. Thus, the gap of manufacturing level with the world's advanced technology will continue to shrink.

According to Wu Jinhua's point of view, after Wanfeng acquired Paslin, they will take full advantage of the accumulated top technology and customers of Paslan in the field of welding automation, to provide integration of automation solutions for customers, to break the limitations in domestic welding robot technology, and to get rid of controlled situation by foreign companies in the field of industrial automation.

Of course, after the completion of cross-border mergers and acquisitions, management became the real test. Paslin was still full of doubts, though there had been several previous in-depth communication between the two sides. Where will the private enterprises from a mountainous county in China take Paslin with a long history?

In August 2016, Chen Ailian led the senior management team to visit U.S. Paslin. After the symposium with them, managers of Paslin quickly unified their thoughts and reached a consensus.

"What is the real reorganization? It is to form a kind of culture that we all agree with, and to realize the enterprise's self-identity." Chen Ailian believes that, the key to achieve this goal is that, both sides' values can be highly integrated. Wanfeng has to trust and respect capable person from worldwide with broad mind.

"We are delighted to join Wanfeng Group, and believe that this integration will benefit our customers, employees and business partners to help us achieve significant growth and expansion quickly. Financial strength, operational capacity and excellent research and development spirit of Wanfeng will promote Paslin to grow up continually." The senior management team of Paislin said.

To further release the synergies of mergers and acquisitions to enhance the competitiveness of products and production capacity, and leveraging the rise of China's industrial robot industry, Wanfeng Group immediately set up China Paslan company after the acquisition of U.S. Paslan. On May 18th, 2016, Wanfeng Jinyuen high-end equipment industrial park with a total investment of 1.5 billion laid the foundation stone.

"How big the heart is, the stage is as big". The following five strategic layout drived Wanfeng Jinyuan Group to achieve development, transformation and upgrading: introduction of SDIC strategic investment, implementation of overseas mergers and acquisitions, construction of production base in China, listed company platform, and purchase of building in Shanghai.

Tracing the roots, a series of successful overseas mergers and acquisitions are not accidental. As the Rotating President of the Zhejiang Chamber of Commerce in Shanghai, Chen Ailian was amazed with the charm of capital from other president, such as Guo Guangchang, Jack Ma, Zhou Chengjian, and Zheng Yonggang. Guo Guangchang, who is in charge of Fosun Group, ennabled the group to become one of the world's most influential investment holding groups with the philosophy of "China resources grafting with global power", which makes the company a benchmark for Wanfeng entering into financial investment industry.

The cornerstone and the new dream

On the second floor of Wanfeng Hi-Tech Park, locates Chen Ailian's office, at the end of a long passage decorated with photographs demonstrating the history of Wanfeng Auto . In her big European style office, visitors are always attracted by a large painting of peony behind her seat. But outside the reception area of the office which witnessed frequent business activities, there is a small door.

Behind the small door is a quite different world. It is a roughly 300-square-meter roof garden with big green grassland. A cobblestone path which looks like a Chinese character "(human)" goes across in the middle of the grassland. At the intersection stands a lush, sweet-scented osmanthus tree which is like an opened umbrella. The yellow osmanthus in clusters hanged on the branches, giving off pleasant aroma. Under the tree is a set of European-style white tables and chairs.

In the autumn of 2016, a season for harvest, Chen Ailian, who had been fought for the dream of Wanfeng Auto for 22 years, squeezed a little time from her tight schedule to sit under the osmanthus tree, reviewing the past and looking ahead.

Looking back to the past, Wanfeng is brilliant. Wanfeng people like to dream. Chen Ailian, as the founder led them to make these beautiful dream into brilliant reality. "We did have made achievements due to good timing, geographical convenience and good human relationship. Good timing means that Wanfeng was born and has grown up in the era of China's reforms and opening up which started from more than 30 years ago. Zhejiang, a birthplace and important province of Chinese private economy, is the geographical convenience where private enterprises received supports from all-level of governments. Good human relationship refers to the love from distinguished consumers and efforts from Wanfeng outstanding team at all levels. Without consumers' trust, the development of Wanfeng would become water without a source. Wanfeng started with only ten people, while now has a staff population of 10,000. All of them have converged on the big stage of Wanfeng, showing their talents, realizing their values and jointly building a more brilliant future for the big family of Wanfeng."

Today, Wanfeng is sound. In the first year of the 13th Five-Years Plan, Wanfeng has made five scientific layout. Firstly, in the system, two groups, Wanfeng Auto and Wanfeng Jinyuan have already been set up, and develop together. Secondly, in the mechanism, both of the two groups have formed a perfect four committee governing system, information management and control system, culture system, and the concept of governing Wanfeng according to law. Thirdly, in the industry, Wanfeng Auto take advanced manufacturing as the core, and take "big traffic" industry such as automobile parts and general aviation as industry positioning. While Wanfeng Jinyuan take financial industry as the core, and take intelligent equipment (integration system of industrial robot) and advanced manufacturing as supporting industry. Fourthly, in the capital, both groups are committed to the vision of "create an international brand, build a century enterprise", to achieve globalization of science and technology, talent, capital, management and brand through combination of industrial capital and financial capital. Fifthly, in the team, excellent teams at all levels are cultivated to achieve younger, better educated, professional and global. Just like in Yangtse River, the waves behind drive on those before, so the new generation excels the last one.

Looking to the future, Wanfeng is brilliant. The blueprint of the 13th Five-

Year Plan of Wanfeng has been described. Wanfeng Auto and Wanfeng Jinyuan will rely on their listing platform to achieve double-100 billion market value target respectively through continuous mergers and acquisitions, and then further enhance their global leadership position.

It can be said that, the 22 years entrepreneurial history of Wanfeng, actually is a miniature of the great history of China's reform and opening up. In the 20th anniversary of Wanfeng, Chen Ailian cannot help but excitedly said: "We fortunately catch up with the era of China's reform and opening up, and contributed our wisdom and sweat. The great era not only created thousands of enterprises, but also created our happy life today!"

When you actually get to know Chen Ailian, you will find that the idea "listen to the Party and follow the Party" is deeply rooted in her soul since childhood. Chen Ailian was born in a revolutionary family and her parents are all Party members since the era of China's revolution. Chen Zhongyan, Chen Ailian's frank and forthright father, named her after a very famous Chinese ancient essay < Ode to Lotus>. Her name bear the hope of her father who wished that his daughter could be like a lotus whose beauty has no trace of kitsch, and whose manner is neither humble nor arrogant. Therefore, at company conferences, Chen Ailian always calls for that Wanfeng people shall keep reverence (reverence for the laws of the country, reverence for the regulations of the company, and reverence for the principles of the organization) in mind. Meanwhile, every staff of Wanfeng shall have a sense of gratefulness. They shall be grateful for the motherland's powerfulness, for the nurturing of the enterprise, and for the devotion of the teams. Only when every Wanfeng staff can really understand the kindness, thank for the kindness and reward the kindness, will they better cherish the environment provided by the government, the resources endowed by the society and the market given by consumers. And in turn, they will see the world with their beautiful eyes and work with happiness.

Therefore, Chen Ailian believes that, entrepreneur's responsibilities and mission is to maximize the value of social resources by innovation and creativity. She asks the general managers at all levels to follow the values of "enhancing value forever and rewarding society constantly", and to take six historical responsibilities: achieving sustainable development, offering quality products for customers, creating more revenue for the country, raising life quality for employees, improve investment reward for shareholders, and supporting social welfare undertakings.

In order to reward the society, Wanfeng has invested over 300 million RMB in education, sports, culture and new countryside construction: building hope primary schools, establishing charity funds and donating 10 million RMB to build water treatment facilities in local rural areas etc. Chen Ailian also personally created the first construction fund of beautiful countryside of Zhejiang. The elders who are over 60 years old, the kids who go to kindergarten, the students who are admitted by college and young couples who get married, will receive longevity benefit, scholarship and happiness benefit respectively every year. Xu Gaosong, chairman of the Foundation can feel deeply about the love Chen Ailian holds. On every year's Chung Yeung Festival, "longevity benefit, scholarship and happiness benefit" will be distributed to the villagers. Seeing their smiling faces is his happiest time.

The happiest time for Chen Ailian is with her 'strong eagle' students together, helping them to achieve their dream. Qiushi Eagle Club is a new mentor model founded by Ruan Junhua from Zhejiang University for the purpose of promoting youth innovation and entrepreneurship, leading the youth positive energy. In Chen's team, there are a lot of talented persons, and many of them have successfully embarked on the road to entrepreneurship. Wang Mengqiu who established ZeroZero Technology, developed the world's first truly portable self-timer Unmanned Aerial Vehicle. Leaper Technology, founded by Wang Xulongqi, successfully started the brand with Wanfeng financing and supporting platform. Xu Shubin started a business on the base of his father. Chen Ailian personally went to the factory of her students, and give them guidance and support in strategy, research and development, marketing, financial, etc. The strong feelings between teacher and students make the entrepreneurial spirit continue to carry forward and develop.

In the entrepreneurial road, Chen Ailian is always busy and happy. "I have full confidence in the future of Wanfeng!"

Every year on Chen Ailian's birthday, the secretary team following her for years, always send her some special gifts: a rose, a red apple, a lollipop, a music disc, a leisure book. The blessing to their chairman titled as "mother and mentor" is permanent health, beauty, happiness, elegance...

In the spring of 2014, the 20th anniversary of Wanfeng, Ailian's description of Wanfeng's blueprints brought an even more brilliant future of the enterprise, just as the blossom that was about to bloom on the roof garden.

The team of secretaries who have served Chen Ailian for years will offer a special gift on her birthday, such as a rose, a red apple, a lollipop, a CD, a book, sincerely wishing the president who they see as "mother and mentor" healthy, happy, beautiful and elegant forever!

The manufacturing level is the symbol of the national strength, a key indicator of comprehensive productivity when comparisons are made between nations, region or enterprises. As the backbone in China's process of industrialization, industrialists must take up and accomplish the historical mission of managing to catch up with the high-level manufacturing in other countries.

Wanfeng Auto has grown in the market-oriented economy brought by the reform and opening-up. It has created what the media called "Wanfeng Auto phenomenon", the key to which are as follows: First, Wanfeng has been persisting in taking the road of developing high-level manufacturing. It has turned into a manufacturing enterprise with ten-billion-yuan asset by adhering to the strategic positioning of being "the one and only"in high end industry and high end market. Second, It has kept the goal in mind and stayed focused by engaging in what Wanfeng is best at — "the multi-modal transportation"which ranges from auto parts and whole vehicles, to aerospace parts and aircraft. Third, Wanfeng has been persisting in the road of globalization. By making the utmost of capital market and integrating international resources, it has taken the course of internationalizing operations as well as capital, management, personnel, technology and brand.

Innovations have filled private-owned businesses with vitality and chances to and provided them with motivation and urges for the fruits of science and technology development which in turn will foster the growth of companies, the industries and the nation. Chen Ailian and her teams on all levels has survived the ever on-going competitions, bravely embraced reforms and shared the valuable lessons learnt in the growth without reservations, making Wanfeng Auto a classical case in China's manufacturing. This is a great gift for either managers of corporate or those who have just started their own business. It is easy to see that Chen Ailian and her teams have been working for the Wanfeng's dream of everyone "working happily and living happily" with gratitude and passion. In the course of realizing Wanfeng's dream, Chen Ailian and her teams has dedicated to the great Chinese dream of the great rejuvenation of the Chinese nation with strong desire, firm belief and endless efforts. This is a brilliant dream about to come true!

机会正在再次来临①

落笔这本万丰奥特控股集团20年公司史的后记文章时，已是2014年的金秋。浙江大地，虽然还有盛夏热烈的余温，更多时候都已经是蓝天高渺、桂树飘香的秋意了。

现在来回顾一年半之前，我走进了位于新昌的万丰奥特办公大楼，第一次与万丰奥特多位高管约谈创作公司史的时候，内心多少是有点惊讶的。

这是因为，在我诸多的公司史写作当中，陈爱莲是第一位女性的企业掌舵者，而且她是如此愿意信任人。

我记得很清楚，首次见面是在万丰奥特办公大楼的一间会议室里，经过简单的事前讨论之后，一位身材高挑，虽经时间磨砺，却仍容颜秀丽、举止优雅的女士走进会议室。她强大的气场让我知道，这就是万丰奥特的创始人陈爱莲。她的身高有一米七，是个性格爽朗之人。

① 本文写于2014年，本书初次出版时。——编者注

　　我的工作决定我有很多机会接触企业的高级管理者。他们决定公司战略、把控公司方向、判断并使用公司最为关键岗位上的人选，等等。可以说，企业的每一个决策都是不容易做好的。因此，处于公司决策层核心的女性，可谓少之又少。

　　而更让我有些意外的是，陈爱莲虽已跻身国内为数不多的优秀企业家行列，在创作会上却又那么愿意信任我。通常在第一次会议当中，我都需要对创作原则、大致构想和企业所需要调动的资源做细致说明，而且常常需要与管理者们就存在的分歧进行沟通。

　　而在万丰奥特，陈爱莲只听到我的创作理念和原则，就明确表明了她支持的态度：每一家公司的创业和发展史都是一笔巨大的社会财富，对一家公司的历程进行经验和教训的总结，就是在为社会积累和发展这笔财富。

　　那是一种很温暖的感觉，就好像两个陌生人偶然在一个地方相遇攀谈，结果却发现原来两人来自一个故乡、认识同一群朋友、有着相同的思念一样。那天下午，随着会议迅速地在关键环节上取得共识，我们也谈得越来越开心。最后，大家都不约而同地鼓起掌来。

　　对，这就是他乡遇故知的感受。

　　其实我的惊讶是正常的。在读者完成这次万丰奥特之旅之后会发现，真正罕见的，是在经历 20 年风雨之后，作为万丰奥特的领导者，陈爱莲仍然保持着敏锐和敏感的内心。

　　企业的领导者和决策者其实不是一个容易驾驭的岗位。因为在他们做出决定的背后，常常意味着各种各样的牺牲。

　　万丰奥特另一位女性高级管理者梁赛南告诉我，在一次重要岗位的人选替换当中，她被派出接任岗位。而被替换的是一位老资格的万丰奥特创业者，她的爱人为公司献出了生命。梁赛南回忆说，因为这份朴素的情谊，她当时不想接手这个职位。

　　陈爱莲批评她说："要论情谊，我与她的感情不比你深？在内心当中，我不比你难过？但那是一大笔公司的资产，是一大群股东的信任，是一大帮同事的饭碗，这不比我们的情谊和感情重要？关键是，你把什么放在第一位！"

这其实就是公司决策者的困境。他必须做出很多看似无情的决定，而背后都有一个根本的原因——那就是公司和整个公司团队的集体利益。

但同时，我也见过很多企业领导者，由于经历了太多这样的决定，所以内心开始变得坚硬、有壁垒，不再轻易地信任他人。

说到底，这就是我在经历万丰奥特公司史创作第一次会议之后，内心有所惊讶的根本原因：作为公司的核心决策者，陈爱莲在这个岗位上已经奋斗了20年，在有过这样的经历之后，仍然保持着初心，真是罕见的。我认为人与人之间的信任，是世界上最宝贵的财富。

陈爱莲所特有的这种女性管理者的敏锐、感性而又层次丰富的内心，在产业变局时刻是有利于她抓住机会的。

就当下而言，万丰奥特的核心产业属于大交通领域。改革开放30多年，由于人的流动需求激增，总体而言，交通业的需求是成倍上涨的。万丰奥特的公司历程让我们不难看出的是，正是因为这种交通需求的大幅上涨，陈爱莲领导下的万丰奥特，其艰苦卓绝的努力得到了市场的认可，实现行业的全球领跑。

而到了当下，在市场高度增长的同时，产业的变局已经隐约可见。中国作为一个人口大国，进入汽车社会则标志着传统汽车产业在规模上达到了顶峰，同时也意味着传统能源的使用进入了瓶颈期，新能源汽车时代已经来临。

我们已经在书中看到了陈爱莲领导下的万丰奥特的新动作：与央企战略合作进军新能源混合动力总成项目；通过国际并购全球镁合金制造巨头镁瑞丁公司，占据新材料轻量化高地；抓住中国正在迎来通用航空产业黄金时代的机遇，意欲通过与国际高端品牌的战略合作，试水航天航空、飞机及零部件制造、航空物流……就在本书出版前几个月，陈爱莲悄然出现于万丰奥特的战略合作伙伴——电动汽车巨头企业特斯拉的美国总部。这家从贷款50万元资金起步的浙江本土民营企业，现在已经为未来做好了充分准备。

这是一个巨大的产业机会。

在自身发展的前 20 年里，万丰奥特已经显示了它是一家极富进取精神、同时不断获得社会尊重的企业。就在产业变革的同时，陈爱莲已经提出，万丰奥特未来要向"百强万丰、百誉万丰、百年万丰"的目标前进。

"不忘初心，方能阔步向前。"

当下，中国社会中的企业人，现在承担越来越大的社会使命。因此在万丰奥特创立 20 周年时刻，将公司 20 年的历程写作成书，不仅是万丰奥特奉献给社会的一笔财富，也是万丰人重读公司"初心"的机会。

如果说万丰这 20 年的经历是一笔宝藏的话，那么下列万丰奥特的管理者和员工，都在本书把它呈现给读者的过程当中起到了至关重要的作用。没有他们的实践和耐心的帮助，作者无法将全书完成。在此，我要诚意致谢：朱训明、张锡康、杨旭勇、盛晓方、吴兴忠、俞利民、俞林、陈滨、盛建锋、赵亚红、陈伟军、梁赛南、余登锋、吴军、杨铭鑫、徐高松、杨慧慧、章益丹、陈国栋、梁品松、童胜坤、袁林刚、丁金潮、吴延坤、杨华声、陈宝根、陆秀雅等，不仅是这些在职的万丰奥特管理者和员工给本书的创作给予了极大的支持，连退休的老万丰人吕永新、蔡竹妃也接受了作者的采访，为万丰奥特早期创业历程中的细节提供了丰富资料。

还要特别感谢夏越璋、吴艺、徐志良、杨晓英、陈春骁等人，他们在本书的创作过程当中，直接参与了创作支持，为本书的顺利出版，做足了保障工作。

作为国内市场化进程的产物，万丰奥特 20 年波澜壮阔的创业历史，其实只是掀开了当下这家企业的第一页篇章。如果就"百年企业"的目标而言，20 年只是弹指一挥间。在改革开放进入"深水区"的当下，万丰奥特的年轻管理层已经完成自身成长和责任交接的过程。因此我们有理由信任这家生长于浙江的民营企业，必将肩负起振兴民族工业的使命，在国际竞技舞台上高举中国创造的品牌大旗，未来会有被中国和世界所骄傲的更大的辉煌！

postscript

The opportunity is coming again.[1]

It is autumn of 2014 when I am writing this article to commemorate the 20-year history of Wanfeng Auto Holding Group. The breeze is more of the laurel fragrance than the summer heat.

Looking back to a year and a half ago when I first walked into the office building located in Xinchang Wanfeng Auto and interviewed a number of Wanfeng's executives for my creation of this biography, I was somewhat amazed by their stories.

Among many of leaders of company I wrote biography for, Ailian is the first female, and she is so willing to trust people.

I could remember clearly about the first meeting in a conference room of Wanfeng Auto, after a simple discussion

---

[1]　This article was written in 2014, when the book was first published.— editor's note

beforehand with a staff member, a tall, tempered by time, but still charming and elegant lady presented with powerful aura. My tuition told me that this must be Chen Ailian, the founder of Wanfeng Auto. Her height is over 1.7 meters and she has a forthright personality.

My job of writing company biography grants me opportunities to know senior business executives. They decide the company's strategy, control the direction of the company, choose and use personnel of the most critical positions in the company. No such decisions are easy to make. Female decision makers at such level are even rare.

It made me more amazed that as one of the few outstanding entrepreneurs in China, Ailian is so willing to trust me in the creation meeting of the book. Usually in the first meeting, I would specify my principles, rough ideas and resources for creation, generally need to communicate with the executives with the existing conflicts on creation.

In Wanfeng Auto, however, after hearing my creation ideas and principles, Ailian clearly expressed her support: history of entrepreneurship and development of each company is a huge social wealth, to sum up experience and lessons of a company is to contribute to the accumulation and development of the wealth.

It was as warm as two strangers met by chance only to find after conversation that they are the same native land, knowing a same group of friends and sharing the same thoughts. That afternoon, with consensus on the key details quickly reached, we talked more and more happily and all invariably applauded.

Yes, that is the feeling to meet old friends in a foreign land.

My amazement is understandable. After reading this book, you will find that the really rare thing is that after going through 20 years of trials, as Wanfeng Auto's leader, Ailian remained a keen and sensitive heart.

Business leader and policy maker in fact is not an easy job to manage. Behind these decisions, there often lies a variety of sacrifice.

Liang Sainan, another senior female manager of Wanfeng told me her experience of being chosen as the candidate taking over an important position. She was reluctant for the original person in charge was one of Wanfeng's veteran entrepreneurs, whose husband gave his life for the company. Liang Sainan recalled that, because of their friendship, she did not want to take over this position.

Ailian scolded her: "Speaking of friendship, don't you think mine with her are less than yours? Deeply down, wouldn't I be more sentimental than you? But we are responsible for a huge sum of the company's assets, trust of a large group of shareholders and the life-making of a bunch of colleagues. Aren't these far more important than our personally feelings and emotions? The point is, what is your top priority?"

In fact, this is the common dilemma company decision makers have to face. They have to make seemingly heartless decisions for the collective interests of the company and the entire team.

But at the same time, I have seen many business leaders, having experienced many such decisions, their heart have became hard, no longer trust people easily.

After all, this is what I was amazed for after the first creation meeting for Wanfeng Auto's company biography--as the company's core decision maker, Ailian has been fighting on this post for 20 years and after all these experiences, she can still maintain her original heart, which is really rare. Trust is what I hold the world's most valuable asset between people .

Ailian's peculiar keen and emotional heart as a female manager is in favor of her detecting and seizing opportunities in the change of situation in the industry.

Currently, Wanfeng Auto's core industry is within a multi-mode-transport sector.

30 years of reform and opening up have led to the surge in peoples' need to travel. In general, demand for transportation is rising exponentially. Wanfeng Auto's history has shown that with such increase of transportation demand, after its arduous efforts, Wanfeng with the leading of Ailian, has gained recognition by the market and become a global industry leader.

By the moment, at the height of explosive market growth, the industry change has been looming. China as a populous country has entered the automobile society, which marks the peak of traditional auto industry and bottleneck of the use of traditional energy, in other words, new energy automotive era has arrived.

In the book, Wanfeng has made its new move to new energy hybrid project: by merging manufacturing giant MLTH, it is occupying the highlands of new lightweight materials and trying to seize the opportunity in the coming golden age of China's general aviation; it is intended to try aerospace, aircraft and parts manufacturing, aviation logistics by strategic co-operations with international high-end brands... Just a few months before the book was published, Ailian went to the United States and quietly appeared in the headquarters of Tesla, an electric car giant, Wanfeng's strategic partner. This local private enterprise in Zhejiang started with an initial funding of 500 thousand yuan loan is now well prepared for the future.

This is a huge industry opportunity.

In its first 20 years, Wanfeng Auto has shown its ambition and won social respect. In the industrial revolution, Ailian has proposed Wanfeng's goal as becoming an enterprise with century-year's reputation.

"Cherish your original heart in order to stride forward."

At the moment, entrepreneurs in China are now taking greater social missions. To complete the biography is to present not only an asset to the society, but also to provide the opportunity for Wanfeng people to recall their "original heart".

If Wanfeng's 20 years of experience is a treasure, then the following Wanfeng Auto's managers and employees played critical roles in presenting the treasure to the readers. Should it not for their practice and patience, the biography won't be complete. My sincere thanks go to: Zhu Xunming, Zhang Xikang, Yang Xuyong, Sheng Xiaofang, Wu Xingzhong, Yu Limin, Yu Lin, Chen Bin, Sheng Jianfeng, Zhao Yahong, Cheng Weijun, Liang Sainan, Yu Dengfeng, Wu Jun, Yang Mingxin, Xu Gaosong, Xu Xiaofang, Yang Huihui, Zhang Yidan, Chen Guodong, Liang Pinsong, Tong Shengkun, Yuan Linfang, Ding Jinchao, Wu Yankun, Yang Huasheng, Chen Baogen, Lu Xiuya etc. Besides those managers who are still serving, employees who have retired from Wanfeng Auto like Lv Yongxin and Cai Zhu Fei have also provided great resources and support to the creation during my interview. Special thanks go to Xia Yuezhang, Wu Yi, Xu Zhiliang ,Yang Xiaoying and Chen Chunxiao who participated directly in supporting my creation, ensuring the successful publication of the book.

As a product of China's marketization, Wanfeng Auto's 20-year magnificent business history only lifts the curtain of this company's entrepreneurship. Comparing with their goal to win centuries' fame, 20 years is just a blink. With the deepening of the reform and opening up, it comes the time for Wanfeng's young management to grow and take over. We have reason to trust this locally grown private enterprise in Zhejiang Province to take up the mission to revitalize national industry and hold high the banner of the brand created by China in the international arena. It is expected to have more brilliant future and become pride of China and the world!